Incest and the Medieval Imagination

Incest and the Medieval Imagination

ELIZABETH ARCHIBALD

CLARENDON PRESS · OXFORD

*This book has been printed digitally and produced in a standard specification
in order to ensure its continuing availability*

OXFORD
UNIVERSITY PRESS

Great Clarendon Street, Oxford OX2 6DP

Oxford University Press is a department of the University of Oxford.
It furthers the University's objective of excellence in research, scholarship,
and education by publishing worldwide in

Oxford New York

Auckland Bangkok Buenos Aires Cape Town Chennai
Dar es Salaam Delhi Hong Kong Istanbul Karachi Kolkata
Kuala Lumpur Madrid Melbourne Mexico City Mumbai Nairobi
São Paulo Shanghai Taipei Tokyo Toronto

Oxford is a registered trade mark of Oxford University Press
in the UK and in certain other countries

Published in the United States
by Oxford University Press Inc., New York

ISBN 0-19- 811209-2

Jacket illustration: A tree of consanguinity from a copy of *La Somme rurale de Jean Boutillier* made in
Bruges in 1471 and illuminated by Loyset Liedet, Bibliothèque Nationale, Paris, MS francais 202,
fol.15ʻReproduced by kind permission of Bibliothèque Nationale, Paris.

FOR JEB

in grateful and loving memory

'There is a friend that sticketh closer than a brother'
Proverbs 18: 24

Acknowledgements

THIS book has been a very long time in the making, time enough, indeed, for a medieval foundling to grow up and marry his unrecognized mother. My research into medieval attitudes to incest began at Yale, where material I read for my Ph.D. dissertation on the Apollonius of Tyre tradition first made me wonder about the popularity and uses of the incest theme in medieval literature. I continued this work at King's College Cambridge, and completed it at the University of Victoria; I am grateful to both these institutions for supporting my research through sabbatical leaves, and grants for conference travel, computer equipment, and research assistants. I have incurred so many other debts during my literary quest that acknowledgement of every individual contribution is impossible. I am very grateful to all who have helped me, and especially to the following colleagues and friends for asking questions, supplying references and texts, reading drafts, checking translations, and giving encouragement: Chris Baswell, Julia Boffey, Danielle Bohler, Laurel Bowman, Keith Bradley, Patricia Clark, Victoria Cooper, David Dumville, Elizabeth Edwards, Tony Edwards, Juliet Fleming, Rob Foley, Jane Gilbert, Paloma Gracia, Patrick Grant, Dick Helmholz, Ralph Hexter, Anne Higgins, Iain Higgins, Amanda Hopkins, Keith Hopkins, David Hult, Sarah Kay, Michael Lapidge, Marilyn Lawrence, Marianne Legault, Jill Mann, Randall Martin, Judith Mitchell, Kathleen Morrison-Bell, Barbara Newman, Joan Noble, Puri Pazó Torres, Ad Putter, Michael Reeve, Nancy Regalado, Miri Rubin, the late and much missed Dadie Rylands, Jim Schultz, Leslie Shumka, John Tucker, Dick Unger, and Joanna Waley-Cohen. Every chapter was read and improved in an early draft by a generous friend who wishes to remain anonymous because of our unresolvable differences over punctuation. The anonymous reader for Oxford University Press made many helpful suggestions about a later draft, as did Simon Gaunt, whose advice and support throughout this project have been invaluable.

I have been fortunate in my research assistants in Victoria, Tina Hamer, Catherine May, and Dorothy Rogers, who worked enthusiastically at a series of arduous tasks including proofreading, bibliography, and indexing, and also solved some technological problems. In Bristol Demelza Curnow did sterling work on the index. The staff of various libraries, most notably the Cambridge University Library and the Macpherson Library at the University of Victoria, have been unfailingly courteous and helpful, as have the staff of the English Department at Victoria. Kim Scott Walwyn commissioned the book, and has remained enthusiastic and encouraging during its long years of gestation. Sophie Goldsworthy and Matthew Hollis have been patient and helpful editors and Heather Watson a meticulous copy editor.

Part of Chapter 5 appeared in a slightly different form in 'Arthur and Mordred: Variations on an Incest Theme', in *Arthurian Literature* 8, ed. Richard Barber (1989), 1–27. I am grateful to Boydell & Brewer for permission to reuse this material.

The dedication expresses my greatest debt; I might not have written this book had I not had the extraordinary good fortune to be the pupil and friend of John Boswell. My classes with him, his own work, and our wonderfully stimulating conversations over the fifteen years of our friendship were crucial in directing my ideas and my research. Alas, he did not live to read the work that he inspired in its present form—it would have been greatly improved had he been able to do so—but nonetheless this is very much his book.

E.A.
Victoria
June 2000

Contents

Abbreviations

AASS	*Acta sanctorum*, ed. J. Bollandus, revised by J. Carnandus, 69 vols. (Paris, 1863–1948)
CA	John Gower, *Confessio Amantis*, ed. G. C. Macaulay as *The English Works of John Gower*, 2 vols., EETS 81–2 (Oxford, 1900–1)
CFMA	Classiques français du moyen âge
CT	Geoffrey Chaucer, *Canterbury Tales*, *The Riverside Chaucer*, ed. Larry D. Benson *et al.*, 3rd edn. (Boston, Mass., 1987)
EETS os	Early English Text Society (original series)
EETS es	Early English Text Society (extra series)
EETS ss	Early English Text Society (supplementary series)
HA	*Historia Apollonii regis Tyri*
L-G	*Lancelot-Grail: The Old French Arthurian Vulgate and Post-Vulgate in Translation*, ed. Norris. J. Lacy, 5 vols. (New York, 1992–6)
MGH	*Monumenta Germaniae Historica* (Hanover, 1828–) LL Leges nationum germanicarum
OM	*Ovide Moralisé*, ed. C. de Boer, *Verhandelingen der Koninklijke Akademie van Wetenschapen te Amsterdam: Afdeeling Letterkunde*, 15, 21, 30, 36, 37, 43 (Amsterdam, 1915–38)
PL	*Patrologia cursus completus, series latina*, ed. J.-P. Migne, 221 vols. (Paris, 1844–64)
PMLA	*Publications of the Modern Language Association of America*
SATF	Société des anciens textes français
TLF	Textes littéraires français

Conventions

TEXTS AND TRANSLATIONS

In view of the large amount of primary and secondary material that I discuss in this study, I have tried to keep the bibliographic information in my chapters and footnotes to the minimum consonant with user-friendliness and also standard practice in the field. Short titles have been used for all primary and secondary sources; full references to all works cited are given in the bibliography. All secondary sources are cited in the usual way by author, short title, and page number. Primary sources are cited by author (if known) and short title; the editor is named in the first citation only (except in the case of different editions of the same text). References to specific passages in verse texts are to line numbers only; references to prose texts are to page numbers (chapter divisions are sometimes given too where appropriate). There are some exceptions to these rules, however. All classical and patristic texts are cited from the Loeb Classical Library editions, unless otherwise stated, and references are given by chapter or division number only. These Loeb editions are not listed in the bibliography. I also cite some standard legal texts, such as Justinian's *Codex* and Gratian's *Decretum*, by chapter or division numbers only. Malory is cited simply as Malory, since there is some dispute over the title and number of his work(s).

I have used the Loeb translations, where available, for classical and patristic texts, though I have sometimes modified them where they seem too old-fashioned or inaccurate. Translations of all other texts are my own unless otherwise indicated.

NAMES

I have generally preferred to use one standard spelling for proper names which appear in several texts in slightly different forms, though I sometimes give a variant form if it differs significantly from the standard (e.g. Gower's Thaise for the Tarsia of the *Historia Apollonii*). The Anglicized forms of classical names are taken from standard reference works.

A Note on Terminology

It is striking how often incest is discussed or alluded to by modern historians and literary critics, and yet they do not include an entry under *incest* in the index. Sometimes the topic is subsumed under *consanguinity* or *endogamy* or *marriage*. It is more likely to appear in its own right in very recent works, perhaps because incest has 'come out of the closet' in our own society over the last decade both as a serious social problem and as a prominent theme in autobiography, biography, and fiction. Possibly this previous reluctance to confront the subject explicitly also accounts for the small number of references to words derived from the Latin *incestum* in the specialist dictionaries for the major vernacular languages of the medieval West, most of which were compiled many decades ago. But it may also be that the word in its various forms, Latin and vernacular, was not very commonly used in the Middle Ages. In Old French and Middle English dictionaries, for instance, the examples given for the noun *incest(e)* are almost all from the mid-fourteenth century or later, though the subject was certainly mentioned in earlier didactic and fictional texts.

My own reading suggests that the Latin *incestum* and its derivatives were generally used as technical terms. Latin didactic texts written mainly for use by ecclesiastics—law codes, confessional or penitential manuals, theological treatises—often include a rubric *de incestu* (about incest), but the description of the sin or penance is more likely to use verbs like *fornicare* (to fornicate) or *stuprare* (to debauch or ravish), and related nouns and adjectives. In didactic texts, both Latin and vernacular, the convention is to explain each concept under discussion, however familiar it may in fact be to the reader or listener. But the comments on incest in some vernacular didactic texts give the impression that it was a learned term not much used in common parlance.

Often the sin is explained or discussed without any mention of the word 'incest', under the heading of fornication or adultery or lechery. In Robert Mannyng's *Handlyng Synne*, which was intended for a lay audience, incest is laboriously explained and flagged as a clerical term; but it is not mentioned in the French source, which was intended for priests.[1] We know that the medieval Church worried constantly about breaches of the very complicated incest prohibitions (see Chapter 1); one problem may have been that many of the faithful did not understand what incest was.

The nobility were probably better informed, but the evidence of romances and other fictional narratives suggests that the term *incest* was not widely used in the courtly world either. The very popular story of Apollonius of Tyre begins with a father's rape of his daughter, but this is seldom described as incest in the many Latin and vernacular versions, or in allusions to the story in other texts (see Chapter 2). In Hartmann von Aue's *Gregorius*, written at the end of the twelfth century by a pious layman, sibling incest is followed by mother/son incest (see Chapter 3); the narrator and the protagonists refer to *schulde* (guilt), *missetât* (misdeed), and *sünde* (sin), rather than using a more specific term. Sometimes in such stories incest is subsumed into some other sexual sin, adultery or fornication or lechery, as in the didactic texts; sometimes it is described by a derogatory term for irregular or unnatural sexual behaviour such as *putage* (debauchery, prostitution), or by a more general term or phrase such as *hontage* (shame) or *ageyn kynde* (against nature). A sample survey of some of the versions of the popular Flight from the Incestuous Father story (discussed in Chapter 4) indicates that Latin writers were readier to use strong terms such as *incestum* or *stuprum* (violation, debauchery). In the vernacular versions of this story, when the father declares his intention of marrying his daughter, she tends to reply in horror that this would be a sin, without giving the sin a specific name.

Both medieval and modern writers distinguish between various different kinds of incestuous impediment to sexual relations inside or outside marriage, though in the Middle Ages the degrees of prohibited relationship were much more numerous. This is a complex topic, and so is the terminology: here I mention only some frequently used Latin terms and their modern English equivalents. Words for 'relationship' in medieval Latin include *propinquitas* and

---

[1] *Handlyng Synne*, 7367–72, ed. Furnivall (the French source is printed beside the Middle English): 'The thryddë synne ys the werst, | The clerkes calleth hyt 'yncest' . . .' (The third sin is the worst, | Clerics/learned men call it incest). Elsewhere Mannyng often uses the formula 'men call it', but not 'clerks call it'.

cognatio; *parentela* can mean both the concept of relationship and the actual kin-group. *Consanguinitas* (consanguinity) means a blood relationship. *Affinitas* (affinity) is the relationship created between the families of a married couple, what we would think of as the 'in-law' relationship. In medieval thinking, a permanent relationship of affinity was created by any act of sexual intercourse (*copula carnalis*). If a man slept on different occasions with two sisters, or with a mother and her daughter, he not only committed incest but also created a relationship of affinity between these women and his extended family, and between himself and their family. Affinity created by legitimate marriage extended much further than we would expect, beyond the nuclear family to the in-laws of one's in-laws (and for several centuries to their in-laws too). *Cognatio spiritualis* (spiritual kinship) had several meanings. It could mean kinship with one's godparent or godchild, and with his/her immediate family; a special vocabulary was developed to describe these relationships which paralleled those of the biological family. It could mean the relationship between any person in religious orders and a lay person, or between two religious. In this spiritual context, incest could also mean intercourse with a nun or other religious. For further discussion of the complex and changing definition of incest in the Middle Ages, see Chapter 1.

Introduction: Dangerous Propinquity

> Home, home—a few small rooms, stiflingly over-inhabited by
> a man, by a periodically teeming woman, by a rabble of boys
> and girls of all ages. No air, no space; an understerilized
> prison; darkness, disease, and smells . . . And home was as
> squalid psychically as physically. Psychically, it was a rabbit
> hole, a midden, hot with the frictions of tightly packed life,
> reeking with emotion. What suffocating intimacies, what dan-
> gerous, insane obscene relationships between the members of
> the family group!
>
> > Aldous Huxley, *Brave New World*[1]

EVERY society has taboos about incest, but they differ considerably,
and so do literary representations of incest. In this book I shall
explore medieval uses of the incest motif in a variety of literary
genres, including romance, hagiography, and *exempla*. In order to
establish the social and literary context, in the first chapter I consider the historical development of medieval incest laws by the
Church and the extent to which they were accepted and observed by
the laity; in the second chapter I discuss classical myths and legends
about incest, and their reception and adaptation in the Middle
Ages. I have arranged the homegrown medieval narratives discussed
in Chapters 3 to 5 according to the main type of incestuous relationship they include: mother–son, father–daughter, sibling, and
other (more distant blood-relatives, relatives by marriage, 'spiritual' relatives). In each of these three chapters I focus on one major
text in considerable detail, but I also discuss a range of other texts
which offer variations on the theme and indicate patterns of influence. Just as incest creates convoluted and ambiguous family relationships, incest stories do not necessarily fall into clear-cut literary

---

[1] This epigram is taken from the discussion of old-fashioned family life in ch. 3 of
Brave New World. The title of this chapter, 'Dangerous Propinquity', is borrowed from
Elizabeth Smart, *By Grand Central Station*, 25; though she uses it in a different context,
it seems a most appropriate metaphor for incest, not least because *propinquitas* in Latin
means closeness in kinship, as well as in space or time.

categories. One can arrange them by genre, by date of composition, by type of source, or by type of relationship, but none of these schemes proves entirely satisfactory, and there is often some overlap or repetition when several types of incest appear in a single text. I have found it necessary to use two different and somewhat inconsistent approaches in order to separate medieval treatments of classical plots from stories apparently invented in the Middle Ages by Christian writers. The stories of classical origin in Chapter 2 are not categorized by the type of incestuous relationship, and are not discussed again in the later chapters.

The use of the incest motif in medieval literature is a huge topic. My main aim here is to show the remarkable popularity of the motif and the variety of ways in which it was used by medieval writers. Medieval incest stories are so numerous that it is impossible even to mention them all, let alone to discuss them all in detail. Nor have I attempted to interpret them systematically in the light of current thinking about incest by anthropologists, sociobiologists, psychoanalysts, and social workers; this would require several more volumes, and also would be inappropriate for my purpose of trying to understand medieval attitudes to incest. I share the view expressed in a recent essay on Artemidorus' manual on the interpretation of dreams, which was written in the second century AD:

Incestuous dreams and their indigenous interpretation are mutually dependent, and a Freudian interpretation of the alleged latent content is an arbitrary intrusion into the patterns of thought of another culture.[2]

I think of my project as literary archaeology, and I hope that other literary critics will build on the foundations I have excavated, using whatever approach they find most useful, just as historians build on the fieldwork of archaeologists. My discussion of the cultural context in which the medieval narratives were produced and of the classical tradition in myth and literature which lay behind them can only be brief overviews; each of these chapters could be expanded into a book. As for the medieval texts, the critical literature about some of them is vast (for instance Hartmann von Aue and the Arthurian legend). I have largely confined myself to the areas I know best—medieval Latin, Old French, and Middle English—with occasional excursions into German, Spanish,

---

[2] Price, 'Future of Dreams', 22.

Italian, and Celtic material. I have tried to suggest patterns, both in terms of literary structure and of historical development, but also to emphasize differences. The same basic plot may be very differently treated in a romance and a saint's life. In one narrative a protagonist may be harshly punished for an unwitting sin, while in another version the same sin is easily absolved. Broad questions which run through this study, and which will be discussed again in the final chapter, include the ways in which Christianity affected the retelling and inventing of incest stories in the Middle Ages; the representation of women in medieval incest stories; and the relationship of incest literature to real life in this period, in so far as it can be reconstructed.

It is also revealing to compare medieval attitudes to incest with our own today. In 1997 Kathryn Harrison published *The Kiss*, a memoir of her affair as a 20-year-old with her father, whom she had not seen since she was 4 (both were aware of their relationship). One review appeared under the headline 'The lust that dare not speak its name'.[3] Homosexuality is no longer shocking and unmentionable in our society; incest is still shocking, and has only recently become mentionable. It has been found to be alarmingly widespread in late twentieth-century society, and it is explicitly and publicly discussed in two main aspects. At the macro level, we ask what circumstances permit or encourage incest: clearly poverty is not the only cause, as was once supposed. Do abusers tend to come from dysfunctional families themselves? To what extent do mothers collude in abuse of young girls by fathers or male relatives? What are the effects of incest on 'survivors' (self-mutilation, promiscuity, difficulty in maintaining relationships or raising children)? How should abusers be treated? At the micro level, many women (and some men too) are declaring themselves to be incest survivors; indeed it could be argued that incest has become the 'flavour of the month' in terms of a childhood trauma which 'explains' later difficulties in life. False memory syndrome is a new problem caused by the 'outing' of incest as a mentionable trauma; it is not only the abused child who is seen as a victim, but also in some cases the parents who are—or claim to be—falsely accused.

One catalyst for the 'outing' of incest has been the women's movement. Feminists see incest as one of many forms of violence

---

[3] See the *Independent* (London), 17 Apr. 1997.

against women, an example of the patriarchal domination and male sexual aggression which have been accepted for so long but are now being vociferously challenged. In a study of feminism and incest, Vicki Bell comments on this new approach:

Sociologists and anthropologists have traditionally regarded incest as disruptive of the family and therefore as disruptive of the social order. Feminism has suggested that, paradoxical as it may seem, incest is actually produced and maintained by social order: the order of a male-dominated society.[4]

The feminist approach mirrors general attitudes to incest in assuming that it is largely a problem of male aggression towards vulnerable women, many of whom are below the age of consent. Judith Herman, author of an important early study of father–daughter incest, takes a similar line: 'The terms "offender" and "victim" describe the situation accurately, even though many people find this language objectionable . . . Father–daughter incest is not only the type of incest most frequently reported but also represents a paradigm of female sexual victimization.'[5] Feminists naturally reject the charge that some young women 'ask for it', and they have little to say about mothers and other older women who seduce young male relatives. Mother–son incest certainly does happen; but in our society both feminists and the more traditional find it hard to accept the idea of women, especially mothers, as sexual predators and seducers of adolescent boys in their care.

Bell gives a very interesting account of the debates in England in the early twentieth century and in the 1980s over incest legislation, and the attitudes to incest that they reveal.[6] Much was made of the genetic argument that inbreeding produces defective offspring who are imperfect human beings, and also a burden to society. As Bell points out, this was an argument for treating incest legislation separately from that relating to rape. But as she also points out, it presupposes that incest involves a man and a fertile woman, and that they are blood relatives. Another prominent feature of these debates was the emphasis on the family as a valuable institution which should be protected: incest was understood not as morally repugnant in itself, but as detrimental

---

[4] Bell, *Interrogating Incest*, 57.   [5] Herman, *Father–Daughter Incest*, 4.
[6] See also Wolfram, *In-Laws*, part II.

to family life. This affected the parameters of incest legislation: it was argued in the 1986 debate that there was no need to include in-laws among the prohibited partners, since nowadays they seldom form part of the nuclear family; adopted children, on the other hand, were included, although they are not blood relatives. One speaker in the debate pleaded, 'If the law is to be sensible it will not prosecute wrongs because they are nameless wrongs, but wrongs which do harm.' Bell compares this with attitudes to sexuality in the eighteenth century, when, according to Foucault, it was seen in relation to the problem of governing society, rather than as a question of individual behaviour or morality. Furthermore, the incest debate in the early part of the twentieth century considered incest as a form of child abuse, and invoked the expertise of the National Society for the Prevention of Cruelty to Children; in the 1980s there was more discussion of the long-term psychological effects on young female victims.

The situation in the Middle Ages can be contrasted with that of the twentieth century in almost every respect, at both the macro and the micro levels. In fact it is hard to differentiate these two modern levels in relation to medieval thinking; although writers like St Augustine and St Thomas Aquinas did discuss the incest taboo in terms of family and social structure and the value of exogamy, it was Christian spiritual values which predominated. While the medieval Church certainly wanted to support the family as a Christian institution, the fate of the individual soul was its first concern (at least, this is always the claim in literary works about incest, but some modern scholars argue that the taboo had more material advantages for the Church—see my discussion in Chapter 1). Incest, which was much more broadly defined in the Middle Ages than it is today, was a matter for private rather than public confession. There was no concern for the safeguarding of the family from an incestuous member, the emotional and physical damage to young victims, or the social rehabilitation of either victims or abusers. The dismantling of a family unit was much less serious than the damnation of a soul, and punishment mostly took the form of contrition and penance (though the latter was sometimes to be performed publicly).[7] The dangers of inbreeding

---

[7] This was the theory, at least, and is certainly the impression conveyed by medieval literature. In real life, churchmen seem to have been prepared in some cases to tolerate

are almost never mentioned by medieval writers, for whom incest included intercourse between relatives not linked by blood.[8] Incest was seen as the most extreme manifestation of lust and bodily appetite, the constant enemies of the soul; the gender of the sinner was immaterial. In fact in the many cautionary tales about incest produced by clerical authors, the initiator of a consummated liaison known to both partners to be incestuous is more likely to be a woman than a man: women's sexual appetites were notoriously insatiable, and like their ancestor Eve they had no self-control. But it was not only clerics who described women as initiating incest. In a digression on the power of love in *Parzival*, Wolfram von Eschenbach uses incest to illustrate the lengths to which passion can drive women:

> frou Minne, ir pflegt untriuwen
> mit alten siten niuwen.
> ir zucket manegem wîbe ir prîs,
> unt rât in sippiu âmîs.[9]

(Mistress Love, with old ways ever-new you foster disloyal ties. You snatch their good name from many women; you prompt them to take lovers over-near of kin.)

The example that follows to show the power of love over men concerns a very different kind of transgression, against feudal vows and the bonds of companionship.

Medieval incest stories differ significantly from classical ones, which were well known in the Middle Ages, because of Christian attitudes to sex, sin, and salvation. Medieval writers were much more explicit about incest than our supposedly liberal society has been till very recently. They had no doubt that it was a severe social and spiritual problem which had to be confronted and discussed. Not only was it frequently cited as a branch of Luxuria or Lechery in definitions of the Seven Deadly Sins, but from the twelfth century on it became very popular among clerical writers as the literary 'péché monstrueux' or monstrous sin which demonstrated that

---

incestuous relationships if the spouses were not too closely related and the incest had been committed in ignorance—see Ch. 1.

[8] For further discussion see my comments in Ch. 1 and the Conclusion.

[9] Wolfram von Eschenbach, *Parzival*, VI. 219.19–22, ed. Lachmann, revised Nellmann, trans. Hatto, 152. He could have found this argument in clerical writing and also in classical sources such as Ovid and Juvenal (see Ch. 2).

divine grace is available to even the most wicked sinner, as long as s/he is truly contrite.[10] It also became a popular motif in secular stories of adventure, which often feature foundlings and separated families: the hero may or may not recognize his mother or sister in time to avoid disaster (the fall of Camelot is attributed to Arthur's incestuous begetting of Mordred in some versions of the Arthurian legend).

There seems every reason to believe that the incidence of incest does not change much over the centuries; what does change is the level of public acknowledgement that it happens, and discussion of what to do about it. One might have expected that the medieval Church would have avoided telling stories about incest for fear of putting dangerous ideas into people's heads. On the other hand, to be plausible and powerful, cautionary tales must bear a strong resemblance to real-life situations, must be recognizable as within the bounds of possibility. The frequent use of the incest theme by clerical writers shows that incestuous desire was not regarded as a rare and barbaric perversion, but rather as a constant danger for all, rich and poor, powerful and humble, male and female.[11] Some writers went so far as to acknowledge the possibility of consensual incest between close relatives who love each other deeply, though of course this was no excuse for sin. By insisting that even this heinous sin could be absolved through contrition and grace, Christianity put a new spin on the incest theme, and on plots which must have been circulating for a long time in oral literature as well as in written sources.[12] The late classical story of Apollonius of Tyre, which begins with the brutal rape of a princess by her father, elicited from several medieval writers the comment that just as one can find gold or a jewel in a dungheap, according to proverbial wisdom, so such a

---

[10] See Payen, *Le Motif*, esp. 54 ff.

[11] Bell offers the analogy of 19th-cent. discussion of children masturbating, paraphrasing Foucault's comments (*Interrogating Incest*, 18): 'masturbation was simultaneously spoken of as a natural inclination and as a danger, both physical and moral, individual and collective'.

[12] Indeed, some modern critics consider that the shadow of incest hangs over a great deal of medieval literature. According to Méla, 'par surimpression des images, les amours médiévales prennent-elles toujours peu ou prou coloration incestueuse' ('Œdipe', 23: by a superimposition of images, medieval love stories always take on a slightly incestuous colouring). He sees the influence of the Oedipus legend in a great deal of medieval narrative, including the Arthurian legend.

shocking story can have moral value for the Christian reader.[13] But even without the moralizing Christian angle, the incest theme would still have had considerable appeal, for as Shelley wrote to a friend, 'incest is like many other *incorrect* things a very poetical circumstance'.[14]

[13] For references see Archibald, *Apollonius*, 205 (V31) and 224 (A16).
[14] *Letters*, ii. 154; he is discussing the work of Calderón in a letter to Maria Gisborne.

I

Medieval Incest Law—Theory and Practice

> Although the Church holds that certain impediments are of
> divine law origin, the precise nature and effects of these
> impediments have not been clear throughout history. There
> has also been debate over the dispensing power of the bishops
> and even the Holy Father in certain cases.
>
> *The Code of Canon Law*[1]

IT is often claimed that the incest taboo is universal, but as anthropologists have demonstrated, kinship structures are socially constructed: rules about endogamy and exogamy and prohibitions on
intercourse or marriage between certain members of the kin-group
vary from culture to culture and from century to century. It is a
considerable over-simplification to say, as does a recent commentary on the contemporary code of canon law, that 'Societies have
generally condemned sexual relations between blood relatives as a
sort of perversion'.[2] Most communities forbid marriage between
persons related in a vertical line—parents and children, grand-
parents and grandchildren; but beyond that practices have varied
widely over the ages, and still do today. In some societies sibling
marriage has been allowed in the royal family (in ancient Egypt,
Peru, and Hawaii); in Egypt in the Graeco-Roman period (300 BC to
AD 300) brother–sister marriages among non-royal citizens were
recorded quite frequently in the census records.[3] Relatives by marriage may or may not be counted as full family members; the paternal kin-group may be privileged over the maternal, or vice versa.
When it comes to uncles and aunts, nephews and nieces, cousins,

---

[1] *Code of Canon Law*, ed. Coriden *et al.* 758.

[2] *Code of Canon Law*, canon 1091, 772.

[3] See Taubenschlag, *Law of Greco-Roman Egypt*, 111–12; Hopkins, 'Brother–Sister
Marriage'; Shaw, 'Explaining Incest'; Frier and Bagnall, *Demography*, 127–37.
Taubenschlag notes that in some families sibling marriage occurred in two successive
generations.

relatives by marriage, and adopted, illegitimate, and stepchildren, there has been much variation over the centuries in the application of the incest taboo. In the ancient world, for instance, levirate marriage, the practice whereby the widow of a man who died childless was married to his brother, or even his father, was common among the Hittites as well as the early Israelites.[4] In Catholic Europe in the Middle Ages such marriages were forbidden (hence Henry VIII's difficulties). In nineteenth-century England marriage to a brother's widow was not permitted, but marriage with a dead wife's sister was legal till Lord Lyndhurst's Act of 1835, then forbidden for seventy years till the unpopular act was repealed in 1907.[5] In England incest remained under the jurisdiction of the ecclesiastical courts till 1908; in Scotland, however, it has been under the control of the common law courts since 1567. At present, English law defines incest in the Sexual Offences Act of 1956 as sexual intercourse between a man and his mother, sister (full or half), daughter or granddaughter, and between a woman over 16 and her father, brother (full or half), son or grandfather.[6] According to the Church of England, the range of relatives whom one may not marry is considerably more extensive, including adoptive daughter, aunt, niece, mother-in-law, grandmother-in-law, daughter-in-law, granddaughter-in-law, stepmother, and stepdaughter (and the corresponding male relatives for a woman).[7] In Scotland a wider range of relatives by blood and by marriage is included in the prohibited degrees according to the Incest and Related Offences (Scotland) Act of 1986. In the United States the incest laws vary from state to state; some but not all prohibit marriage to a first cousin, or to an adoptive child.[8]

The Catholic commentary quoted at the beginning of this chapter is refreshingly honest about the difficulties surrounding the incest prohibitions, which are by no means peculiar to Christianity.

[4] See Ziskind, 'Legal Rules'; and also Hoffner, 'Incest'.

[5] See Wolfram, *In-Laws*, 30 ff., and Gullette, 'Puzzling Case'. Marriage to this sort of sister-in-law was legal in many continental countries and in America during this time; some English couples perjured themselves to marry in England, while others fled abroad.

[6] On incest law in Britain see appendix 1 in Bell, *Interrogating Incest*, 186–8, and the excellent discussion in Wolfram, *In-Laws*, esp. ch. 2. English law has changed considerably in this century, and is still changing, so that it is now possible to marry a relative by marriage such as an ex-mother-in-law.

[7] See *Canons of the Church of England*, B 31, 22–3.

[8] There is a convenient list arranged by state in the appendix of Herman, *Father–Daughter Incest*, 221–59.

As Mary Douglas notes in her broad-ranging study of pollution and taboo, 'It is the nature of a moral rule to be general, and its application to a particular context must be uncertain.'[9] Some societies appeal to natural or divine law as a justification for their own practices, but many writers recognize, as medieval authorities did, that their laws are in fact human constructs, and subject to change for a variety of reasons. These reasons may not always be rational, nor the changes logically consistent. Alan Watson argues that 'though there is a historical reason for every legal development, yet to a considerable extent law in most places at most times does not progress in a rational or responsive way'.[10] He notes that 'the divergence between law and the needs or wishes of the people involved or the will of the leaders of the people is marked', and that laws do not always reflect the people's best interests:

Rules of law which produce results which are intolerable to the society or its ruling class will no doubt be replaced. But to argue that in consequence any given system of law will reflect the needs and desires of society or its ruling class is a *non sequitur* unless we take that proposition in a very restricted sense indeed. Society and ruling classes are, in practice, able to tolerate a great deal of private law which serves neither the interests of society at large or its ruling class nor the interests of anyone else.

In the Middle Ages the prohibitions relating to marriage and also intercourse with relatives were extended to a degree unprecedented in any other society; the family was defined so broadly as to include not only biological and social relationships but also spiritual ones. At their most draconian, in the tenth, eleventh, and twelfth centuries, these prohibitions banned sexual intercourse between all relatives connected by consanguinity or affinity to the seventh degree, and between persons linked by compaternity (spiritual affinity) to the fourth degree. This was disadvantageous for most of the population, and the rules were often broken, sometimes through ignorance but sometimes quite deliberately. How did such an unworkable system develop, and whose interests did it serve? In this chapter I shall briefly consider the medieval inheritance from Graeco-Roman and Judaic law, the ways in which the medieval rules about incest developed and changed, and attitudes to incest in medieval society (whether attempted or

---

[9] Douglas, *Purity*, 131.   [10] Watson, *Society*, 5–6.

achieved, actually committed or merely imputed), in so far as they can be reconstructed.[11]

THE GRAECO-ROMAN TRADITION

The Greeks, like most other societies, forbade both marriage and sexual intercourse between ascendants and descendants; Glotz notes that in their attitudes to incest they were less free than oriental societies, but less rigorous than Roman society.[12] In Xenophon's *Memorabilia* Socrates reminds Hippias that those who transgress this unwritten law of the gods are punished by having bad children; he implies that the incestuous child will be immature and therefore will produce unsatisfactory offspring.[13] In Plato's *Laws* the Athenian argues that unwritten law and the force of public opinion restrain parents from sleeping with children, and men from intercourse with attractive siblings (7. 838a–839a). But Just notes that there were few specifically prohibited relationships, and Harrison comments that 'we hear of no action at law which either was or could be brought against those guilty of incest, and in fact there is in Greek no technical term for incest'.[14] Parker discusses incest in his study of pollution and purification in Greek society, but notes that the word *miasma* (pollution) is never in fact used to refer to incest.[15] In Sophocles' play Oedipus is exiled from Thebes for parricide, not for incest. Athens was notably tolerant in its interpretation of the taboo, and indeed favoured endogamy, as Just notes: 'An Athenian's first loyalties were towards his kin . . . It was thus among his kin that he first sought for a husband for his daughter, sister, or

---

[11] I mean by this the evidence for actual occurrences of incest, and historical responses to potential or actual incest, rather than commentary in the form of myth or fiction; such commentary is discussed in the chapters that follow. Throughout this chapter I am indebted to the magisterial study of Brundage, *Law, Sex*, and also to part 1 of McCabe, *Incest, Drama*, 3–63.

[12] I am much indebted here to the excellent entries by Glotz (Greece) and Humbert (Rome) in *Dictionnaire des antiquités*, s.v. *incestum*.

[13] *Memorabilia*, 4. 4. 19–23; see also *Republic*, 461b. Aristotle in the *Politics* criticizes Plato for proposing a communal life which would obscure family relationships and therefore permit incest (1262ᵃ); the potential liaisons he mentions are exclusively homosexual (father and son, brothers).

[14] See Just, *Women*, 76 ff.; and Harrison, *Law*, 22–3. Glotz cites a number of Greek terms used for incest, including *gamos anosios* (unholy marriage).

[15] Parker, *Miasma*, 97.

any girl in his *kyrieia*.[16] Siblings could marry if they were born of
different mothers, and a number of examples of such marriages are
known.[17] Uncles and nieces could and did marry each other, and so
did adoptive siblings.[18] There seems to have been no concept of
affinity in Athenian law; if Phaedra had succeeded in seducing her
stepson Hippolytus, in legal terms she would have been guilty of
adultery rather than incest. Glotz notes that there was no formal
punishment for incest in Athenian law, unless a third party was
injured by it (as Theseus would have been in Phaedra's case).

Rome was less endogamous than classical Greece in its marriage
practices, and stricter in its legislation about incest.[19] The Romans
did have a specific word for incest, though in classical Latin *incestum* had much broader connotations than its modern equivalent. In
the sense of 'unchaste behaviour' this term covered a variety of
offences relating to pollution and incontinence, though clearly
sexual incontinence was the most important.[20] For instance, Horace
refers to Paris as 'incestus iudex' (unchaste judge) because lust
influenced his decision to bestow the apple of discord on Venus,
who had promised him as a reward Helen, the most beautiful
woman in the world.[21] But the term was also applied to intercourse
with a Vestal virgin, a usage which was continued in the Middle
Ages when incest was used to mean intercourse with nuns or clerics
as well as with relatives. Lactantius Placidus explained in his influential commentary on the *Thebaid* of Statius, written in the fifth or
sixth century AD, that *incestum* is derived from the *ceston* or girdle

---

[16] Just, *Women*, 80.
[17] Themistocles' son by his first wife married his daughter by his second wife; see Cox,
Household Interests, 216–19. When sibling incest is discussed in Seneca's
Apocolocyntosis, a character remarks 'Athenis dimidium licet, Alexandriae totum' (ch.
8; half is alright in Athens, and whole in Alexandria). Curiously, at Sparta the situation
was reversed: siblings with a common father were not permitted to marry. Sparta also
permitted a form of levirate marriage during the first husband's lifetime.
[18] See Just, *Women*, 80 and 95; and Pomeroy, *Families*, 34–5. An Athenian could adopt
his daughter's husband, and could also marry his daughter to his adopted son.
[19] See Treggiari, *Roman Marriage*, 37–9; and Shaw, 'Explaining Incest', 269–70.
Humbert attributes this Roman rigour to the fact that the *paterfamilias* stood *in loco
parentis* to all the members of his *gens* or clan, so that they could be regarded as closely
related to one another.
[20] By the beginning of the empire the idea that incest created pollution may have been
regarded as old-fashioned; Tacitus reports that Claudius was mocked for ordering
purification ceremonies after the suicide of a man accused of incest with his sister
(*Annals*, 12. 8).   [21] *Odes*, 3. 3. 19.

14MEDIEVAL INCEST LAW

of Venus, which binds mortals in matrimony; adultery is an undo-
ing of this girdle, thus *incestum*.[22]

Although there is no reference to incest in the Twelve Tables, an
early codification of Roman law, a remark of Cicero's suggests that
it was in fact a capital crime, and Tacitus refers to a Spaniard who
was thrown from the Tarpeian rock for committing incest with his
daughter.[23] Claudius had the law forbidding marriage between
uncle and niece changed in order to marry his brother's daughter
Agrippina; Tacitus describes the embassy of Vitellius to the Senate
on behalf of the emperor, and attributes to him an argument which
places incest firmly under the rubric of customary law, rather than
natural law.[24] According to Plutarch, the marriage was justified on
the grounds of public necessity.[25] By the second century AD a man
was not permitted to marry his sister's daughter or granddaughter,
his aunt, stepmother, stepdaughter, mother-in-law, or daughter-in-
law, nor a woman her equivalent male relatives; marriage between
siblings by adoption was valid only if one had been previously
emancipated.[26] Gaius notes that because of Claudius' example
marriage to a brother's daughter was permitted, but not to a sister's
daughter; no reason is given for this discrepancy. It may have been
connected to questions of inheritance (marriage with an aunt was
strictly forbidden, perhaps because it carried fewer financial advantages); or it may be that there was greater certainty about the blood
relationship with a sister's daughter than with a brother's (this is
presumably the logic behind the Athenian prohibition against marriage between uterine siblings). Watson cites Claudius' success in
changing the law as an example of the random way in which laws

---

[22] *Lactantii . . . commentum*, 5. 62, ed. Sweeney.
[23] Cicero, *De legibus*, 2. 9. 22; Tacitus, *Annals*, 6. 19. See the comments of Gardner
(*Women*, 125–7), who suggests that nuclear family incest was a matter for the family or
for the pontifices, and that 'marriages within the forbidden degrees would simply be void
in law; sexual relations between the couple did not in themselves constitute an offence'
(126). But incest cases do seem to have come to court on occasion. Cicero refers to a
famous speech by Curio in defence of Servius Fulvius, who was accused of incest
(*Brutus*, 122); he also notes that slaves could be tortured to produce evidence in cases of
incest and conspiracy (*De partitione oratoria*, 122).
[24] *Annals*, 12. 5–7; the word *incestum* is not used. Tacitus comments that only one
senator, a notorious toady, took advantage of the new licence.
[25] *Quaestiones romanae*, 6; discussing why it is customary for women to kiss relatives
on the lips, Plutarch notes that the ancients did not marry blood relatives, just as marriage to aunts and sisters is forbidden at Rome, though the marriage of cousins has
recently been allowed. [26] See Gaius, *Institutes*, 1. 58–62, ed. Seckel and Kuebler.

can come into being, in this case to suit the needs of a particular individual, without any thought for the needs of society in general, or for any supposed rationale for the previous ban on uncle–niece marriage, and comments: 'The same senators, moreover, would have favoured any different rule of law if that would have enabled them to please Claudius. In slightly altered circumstances, one could easily imagine that the decree of the senate would have allowed marriage with a sister's daughter, but not with a brother's daughter.'[27] Marriage with a niece, whether brother's or sister's daughter, was pronounced a capital crime by Constantius and Constans in AD 342, but in 396 Arcadius and Honoriuṣ reduced the penalty to disinheritance of the wife and the children (who were considered illegitimate). There seems to have been considerable dis-agreement about how bad this type of incest was. Marriage between first and second cousins was legal, but apparently fairly rare.[28]

In Gaius' *Institutes* all the rules about incest are grouped together and clearly laid out. Diocletian seems to have had cause for anxiety about the inefficacy of the incest laws, for in AD 295 he issued a stern edict spelling them out again and insisting on their obser-vance; he notes that the gods will continue to favour Rome only if Romans live piously and chastely.[29] In the *Codex Theodosianus* (issued in 438) there is a section on incestuous marriages, but in the *Digest of Justinian* (issued in 533) the incest laws are interspersed with many other aspects of marriage law.[30] In Justinian's code only the most vague justification for the rules is given (natural law and *pudor*, decency). In some cases blood relationship seems to be the crucial factor—it is legal to marry an adopted sister's daughter—but by no means in all: it is illegal to marry an ex-stepmother, a grandmother-in-law, a step-granddaughter, the mother of an ex-fiancée, or an adoptive aunt. It is legal to marry an adoptive sister who has since been emancipated, but unthinkable to marry an adoptive daughter or granddaughter. Treggiari notes that the treat-ment of incest in the works of Roman jurists is confusing; some cases seem to have been treated as adultery or fornication. She also notes that ignorance of the law, or of the relationship, constituted grounds for acquittal, especially for women, though the marriage

---

[27] Watson, *Society*, 37–40 (the quotation is taken from 40).
[28] This is the argument of Shaw and Saller in 'Close-Kin Marriage'.
[29] See *Mosaicarum . . . collatio*, 6. 4, ed. Hyamson.
[30] *Codex Theodosianus*, 3. 12; *Digest of Justinian*, 23. 2.

would still be considered invalid and the children illegitimate. Charges against women were dropped if the incest was of a type forbidden by Roman law rather than *iure gentium* (by the law of mankind), though they might still be charged with adultery.[31] The distinction between *ius gentium* and local Roman law was important for Roman attitudes to incest, but there is no clear rationale for the taboo. There seems to have been some sense that incest caused pollution and offended the gods, but it was not widely or clearly articulated. Justinian was responsible for a very significant innovation when he forbade marriage between children and their baptismal sponsors on the grounds that God had already sanctioned intercourse between their souls.[32] This is the first overtly Christian reference in justification of an incest law (for further discussion see below). The prime consideration in the structuring of the Roman incest laws during the early Empire seems to have been the moral responsibility of a male in authority over female family members (*in loco parentis*), though this principle was ignored in the case of Claudius and Agrippina, and could also lead to some curious anomalies. Treggiari cites the marriage of Nero, the adopted son of Claudius, to Octavia, Claudius' natural daughter who had been emancipated; this was quite legal in Roman eyes, since Claudius was no longer in authority over his own daughter.[33]

As a result of these complicated considerations of the nature of kinship and familial responsibility, Roman law never acknowledged a set number of degrees of prohibited relationship, as medieval canon law would. What did medieval Christians inherit from Roman incest law? That the incest prohibitions included relatives beyond the nuclear family; that there were different kinds of incest, some forbidden universally by natural law and some only by local law, and therefore that the laws against incest could allow some flexibility; that ignorance was an excuse for incest, especially for relationships forbidden by Roman as opposed to natural law, and that in some circumstances incestuous marriages might be tolerated.

---

[31] Treggiari, *Roman Marriage*, 38–9 and 281.

[32] *Codex Justinianus*, 5. 4. 26. This prohibition follows a discussion of the doubts of earlier jurists as to whether it was permissible to marry an emancipated *alumna* (foster-daughter); Justinian argues that anyone who has been raised *in loco filiae* (in the place of a daughter) is ineligible as a wife, and goes on to add the prohibition on marrying a goddaughter. See the comments of Lynch, *Godparents*, 224–6.

[33] Treggiari, *Roman Marriage*, 38.

OTHER EVIDENCE FOR CLASSICAL ATTITUDES TO INCEST

What historical evidence is there for classical attitudes to incest other than law codes?[34] Greek and Roman writers tended to sneer at incest as characteristic of barbarians. Herodotus tells how the Persian king Cambyses insisted on marrying his sister; the royal judges could find no precedent for such a marriage, and so declared diplomatically that legally the king of Persia could do whatever he liked.[35] Strabo reported that the Persian magi slept with their own mothers, as did the Irish, who also ate their dead fathers.[36] Tertullian repeats a story from Ctesias' lost *History of Persia* about some Macedonians who saw a performance of *Oedipus Tyrannus* and could not understand why Oedipus thought it necessary to mutilate himself after discovering the truth about his birth; they booed the actor, and urged each other 'Go for your mother.'[37] In Seneca's *Hippolytus* Theseus, believing that his son has propositioned Phaedra, can only think that it must be the barbarian blood of Hippolytus' Amazon mother coming out in him, for even animals avoid incest (906–14). Ovid's Myrrha, who fell in love with her own father, takes the opposite view, envying animals for enjoying a sexual freedom denied to humans (*Metamorphoses*, 10. 321 ff.). But the view of incest as bestial in a negative sense was widespread in the classical world. Ovid refers in passing to Menephron, who slept with his own mother 'saevarum more ferarum' (*Met*. 7. 386: as wild beasts do). In *The Republic* Socrates remarks that in sleep men's animal instincts are released in dreams: this savage aspect 'does not shrink from attempting to lie with a mother in fancy or with anyone else, man, god, or brute' (9. 571).

Dreams about incest seem to have been common in the classical world, and much discussed. Artemidorus covers every possible variety in his famous treatise on the taxonomy and interpretation of dreams written in the second half of the second century AD, the only classical dream book now extant; he challenges the views of other interpreters in relation to dreams of intercourse with one's mother, and refers to a book on Oedipal dreams by Apollodorus of

---

[34] Classical myth and literature are discussed in Ch. 2.   [35] *Histories*, 3. 31.
[36] *Geography*, 15. 3. 20 and 4. 5. 4. Similar charges against the Irish were still circulating at the time of the Norman Conquest of Ireland in 1172; see the letter of Pope Alexander III to Henry II, quoted in translation by Sheehy in *When the Normans*, 18.
[37] *Apologeticus*, 9. 16, quoted by McCabe, *Incest, Drama*, 7.

Talmessus, which is otherwise unknown.[38] Artemidorus divides his
discussion of dreams about sex into three categories: 'the natural,
legal and customary', the illegal, and the unnatural. In some cases
he cites, the illegality and horror of the incest correlate with the
significance of the dream: possessing a young child means either the
death of the child or the disgrace of the dreamer, 'for no man with
any self-control at all would possess either his own son or any other
child of so tender an age' (1. 78). He devotes one whole section
(1. 79) to dreams of incest with one's mother, which can be auspicious, depending on the precise circumstances (and positions): is
the mother alive or dead in real life, and is she face to face with the
dreamer, looking away, or in the 'rider' position? Sophocles' Jocasta
says that Oedipal dreams are quite common; they are mentioned by
various classical historians in connection with famous political
figures.[39] According to Herodotus, for example, the exiled tyrant
Hippias dreamed of sex with his mother and mistakenly interpreted this to mean that he would reconquer Athens; instead he
died.[40] According to Plutarch, Julius Caesar had a similar dream the
night before crossing the Rubicon; according to Suetonius, this
dream occurred when Caesar was in Spain, and was taken to mean
that he would conquer the whole earth, the universal parent.[41]

Dreams of incest may have been auspicious in some cases, but
charges of incest were often made in the classical world to blacken
the characters of unpopular figures, especially tyrants: the transgression of the incest taboo is a common metaphor for the misuse
of political power.[42] The enemies of the conservative fifth-century
Athenian politician Cimon accused him of both political and moral
crimes, pro-Spartan sympathies and incest with his sister Elpinice;
there had been rumours about their relationship when he was
young, and these were revived to blacken his name.[43] Alcibiades, the
controversial politician, soldier, and friend of Socrates, was a natural target for similar gossip: Athenaeus reports the comment of
Antisthenes that Alcibiades was so perverted and promiscuous that

[38] Artemidorus, *Interpretation*, trans. White; see also Price, 'Future of Dreams', and
Foucault, *History of Sexuality III*, 3–36.
[39] *Oedipus Tyrannus*, 981–2; and see White's notes on Artemidorus 1. 97.
[40] *Histories*, 6. 107.
[41] Plutarch, *Life of Caesar*, 32. 6; Suetonius, *The Deified Julius*, 7.
[42] See McCabe, *Incest, Drama*, 25: 'Perversions in the sexual politics of the family provide ready analogies for corruptions in the power politics of the state or the ideological
politics of church and academy.'   [43] Plutarch, *Cimon*, 4. 5, 15. 3.

he slept with his mother, his daughter, and his sister, 'as Persians do'.[44] A fragment of a speech by Lysias offers more evidence of Alcibiades' immorality: he and Axiochos shared a woman in Abydos and did not know which of them was the father of her daughter, so when the girl became nubile they took turns to sleep with her, each claiming that she was the child of his friend.[45]

In late Republican Rome, the tribune P. Clodius was believed to have slept with one or more of his sisters. Cicero frequently refers to this gossip, though ironically he himself was accused of incest with his daughter Tullia, to whom he was famously devoted.[46] The satirists quite frequently mention rumours of incest (though according to Richlin, they seem to have been much more fascinated by oral sex).[47] Juvenal includes affairs between stepmothers and their stepsons in his list of female failings in *Satire* 6 (402–4). Augustus, the first Roman emperor, exiled his only daughter Julia because of her adultery; but his great-grandson Caligula spread a rumour that Augustus had committed incest with Julia, and that Agrippina (mother of Caligula) was the result. Apparently Caligula preferred to be the descendant of an incestuous emperor rather than of his real grandfather, the soldier Agrippa.[48] Caligula himself was widely rumoured to have committed incest with his sisters; Nero was reputed to have desired his mother Agrippina, and to have had sex with her when they travelled together in a litter.[49] Suetonius, the purveyor of this gossip, also claims that Titus had an affair with his sister-in-law, and Domitian with his niece (Plutarch makes this latter charge too).[50] As in Athens, powerful public figures in Rome were often accused of incest, which was perceived as symbolizing excessive appetite and abuse of power (see the discussion of Periander and Semiramis in the next chapter). Incest was also a charge used by rulers to remove enemies or obstacles. Agrippina wanted her son Nero to marry Octavia, daughter of the emperor Claudius, but Octavia was already engaged to Silanus.

[44] *Deipnosophistae*, 5. 220 c–d.

[45] Lysias, Fragmenta xxx, in *Discours*, ed. and trans. Gernet and Bizos. It is possible that Athenaeus is referring to the same situation: since there is no possessive pronoun in the Greek, it could mean 'he slept with a mother and her daughter', rather than referring to his own relatives. But clearly anything could be believed of Alcibiades!

[46] On Clodius see also Catullus, 79. 1–2. On Cicero see Richlin, *Garden*, 96–7.

[47] See Richlin, *Garden*, 15; incest does not appear in her index.

[48] Suetonius, *Caligula*, 23.   [49] Suetonius, *Caligula*, 24 and 36; *Nero*, 28.

[50] Suetonius, *Titus*, 10, and *Domitian*, 22.

Agrippina accused Silanus of incest with his sister, to whom he was well known to be devoted; Silanus was struck off the senatorial roll, and committed suicide on the day that Claudius married Agrippina.[51]

Given that incest charges were so popular as polemical instruments, it is hardly surprising that accusations of incest were made against the early Christians. Pagan writers pounced on the novel Christian emphasis on the importance of love, the use of 'brother' and 'sister' as a standard form of address between Christians, and their communal meals or 'love-feasts'; these practices were interpreted as conclusive evidence of cannibalism and incest. Minucius Felix is one of the early Christian writers who gives examples of these charges:

They fall in love almost before they are acquainted; everywhere they introduce a kind of religious lust, a promiscuous 'brotherhood' and 'sisterhood' by which ordinary fornication, under cover of a hallowed name, is converted to incest.[52]

Similarly, Tertullian makes frequent and mocking reference to the supposed orgies in the dark at Christian feasts:

We are said to be the most criminal of men, on the score of our sacramental baby-killing and the baby-eating that goes with it and the incest that follows the banquet, where the dogs are our pimps in the dark, forsooth, and make a sort of decency for guilty lusts by overturning the lamps.[53]

He asks his pagan interlocutor to imagine the situation for a Christian who is certain of eternal life:

. . . catch the infant blood; steep your bread with it; eat and enjoy it. Meanwhile, as you recline on your couch, reckon the places where your mother, your sister, may be; make a careful note so that, when the darkness of the dogs' contriving shall fall, you can make no mistake. You will be guilty of a sin, unless you have committed incest. So initiated, so sealed, you live for ever. I wish you to answer: is eternity worth it?

It is striking that the tendency to accuse minority or unpopular religious groups of incest has continued down the centuries; later

---

[51] Tacitus, *Annals*, 12. 4. 2; this sad episode is the background to Seneca's comment on the diversity of attitudes to sibling incest at Athens and Alexandria which was quoted earlier (*Apocolocyntosis* 8—see n. 17).   [52] *Octavius*, 9. 2.
[53] *Apologeticus*, 7. 1 and 8. 2–4. See Rousselle, *Porneia*, 107–13.

targets include the Albigensians, the Quakers, and recently the Branch Davidians of Waco. It may be that one reason why medieval Christian writers did not use incest as a major theme in exemplary and hagiographical tales until the eleventh or twelfth centuries was that it had taken them so long to dismiss these pagan accusations. Early Christians felt no compunction, however, about replying in kind rather than turning the other cheek. Patristic writers poured scorn on pagan Romans for allowing such shocking stories to be told of the promiscuity of their gods, including incestuous affairs (see my discussion of the Christian reception of classical mythology in the following chapter).

THE JUDAIC, BIBLICAL, AND PATRISTIC TRADITION

Christians in the Middle Ages inherited a complicated and often contradictory series of attitudes to incest from Jewish and biblical tradition. The crucial biblical texts were Leviticus 18: 6–18 and 20: 10–21, which list the relatives with whom sexual relations are forbidden: the taboo is explained in the context of distinguishing the Jews from neighbouring races, specifically the Egyptians and the Canaanites (18: 3).[54] The list of prohibited relatives includes mother, stepmother, sister (father's or mother's daughter), granddaughter, aunt (by blood or father's brother's wife), daughter-in-law, sister-in-law (brother's wife, and also the sister of a living wife); but curiously daughters are not mentioned, nor are nieces.[55] It is also forbidden to sleep with a woman and then with her daughter or granddaughter; in 18: 12, 13, and 17 the prohibited person is said to be 'near kinswoman' of another close relative, by way of explanation. It is striking that both here and at 20: 19–20 aunts are

[54] R. H. Helmholz has pointed out (in correspondence) that medieval commentators on canon law did not often refer to the Leviticus texts; he doubts whether they played much part in the development of the medieval incest laws. There is a huge literature on the interpretation of Leviticus; I have not attempted an extensive survey.

[55] Ziskind considers the omission of daughters insignificant, arguing that few Near Eastern incest laws are comprehensive ('Legal Rules', 100–1). But it must have provoked some debate, judging from the tone of St Ambrose's letter to Paternus in which he insists that father–daughter intercourse is obviously prohibited by natural law, divine law, and individual piety (*Epistolae*, 1. 60 (PL 16: 1185)). Leviticus also appears to ban only half-sisters. Rabanus Maurus, writing in the early 9th cent., found this puzzling, but argues, like St Ambrose, that full sisters must be intended here too; see his *Expositionum in Leviticum*, 5. 9.

singled out; at 20: 19–20 relations with an aunt are said to constitute 'iniquitas' (wickedness) and 'peccatum' (sin), terms which do
not appear in all the other prohibitions, though 'iniquitas' is
applied to a half-sister in 20: 17 (I discuss the Latin terms here,
rather than the Hebrew ones, since the Vulgate was the standard
text used in the Middle Ages). This seems to imply that natural
shame and reverence will only prevent relations with very close
family members, and that the prohibition against aunts, half-
sisters, and step-relatives has to be reinforced by further injunc-
tions, explanations, and threats (it is not a simple distinction
between relations by consanguinity and by affinity). Incest is one of
several pollutions prohibited in Leviticus; others include intercourse with a menstruating woman, adultery, masturbation, blasphemy, and bestiality. In Chapter 20 the penalties for breaking the
various taboos are spelled out. It is striking that some forms of
incest are to be punished by death (as are adultery, homosexuality,
and bestiality): intercourse with the father's wife, with a daughter-
in-law, with a wife and also her mother. Incest with a sister incurs
exile. Surprisingly, it is only in relation to incest with an aunt by
marriage or sister-in-law that the issue of children is raised: in both
cases the transgressors will die childless. This could suggest that the
children will not survive, or it might mean sterility—but as a divine
punishment rather than the biological consequence of incest, since
the sinners are related by affinity, not consanguinity.

Ziskind stresses that these prohibitions are all addressed to
men and that the prohibited family members are all female.[56] He
concludes that 'the priestly writer was not only compiling rules
relating to the purity of family life but was reforming them with the
objective of improving the status of women within the framework
of ancient Israel's patriarchal structure'. The prohibitions in
Leviticus include various widows of male relatives: 'the option of
handing around these women either as wives or concubines to other
men within the family was foreclosed . . . The women could not be
forced to remain within the extended family as cheap laborers or
child bearers . . .' Mitterauer agrees that there was a strong tendency to exogamy among the Israelites, but points out that they
were also very concerned about pure bloodlines, especially in
priestly families, a concern which encouraged endogamy.[57]

---

[56] Ziskind, 'Legal Rules', 104.   [57] Mitterauer, 'Christianity', 310–13.

Carmichael argues that the inclusion of some relationships in the Leviticus prohibitions and the omission of others can be explained by reference to the stories about incest in the preceding books of the Old Testament; in his reading, the writer is responding to those narratives (Lot, Abraham, Judah, Amnon, etc.), and also adding some contrasting examples, rather than offering solutions to real-life problems.[58] Whether or not they provide the explanation for the rules in Leviticus 18 and 20, narratives involving incest in the first section of the Old Testament presented serious problems for early Christian theologians. The dying Jacob curses his son Reuben for having sex with his stepmother, the concubine Bilha (Gen. 49: 3–4), and Absalom has his half-brother Amnon murdered for raping their sister Tamar (2 Sam. 13). But other incestuous characters are not punished in any way. No moral comment is made in the Genesis account of Lot's seduction by his daughters after the destruction of Sodom (Gen. 19: 30–8), though later we learn that their descendants, the Moabites and Ammonites, are excluded from the congregation of the Lord (Deut. 23: 3). Lot's incest is often mentioned in medieval commentaries as an example of the evils of drunkenness; patristic writers stressed that the daughters thought that Lot was the only surviving man in the world, and that it was their duty to continue the human race.[59] Tamar, the widowed daughter-in-law of Judah, deliberately disguises herself as a harlot to tempt her father-in-law, and bears him twins (Gen. 38). Perhaps she is justified in that he had promised her to his youngest son, but the marriage had never taken place; she does not seem to incur any punishment, nor does Judah. Particularly striking is Abraham's open admission that his wife Sarah is in fact his half-sister (Gen. 20: 11–12). No further comment is made in Genesis, but according to Leach, '[t]he barrenness of Sarah is an aspect of her incest. The supernatural intervention which ultimately ensures that she shall bear a child is evidence that the incest is condoned.'[60] This marriage appears to put Abraham on a par with the reviled Pharaohs, but Leach argues that other biblical episodes make Abraham's sin seem minor:

The myth requires that the Israelites be descended unambiguously from Terah the father of Abraham. This is achieved only at the cost of breach

---

[58] Carmichael, *Law*, 39 ff.
[59] See for instance Origen, *Homilies on Genesis*, Homily 5; Chrysostom, *Homilies on Genesis*, Homily 44. 17–23.   [60] Leach, 'Genesis', 10.

of the incest rule; but by reciting a large number of similar stories which entail even greater breaches of sexual morality, the relations of Abraham and Sarah stand out as uniquely virtuous. Just as Adam and Eve are virtuous as compared to Cain and Abel, so Abraham's incest can pass unnoticed in the context of such outrageous characters as Ham, Lot's daughters, and the men of Sodom. [61]

Certainly this prominent instance of incest appears to pass without comment in the Old Testament.

Medieval theologians were well aware of the problem of incest among the patriarchs, and dealt with it ingeniously. St Augustine provided a determined lead. In a passage in the *City of God* much quoted by later writers (15. 16), he acknowledges that there is a discrepancy between biblical example and current Christian teaching, and even credits pagans with a growing desire to avoid incest (here he shows a generosity rare in patristic writers, who were usually quick to criticize pagans for their lack of inhibition in relation to incest). He explains that incestuous marriages—by this he means sibling marriages—were acceptable in the newly created world 'compellente necessitate' (by force of necessity); but as soon as the population expanded sufficiently, it became necessary to spread the net of 'socialis dilectio' (social affection) by marrying outside the immediate kin-group. He shows in detail how incest restricts social networking through the doubling of father and father-in-law, or even of father, father-in-law, and brother. Thus through 'lex humana' (human law) and the encouragement of the 'patres antiqui' (ancient fathers), instinctive shame was activated and incest became 'nefas' (taboo). Augustine has great faith in instinctive revulsion against incest, 'humanae verecundiae quiddam naturale et laudabile' (a certain natural and admirable human shame); but he does not insist that such shame always functions properly of its own accord. He does comment with some pleasure that though marriages between cousins are legal in his own time, they are in fact very rare: 'Verum tamen factum etiam licitum propter vicinitatem horrebatur illiciti' (Nevertheless there was a revulsion from doing something which, lawful though it was, bordered close on the unlawful). But like the theologians and lawyers who later drew on his argument, he acknowledges that laws are needed to enforce this taboo, and that they are human laws, not natural ones.

[61] Leach, 'Genesis', 12.

Augustine's account of the incest taboo was immensely influential; the twelfth-century canonist Gratian, for instance, quotes it as his only authority in the section on incest in his great codification of canon law, produced in the late twelfth century.[62] Many other writers repeat Augustine's arguments, and they are not only theologians and lawyers; for instance, Chaucer's friend and contemporary Gower begins Book 8 of his *Confessio Amantis* (late fourteenth-century) with a discourse on the laws of marriage.[63] He notes that Cain and Abel married their sisters Calmana and Delbora, 'Forthi that time it was no Sinne | The Soster forto take hire brother | Whan that ther was of chois non other' (68–70: because at that time it was no sin for the sister to take her brother, when there was no other choice). He dates the first change in this situation to the third age, the time of Abraham, when sibling marriage became forbidden because 'The nede tho was overrunne, | For ther was poeple ynough in londe' (100–1: the need was superseded, since there were enough people in the land). At this point marriage between cousins became the rule, as shown by the choices of Isaac and Jacob. Gower attributes the expansion of the consanguinity prohibitions to exclude all relatives to an unspecified Pope in the early Christian era (142 ff.). But he does not share Augustine's optimistic view that there is natural respect for the incest taboo: the narrator, Confessor, remarks that the rules are widely ignored by those who 'taken wher thei take may' (take wherever they can), and urges the shocked Amans (Lover) to confess forthwith any sins of incest he has committed (148 ff.).

Gower was by no means the first to express such mixed views on the incest laws. One distinguished predecessor a century earlier was Thomas Aquinas in his comments under the rubric 'utrum incestus sit determinata species luxuriae' (Is incest a determinate species of lust?)[64] At the beginning of this section he notes that 'accedere ad consanguineas vel affines non est secundum se deforme; alias nullo tempore licuisset' (to lie with relatives, whether by blood or by spiritual ties, is not ugly in itself, else it would never have been lawful). And at the end he quotes Augustine from the *City of God* (15. 16): 'commixtio sororum et fratrum quanto fuit antiquior, compellente

[62] *Decretum*, Pars Secunda, C. 35 q. 1, ed. Friedberg.
[63] I cite the edition of Macaulay.
[64] Aquinas, *Summa Theologiae*, 2a2ae.154, 9, ed. and trans. Gilby, xliii. 236–41.

necessitate, tanto postea facta est damnabilior, religione pro-
hibente' (the union of brothers and sisters goes back to olden times,
when necessity compelled it; all the same so much more damnable
did it later become when religion forbade it). The arguments in
between are curiously contradictory: he invokes innate respect for
parents as a natural deterrent to incest, yet his next point is that living at close quarters is bound to inflame lust and offer irresistibly
tempting opportunities, and so the incest taboo is necessary. As a
modern saying puts it, 'Nothing propinks like propinquity'; for
Christian theologians, such propinquity was inevitably dangerous.
Aquinas repeats Augustine's argument about the benefits of
exogamy in widening the social network, then quotes Aristotle's
view that natural affection for one's own kin could easily become
blazing lust. Aristotle is invoked again to support Aquinas' claim
that 'in commixtione personarum conjunctarum aliquid est quod
est secundum se indecens et repugnans naturali rationi' (there is
something indecent and repugnant to natural reason in the sexual
intercourse of relatives). Aquinas reports that in the *De animalibus*
Aristotle told the story of a stallion who covered his mother without knowing it, and on discovering what he had done jumped off a
cliff out of horror. It seems curious that the main ammunition for
Aquinas' important and indeed controversial argument about natural reason should be a prime example of the pathetic fallacy taken
from the animal world. One wonders if he had in fact read the
whole of Aristotle's work: the noble companion and helper of man
provides a less satisfactory analogy in an earlier part of the treatise,
where Aristotle comments that horses are the most lascivious of
creatures (after men), and that stallions even cover their own
mothers and daughters, a match which is considered particularly
desirable by breeders.[65]

THE DEVELOPMENT OF MEDIEVAL INCEST LAWS[66]

Christianity is not opposed to marriage; after all, Christ's first miracle was performed at the marriage at Cana, and there is no record

---

[65] The story quoted by St Thomas is told in Aristotle's *Historia animalium*, 9. 47
(631^{a}21); for the comments on inbreeding see 6. 22 (576^a).

[66] This is a very complex subject, so my discussion here is of necessity very selective.
There is a useful survey by Mangenot in *Dictionnaire de théologie catholique*, s.v.

of His forbidding His followers to marry.[67] St Paul urged all married Christians to pay the 'marriage debt' to their partners (an order that greatly pleased Chaucer's Wife of Bath), and Augustine declared that there were three grounds for sex in marriage: procreation of children, social stability, and the avoidance of extramarital fornication or adultery.[68] On the other hand, asceticism was a very important aspect of early Christianity, and patristic writers regarded sex as sinful and polluting: 'Lust was an infirmity of the flesh which somehow contaminated the soul and caused disorder both in the human spirit and in the human frame.'[69] As a particularly inappropriate and unbridled form of lust, incest was especially unacceptable to Christians; indeed in some medieval texts, as we shall see, it was taken to represent original sin. One can understand why the Church might have been disturbed by nuclear family incest, and by any kind of incest that involved the abuse or exploitation of children. But the legislation about incest that developed in the course of the Middle Ages goes well beyond the nuclear family, and indeed beyond the kin-group linked by blood; and it ignores the problem of child abuse which is of such great concern to us today.[70] By the twelfth century the impediments to marriage on the grounds of kinship had been extended to what we would consider ludicrous lengths, and were a source of constant debate and discussion. How did this situation arise?

St Augustine, followed by many other writers including Thomas Aquinas, acknowledged that the supposedly natural and universal law prohibiting incest was in fact socially constructed, and thus open to interpretation and alteration by the Church authorities.

---

inceste. Apart from Brundage's indispensable *Law, Sex*, some specialized studies which I have found useful are Esmein, *Mariage*; Fleury, *Recherches*; and Smith, *Papal Enforcement*, chs. 1–3. There is a valuable survey of sources in Gaudemet, *Sources*. For the Eastern church, which does not concern me here, see Dauvillier and de Clercq, *Mariage*, and also the admirably clear account in Levin, *Sex and Society*, 136–59.

[67] There is no record of comment on incest by Christ. In 1 Cor. 5 St Paul reprimands the Corinthians for tolerating a case of incest between a man and his stepmother; and John the Baptist's death was the result of his criticism of Herod for marrying his brother's wife (Luke 3: 19–20, Mark 6: 14–29).

[68] For St Paul's views see 1 Cor. 7; for Augustine's views, see his *De nuptiis* and *De bono coniugali*.

[69] Brundage, 'Carnal Delight', 365. See the excellent introduction in Brundage, *Law, Sex*, and also Brown, *Body and Society*.

[70] On the treatment of children in medieval law codes, see Helmholz, 'And were there Children's Rights'.

The taboo in Leviticus covered only close relatives (including some affines); this seems also to have been the case in Rome in antiquity. Yet by the twelfth century, the Church insisted that no marriages could be contracted between persons related by blood or affinity to the seventh degree, and between persons related by spiritual affinity to the fourth degree.[71] This was sometimes summarized as a ban on intercourse or marriage with any relative, since memory and family lore were unlikely to extend beyond seven degrees. The laws which 'placed most medieval men and women in an impossible legal position' were often presented as if based on unassailable principles, but the constant requests for clarification by churchmen and the idiosyncratic interpretations and explanations of Popes, jurists, and theologians reveal the uncertainty and confusion which continued to prevail throughout the Middle Ages.[72] Not only was explicit biblical sanction lacking for many of the prohibitions pronounced by medieval theologians, but drastic changes in the laws were made over the course of a thousand years; and these laws were not always strictly observed or enforced, creating contradictory precedents.

The confusion was augmented by the fact that there were two very different systems of calculating relationships in Europe at the beginning of the Middle Ages. The Roman system was to count back from one collateral up the family tree to a common ancestor, and then down again to the other collateral relative in question; the total number of generations, counting both sides, represented the degree of relationship. So a man would be related to a first cousin in the fourth degree (via his father, his grandfather, and his uncle). The Germanic system, however, was to count back by parallel generations or 'joints', so that two Germanic degrees were the

---

[71] Affinity included one's own in-laws (the first degree), the in-laws of one's in-laws (the second degree), and the in-laws of the in-laws of one's in-laws (the third degree). Pope Gregory I (590–604) was supposedly the first authority to specify the number of degrees as seven, though in this period when Europe was still being converted to Christianity, some flexibility was needed in dealing with more endogamic peoples.

[72] The quotation is taken from Baldwin, *Masters, Princes*, i. 333. A great deal has been written recently about the reasons for the complex medieval system of prohibited relationships: see Duby, *Medieval Marriage* and *Knight*; Guerreau-Jalabert, 'Sur les structures'; Goody, *Development*; Lynch, *Godparents*; Brooke, *Medieval Idea*; de Jong, 'To the Limits'; Archibald, 'Incest'; Herlihy, 'Making Sense'; Mitterauer, 'Christianity'; and Shell, 'Want of Incest'.

equivalent of four Roman degrees.[73] In the second half of the eighth century the Church shifted from the Roman system to the Germanic system (though it was not universally accepted for some time); the pool of eligible partners was thus dramatically reduced, particularly in small communities where most people were related to their neighbours in some way.[74] A key concept in this quagmire of shifting rules and regulations is the Christian notion of *unitas carnis* (one flesh), which differentiates medieval incest legislation distinctively from that of other societies, including our own. In medieval thinking, once a man and a woman had sexual intercourse, they became one flesh, whether or not they were married and whether or not their sexual relationship continued; therefore the man's relations became the woman's too, and vice versa. The authority cited in support of this concept was Gen. 2: 24: 'Therefore shall a man leave his father and mother, and shall cleave unto his wife: and they shall be one flesh.'[75] The prohibitions in Leviticus indicate implicit recognition of the principle of *unitas carnis*. This idea was quite foreign to the Graeco-Roman world, but the early Christians took it very seriously, and it was to complicate greatly the medieval Church's list of prohibited marriage partners. The source of this doctrine, as of so many others dealing with sex and marriage, was St Paul, who first argued that marriage made man and wife one flesh (Eph. 5: 31–2); it then seemed a logical consequence that the relatives of one spouse should be related by affinity to the other spouse. This idea was extended by later writers such as Isidore of Seville so that any act of sexual intercourse created a lasting relationship between the two persons involved (and therefore an impediment to marriage between their families). Once this principle was established, logic demanded that the prohibited categories of relationship be extended inexorably as far as possible,

---

[73] These relationships were often schematized pictorially as trees of consanguinity (an example is reproduced on the dust jacket); see Klapisch-Zuber, 'Genesis', and Guerreau-Jalabert, 'L'Arbre'.

[74] In the 11th cent. the jurists of Ravenna incited the citizens of Florence to rebel against the now established Germanic method; the revolt was crushed, but confusion and discontent continued. It is surprising that there was not more public outcry against a system which doubled the already oppressive restrictions imposed by the Church without any obvious authority.

[75] See Crouzel, '"Pour former une seule chair"'. Helmholz remarks that the canonists 'did not treat biblical texts as direct sources or as statutes . . . Instead, they drew legal lessons and legal principles from them' ('Bible', 1565).

even to in-laws of in-laws of in-laws (though when these laws proved unworkable, the prohibited degrees were in fact reduced by the Fourth Lateran Council—see below).

In late antiquity the incest taboo was not expressed in terms of a standard number of forbidden degrees of relationship, nor was there any logical or consistent basis for the various incest laws. To some extent the Romans thought of incest as pollution and as offensive to the gods, but religious values were rarely invoked in connection with incest laws. Early Christian councils increasingly condemned various forms of incestuous liaisons, but the laws about incest introduced by the early Christian emperors 'seem to reflect broad considerations of social policy, rather than specifically Christian viewpoints'.[76] Justinian was the first emperor to give a specifically Christian rationale for an incest law in his *Codex* (published in 529): he prohibited marriage between a baptismal sponsor and his godchild on the grounds that the appropriate relationship is paternal affection on the part of the sponsor, and a spiritual bond brokered by God.[77] This notion of spiritual kinship or 'compaternity' seems to have taken root early in Byzantium, by the sixth century, and probably spread to the West from there; Byzantine influence was strong in the Lombard kingdoms of Italy.[78] In Byzantium, where priests could be married, a priest's child could not marry anyone the priest had baptized.[79] In the beginning of the Christian era, it was usual for a parent to sponsor his or her own child at baptism. For social reasons, it became increasingly usual from the sixth century on to invite an outsider to be godparent, as Lynch notes: 'Baptism was the occasion for the creation of a web of kinship, a family that was the mirror image of the natural family.'[80] He suggests that in the early centuries of Christianity there was no

[76] Brundage, *Law, Sex*, 107.

[77] *Codex Justinianus*, 5. 4. 26. Antonina, wife of the great Byzantine general Belisarius, was accused of having an affair with their joint godson and adopted child, Theodosius; see Procopius, *Anecdota*, 1. 1, and the comments of Lynch, *Godparents*, 226–8.

[78] It was first promulgated in the East at the Council in Trullo of 692, and in the West at the Council of Rome in 721. Mayke de Jong suggests that this legislation accorded with traditional Germanic fears of pollution in the kin-group ('To the Limits', 37–8). For a detailed study of spiritual kinship see Lynch, *Godparents*, to which I am much indebted. He notes that it is hard to find suitable words in English for this spiritual relationship (6–7); 'godfather' is an inadequate translation of *compater*, and he prefers 'cofather'.   [79] Lynch, *Godparents*, 202.

[80] Lynch, *Godparents*, 275.

need to invoke the incest taboo in relation to godparents, since there was usually only one, of the same gender as the person baptized. But once it became usual to have several godparents, both male and female, from the ninth century on, the ban was considered necessary. The language of the family was already used to describe the Christian community: God is the universal Father, the abbot is the spiritual father of his community and the priest of his congregation; the Church is the bride of Christ and the mother of all Christians, who regard each other as brothers and sisters.[81] Special names for the sponsors based on the Latin terminology for parents and children became current in the West in the eighth century, *patrinus, matrina,* and *filiolus/a* (little father/mother/son/daughter). As Lynch notes, this kingroup was considered morally superior to the natural family: 'The spiritual family was no less real than the carnal family, but it was thought to originate and function in a higher realm, that of grace and purity.' The Byzantine Council in Trullo of 692 had decreed that 'a spiritual relationship takes precedence over a carnal one: it was not permitted to maintain both'.[82] Parents who acted as sponsors to their own children, intentionally or unintentionally, were therefore required to separate; this rule was cynically manipulated by those who wanted to end an unsatisfactory marriage.[83]

By the time of Justinian's legislation the empire had long been Christian, yet Christian rationales were not generally applied to the incest laws. In the following centuries, however, some imperial scandals at Byzantium indicate that incest was being viewed from an explicitly Christian perspective.[84] But it is in the barbarian codes of the West that spiritual grounds for the incest laws were first explicitly adduced. At first their rulings on incest made no mention

[81] Guerreau-Jalabert regards this language as a significant source for the invention of 'compaternity', or 'pseudo-parenté', as she calls it ('Sur les structures', 1036).

[82] Lynch, *Godparents,* 177 and 209; he notes that in Latin America and the Mediterranean today, compaternity is considered to be a very important relationship.

[83] Lynch, *Godparents,* 279–81; and see Gratian, *Decretum,* C. 30 q. 1 c. 4. Some manuscripts of the *Decretum* include illustrations of crowds around the font at mass baptisms when parents sometimes sponsored their own children, either by mistake or by design: see Melnikas, *Corpus,* iii. 943 ff.

[84] There was considerable criticism when the Byzantine emperor Heraclius (d. 641) married his niece Martina, and the deformity or early deaths of a number of their children were interpreted as divine punishment for the sin of the parents; Bardas Caesar, uncle and effective regent for Michael III, was excommunicated in 858 for abandoning his wife in favour of his own daughter-in-law (for the sources see *Oxford Dictionary of Byzantium,* s.v. *Heraclius* and *Bardas*).

of Christian values, and the penalties were entirely secular (for instance, disinheritance or the payment of wergeld). But in the mid-eighth century the Lombard king Liutprand cited the Christian canons as authority for the ban on marriage with a sister-in-law, and forbade marriage with a cousin's widow 'deo iubente' (at God's command), noting that this was done at the special request of the Pope.[85] This comment implies that no natural instinct or shame would have suggested the prohibition to the Lombards without papal intervention—and indeed early Christian missionaries in Europe spent much of their time dealing with local marriage customs which were unacceptable to the Church. For instance, Pope Gregory authorized Augustine of Canterbury to sanction marriages in the fourth and fifth degrees among the newly converted Anglo-Saxons, a compromise which was frequently questioned and disputed by later writers.[86] At the Roman Council of 743 Pope Zachary had to explain it away as best he could as an extraordinary concession in the interests of the successful evangelization of the Germanic peoples, 'dum rudi erant et invitandi ad fidem' (at a time when they were ignorant and needed to be encouraged to believe).[87]

By the time of the Lombard king Aistulf (mid-eighth century), the crown was at one with the Church. In his laws Aistulf ordered an immediate end to any marriage prohibited under canon or secular law, because 'qui talia consentiunt, contra Deum et animam suam faciunt, et malitia amplius crescit' (those who agree to such things act against God and their own souls, and evil grows greater).[88] The most fanatical of these barbarian codes, from the point of view of Christian zeal, was produced by the Visigothic kings. Their civil laws specified not only immediate separation for the incestuous couple, but also perpetual penance and entry into a monastery (though the king could reduce this sentence).[89]

---

[85] *Leges Liutprandi regis*, 32. III and 33. IV, in *Leges Langobardorum*, ed. Bluhme, 123–4.

[86] Bede, *Ecclesiastical History*, i. 27. V, ed. Colgrave and Mynors, 84–7; see also the editors' comments at lxii ff., and 79 n. 4. Some manuscripts of Bede's *Historia* have appended an extract from Isidore's definition of incest in the *Etymologiae*, and another from the Roman Council of 721, to represent the orthodox point of view. See Deanesly and Grosjean, 'Canterbury Editions', and Chadwick, 'Gregory the Great', 207–11.

[87] Mansi, *Sacrorum conciliorum*, XII. 366, canon 15. This answer did not put an end to discussion of the concession: see Gratian, *Decretum*, C. 35 q. 2–3 c. 19–20.

[88] *Leges Ahistulfi*, 8, in *Leges Langobardorum*, ed. Bluhme, 197.

[89] *Leges Visigothorum*, III. 5. I–II, ed. Zeumer, 158–61.

According to this code, charges of incest could be incurred not only through illegal marriage, but also by *copula carnalis* (physical connection), or affinity; previous intercourse with one member of a family was an impediment to marriage with any other member of that family, to the sixth degree. In the early Anglo-Saxon civil codes there was little reference to incest; no doubt it was regarded as part of the ecclesiastical sphere. But it is clear that Christian ethics controlled the laws about incest by the time of Æthelred (*c*.1000), whose code prohibited breaches of spiritual consanguinity on the authority of God's law, with threats about personal salvation.[90]

Law codes offer one type of evidence for the incest laws of the early Middle Ages, and Church councils constantly harped on the problem of enforcing these laws. Another type of evidence is found in the penitentials, lists of the penalties imposed by the Church for various kinds of sins (including incest) which date from the sixth century on, though it is hard to know how to assess the relationship between these texts and actual practices in this period. The earliest extant penitentials were written in the British Isles and contain references to incest, as do most later penitentials, though they are often arranged in a curiously unsystematic way.[91] The Irish *Penitential of Cummean* (*c*.650) prescribes three years of penance and perpetual pilgrimage for a man who commits incest with his mother; no other form of incest is mentioned, though the following items concern oral sex, sodomy, and masturbation. The Anglo-Saxon *Penitential of Theodore* (*c*.690) demands fifteen years of penance, or seven years of penance and perpetual pilgrimage, for incest with one's mother; fifteen (or possibly twelve) years of penance for incest with one's sister; abstinence from flesh for fifteen years for incest between brothers; and the mother who 'imitates acts of fornication with her little son' is to eat no flesh for three years and also to fast one day a week. It is curious that mother–son incest appears fairly frequently but father–daughter not at all; and marriage to an affine is discussed only in the so-called *Roman*

---

[90] *Laws of Æthelred*, VI. 12, ed. and trans. Robertson, 94–5; the main author was probably Archbishop Wulfstan.

[91] R. H. Helmholz has pointed out (in correspondence) that since the pentitentials consisted largely of answers to questions or problems, the lack of systematic coverage is not so surprising. The texts mentioned here are all conveniently available in McNeill and Gamer, *Medieval Handbooks*. For useful discussions of the penitentials and their relationship to actual life see Manselli, 'Vie familiale', and Payer, *Sex*; there is also further comment later in this chapter.

Penitential of about 830, which condemns those who marry a wife's daughter, a stepmother, an uncle's widow, or a wife's sister. There does not seem to be a standard list of forbidden liaisons, and the early penitentials do not seem to conform with what we know of civil legislation about incest in the barbarian law codes.

By the eleventh century the prohibitions on marriage between kin had reached their most extended range. No one might marry any relative by blood or marriage within seven degrees of kinship, or any spiritual relative within four degrees of kinship. But this extraordinarily restrictive taboo was not established without resistance, and was honoured as much in the breach as in the observance. The correspondence of medieval ecclesiastics is full of queries about the prohibitions on marriage with kin. St Boniface, evangelist to the Germanic peoples in the first half of the eighth century, wrote to several Popes requesting guidance on these matters; his letters make it clear that the new and expanded prohibitions were not immediately accepted, and indeed were challenged by pillars of the Church. Boniface was particularly baffled by the vexed question of spiritual consanguinity, and begged several Anglo-Saxon bishops to identify for him the source of the prohibition, complaining that he had never come across it in any old canons or papal decrees or lists of sins. He attacked this recent law with devastating logic:

Quia nullatenus intelligere possumus quare in uno loco spiritualis propinquitas in conjunctione carnalis copulae tam grande peccatum est, quando omnes in sacro baptizmate Christi et Ecclesiae filii et filiae, fratres et sorores comprobamus.[92]

(For in no way can I understand why in one place spiritual relationship in marital intercourse should be so great a sin, when we are all known to be sons and daughters, brothers and sisters of Christ and of the Church in holy baptism.)

According to his logic, either all incest taboos are unncessary, or the entire human race should abstain from sex. Pope Gregory II told him that the taboo could be reduced to four degrees for new converts who were used to very different practices. But a much harder line was taken by Peter Damian, who in 1046 wrote a long and detailed letter to the Bishop of Cesena and the Archdeacon of

---

[92] Boniface, Epistle 32, quoted and translated by Lynch, *Godparents*, 245. See also Shell, 'Want of Incest', esp. 631–9.

Ravenna criticizing a recent argument that allowed marriage between relatives in the fourth degree, and insisting on adherence to the full range of prohibitions.[93]

One of the first systematic discussions of the problem of defining and dealing with incest, and one of the most influential, is found in Gratian's *Decretum*, written about 1140 in order to systematize contemporary law at a time when jurists were returning to the model of Roman law. In Causa 35 of the Second Part of his *Decretum*, Gratian posits a hypothetical but no doubt frequent problem. A widower marries a woman related in the fourth degree to his dead wife and in the sixth degree to himself, and children are born to them; three years later he is denounced to the Church, and pleads ignorance. Gratian poses ten questions:

1. Can one marry one's relatives?
2. Can one marry one's wife's relatives?
3. What are the prohibited number of degrees?
4. Why are there seven?
5. How are they calculated?
6. Who can confirm relationships on oath?
7. What is the status of the children of an incestuous marriage?
8. If a couple marries illegally through ignorance, is separation necessary?
9. What is the status of a second marriage, if the church dissolves the first marriage in error?
10. Can a woman's children by her second husband marry relatives of her first husband?

I shall concentrate here on the first five questions, which involve the historical development and rationale of medieval incest law.

Gratian's answer to question 1 is that although there were marriages between blood relatives in Old Testament times, they are no longer permitted. He quotes at length Augustine's arguments in the *City of God*, and ends firmly: 'Consanguineorum ergo coniunctiones, quamvis evangelicis et apostolicis preceptis non inveniantur prohibitae, sunt tamen fugendae, quia ecclesiasticis institutionibus inveniuntur terminatae' (So although marriages between blood-relatives may not be forbidden by the commands of the gospels and the apostles, nevertheless they are to be avoided, because they are

---

[93] *Briefe*, 19, ed. Reindel, i. 179–99.

considered invalid according to the doctrine of the Church). Gratian then takes questions 2 and 3 together: can a man marry relatives of a previous wife, and how many degrees of relationship are forbidden? It is obvious that this is a much thornier problem: he cites twenty-two different authorities. He starts confidently with Pope Gregory's ruling that seven is the number of forbidden degrees, and Pope Callixtus' ruling that one may not marry blood relatives (this is confirmed by both divine and earthly law). As for the wife's relatives, Pope Fabian ruled that affines in the fifth degree may lawfully marry, and that if they marry in the fourth degree, they will not be separated. In canon 5, Gratian raises the problem of ignorance, using the examples of a woman who sleeps on separate occasions with two brothers, or a man who sleeps with a woman and then with her daughter; if a person unwittingly commits incest, s/he is not barred from marriage for ever, though penance may be necessary, and all those involved may be barred from taking communion. In canon 14 he introduces the idea of *unitas carnis* (one flesh) as the explanation for the rules: 'quia constat eos duos fuisse in carne una, ideoque communis illis utraque parentela credenda est, sicut scriptum est: 'Erunt duo in carne una'' (Because it is agreed that the two have become one flesh, and so each one's family should be considered related to the other, just as it is written: 'They shall be one flesh' [Gen. 2: 24]).

All the authorities cited so far agree on the seven-degree principle, but in canon 19 Gratian introduces the concession of Pope Gregory to the English, and in canon 20 he muddies the waters further by pointing out that the calculation of degrees varies: some people count a parent as one degree removed, but for others who do not (on the principle of *unitas carnis*) the prohibited degrees are six, not seven. In question 4 he pursues the problem of numbers, citing Isidore's argument that the prohibited degrees of relationship are six because of the six ages of the world.[94] He gives more details of the computation of the degrees in question 5, quoting at great length from Pope Alexander II and again from Isidore, and declares the matter sufficiently demonstrated. One can understand why the Council of Worms of 868 took the line that consanguinity is to be measured not by degrees but by the extent of memory. Another even simpler solution had been advocated at the Council of Toledo in

---

[94] Isidore, *Etymologiarum libri*, 9. 6, ed. Lindsay.

531, which banned marriage between all relatives, regardless of degree, on the basis of Leviticus 18. In practical terms the seventh degree, the extent of memory, and all known kin probably came to much the same thing for many people in the Middle Ages.

Writers of penitentials in the period of the great twelfth-century codification of the laws tended, like Gratian, to focus more on distant relatives and problems raised by affinity than on the nuclear family. Bartholomew of Exeter and Robert of Flamborough (both writing in the late twelfth century) begin their discussions of incest with what we would consider marginal cases: intercourse with two sisters, or a stepmother, or an aunt, or a first cousin, or a niece, or the mother of a godson, or a goddaughter.[95] Serlo of Wilton has a similar list, but begins with two brothers or an uncle and nephew who sleep with the same woman.[96] Robert of Flamborough gives a sample confessional interrogation under the heading 'Luxuria' (Lechery):

Ad consanguineam tuam accessisti? Dic ad quot, et quam propinquae erant tibi . . . Ad duas sibi consanguineas accessisti? Dic ad quot paria, et quam propinquae sibi [tibi] erant . . . Aliquas habuisti post consanguineos tuos? Dic quam propinqui tibi erant . . . Ad monialem accessisti vel aliam conversam? Dic cujus religionis erant . . . Virginem deflorasti? Ad commatrem tuam accessisti? Ad matrinam tuam? Ad filiolam patris tui? Ad filiolam patrini tui? Ad menstruatam? Ad infidelem, scilicet judaeam, gentilem, haereticam?[97]

(Have you slept with a blood-relative? Say how many times, and what relation she was to you . . . Have you slept with two women related to each other by blood? Say how many times, and what relation they were to you . . . Have you slept with women after male relatives of yours? Say how closely related they were . . . Have you slept with a nun or some other woman vowed to religion? Say what order they belonged to . . . Have you deflowered a virgin? Have you slept with the mother of your godchild? With your own godmother? With your father's goddaughter? With your godfather's daughter? With a menstruating woman? With a pagan, that is a Jewess, gentile or heretic?)

Similarly Alain of Lille mentions, in this order, sex with the mother of a godchild or with a goddaughter, with one's mother, with a

[95] Bartholomew of Exeter, *Liber*, ed. Morey, 231–2; Robert of Flamborough, *Liber*, v. ii. 276, ed. Firth, 232. Many penitentials survive; my comments are not intended to be comprehensive.   [96] Serlo, *Summa de Penitentia*, ed. Goering, 33–4.
[97] Robert of Flamborough, *Liber*, IV. viii. 225, ed. Firth, 197.

partner of one's father, with one's future daughter-in-law, with a mother and her daughter, or a partner of one's father or brother, with two women linked as co-godmothers, with the wife of a blood relative, and with any female relative by consanguinity, affinity, or compaternity.[98] There is little sense in these texts of a hierarchy of forms of incest in which partners within the nuclear family are differentiated from more distant relatives, or from spiritual kin. It seems curious that so many varieties of incest in the broad medieval sense are mentioned here, and yet there is no reference to sisters or daughters. Possibly more distant relationships are listed so carefully because these were the impediments to marriage which frequently came up in court cases (discussed later in this chapter); nuclear family incest has little to do with marriage, though everything to do with sin. And since the list of persons with whom sex was prohibited must have covered every possible partner in many small communities, there was no doubt plenty of confessional discussion of these more distant relationships, which seem innocuous to us today.[99]

In the later Middle Ages there was a proliferation of confessors' manuals and penitentials in the vernaculars.[100] They are often arranged around the Seven Deadly Sins; incest appears as a branch of Lechery. In the fourteenth-century Middle English *Book of Vices and Virtues*, which is based on the popular French manual *Somme le Roi*, the branches of Lechery are listed in more or less regularly ascending order of gravity according to the status of the two persons concerned, and also what they do together:[101] persons who are not bound in any way to one another; a man and a prostitute; an 'unbound' man and a woman bound by some kind of vow; a man and a virgin; a man and a married woman (doubly sinful when the man is married too); unnatural sex between a man and his own wife; a man and his mother or daughter, or the children of his godfather or godmother; a man with a kinswoman (more or less

---

[98] Alain de Lille, *Liber*, II. CXXVII ff., ed. Longère, 112–17.

[99] McLaughlin argues that father–daughter incest was not mentioned by Gratian because it was not a disputed area of the law ('"Abominable Mingling"'). She admits that references to this form of incest in canon and secular law codes are rare, but notes that the few records which do survive show that when cases were prosecuted, the fathers were severely punished.

[100] The literature on this subject is vast. For useful summaries and discussion of confessional practice, see Michaud-Quantin, *Sommes de casuistiques*; for further discussion see also Biller and Minnis (eds.), *Handling Sin*.

[101] *Book of Vices*, ed. Francis, 44–6.

serious according to the degree of relationship); a man and relatives of his wife, or a woman and relatives of her husband; a lay woman and a clerk; a lay man with a nun, or a lay woman with a monk; two religious (more or less serious according to their status); a prelate of the church, who should be setting a good example; unspeakable unnatural sex. There does seem to be a hierarchy here, of a kind; it is worse for religious to succumb to lechery than for lay people, and although incest is never actually mentioned, it seems to rank only just below unnatural acts as a heinous sin. Chaucer's Parson in the *Canterbury Tales* lists what we would call incest as the fourth category of adultery, and places it between two other types of unnatural sex (*CT* 10. 903–9): marital intercourse motivated by desire for pleasure rather than for children, and 'thilke abhomynable synne of which that no manne unnethe oghte speke ne write' (that abominable sin which should scarcely be spoken or written about by anyone). He remarks of incestuous sinners that 'this synne maketh hem lyk to houndes, that taken no kep to kynrede' (this sin makes them resemble dogs, which pay no attention to kinship). He too emphasizes spiritual incest, commenting that it is as sinful for a woman to sleep with her 'godsib' (child of her godparent or parent of her godchild) as with her own brother.

Although incest is frequently discussed in the penitential and confessional material, it is often not identified by that name, but simply treated as one of many aspects of lechery. When it is explicitly named, the connotation is not always what we would expect. When Gower introduces Dame Incest, fourth daughter of Lechery, in his *Mirour de l'Omme*, he talks about monks and nuns; all his examples under this heading relate to the activities of persons living under an ecclesiastical rule, whether it is a priest corrupting his spiritual daughter (presumably this means through baptism or confession), or mendicants seducing married women, or nuns betraying their vows of chastity. It is only in the last few lines of this section that he turns to nuclear family incest.[102] This concept of incest as incontinence on the part of those who have taken religious vows of chastity may be influenced by the Roman use of *incestum* to mean intercourse with a Vestal virgin. In the fifteenth-century *Fall of Princes* Lydgate follows Laurent de Premierfait, one of his sources, in commenting on the disturbing

---

[102] Gower, *Mirour*, 9083 ff., ed. Macaulay.

origins of Rome.[103] Romulus and Remus were the twin sons of the Vestal virgin Rhea Silvia who mysteriously became pregnant; thus the ruling dynasty of the city came

> off such incontinence
> As clerkis call incestus in sentence.
>
> Incestus is a thyng nat fair nor good,
> Afftir that bookis weel deuise cunne,
>
> As trespasyng with kyn or with blood,
> Or froward medlyng with hir that is a nunne.

(from that incontinence which scholars/clerics call *incest* in their teaching. *Incest* is something that is neither attractive nor good, according to the expert books, such as transgressing with family or blood relatives, or wicked meddling with a nun.)

Shell argues that one reason (the main one, apparently, in his view) for the concept of spiritual incest is that Christians committed to a life of perfection regard all humankind as their siblings, and therefore all intercourse between them is incestuous; this is the argument advanced in jest by Boniface. But another explanation is given in a gloss on Gratian's *Decretum*: since nuns are the brides of Christ and God is the father of all humans, there is a relationship of affinity between all men and all nuns, and therefore any sexual activity is for them a form of incest.[104]

In spite of the certainty of Gratian and other canonists in the twelfth century about the extent of the prohibitions (six or seven degrees of blood relationship and affinity), the Fourth Lateran Council of 1215 promulgated a canon reducing the prohibited degrees of affinity from seven to four, and abolishing affinity in the second and third degrees, on the remarkable grounds that the existing prohibitions were causing considerable hardship.[105] It is noted that human laws can change according to varying circumstances.

---

[103] *Fall*, ii. 4066–71, ed. Bergen; for Laurent's version, see Bergen's note.

[104] Glossa ordinaria on Gratian, *Decretum*, C. 27 q. 1 c. 14 ('Virginitas'), s.v. *incesta*. I am indebted for this reference to R. H. Helmholz, who commented (in correspondence): 'really quite simple—if far-fetched—once you think about it'. Gower remarks that nuns are married to God, and that when they stray, they corrupt their marriages (*Mirour*, 9157–62). Shell, 'Want of Incest', 631–2.

[105] Fourth Lateran Council, canon 50, in *Constitutiones Concilii*, ed. García, 90–1. Perhaps the justification for the new number is borrowed by analogy from Isidore's reference to the six ages.

The explanation of the choice of four as the new limit is equally remarkable: 'quia quatuor sunt humores in corpore, quod constat ex quatuor elementis' (because there are four humours in the body, which correspond to the four elements). The injunction that this new law should stand in perpetuity seems at odds with the opening remarks of the canon that human laws should be changed in accordance with changing times, especially in cases of 'urgens necessitas' (pressing necessity) or 'evidens utilitas' (obvious usefulness). Here is yet another acknowledgement that the incest taboo is not a natural law, but one established by the wise Church for the benefit of its members. Each time that the legislation is revised, the Church hopes that the new laws will last for ever; but if they do not work, it is flexible enough to revise them.[106] In fact the medieval laws were not revised substantially again until the sixteenth century, when very different rules were produced by the Council of Trent for Catholic Europe, and by Henry VIII for Protestant England.

OBSERVANCE OF THE INCEST RULES IN THE MIDDLE AGES

From the early centuries of Christianity to the beginning of the thirteenth century, a period of nearly a thousand years, the prohibited degrees of relationship grew to the point where most people living in small communities could not legally marry anyone they knew. From the early thirteenth century to the end of the Middle Ages, the prohibited degrees of relationship were somewhat reduced, but still seem startlingly numerous and constraining by our modern standards. Nor did everyone in the Middle Ages find them plausible. The criticisms of Boniface mentioned earlier were repeated and expanded much more forcefully by Luther, who was outraged both by the arrogance of the ecclesiastics who claimed the power to prevent or annul marriages, and by the shamelessness with which they allowed themselves to be bribed:

Who gave this power to men? Granted that they were holy men and impelled by godly zeal, why should another's holiness disturb my liberty? Why should another's zeal take me captive? . . . Yet I am glad that those

---

[106] Guerreau-Jalabert argues that by this time the Church's rulings had been established and accepted, and thus could be reduced to conform with actual practice ('Sur les structures', 1041–2).

shameful laws have at last reached their full measure of glory, which is this: that the Romanists of our day have through them become merchants. What is it that they sell? Vulvas and genitals—merchandise indeed most worthy of such merchants, grown altogether filthy and obscene through greed and godlessness. For there is no impediment nowadays that may not be legalized through the intercession of mammon.[107]

He goes on to argue that only the relationships mentioned in Leviticus should be regarded as prohibited, and that the concept of spiritual affinity is nonsense. He maintains that marriage as a divine institution is much more important than man-made laws, and urges priests and friars to confirm any marriage which is contrary to canon law but not to the biblical rules.

Luther was particularly outspoken in his defiance of the medieval incest laws and his criticism of the abuse of dispensations, but many people agreed with his views. However much the Church rationalized its system and strove to enforce it, it is evident from ecclesiastical correspondence, court records, and well-known scandals of the time that the rules were ignored or honoured in the breach by many Christians throughout the Middle Ages, or were manipulated for personal advantage to get round the principle of the indissolubility of marriage. As McCabe notes, 'Details of kinship were often suppressed with a view to future annulments, and the "horror of pollution" was cultivated as much as a political tool as an expression of natural revulsion.'[108] In spite of the determination with which the Church insisted on its complex rules about who could marry whom, in practice the ecclesiastical authorities were often remarkably lenient in interpreting many parts of the incest legislation, especially in regard to more distant relations and affines.[109] It is also clear that many people in the Middle Ages were not particularly bothered by breaches of the incest rule such as the marriage of second cousins. These cases sometimes came before the ecclesiastical courts, and many aristocrats obtained dispensations for such marriages. Eleanor of Aquitaine was divorced from Louis of France after fifteen years of marriage and numerous children on the grounds of their close relationship (which was of course well known both to them and to many others); she was related in a comparable degree to her next husband, Henry II of England, but

---

[107] Luther, *Babylonian Captivity*, trans. Steinhäuser *et al.* 97.
[108] McCabe, *Incest, Drama*, 40.   [109] See for instance Duggan, 'Equity'.

the Church made no attempt to block their marriage, or to declare their children illegitimate. There is presumably considerable irony in the harsh ruling on incest which she is made to give in Andreas Capellanus' treatise on courtly love:

Satis illa mulier contra fas et licitum certare videtur, quae sub erroris cuiuscunque velamine incestuosum studet tueri amorem. Omni enim tempore incestuosis et damnabilibus tenemur actibus invidere, quibus etiam ipsa iura humana poenis novimus gravissimis obviare.[110]

(This woman, it seems, is certainly striving against what is lawful and permitted when she strives to maintain an incestuous love under the pretext of some mistake. We are perpetually bound to loathe acts which are incestuous and merit condemnation, for we know that the laws of men oppose them with the harshest of punishments.)

The Church walked a tightrope here. The indissolubility of marriage was a central part of Christian doctrine, yet incestuous marriages were clearly improper and invalid. In practice, the authorities tended to do nothing about marriages of fairly distant relations who had not known of their relationship, especially if they had been married for some time. Brundage attributes to the twelfth-century Bolognese canonist Rolandus the subtle distinction between a 'diriment impediment', a relationship which causes the immediate dissolution of an existing marriage, and an 'impedient impediment', a relationship which would prevent a forthcoming marriage.[111] In the late twelfth century, for instance, Bartholomew of Exeter was instructed by Pope Alexander III to do nothing about the long-standing marriage within the prohibited degrees of a respectable sheriff of Devon; the Pope ruled that 'tolerabilius est enim aliquos contra statuta hominum copulatos relinquere, quam coniunctos quoslibet legitime contra statuta domini separare' (it is more tolerable to leave some people married in contravention of the laws of man than to separate those who are legitimately married, in contravention of the laws of God).[112] Duby notes that the Church's insistence on consent as a crucial factor in establishing a valid marriage induced a certain degree of tolerance of incestuous marriages: ' . . . the fact that they attributed decisive value to consent (*consensus*) between the spouses, to what we might call love, gave pause to

---

[110] *Andreas Capellanus on Love*, ed. and trans. Walsh, 256–7.
[111] Brundage, *Law, Sex*, 289.
[112] Quoted by Morey in his introduction to Bartholomew of Exeter, *Liber*, 67–8.

the prelates when it came to dissolving a union based on the mutual understanding of two hearts, even if it was sullied by incest'.[113] But he also notes that the Church insisted on being the final authority in such cases.

The ambivalent reaction of the Church to the enforcement of the laws led to many abuses, especially among the aristocracy. Peter the Chanter (d. 1197), who lobbied for a reform of the consanguinity laws because they were constantly exploited, indignantly quotes a noble whom he overheard discussing his imminent marriage:

Bene est michi quia magna dos est. In tercio genere affinitatis forsitan est illa mihi, et ideo non ita mihi proxima, quo ab ea separer. Sed si voluero et non placebit michi, per affinitatem illam discidium procurare potero.[114]

(It suits me because there is a big dowry. She may be related to me in the third degree of affinity, but she is not so close that I would be separated from her. But if I choose, and she does not please me, I shall be able to obtain a divorce because of this relationship.)

Peter goes on to argue that this sort of behaviour gives the Church a bad name, and that the complexity of the rules about impediments to marriage results in innumerable such transgressions. Indeed, as Helmholz comments, the aristocracy married 'sub spe dispensationis' (in hope of a dispensation).[115] What the Church gave with one hand, it took away with the other: canon law insisted (in principle, at any rate) on the separation of incestuous couples, yet many such separations were clearly just what at least one partner wanted. The impediments of consanguinity and affinity were exploited from an early date by spouses who wished to divorce (often kings who wanted male heirs, like Louis). Duby has documented at length the struggles of various French kings in the eleventh and twelfth centuries to get the Church to recognize separations and second marriages which were motivated by political or emotional needs, but were justified on the grounds of breach of the incest laws.[116] The battles over aristocratic and royal marriages within the prohibited degrees of kinship continued throughout the later Middle Ages. Papal responses could vary considerably. In 1392

---

[113] Duby, *Medieval Marriage*, 21–2.
[114] *Verbum Abbreviatum*, quoted from manuscripts by Baldwin, *Masters, Princes*, i. 335 and note.   [115] Helmholz, *Marriage Litigation*, 87.
[116] See Duby, *Medieval Marriage* and *Knight*.

Bernard, Count of Armagnac, was refused papal permission to marry his elder brother's widow; but in 1410, under a different Pope, Thomas of Lancaster was allowed to marry his uncle's widow, and in 1500 Emanuel of Portugal was given permission to marry his deceased wife's sister (who was also the sister of Catherine of Aragon). Emboldened by such rulings, Jean, Count of Armagnac, actually tried in the mid-fifteenth century to marry his own sister (whom he had already seduced), making use of a forged papal dispensation.[117] The Pope refused to sanction this indubitably incestuous marriage; but the same Pope did allow a nobleman to marry his sister's daughter, as Richard III tried to do.[118] Such cases formed the background to Henry VIII's attempts to get rid of his first wife, Catherine of Aragon, the widow of his older brother Prince Arthur, in order to marry Anne Boleyn.[119] Among other arguments put forward on the king's behalf, Cranmer claimed that the prohibited relationships in Leviticus were indispensable (Luther's argument), and therefore that Catherine had been ineligible as a bride for Henry. He had already slept with Anne's sister, and possibly with her mother too, thus creating an impediment of affinity; Cranmer resolved this for him by arguing that affinity could only be created by intercourse within marriage. It seems sadly ironic that after evading the charge of incest himself, he used it later to get rid of Anne, whom he accused of sleeping with her own brother. A further dispensation was needed for his marriage to Catherine Howard, since she was a first cousin of Anne Boleyn. This is an extreme example of the complexities of the prohibitions based on consanguinity and affinity.

We have a considerable amount of information about the flouting and exploitation of the incest regulations by the aristocracy, because their doings were of interest to chroniclers and historians, and the subject of correspondence by high-ranking churchmen.[120] But what about the man and woman in the street, or in the field? Did they feel the natural shame over incest and respect for kinship

---

[117] I am indebted to Arjo Vanderjagt for bringing this remarkable case to my attention. For further details see *Commentaries of Pius II*, trans. Gragg, 315–20 (this section was omitted from earlier editions of the *Commentaries*); also Kelly, 'Canonical Implications', which is usefully summarized in McCabe, *Incest, Drama*, 48 ff.

[118] See Kelly, 'Canonical Implications'.   [119] See Kelly, *Matrimonial Trials*.

[120] Some of the reported cases may be pure gossip. As in previous eras, notorious characters of high status tended to attract charges of incest in addition to their other crimes, for instance Pope John XXIII and the Borgias.

invoked by Augustine and Thomas Aquinas? Were they obedient to the rulings of the Church? When Ivo of Chartres (d. 1116) quoted St Augustine as saying that it is worse for a man to sleep with his own mother than with an unrelated married woman, or when Robert of Flamborough (d. 1219) wrote that it is worse for a man to sleep with his own sister than with two sisters who are unrelated to him, were the examples intended to be easily recognizable from everyday life?[121] Peter Abelard in his *Ethics* used incest with an unrecognized sister as an example of the importance of intention in defining sinful actions, and remarked: 'nemo est qui hoc preceptum servare possit, cum sepe quis sorores suas recognoscere nequeat, nemo, inquam, si de actu potius quam de consensu prohibitio fiat' (there is no one who can keep this ordinance, since one is often unable to recognize one's sisters—no one, I mean, if the prohibition refers to the act rather than to consent).[122] Failure to recognize an attractive sister is a frequent problem in folklore and literature, but was it really so common in real life?

The incidence of nuclear family incest in the later Middle Ages is very hard to estimate, since it is hardly ever mentioned in court records.[123] It seems likely that cases of this kind of incest very rarely came to court, but were handled largely in the confessional—or else ignored. Plenty of people seem to have ignored the rules on incest in the broader sense; though some were brought to court, the evidence of the many decrees, the ecclesiastical correspondence, and the manuals about confession and penance suggest that many people broke the laws with impunity and without guilty consciences, whether through ignorance of the law or of precise degrees of relationship. The insistence on questions about incest in manuals for confessors and explanations of the prohibitions in handbooks for the laity suggests that the faithful needed constant reminding about the complex laws. Sheehan notes that in the cases concerning marriage he studied in a fourteenth-century register from Ely, the revelation of a previous marriage was a more frequent problem than the

---

[121] Ivo of Chartres, *Decretum*, 9. 10, in *PL* 161: 686, quoting Augustine, *De bono coniugali*, ch. 8; Robert of Flamborough, *Liber*, II. 39–42, ed. Firth, 79–80.

[122] Abelard, *Ethics*, ed. and trans. Luscombe, 26–7.

[123] Two cases of incest do appear side by side in the records of the ecclesiastical court in Durham for 1313, one father–daughter, the other brother–sister (*Registrum Palatinum*, ed. Hardy, i. 464 and 484). I am grateful to Paul Brand for this reference. On the scarcity of records of incest cases in the early modern period see Ingram, *Church Courts*, 245–9.

impediments of consanguinity or affinity.[124] But in the consistory court records from Rochester in Kent for an eighteen-month period in 1347–8, there are numerous cases of couples trying to marry although related in the third and fourth degree of consanguinity, or by affinity through fornication (often the guilty couple was given a public punishment of being whipped around the church).[125] We find the same thing at a rather higher level of society in the register of papal letters relating to cases in Great Britain and Ireland from the same period, though there is little reference to punishment other than the founding of chaplaincies.[126] These papal letters suggest a surprising degree of tolerance for transgression of the rules. In 1342 the papal nuncios were allowed to offer dispensations to ten men and women married unwittingly in the fourth degree of consanguinity or affinity (73). In 1345 the Bishop of St Asaph was empowered to lift the sentence of excommunication imposed on the Earl of Surrey for marrying the niece of a woman he had previously slept with (169). In 1351 the Bishop of Worcester was permitted to remarry a couple who had married illicitly and without banns because the man was godfather to the woman's son by a previous marriage; their excuse was that it was a time of pestilence and he knew no one else whom he could marry (460). In 1353 absolution was granted to a couple who knew that the wife's ex-husband had been godfather to her current husband's son, on the grounds that they did not realize that this constituted an impediment to their marriage (489–90). Records of this sort suggest that the strict rules laid out in the penitentials and other handbooks did not bear much relation to real-life practices, at least in cases of incest outside the nuclear family.

There is certainly evidence to suggest that some people who committed or abetted incest in the Middle Ages felt the prick of conscience, no doubt in part at least as a result of the clergy's constant harping on the sin. Helmholz argues that though the aristocracy may have married 'sub spe dispensationis' (in hope of a dispensation),

---

[124] Sheehan, 'Formation', 257.

[125] *Registrum Hamonis Hethe*, ed. Johnson, ii. 911–1043. The records from Ely and Rochester are paired by Kelly in *Love and Marriage*, 168–73. There are far too many records to survey in the space available here; the examples discussed in this section are merely a selection.

[126] *Calendar of Entries*, ed. Bliss and Johnson; page references are given parenthetically.

the common people were more reluctant to break the rules; he cites as evidence the case of a man who was troubled on his deathbed in 1462 by the fact that his son had married many years earlier within the prohibited degrees.[127] In Montaillou, the Pyrenean village whose inhabitants were interrogated about their heretical Cathar beliefs in the early fourteenth century, there seems to have been a great deal of incestuous fornication and marriage which caused concern to some but by no means all of the inhabitants.[128] Bélibaste, the Cathar holy man of the village, condemned incest with relatives by consanguinity or by affinity as sinful (179); Raymond de l'Aire, on the other hand, is quoted as saying that incest even within the nuclear family is shameful but not sinful, and that incest with second cousins does not count at all (185). Pierre Clergue, the priest and Casanova of the village, desired his own sisters and sisters-in-law (154), and slept with women who were closely related to each other (155). Not everyone thought this incestuous behaviour acceptable, however; Raymonde Testanière was so shocked when the cousin of a previous partner of hers tried to rape her that she rejected the Cathar faith (150). It seems that many villagers were ignorant of the complex relationships that linked them all; Grazide Lizier claimed that she would not have slept with the priest Pierre Clergue if she had known that he was the illegitimate first cousin of her mother (185–6). A more sophisticated kind of evidence for popular attitudes is offered by Boccaccio. His *Decameron* may not be an entirely reliable witness to real life, but two of the stories in it suggest that spiritual kinship was not taken very seriously by many people, and indeed could be used as a smokescreen for illicit affairs.[129]

St Augustine argued against endogamy on the grounds that the network of social affection should be expanded as much as possible. It seems that many later ecclesiastical authorities turned this view around to argue that marriages which were in breach of the incest laws should in some instances be tolerated in the interests of public order. In the papal register, settling strife or even ending a war is sometimes adduced as the justification for tolerance of a marriage that was technically incestuous. Bossy has argued that

---

[127] Helmholz, *Marriage Litigation*, 79–80.
[128] See Le Roy Ladurie, *Montaillou*; page references are given parenthetically.
[129] See the discussion in Ch. 5.

both marriage and godparenthood were used to widen social ties, and that it was seen as the role of the Church to settle conflict.[130] Goodich points out that public exposure of illicit sexuality of all kinds constituted a threat to family honour, and was therefore to be avoided if possible:

The dishonour brought upon the family or clan by such acts may partially explain the relative absence of cases involving intrafamilial violence, infanticide, and sexual misdemeanour in the surviving documents of contemporary law courts . . . It would appear that such injustices were more often handled through the informal agencies of religion.[131]

It seems that in spite of all the expressions of clerical outrage, incest was often tolerated in the interests of civil concord, at least when it was outside the nuclear family.

This makes it even harder to see who stood to gain from the incest laws and the changes that were made to them during the Middle Ages. Clearly the Church gained tremendous power by being the judge of who could and could not marry. Goody has also argued, rather cynically, that it stood to gain a great deal of wealth if marriage was made so difficult that many people were never able to find an appropriate partner, and left their money to the Church. This explanation is rebutted by Mitterauer, who argues (among other things) that the avarice of the Church cannot explain the insistence on spiritual kinship as an impediment to marriage: 'such bans can only be explained by religious logic'.[132] He points out that for Christians as opposed to Jews, 'physical descent is without any religious importance'; spiritual relationships were as important as blood relationships, if not even more so (Lynch makes the same point). It is clear that the incest laws were broken by both rich and poor, 'the learned and the lewed', and that the Church was often surprisingly tolerant about these transgressions, condoning incestuous relationships which had been contracted in ignorance, and sometimes turning a blind eye to obvious impediments.[133] Even though the extended prohibitions which included every imaginable relationship were insisted on by the Church for many centuries,

---

[130] Bossy, 'Blood and Baptism'.   [131] Goodich, 'Sexuality', 499–500.

[132] Goody, *Development*; Mitterauer, 'Christianity', 320–1.

[133] In some literary texts the Pope gives permission for a king to marry his daughter (see Ch. 4); this is presumably a dig at the laxity with which the laws were enforced, at least among the aristocracy.

they were changed with remarkably little fuss at the Fourth Lateran Council, when it was agreed that they were causing too much hardship (a tacit admission that they were unenforceable). This about-turn is rather reminiscent of official Communist plans for agriculture or industry which were strictly maintained, even though clearly ridiculous and impossible, until a critical moment was reached when they had to be jettisoned; the replacement plan then became equally sacred, as if it had always been in place. Perhaps one reason why popular medieval incest stories almost always deal with nuclear family incest is that in these cases there can be no argument about the severity of the sin, or the need to regularize the situation. Although cases of affinity produced by illicit intercourse or marriage between second cousins are frequently discussed in the law codes and penitentials, cited in manuals and handbooks, and resolved in the courts, such cases are very rarely described in the exemplary and imaginative literature of the later Middle Ages (see Chapter 5).

An enormous amount was written about the problem of incest during the Middle Ages, and clearly many people did take the prohibitions seriously. Yet among all the contemporary explanations of these complex laws, conspicuous by its absence is any mention of the dangers of inbreeding. This justification for the incest taboo, which was cited by Robert Burton in the sixteenth century, and was popular in the twentieth century, may have been widely accepted in the Middle Ages, but explicit references to it are very rare.[134] One reason may be that any deformity resulting from incest would have been interpreted as divine punishment for sin, rather than biological cause and effect.[135] An example of this is a cautionary tale told by Peter Damian in a letter to Abbot Desiderius and the monks of Monte Cassino, written in 1063 or 1064. In reference to those who commit adultery and incest, he insists that God punishes the wicked in this life, and gives the horrifying example of King Robert of France, who married as his second wife his cousin Bertha, and was therefore excommunicated: their son had a goose's

---

[134] According to Burton, 'the Church & common-wealth, humane and divine lawes, have conspired to avoid hereditary diseases, forbidding such marriages as are any whit allied'; see *Anatomy*, 1.2.1.6, ed. Faulkner *et al.* i. 206.

[135] In Leviticus, for instance, it is stated that if a man sleeps with his uncle's or brother's wife, they will die childless (20: 20–1); it is striking that this warning is not issued in connection with any of the other forms of incest listed here.

neck.[136] The king was shunned by all but a few servants, who treated the dishes from which he ate as polluted, and burned the leftover food. Eventually he ended his incestuous union, and made a legal marriage. Another writer whose comments suggest that there was widespread awareness of the link between incest and physical deformity is Gerald of Wales (Giraldus Cambrensis), though he too emphasizes divine punishment rather than biology. In his description of Ireland, written in the late twelfth century, he reports that incest was widely practised there; he was particularly horrified by the unchristian way in which men married the widows of their brothers.[137] He goes on to say that although many of the Irish are splendid-looking, he has never seen so many people deformed in such particularly horrible ways, a phenomenon which he attributes to the appalling state of Irish morals:

And it is not suprising if nature sometimes produces such beings contrary to her ordinary laws when dealing with a people that is adulterous, incestuous, unlawfully conceived and born, outside the law, and shamefully abusing nature herself in spiteful and horrible practices. It seems a just punishment from God that those who do not look to him with the interior light of the mind, should often grieve in being deprived of the gift of the light that is bodily and external.[138]

Whatever they knew about the effects of inbreeding from observation of both animals and humans, the non-Christian inhabitants of western Europe, both Germanic and Celtic, seem to have favoured endogamy, just as many ancient peoples did. Ellis comments on this tendency in Wales: 'The preference for marriages between near relations found expression in the old Welsh proverb, "Marry in the kin, and fight the feud with the stranger."'[139] Some medieval Christians may have been deterred from incest by the fear of deformity in their children. They certainly associated other forms of immoral behaviour with unpleasant physical consequences; it was widely believed, for instance, that children conceived on a holy day would be deformed, though suitable penance could avert this

---

[136] *Briefe*, 102, ed. Reindel, iii. 132–3.

[137] *History and Topography of Ireland*, 3. 98, trans. O'Meara, 106. He also comments on Welsh immorality and incest in his description of Wales, but he is particularly critical of the Irish; see Bartlett, *Gerald of Wales*, 38–45 and 170–1.

[138] Gerald, *History*, 3. 109, trans. O'Meara, 117–18.

[139] Ellis, *Welsh Tribal Law*, 431.

fate.[140] In view of such beliefs, it does seem surprising that deformity, either as biological consequence or as divine punishment, is not a common motif in medieval incest stories.[141] In exemplary literature, many children of incestuous liaisons are killed at birth because they are a social embarrassment and a sign of sin; in real life, they may also have been killed because they were deformed. In fictional texts, however, those who survive infancy often turn out to be heroes or saints rather than monsters, as we shall see in the chapters that follow.

[140] See Meens's comments on the story of Iso of St Gall in 'Frequency and Nature', 49. See also Jane Gilbert's comments in the context of the deformed baby in *The King of Tars*, and her useful bibliography, in 'Unnatural Mothers', 329–37.

[141] But see the comments of Hopkins on inbreeding in Roman Egypt, which apply equally well to medieval Europe ('Brother–Sister Marriage', 326–7): 'In the conditions of high mortality prevalent in Roman Egypt, the extra deaths caused by inbreeding would probably not have been visible, and they are not remarked in any surviving source. Infant mortality was high already: infants and children suffering from serious congenital malformations may have slightly increased that high death rate.'

2

The Classical Legacy

> Your histories and tragedies boast of instances of incest, and
> you both read about and listen to them with pleasure. So too
> you worship incestuous gods who have had intercourse with a
> mother, a daughter, a sister.
>
> Minucius Felix, *Octavius*, 31. 3

STORIES of incest are universal; no doubt the medieval writers whose
work is discussed in this study were influenced by oral tales circulating in Europe which have not come down to us in written form.
But they were also greatly influenced by classical literature.
Although from the perspective of medieval Christians it was produced by unenlightened pagans, it was still regarded as worthy of
study and imitation: Virgil, Ovid, and Statius were read by all educated persons as standard schooltexts in the Middle Ages, and were
widely glossed, adapted, translated, and quoted.[1] Classical literature was believed to contain a valuable core of truth which could be
discovered by Christian interpreters (see the discussion of allegorization later in this chapter). Medieval readers would have been
well aware of the rich mythographic and commentary tradition on
classical texts, as Blumenfeld-Kosinski points out:

When medieval poets and clerks encountered mythological narratives by
such classical authors as Virgil, Ovid, or Statius, they not only read the
narratives themselves but layer upon layer of commentary and interpretation. Woven into the very fabric of the text, filling every available square
inch of the margin, or appended to the text itself, the interpretive tradition
constantly insinuated itself into the act of reading.[2]

Perhaps this accounts, at least in part, for the rarity of free-standing
treatments of classical incest stories in the Middle Ages; it was
almost impossible for a medieval author to separate the plot itself

---

[1] Few people could read Greek, but Greek myths and legends were transmitted via
Latin writers.

[2] Blumenfeld-Kosinski, *Reading Myth*, 1; I am greatly indebted to this study.

from the moralizing tradition in which it had become cocooned. As we shall see, there are a few examples of such extended reworkings in the twelfth century, perhaps part of the initial response to the new demand at that time for vernacular tales of love; but most of the classical stories are retold briefly as part of a larger narrative, or else merely alluded to in passing—and usually there is a clear moral to be drawn about the dangers of excessive and inappropriate love.

In this chapter I give a brief survey of the incest theme in classical myth, legend, and literature. Then I discuss individually the classical incest stories which were most popular in the Middle Ages, showing how each was treated by classical and medieval writers.[3] This survey cannot be comprehensive; there are far too many allusions to classical protagonists in medieval texts. But it offers a representative range of the major medieval treatments, which show some striking shifts in attitudes to incest, and also suggest sources for at least some of the stories invented by medieval writers.

INCEST IN CLASSICAL MYTH, LEGEND, AND LITERATURE

In classical myth and literature, incest is a frequent theme in stories of gods, heroes, and mortals. Early Christian writers like Minucius Felix were quick to denounce a religion whose gods were so depraved.[4] In the Greek creation myth, as in so many others, incest is central. Cronus married his sister Rhea and was subsequently deposed by their son Zeus, who in turn married his sister Hera. Similarly in Egyptian myth the brothers Osiris and Set married their sisters Isis and Nephthys. The first stages of creation permit, indeed necessitate incest. But it was not just the need to populate the world that caused Zeus to be notably promiscuous in his casual couplings with his sisters and daughters, and the other Olympians enthusiastically followed his lead. It is hard to draw a family tree for

---

[3] These stories will not be discussed again in detail in the three chapters that follow on incest stories invented by medieval writers. All references and quotations are taken from the Loeb Classical Library editions unless otherwise stated; translations are generally those in the Loeb editions, though I have made some changes. I have consulted Grimal, *Dictionary of Classical Mythology*, and Bell, *Dictionary of Classical Mythology*; the Anglicized forms of proper names are taken from standard reference works such as Grimal.

[4] This will be discussed further below. For an overview of both pagan and Christian attitudes to the behaviour of the gods see the invaluable study by Demats, *Fabula*.

them, since marriages and affairs between closely related gods were frequent. For instance, Aphrodite, daughter of Zeus and Dione in some accounts, married her half-brother Hephaestus, son of Zeus and Hera, and had an affair with another half-brother, Ares. Zeus slept with his sister Demeter, and also with their daughter Persephone.[5]

Medieval writers were more familiar with Roman mythology, as reported by the great Roman writers. Virgil candidly describes Juno as 'Iovis et soror et coniunx' (*Aeneid*, 1. 46: both sister and consort of Jove), without futher comment on this unusual marriage. Ovid's attitude to it is more complicated and, as might be expected, often more cynical. At the beginning of Book 6 of the *Fasti*, he sees the goddesses and recognizes one who is 'sui germana mariti' (17: the sister of her own husband). This description, followed by the information that 'stat in arce Iovis' (18: she stands in the citadel of Jove), is enough to identify her as Juno. When she speaks, she draws attention again to her dual relationship to Jupiter:

> est aliquid nupsisse Iovi, Iovis esse sororem:
> fratre magis, dubito, glorier, anne viro.   (27–8)

(It is something to have married Jupiter and to be Jupiter's sister. I am uncertain whether I am prouder of my brother or of my husband.)

She goes on to wonder whether lineage through blood descent trumps lineage acquired by marriage—perhaps a reflection of Roman preoccupations in Ovid's time.

If Juno's boasting about her incest is almost comic here, other references to it could be seen in a more sinister light. Ovid's Phaedra, trying to justify her passion for her stepson Hippolytus, claims that Jupiter's marriage made incest legitimate, and that 'ista vetus pietas' (*Heroides*, 4. 131: such old-fashioned regard for virtue) has long been out of date. She emphasizes the strength of her passion by insisting that she would prefer Hippolytus even to Jove:

> si mihi constat Iuno fratremque virumque,
> Hippolytum videor praepositura Iovi!   (35–6)

(If Juno allowed me her brother-cum-husband, I think I would rank Hippolytus above Jove!)

This is of course intended to be flattering to her beloved; but the

---

[5] This double incest will be discussed further in the final chapter.

description of Jupiter as 'brother-cum-husband' underlines the fact that Phaedra's union with Hippolytus, like that of Jove and Juno, would be incestuous, but without the licence afforded to the gods. Ovid's Byblis, horrified by her erotic dreams about her brother Caunus, also invokes the example of the gods, but recognizes that they are unaffected by human laws:

> an habent et somnia pondus?
> di melius! di nempe suas habuere sorores.
> sic Saturnus Opem iunctam sibi sanguine duxit,
> Oceanus Tethyn, Iunonemque rector Olympi.
> sunt superis sua iura! quid ad caelestia ritus
> exigere humanos diversaque foedera tempto?
>
> (Met. 9. 496–501)

(Or do dreams really have weight? The gods forbid!—But surely the gods have loved their sisters; so Saturn married Ops, related to him by blood; Oceanus, Tethys; the ruler of Olympus, Juno. The gods have their own laws! Why do I try to measure human rites by the quite different contracts of the gods?)

Later she decides to ignore the laws which were clearly made by old men and are not relevant to the young, and to follow 'magnorum exempla deorum' (555: the examples of the great gods). Ovid seems to be drawing attention to the discrepancy between what is thought appropriate for gods and for mortals, to the tolerance of incest in myth but not in legend, to the domesticity and established nature of Juno's marriage to her brother as opposed to the tragedies brought about by human incestuous passions, and to the dangers of mythological precedents, especially in an age so devoted to the art of rhetoric and debate.

For the gods may get away with multiple incest, but there is no hope for mortals: in classical stories consummated incest usually leads to violent death or metamorphosis, and is often the cause, and/or a significant example, of a series of disasters over several generations in a doomed family.[6] The mythographer Hyginus, writing in the first or second century AD, includes many incest stories under the rubrics 'Fathers who killed their daughters' (ch. 238), 'Mothers who killed their sons' (ch. 239), 'Men who committed sui-

---

[6] An exception to the rule that incest leads inevitably and swiftly to death or metamorphosis is Oedipus, in some versions of his story at least; see below for more detailed discussion.

cide' (ch. 242), and 'Women who committed suicide' (ch. 243); all the entries in ch. 246, 'Men who ate their sons at banquets', and ch. 253, 'Women who had unlawful sex', also involve incest.[7] The most famous example is of course that of Oedipus, whose father Laius had already begun the pattern of unnatural acts by abducting Chrysippus, the young son of Pelops, and thus incurring Pelops' curse. Oedipus' predestined parricide and incest led to the suicide of his wife/mother Jocasta, his own blinding, and internecine civil war between his sons for the throne of Thebes which brought the dynasty to a bloody and tragic end. Pelops' own family had an even more complex and horrific history, beginning with Tantalus' crime in cooking the young Pelops and serving him to the gods at a feast. The feud between Pelops' sons Atreus and Thyestes included the seduction of Atreus' wife by Thyestes; the killing and cooking of Thyestes' children by Atreus; Thyestes' seduction of his own daughter Pelopia to beget a son (Aegisthus) who, according to an oracle, would avenge him on his brother; the suicide of Pelopia when she discovered what her father had done (though in some accounts she did not kill herself, but married her uncle Atreus); the murder of Atreus and also (in some versions) of his son Agamemnon by Aegisthus, who had already seduced Agamemnon's wife Clytemnestra; and the murder of Aegisthus and Clytemnestra by Agamemnon's son Orestes. Atreus and Thyestes were the children of Hippodamia, won by Pelops through a murderous trick from her possessive and possibly incestuous father, Oenomaus. Incest here is merely one repeated element in an ongoing pattern of feuding, transgression, and violent vengeance. Another, more limited, example of this pattern occurs in one version of the story of Sisyphus, condemned for eternity to roll a stone up a steep hill in the underworld in punishment for seducing his niece Tyro. An oracle had told him that if he had sons by her, they would avenge him on his brother Salmoneus; when Tyro discovered this, she killed her children.[8]

---

[7] Hyginus, *Fabulae*, ed. Marshall; he also tells many incest stories in earlier chapters under individual names. Further details about some of the more obscure stories are offered in the excellent article by Rudhardt, 'De l'inceste'. See also the comments of Vernier in 'Théorie'.

[8] Uncle–niece marriage was not forbidden, or even discouraged, in Athens; in fact it was required when the niece was her father's sole heir, in order to preserve the family estate. Presumably what made Sisyphus' callous seduction outrageous to Greek

Incest is similarly linked with vengeance and also with cannibal-ism in the story of Philomela (more often spelled Philomena in the Middle Ages) and her sister Procne.⁹ When Procne discovered that her husband Tereus had raped Philomela and cut out her tongue to ensure her silence, she took revenge by cooking their only son, Itys, and serving him to her errant husband; when the furious Tereus tried to attack the sisters, the gods transformed all three into birds. A similar pattern of incest, cannibalism, and metamorphosis is found in the story of Clymenus, who seduced his daughter Harpalyce; in revenge she cooked their son (or possibly her brother) and served him to her father, who then killed her. According to some sources father and daughter were both turned into birds. The incest of Myrrha (or Smyrna) with her father Cynaras and her sub-sequent metamorphosis are also part of a longer revenge story, though here the gods are the avengers. Myrrha's mother had rashly claimed that her daugher was more beautiful than Aphrodite; in punishment, the goddess made Myrrha desire her own father. She tricked him into sleeping with her, but then, pregnant and over-whelmed by shame, she took refuge in a forest and begged the gods to remove her from mortal life; she was turned into a myrrh tree. The product of her incest was rescued from the bark of the tree— Adonis, beloved of Aphrodite, whose death was caused by the curse of a deity angry with Aphrodite (Artemis or Apollo or Ares). Phaedra's story is also part of a larger history of human trangres-sion and divine vengeance: her father was Minos, her mother Pasiphae, whom an angry deity (Poseidon offended with Minos or Aphrodite with Pasiphae) punished by making her fall in love with a bull and give birth to the Minotaur. Phaedra's stepson Hippolytus, son of Theseus and an Amazon, was devoted to the virgin goddess Artemis, so Aphrodite, offended by his rejection of love, made Phaedra besotted with him. When Hippolytus spurned her advances, she accused him to her husband Theseus of trying to rape her. Theseus appealed for vengeance to his protector (or father) Poseidon, and the innocent Hippolytus was killed when a

---

readers/writers was his motive, revenge on his brother; the result was indeed the proph-esied destruction of Salmoneus' line, but not in the way that Sisyphus had expected. I am grateful to Laurel Bowman for pointing this out to me.

⁹ Lévi-Strauss described cannibalism as 'inceste alimentaire' (incest as food) in *L'Homme nu*, 123 (quoted by Roussel, *Conter de geste*, 153).

bull from the sea frightened his horses. Phaedra then hung herself out of shame.

Even when there is no further twist to the story, those who have committed incest often commit suicide, though not always by their own choice. Pelopia, the daughter of Thyestes, killed herself, and so in some accounts did Byblis, whose brother Caunus rejected her advances in horror (though according to Ovid she was turned into a fountain). When Aeolus discovered that his daughter Canace had had a child by her brother Macareus, he had the baby exposed, and sent his daughter a sword with which she reluctantly killed herself; according to some versions Macareus committed suicide too.[10] Jocasta hung herself; Oedipus put his eyes out (in Sophocles' version he feared recriminations in the underworld; in some versions his own servants blinded him on Creon's orders, though in Homer he is not blinded at all). There can be no future for those who have committed incest; though Oedipus survived, he was marginalized by his blindness, and by the contemptuous treatment of his sons; and in Sophocles' version he was exiled, a form of social death.

While the famous stories are preserved in detail (Oedipus, Canace, Myrrha, Phaedra, Byblis, Philomela), many others survive only as brief allusions. Nyctimene was turned into an owl after being seduced by her father (or seducing him, in some versions); Phlegyas slept with his own mother and begot Coronis, later murdered by her lover Apollo for her infidelity; Menephron of Arcadia lived incestuously with both his mother and his sister (history does not relate how their story ended); Evopis fell in love with her brother and hung herself for shame. Ovid included both famous and little-known incest stories in the *Metamorphoses*, as did Parthenius, an Alexandrian writer who produced a collection of love romances in the second century AD. Very few of these stories involve unwitting incest; one if not both partners are usually aware of their relationship. Brother–sister liaisons may be consensual, but for the most part consummated incest involves coercion or deception, and the stories end badly, with death or metamorphosis for the protagonists, and often tragedy for the whole family. While the incest is definitely shocking, it is not entirely clear what sort of

[10] In the *Odyssey* Aeolus has fifty sons and fifty daughters who marry each other without any fuss, but by the fifth century this was no longer acceptable; see the discussion later in this chapter for other variations.

crime it is. Sometimes it is inflicted on mortals by offended gods as punishment for some slight; sometimes an oracle suggests it as a means of vengeance. Once it is initiated, the gods seldom interfere, and when they do intervene, it is not clear why. They do not save the innocent Hippolytus from his unjust fate, but they do respond to the guilty Myrrha's prayer to be removed from the human world, and they allow the child of her incest to be born, though later a god's anger causes his death.

Another category of classical incest story concerns historical or pseudo-historical characters. Parthenius tells the story of Periander, tyrant of Corinth, whose mother Krateia fell desperately in love with him.[11] She persuaded him that a beautiful woman longed to sleep with him but wished to remain unidentified and insisted on total darkness. Periander accepted the conditions and enjoyed the affair, but after some time decided to conceal a light in his bedroom in order to look at his mysterious lover. On discovering that she was in fact his own mother he tried to kill her, but was deterred by a divine apparition. Maddened by these experiences, he turned into a cruel and violent tyrant; his mortified mother killed herself. Parthenius' story does not seem to have caught the popular imagination, but it is an example of a frequent theme in classical incest stories: the link between incest and tyranny. Krateia, the name of Periander's mother, means sovereignty; once he has possessed sovereignty, he becomes a tyrannical ruler. The nurse in Seneca's play *Hippolytus* (sometimes edited under the title *Phaedra*) remarks that power breeds a desire for the forbidden: 'quod non potest vult posse qui nimium potest' (215: the man with too much power wants to be able to do the impossible). As I noted in the previous chapter, various historical Greek and Roman rulers (Caligula, Nero) and politicians (Cimon, Alcibiades, Clodius) were accused of incest, and so was a legendary eastern empress, Semiramis, builder of the hanging gardens of Babylon.[12] In the case of Semiramis, confusion may have been caused by the fact that her husband and her son were both named Ninus; but to classical and medieval readers it seemed quite plausible that a powerful woman ruler (and a barbarian to boot) would be tyrannical and transgressive in her lust,

---

[11] *Love Romances*, no. 17; on parallels between Oedipus and Periander see Vernant, 'Le Tyran boiteux'.

[12] Her story is discussed in more detail later in this chapter.

and that her violent delights would have a violent end. A very influential late classical example of incest linked to tyranny occurs in the 'romance' of Apollonius of Tyre, perhaps composed in the third century AD, popular throughout the Middle Ages, and more familiar to modern readers as Shakespeare's *Pericles*.[13] This story begins with the familiar motif of the over-possessive royal father, Antiochus, who seduces his own daughter. The shadow of incest hangs over the story till the very end, when the hero does not act on his attraction to a young courtesan who then turns out to be his long-lost daughter; he becomes a good king and is reunited with his long-lost wife too.

The first incest motif in *HA*, the possessive father who drives away or kills all suitors for his daughter's hand, is found in classical legend even when the incest is not explicitly recognized (e.g. Oenomaus and Hippodamia). The separated family is also a familiar theme: it appears in *Oedipus*, of course, and also in Euripides' lost *Alcmaeon of Corinth*, in which a father buys his unrecognized daughter and narrowly avoids committing incest with her before they discover their true relationship. Another example is the story of Auge and her son by Heracles, Telephus, who were separated for many years and then entered into an arranged marriage without recognizing each other. Auge wanted to remain faithful to the memory of Heracles and entered the bridal chamber with a sword, but by divine intervention a huge snake appeared to separate them until their true relationship was revealed. The theme of unwitting near-miss incest resolved by a recognition scene is relatively rare in classical myths and legends. In New Comedy, however, near-miss incest in a contemporary setting is a common theme, and often plays a crucial part in resolving the problems of the protagonists and bringing about the happy ending.[14] In these comedies the potential incest is averted as a result of recognition rather than revulsion, and love often triumphs because the lovers are not who they think they are. In Plautus' *Rudens* the shipwrecked courtesan heroine attracts the unwelcome attentions of an old man who turns out to be her long-lost father; after the recognition scene she is safely united with

[13] The standard Latin text and some medieval adaptations are discussed later in this chapter; the Latin version will be cited as *HA*; when the story is discussed without reference to a specific text, it will be cited as Apollonius.

[14] This was the more realistic form of comedy popular in the 4th cent. BC at Athens, and imitated in Rome by Plautus and Terence.

her lover. In his *Curculio* (probably derived from a play by Menander) the unwelcome suitor finds that the courtesan he is wooing is in fact his own sister; again the recognition scene frees her to marry her lover. Another popular plot of New Comedy involves a father or husband searching far and wide for his lost daughter or wife; in Plautus' *Poenulus*, a father looking for his daughters, who have been abducted and sold to a brothel, hires courtesans and questions them about their origins, and so in the end finds his children. In such plays the protagonists are usually not royal, but as in the tragedies the recognition scene links the threat of incest to important revelations about identity, lineage, and social status. The comedies offer an inversion of the tragic pattern in which the discovery of the identity of the protagonist(s) brings about a devastating peripeteia. In comedy the peripeteia of the recognition scene is very important, as in tragedy, and often requires a radical rethinking of existing social relations; but it always heralds a happy ending.

Another kind of near-miss incest story involves an initial incestuous proposal which is indignantly rejected by a virtuous protagonist, who then flees from home to escape further incestuous persecution. This plot is surprisingly rare in classical myth and literature; most victimized daughters seem to stay with their incestuous fathers, or else kill themselves. One example of flight from incest is Caunus, brother of Byblis, who left home to escape her advances and founded the city of Caunus in Caria. Apollonius is a borderline case: he runs away from an incestuous father, but is not himself the object of Antiochus' attentions. A third example is the mother of the separated family in the early Christian 'romance' *The Clementine Recognitions*, who flees from her lustful brother-in-law (discussed below). This theme of flight from the improper advances of a close family member is common in folklore from many parts of the world. Perhaps it was mainly an oral tradition in the classical world; as we shall see in Chapters 4 and 5, it became extremely popular in elaborate written forms in the later Middle Ages.

Stories of consummated incest in which neither partner is aware of the incestuous relationship seem to be rare in classical myth and legend; Oedipus is much the most famous and influential example. Sometimes one partner is aware while the other is not: examples of those who are induced to commit incest in ignorance of the truth include Myrrha's father, Thyestes' daughter, and Periander.

Consensual incest, as in the case of the siblings Canace and Macareus, also seems to be fairly rare. More common are stories of incestuous rape (for example, Pelopia and Philomela), or revulsion from an incestuous proposition (for example, Hippolytus and Caunus). This might suggest a moralizing attitude on the part of tellers of incest stories, and in some texts this is indeed the case; but this attitude is not nearly as pronounced, or as universal, in classical texts as in medieval ones.[15] In the classical Oedipus story, the emphasis is on the way in which the shocking truth is revealed, and the consquent crisis of authority in Thebes (though in Homer's account Oedipus continued to rule for many years after Jocasta's suicide). Statius, whose *Thebaid* was the main source for medieval readers, tells the story of Oedipus merely as a prelude to the civil war at Thebes. Ovid's approach to incest is largely psychological, at least in his more extended treatments: he is interested in showing us how women who feel incestuous desire might react, and how their initial horror might change to self-justification.[16] We may disapprove of Phaedra's arguments and Canace's outpouring of love in their letters in the *Heroides*, but theirs are the only voices we hear, and we are quickly caught up in Phaedra's vacillating mood, and Canace's pathetic deathbed declaration of her fatal passion for her brother. We know that they are wrong, and doomed; but we are invited to look into their hearts and 'feel their pain', and to come away with a sense of 'the pity of it', rather than 'the horror, the horror'. In the case of Byblis, we see how innocent sibling affection grows, to her alarm, into incestuous passion. Myrrha too fights hard against her desire for her father before tricking him into sleeping with her.

Although consummated incest usually leads to disaster for the protagonists, they can be presented quite sympathetically, especially if like Oedipus they are unaware of their crimes. There is of course great sympathy for those who are clearly innocent victims, like the luckless Philomela, but there is also some sympathy for

---

[15] Aristotle used the phrase 'Kaunios eros' (Caunian love) to signify a shameful love, indicating that it was proverbial (*Rhetorica*, 1402[b]2), but few other examples of the phrase are known.

[16] Richard Fabrizio comments on the difference between Greek and Roman treatments of incest ('Incest Theme', 653): 'The Greeks used incest as a means to an end—the investigation of the human condition, the relation of self to family. The Romans used incest as an end—the delineation of a mental condition, how the incestuous person feels, thinks, acts. Greek interest in incest was philosophical; Roman interest was psychological.'

those who knowingly embark on incestuous affairs because of irresistible passion, like Canace.[17] Women seem to be treated more gently than men, perhaps because they usually act out of overwhelming and long-resisted passion (sometimes imposed by offended gods), rather than out of brute lust, or as part of some politically motivated plan; another way of putting this is that women are typically presented as acting out of weakness, whereas men usually act out of misdirected strength. Phaedra, Myrrha, Byblis, and Canace all fight for a long time against their outrageous desires, and acknowledge the taboo that they are breaking. If they compound their incest with other sins, however, they forfeit all sympathy; Phaedra's fatal mistake is her false accusation, which leads to the death of the innocent Hippolytus. Men who commit incest knowingly are not given the benefit of the doubt about their struggle to resist the forbidden desire: Tereus makes little effort to fight against his lust for his sister-in-law, and mutilates her to ensure her silence; and Thyestes cold-bloodedly seduces his unwitting daughter in order to beget the prophesied son who will avenge him on his hated brother. In the cases where males instigate the incest, the female may or may not be presented as a victim; her feelings are not always described, though sometimes they are made clear by the terrible revenge she exacts (infanticide), or by her suicide.

Incest is sometimes presented in classical literature as a stereotypically barbarian practice, though when Seneca's Phaedra first reveals her passion for Hippolytus, the horrified nurse comments that not even barbarians would break the taboo (*Hippolytus*, 165–8). However, there is no doubt in the minds of classical writers that it is a form of desire which can be felt by anyone (after all, it affects the gods too!), and that like other kinds of overwhelming emotion, it can be very hard to resist. The classical world was not overshadowed by the concept of sin like the Christian world, nor did it believe in evil spirits tempting weak mortals into transgression. Sometimes incestuous lust is inflicted on mortals by angry

[17] It has been argued that Ovid was the first to make Canace love Macareus, and that in Euripides' lost play about them, *Aeolus*, she died because she was pregnant, not because she had committed incest. Euripides' play apparently caused a scandal in Athens; there are frequent references to it in the comedies of Aristophanes. He parodies one especially notorious line, 'What is shameful, if it does not seem so to those who do it?', in *The Frogs* (1475): 'What is shameful, if it does not seem so to those who view it?' Plato is said to have confronted Euripides with the rejoinder 'Euripides, what is shameful is shameful, whether it seems so or not'. See Verducci, *Ovid's Toyshop*, 198–201.

gods, as in the case of Phaedra and Myrrha; sometimes the lust is motivated by a divine prophecy that a child born of incest will revenge a wronged parent, as if this child were somehow stronger or more heroic because of his incestuous birth. In these cases, the mortal sinners can hardly be held responsible for their actions, and the moral to be drawn might reflect more harshly on the callous behaviour of the gods. But it does seem to be the case that even in the classical period, the female protagonists of certain notorious incest stories had already become a byword for outrageous desire. When Ovid discusses libido in the *Ars amatoria* (1. 269 ff.), he argues that men are bound by convention in relation to their desires, and that they observe 'legitimum finem' (the lawful boundary), but for women no holds are barred: his first examples are Byblis and Myrrha. Whether or not Ovid himself believed in this gender distinction, it is clear that it was a popular one.

A striking example of this misogynistic attitude to female lust is offered by the curious story of Secundus and his mother, apparently composed in the late second or early third century AD, and very popular in the later Middle Ages.[18] Secundus learns during his education that all women are insatiably lustful. He determines to test this theory by returning home incognito and attempting to seduce his own mother. He bribes her successfully through a venial servant and is admitted to her bed for a night, but does not make love to her. In the morning she asks why he has been so restrained, and he identifies himself. She drops dead from horror, and he takes a vow of silence (later tested by the emperor Hadrian, who puts many philosophical questions to him). Though there is little trace of the circulation of the Latin version of this text during the classical period, it—or perhaps its oral sources—had an enormous influence: it was translated into Arabic, Armenian, Ethiopian, Greek, and Syriac, and appears in *The Thousand and One Nights* and in *The Book of Sinbad*, as well as in many widely read medieval exemplary texts. The success of this story testifies to the low opinion of female self-control which is a feature of many classical incest stories, an opinion wholeheartedly shared by medieval Christian writers.

---

[18] On the classical tradition see Perry, *Secundus*, and Philonenko, 'Oxymores'; I am indebted to Keith Hopkins for these references. For medieval versions see Tubach, *Index Exemplorum*, no. 2733.

CHRISTIAN APPROACHES TO CLASSICAL INCEST STORIES

The preceding survey shows how popular and familiar the incest theme was in classical myth and literature. It also suggests a variety of attitudes to incest: classical incest stories include consensual incest with and without tears (Canace, the gods); incest consummated through trickery with disastrous results (Myrrha, Thyestes); tyrannical incest, also ending in disaster (Semiramis, Antiochus); and incest averted (Apollonius, New Comedy). Very few characters in classical literature question the incest taboo. One is Ovid's Myrrha, who (in spite of her shocking desire for her own father) is given some powerful and persuasive arguments against it: far from considering herself a barbarian or an animal because of her unnatural feelings, she envies the sexual freedom of the animal world and complains bitterly of the artificial constraints and 'invida iura' (jealous laws) of human society (*Met.* 10. 321 ff.). Another is his Byblis, who fights desperately against her growing passion for her brother Caunus, but then decides to take the gods as her role models and try to consummate her love (*Met.* 9. 496–501). Such comments as Ovid himself makes are brief; other classical writers were more forthcoming, and more critical, about the immoral behaviour of their gods, long before Christian writers used mythology to attack their opponents.[19] Plato and others blamed the poets, beginning with Homer, for their lack of responsibility. Some writers tried to rationalize the activities of the gods, either by arguing that they were originally men (the Euhemerist argument), or by interpreting the various gods as natural forces (a form of allegory). According to this latter scenario, for instance, the marriage of Jupiter and Juno represents the union of ether and earth. In Cicero's *De natura deorum* both the historicizing argument and the more 'scientific' symbolic argument are discussed and dismissed as 'non philosophorum iudicia sed delirantium somnia' (1. 15: more like the dreams of madmen than the considered opinions of philosophers). The speaker, Velleius, goes on to attack the poets for describing all the shameful goings-on of the gods, including 'effusas in omni intemperantia libidines' (1. 16: the utter and unbridled license of their passions). He is an Epicurean and so fol-

---

[19] For full discussion and references see Demats, *Fabula*, ch. 1.

lows his master in arguing that the gods, being blessed and eternal, can feel no human emotions or anxieties.

In such expressions of disbelief and disapproval, pagan writers show themselves very close to the early Christians, who frequently criticized the official religion of the Empire for allowing such stories to be told of its gods. 'Proinde incesti qui magis quam quos ipse Iupiter docuit?' asked Tertullian (*Apologeticus*, 9. 16: Then again who are more incestuous than the disciples of Jupiter?) Discussing the Euhemerist view, he argues that belief in the elevation to divinity of men who have committed incest, adultery, rape, sodomy, and murder, and who should therefore be in the depths of Tartarus, represents a perverted notion of justice and 'suggillatio in caelo' (11. 12–14: an affront to heaven). He draws attention to the purity of Christ's birth: 'Nec de sororis incesto nec de stupro filiae aut coniugis alienae deum patrem passus est squamatum aut cornutum aut plumatum, amatorem in auro conversum Danaidis' (21. 8: No incest with a sister was here, no pollution of a daughter or another's wife; he had not to endure a divine father, disguised with scales, or horns, or feathers, a lover turned into gold for a Danaë). Minucius Felix also attacks pagan mythology and its incest stories: 'Memoriae et tragoediae vestrae incestis gloriantur, quas vos libenter et legitis et auditis: sic et deos colitis incestos, cum matre, cum filia, cum sorore coniunctos' (*Octavius*, 31. 3: Your histories and tragedies boast of instances of incest, and you both read about and listen to them with relish; so too you worship incestuous gods who have had intercourse with a mother, a daughter, a sister). St Augustine went even further in condemning such myths: 'Etsi fabula cantat crimen numinum falsum. delectari tamen falso crimine crimen est verum' (*City of God*, 18. 12: So legend sings of the false crimes of the gods, but to enjoy a false crime is a true crime).[20] If Christian writers were so shocked by classical incest stories, why did they continue to recount them? One motive may have been pagan accusations that the early Christians were much given to incest; it would have been natural for Christian apologists to respond by pointing out how frequent incest was in classical mythology (see my comments in the previous chapter).

[20] Elsewhere, however, he and other patristic writers admitted that myths do have value in that they conceal truths which must be exegetically understood; see my comments below.

Furthermore, pagan writers continued to be respected as literary authorities long after the triumph of Christianity. But there was another very important reason for the survival of classical incest stories: they provided a most useful model of the dangers of lust. Christian writers regarded women as a constant source of temptation and danger for Christian men (the reverse was apparently not true, or not a problem). They were therefore very willing, on both literary and theological grounds, to take over the traditional catalogues of female vices; the attacks which had been made at least partly tongue-in-cheek by satirists such as Ovid and Juvenal became entirely serious in the hands of patristic writers.[21] This may explain, at least in part, the frequent allusions in medieval texts to Myrrha, Phaedra, Canace, Byblis, and Semiramis, the relative lack of interest in Oedipus, and the almost total lack of interest in other classical incest stories in which men are the aggressors.

But as well as being sexual temptresses, women could also be presented as types of virtue beleaguered by vice in a fallen world, and this may explain the fashion in the later Middle Ages for the motif of the flight from an incestuous father (or brother-in-law); this plot does not seem to appear in classical texts until late in the period. One example is the influential early Christian 'romance' known as *The Clementine Recognitions*.[22]

Clement, later Bishop of Rome, has become separated from his family and travels about the Mediterranean with St Peter. They encounter an old beggar woman who has gnawed her hands to the bone in her misery; she turns out to be Clement's mother Mattidia, who left home years before with her twin sons (Clement's elder brothers) to escape the advances of her brother-in-law, but lost the children in a shipwreck. Travelling on together, Mattidia, Clement, and Peter encounter two young men who turn out to be the long-lost twins. Peter then has an argument with a cynical old pagan who believes in astrology because of the experiences of a friend (so he says): the friend's wife ran away with a slave, taking her twin sons, and the friend later

<hr/>

[21] On ancient and medieval catalogues of women see McLeod, *Virtue*; for a depressing but useful anthology of medieval misogyny (including some seminal biblical and classical sources) see Blamires (ed.), *Woman Defamed*.

[22] Edited as *Die Pseudoklementinen* by Rehm and Paschke; the extant texts date from the 4th cent. AD, but are derived from a 2nd- or 3rd-cent. original which in turn may have been based on a pagan romance. For medieval analogues see Chs. 4 and 5 below.

learned that she had previously made advances to his brother. He set out to find her with his remaining son, but became separated from the boy; now he denies the existence of God and believes in astrology. Peter realizes that this is Clement's father; the family is reunited, Mattidia's virtue is confirmed, and those who are not yet Christian are converted.

Here the familiar theme of family separation and eventual reunion through a recognition scene is reworked in a didactic Christian context with a new protagonist, St Peter, the facilitator who brings about the happy ending. In this Christian tragi-comedy the innocent Mattidia is not actually raped; she has to suffer unnecessarily for many years, but in the end her virtue is established and she regains her family. Clement loses his biological father for many years, but finds a spiritual father in St Peter.

The Christian message in this story is obvious; there was no need to allegorize it. But in many cases allegorization was the Christian response to incest stories, as to many other forms of pagan literature (and also to the Old Testament).[23] This technique had been used in Greece and Rome before the Christian era; it proved to be an invaluable tool for Christian writers, both those who commented on existing texts (scriptural or pagan), and also those who invented new allegorical narratives. It was understood that pagan writing contained hidden truths, both philosophical and specifically Christian—truths hidden in many cases even from the writers themselves, but accessible to interpretation by the Christian reader. Medieval writers subscribed wholeheartedly to the view, already current in classical times, that literature should be instructive and improving as well as entertaining. Although Chaucer's merry Host suggests his tale-telling competition as a way of providing some fun for the Canterbury pilgrims on their journey, his formulation of the competition rules conforms to both classical and medieval literary theory: the prize of a free supper will go to the pilgrim who tells 'tales of best sentence and moost solaas' (CT 1. 798: stories of best [moral] significance and greatest entertainment). Several times in the course of the Canterbury Tales Chaucer (or one of his

---

[23] The use of allegory in the Middle Ages is a vast topic which can only be treated very cursorily here. I have drawn on the following studies: Seznec, *Survival*, esp. ch. 3; Allen, *Mysteriously Meant*, esp. chs. 1 and 7; Heinrichs, *Myths*; Copeland, *Rhetoric*; and Blumenfeld-Kosinski, *Reading Myth*.

narrators) paraphrases the famous passage from Romans 15: 4, 'for whatsoever things were written aforetime were written for our learning' (*CT* 7. 3441 and 10. 1083: 'al that is writen is writen for our doctryne'); in Romans this refers specifically to scriptures, but later it was taken to encompass all texts. In spite of their great reverence for literary authorities, medieval writers felt quite free to add explanatory introductions which gave a decidedly new twist to the classical texts that every schoolboy had to read. These *accessus ad auctores* (approaches to authors) included a confident statement of the intention of the original author, which was always represented as moral and didactic, and also an explanation of the usefulness of the work for Christian purposes.[24] One medieval moralizer of the *Heroides* explains that the depiction of love in this text has three aspects: chaste, illicit, and incestuous.

Intentio est castum amorem commendare, illicitum refrenare et incestum condemnare. utilitas est magna. nam per hoc scimus castum amorem eligere, illicitum refutare et incestum penitus exstipare.[25]

(The intention is to commend chaste love, to rein in illicit love, and to condemn incestuous love. This is very useful, for thus we know we must choose chaste love, reject illicit love, and root out incestuous love entirely.)

This was one way of averting criticism and making Ovid acceptable in a Christian culture. But some moralizers went far beyond this rather obvious analysis in their application of the technique of allegorization, as we shall see in the discussion that follows.

MEDIEVAL ADAPTATIONS OF CLASSICAL INCEST STORIES

Until the twelfth century, there seems to have been little interest in composing new versions of classical myths, though the mythographic tradition flourished. This century in western Europe is often described as a renaissance; it marked the beginning of a spectacular growth in literacy and in the production of vernacular literature (especially what we would categorize in modern terms as romantic and historical fiction); there seems to have been an intense interest at this time in stories of love and in the psychology of love.

[24] For detailed discussion see Minnis, *Medieval Theory*.
[25] Quoted by Born in 'Ovid', 377.

One innovative and influential form of response to classical literature was to expand and medievalize it: the stories of Thebes and Troy, of Alexander and Aeneas were retold in the 'romans antiques' in anachronistic versions which stressed medieval attitudes to war and to love, and shamelessly inserted new episodes and new characters. Ovid reached new heights of popularity, not least because of his emphasis on love and extended description of emotions; indeed this century is often described as the 'aetas Ovidiana', the age of Ovid. Among the classical tales which were adapted or retold with an intense spotlight on the emotions and amorous adventures of the protagonists were incest stories. Few of these stories received lengthy treatments; some are retold in collections of short narratives, but more often the best-known names were simply mentioned as examples of overwhelming passion and its tragic consequences. Some famous classical texts were also subjected to extended allegorizations; the most startling example is the monumental late thirteenth-century poem *Ovide Moralisé*, in which Ovid's metamorphoses of lovelorn pagans were themselves metamorphosed with extraordinary ingenuity into multiple Christian *exempla*, often including propaganda for specific doctrines such as contrition and penance.[26] In the remainder of this chapter, I explore the treatment of the most famous classical incest stories by some secular and exegetical writers in the later Middle Ages.

Oedipus

Classical traditions about Oedipus varied considerably; not all recounted his self-blinding or removal from the throne of Thebes.[27] Today we are most familiar with Sophocles' version, but this was not known in western Europe in the Middle Ages; medieval writers were most likely to know the story from Statius' *Thebaid*, from Seneca's tragedy (but only after the twelfth century), and from references in other classical writers. Both Statius and Seneca are particularly interested in the political aspects of the

[26] I cite the edition of de Boer, hereafter *OM*; I do not include the later prose version in my discussion. For commentary on the approach and techniques of the poet see Copeland, *Rhetoric*, 107–30, and Blumenfeld-Kosinski, *Reading Myth*, ch. 3.
[27] See Constans, *La Légende*; Cingano, 'Death of Oedipus'.

story.[28] For Seneca, though the incest is certainly horrifying, this is very much a story about power and kingship; the sparring between Oedipus and Creon is more marked in his play. Statius retells the story of Oedipus very briefly at the beginning of his epic *Thebaid*, which is mainly concerned with the story of the internecine war between Oedipus' sons.[29] The first reference to parricide and incest comes from Oedipus' own mouth, but the catalogue of his vicissitudes and sins does not suggest much sense of guilt or horror at his crimes. He blames his ill-begotten sons for despising him: 'hisne etiam funestus ego? et videt ista deorum | ignavus genitor?' (79–80: Do these too think me accursed? and the father of the gods sees this, and does nothing?) He appeals to Jupiter as a fellow-father, conveniently disregarding the fact that the king of Olympus too produced children from an incestuous marriage; Jupiter considers that Oedipus has made sufficient atonement by blinding himself, and promises to fulfil his prayers. There are possible analogues here for several distinctive aspects of medieval incest stories: the Christian belief that even incest can be expiated by penance in the form of suffering or deprivation, and the fashion for making the incestuous son himself the product of incest (see the stories of Gregorius and Albanus in the next chapter). The biblical principle of the sins of the fathers visited on the children was well known in the classical world too, though somewhat differently conceptualized and expressed. In Statius, Jupiter sees Oedipus' crime in the greater context of his family history, as one horror among many.

The story of Oedipus attracted surprisingly little attention in medieval literature.[30] It is mentioned in many chronicles, but as in most other medieval accounts it is merely the curtain-raiser to a fuller account of the civil war between Polynices and Eteocles. A moving *planctus* survives in some twelfth- and thirteenth-century manuscripts in which Oedipus describes and laments his terrible

[28] Neither Statius nor Seneca continues the story, as Sophocles does, to show the exiled Oedipus dying as a sort of saint on Athenian territory, where his bones will bring good fortune to those who have taken pity on him.

[29] It may well be that this is the oldest part of the story, and that both Laius' rape of Chrysippus and Oedipus' disastrous parricide and incest were invented later to explain the background of the civil war between Polynices and Eteocles; see Constans, *La Légende*, 11.

[30] See Constans, *La Légende*; Edmunds, 'Oedipus in the Middle Ages'; and Archibald, 'Sex and Power'.

fate as he looks at the corpses of his sons.[31] But Oedipus was not a popular choice as protagonist in medieval narratives; it is the political consequences of his story rather than the personal ones that seem to have fascinated medieval writers, Statius' version rather than that of the tragedians. Civil war was always a worrying possibility in medieval Europe, feuds between royal siblings all too common, and the necessity for an heir to continue the male line of succession a constant preoccupation. In this context it is hardly surprising that many medieval authors keep Jocasta alive till the very end of the story so that she can grieve over her dead sons, the ultimate tragedy for a royal mother. Given the 'rise of romance' in the late twelfth century, and the great interest at this time in exemplary incest stories which warn against despair and emphasize the benefits of contrition and penance, one might have expected to find various lengthy versions of a *Roman d'Œdipe*. But few writers seem to have been attracted by the story's potential for romance treatment—the hero's quest to find his parents, his marriage to his unrecognized mother, the traumatic recognition scene—though all these themes appear in the later Middle Ages in both exemplary and secular stories which are clearly derived from the Oedipus legend (see Chapter 3).

In one of the earliest vernacular medieval texts regarded by modern critics as a romance, the *Roman de Thèbes*, the focus is on the civil war between the sons of Eteocles and Polynices, and Oedipus makes only a brief appearance in the introductory section, as in Statius' *Thebaid*.[32] But whereas Statius has Oedipus himself recount his tragic story in the course of cursing his two over-ambitious sons, the author of the *Thèbes* presents this material as narrative, and fills it out in ways typical of the new genre of romance, with its interest in the expression of extreme emotion and in anachronistic details about daily life and contemporary concerns. There are some striking departures from the classical version. For instance, when Laius orders Oedipus to be exposed in order to avoid the dreadful fate revealed by the oracle, Jocasta is given a long speech in which she expresses her pain and guilt at having to kill her child (53–78); and the baby is left hanging in an oak tree, a form of exposure quite common in the

---

[31] See Clogan, '*Planctus*', and Edmunds, 'Oedipus in the Middle Ages', 148–9.
[32] *Roman de Thèbes*, 33–568, ed. Raynaud de Lage; see also Poirion, 'Edyppus'.

Middle Ages.[33] The recognition scene occurs twenty years later when Jocasta is bathing her husband and sees, apparently for the first time, the wounds on his feet. The story is not Christianized, and there is no reference to Christian incest prohibitions. Statius' references to the previous sins of Oedipus' ancestors are omitted; the responsibility lies squarely on him and on Jocasta. Nevertheless, it is the consequences for Thebes which interest this writer, not the fate of the souls of the incestuous sinners. As Constans has pointed out, there is no attempt to show Oedipus' remorse, to move the reader by an account of his self-punishment, or to stress the ineluctable destiny which brought about these horrors.[34] Moreover, this destiny is watered down because Jocasta already knows when she marries Oedipus that he is the killer of her husband; it is only the incest that remains to be discovered, and that is presented as merely the backdrop for the Theban civil war which so fascinated the Middle Ages. When the princes die, the poet comments that it is because they did not love their father, and callously trampled on his eyes when he tore them out (9811–16); as an aside, the poet reminds us that he tore them out in his distress at the revelation of his incest, but the behaviour of the sons is clearly the most important aspect of the story.

Another influential treatment of the story was that of Boccaccio in his collection of tragic histories, *De casibus virorum illustrium* (written 1355–60), which was translated into French by Laurent de Premierfait as *Des Cas des nobles hommes et femmes* (c.1405), and into English by John Lydgate as *The Fall of Princes* (1430–8).[35] Boccaccio's aim was to show how the hubris of princes inevitably brings disaster: Fortune throws them down from her wheel. The shift in attitudes to Oedipus in the Middle Ages is very clear here; Boccaccio and his followers tell the story of Thebes as the tragedy of Jocasta, even though their books are devoted to the falls of princes. The plot varies somewhat from the traditional version, and Lydgate suggests that it was not well known (this is his excuse for

[33] See Boswell, *Kindness of Strangers*, 365. When the 12th-cent. Jocasta comments that the innocent child is not, after all, the offspring of a prostitute, a monk, or a nun, it is clear that children in these categories were in fact often exposed.

[34] Constans, *La Légende*, 302–3.

[35] Lydgate's version (*Fall*, 1. 3158 ff.) is the most extended, and will be my main focus here. The relevant parallel passages from the Italian and French sources are printed in Bergen's notes; for Boccaccio see also the edition of Ricci and Zaccaria.

giving the Sphinx's riddle at considerable length). It begins and ends with Jocasta's sorrows: she is mourning when we first meet her because Laius has taken away her child to be exposed, and at the end she commits suicide because her sons are dead, rather than because of shame at her incestuous marriage. Although Lydgate describes the two pronouncements of the oracle, the disastrous marriage of Oedipus and his mother is ascribed to the bad influence of 'sum fals froward constellacioun' (3487: some false, hostile constellation). The recognition scene is reduced almost to non-existence. There is no speech of mutual or self-recrimination, no acknowledgement of the horror of what they have unwittingly done. Jocasta does not kill herself until her sons are both dead; Oedipus is exiled, but Lydgate, like Boccaccio, is unable to say anything about his death. At the end Lydgate does insist on the 'onkyndli mariage' (unnatural marriage) as the root of all the trouble, though the 'fraternal envie' of Eteocles and Polynices is certainly a contributing factor (3750–2). But there is no mention of incest in his Envoy, which has a purely political refrain: 'Kyngdamys deuyded may no while endure' (3822: Divided kingdoms cannot last). Lydgate clearly found the story fascinating: in an earlier work, *The Siege of Thebes*, he presents himself as joining Chaucer's pilgrims in Canterbury and telling the story of Thebes as the first tale on the journey home.[36] As in Statius and the *Roman de Thèbes*, the history of Oedipus is the curtain-raiser, but the bulk of the tale concerns his sons. The Oedipus section ends with his death and unceremonious dumping in a ditch by his callous sons. Again there is little reference to incest; Lydgate does comment that it is not acceptable to God for 'blood to touche blood' (788), but follows this with the example of John the Baptist's criticism of Herod for marrying his brother's wife, which hardly seems relevant (794–801). The only explicit moral is that those who do not honour their parents inevitably come to a bad end (1019–43).

Although Boccaccio, Premierfait, and Lydgate downplay the incest part of the story in favour of the political aspects, it is striking that in all three versions the Oedipus story is immediately followed by another complicated family saga involving incest, the story of Atreus and Thyestes, who vie with each other in telling their versions of events to the narrator (*Fall*, 1.

---

[36] *Lydgate's Siege of Thebes*, ed. Erdman and Ekwall.

3844 ff.).[37] Boccaccio describes himself as preparing to write about Theseus when Thyestes interrupts, insisting that his sorrows are much greater than those of Jocasta and Oedipus: his brother Atreus first exiled him, and then murdered his children and served them to their father at a feast. Atreus immediately approaches to set the record straight, arguing that his wife Europa was seduced by her brother-in-law Thyestes, 'a thyng intollerable, | And to the goddis verray abhomynable' (4113–14: an intolerable deed, and absolutely loathsome to the gods); then Thyestes seduced his own daughter to beget Aegisthus, who murdered Atreus and then his son Agamemnon. Curiously, incest is never mentioned here: in Lydgate the introductory rubric and Atreus himself both refer to adultery in relation to Thyestes's seduction of Europa, and Laurent uses the term 'fornication' as well as 'adoultrie' (note on *Fall*, 1. 4181). There is no comment on Thyestes' seduction of his own daughter, but incest seems an obvious link between the two stories, in addition to the internecine rivalry of royal brothers.

The incest connection is used more explicitly in relation to Oedipus in the *Ovide Moralisé*. Ovid only referred very briefly to Oedipus in the *Metamorphoses* without any mention of incest (in the story of Cephalus and Procris, *Met.* 7. 754–61); but the author of the *Ovide Moralisé* gave the story more space, and also a very surprising moralization (*OM* 9. 1437–1996). Immediately before the story of Byblis, who vainly pursued her own brother, he interpolated an account of the story of Thebes based on Statius. In the allegorization Oedipus becomes a martyr, and his blinding a form of penitence. This is startling enough, but in an even more unexpected twist his ambitious and quarrelsome sons are types of the Jews, and Oedipus is represented as a type of Christ, since he was hung up with his feet pierced when he was exposed as an infant, like Christ on the cross, and because his mother also became his spouse, as Mary became Christ's bride.[38] Here Oedipus' fatal incest is turned into something positive, and his story is no longer a cautionary tale

---

[37] In all three versions the narrative is presented as a dream vision in which Fortune herself brings many of the characters to the writer's study, while others push in unannounced, demanding to be heard.

[38] There was a long tradition throughout the Middle Ages of describing Mary as the daughter and bride of her own son (for further discussion see the final chapter). On Oedipus as Christ see Visser-Van Terwisga, 'Oedipe'.

of a downward spiral to disaster in a doomed family, but rather a reminder of the central events in Christian history: the Incarnation and the Resurrection. This is a splendid example of the principle dear to medieval Christian writers that 'al that is writen is writen for our doctryne': any text can be interpreted in a way that is useful for didactic purposes.

The moral offered in the *Ovide Moralisé* is, however, a very unusual reading. As we shall see, incest was sometimes interpreted by medieval writers as original sin; it would have been easy to read the Theban story as another case of original sin followed inevitably by fraternal slaughter, but even this seems to have been rare.[39] The most fascinating aspect of the Oedipus story for medieval readers was the struggle of the rival brothers, rather than the vicissitudes of the father who begot them incestuously. In the *Canterbury Tales* Chaucer uses their civil war as the frame for the *Knight's Tale*, his adaptation of Bocaccio's *Teseida* which opens with Theseus' defeat of Creon and focuses on the disastrous rivalry in love of two Theban cousins previously sworn to eternal brotherhood. Elsewhere in his work he quite often refers to the story of Thebes, but he only mentions Oedipus twice in brief allusions without any comment on his incest (*Troilus*, 2. 101–2 and 4. 300–1); he never mentions Jocasta. Generally the incest story got surprisingly little attention, though it was evidently quite well known. In Constans' useful list of allusions to the *Roman de Thèbes* in later medieval sources, there are far more references to Jocasta and to her sons than to Oedipus; one might argue that Jocasta had the higher profile in the Middle Ages. Dante names her sons and later refers to her double sorrow (their deaths), but never mentions Oedipus.[40] We have seen that her story dominated the versions of Boccaccio in the *De casibus* and of his translators. Boccaccio also included Jocasta in *De claris mulieribus*, his innovative female equivalent of the *De casibus* which was the first collection of biographies of women, as

---

[39] Poirion notes that the poet's sympathy for the younger son, Polynices, suggests an echo of the Cain and Abel story ('Edyppus', 291). The author of *On the Thebaid*, an allegorical text long attributed to Fulgentius but probably written in the later Middle Ages, interprets Oedipus as lust and his sons as greed; but the main focus in this text is on Theseus, who represents God when he conquers Creon (pride), and liberates Thebes (the soul). See *Fulgentius*, trans. Whitbread, 235–44.

[40] See *Inferno*, 26. 52–4, and *Purgatorio*, 22. 56, ed. Singleton; he also mentions her daughters at *Purgatorio*, 22. 110.

the author proudly points out in his prologue.[41] Not all the women he discusses were famous for good or positive reasons, and it was her misfortunes which won Jocasta a place in the book (ch. 25); again she is kept alive till her sons are both dead, and it is this disaster, rather than her unwitting incest, that causes her to commit suicide. This is also the case in the works of Christine de Pizan, who includes Jocasta in her *Book of the City of Ladies*.[42] But although Oedipus was not very popular in the Middle Ages, his story had an important influence on many medieval incest stories, as we shall see in the next chapter.

Ovidian Bad Girls

The female protagonists of classical incest stories who were most often mentioned in the Middle Ages are Myrrha, Canace, Byblis, and Phaedra (Semiramis will be discussed separately since her story is not told by Ovid, and so will Philomena, who is a victim rather than a villainess). Ovid describes Phaedra and Canace in the *Heroides* (4 and 9), and Byblis and Myrrha in the *Metamorphoses* (9. 454 ff. and 10. 298 ff.); both texts were very widely read and commented on in the later Middle Ages. Ovid devotes a great deal of space to the feelings of each heroine as she struggles with her overwhelming incestuous desire. No single extended narrative devoted to any one of these women survives from the Middle Ages, though their stories are told in some collections of short narratives (for instance by Boccaccio, Gower, Chaucer, and Lydgate—see below).[43] But they are frequently invoked in lists of tragic lovers or wicked women, or of examples of the folly of immoderate lust. Their names recur in the work of both Latin and vernacular writers, didactic and secular, mythographers, theologians, and poets of love, such as Walter Map, Petrus Pictor, Bernard of Cluny, Alain of Lille, Dante, Boccaccio, Petrarch, Matheolus, Jean Le Fèvre, Jean

[41] *De claris mulieribus*, ch. 23, ed. Zaccaria, 108, trans. Guarino, 49.
[42] *Book of the City of Ladies*, 2. 61. 4, trans. Richards, 203; see also Régnier-Bohler, 'La Tragédie'.
[43] There is some evidence to suggest that the story of Byblis was expanded to include a courtly admirer, Itis or Iris, but it remained a tragedy, with Byblis committing suicide at the end. See Leclanche, 'Biblis', who shows that Byblis was frequently alluded to in French and Occitan poems of the 12th and 13th cents. as a passionate and tragic lover (she is often linked with Dido), and in some texts was apparently presented as actually sleeping with her brother.

de Meun, Deschamps, Froissart, Machaut, Chaucer, Gower, and Christine de Pizan.[44] Often two or more of Ovid's quartet are named together; sometimes they appear with other notorious women from classical legend such as Pasiphae. They are not always explicitly cited as having committed incest, or as being wicked: for instance, the stories of Canace and Byblis, as well as of Semiramis, Dido, Thisbe, and other famous characters who suffered for love, are painted on the walls of the temple in Chaucer's *Parliament of Fowls* (288 ff., a description borrowed from Boccaccio). But any educated reader in the Middle Ages would have known the details of their incestuous loves and the mythographic and commentary traditions, and would have had no hesitation in identifying these women as sinners who were punished for their outrageous sexual appetites. Heinrichs discusses some of the many references to them and concludes that 'a poetic voice that cites with sympathy or approval the Ovidian heroines Medea, Myrrha, Oenone, Hypsipyle, or certain others from the *Heroides* and *Metamorphoses* is the voice of the irrational, impulsive lover'.[45] When Gottfried von Strassburg makes Tristan and Isolde sing songs about Phyllis, Canace, Byblis, and Dido during their idyllic exile at the Cave of Lovers, it is a reminder that their own love is also doomed.[46]

Canace does not seem to have been so frequently cited as Byblis in medieval literature, but several long accounts of her tragedy do survive. She is sometimes linked with Byblis in lists of tragic lovers, but may have been regarded with more horror than Byblis because she did actually consummate her love for her brother Macareus. In pre-Ovidian texts it was apparently he who seduced her, but after Ovid it is Canace who is usually cited as the main sinner, partly because of her famous letter in the *Heroides*, and partly no doubt because pious medieval writers were always eager to blame the woman in sexual scandals.[47] Canace was clearly well known to English audiences by the end of the fourteenth century. The Man of Law in the *Canterbury Tales*, apologizing in his prologue that all the good tales have already been told by Chaucer, separates her from the other tragic women of the *Heroides* and refers to her with

[44] See Heinrichs, *Myths*, and Blamires (ed.), *Woman Defamed*.
[45] Heinrichs, *Myths*, 47–8; see also ch. 3, 'Classical Lovers and Christian Morality'.
[46] *Tristan*, 17187–99, ed. Ranke, rev. Krohn, ii. 436, trans. Hatto, 267.
[47] See n. 21.

revulsion, protesting indignantly that Chaucer would never write about 'unkynde abhomynacions' such as incest:

> But certeinly no word ne writeth he
> Of thilke wikked ensaumple of Canacee
> That loved hir owene brother synfuly—
> Of swich cursed stories I sey fy!—...[48]

(But certainly he did not write a word about that wicked *exemplum* of Canace, who loved her own brother sinfully—shame on such damned stories, I say!)

It is true that although Chaucer refers to many (in)famous incestuous lovers, he does not tell any of their stories (except for that of Philomena—see below). The comments of the Man of Law may be intended as a satire on the prudery of some self-righteous readers and audiences. The tale he does tell is in fact analogous to the popular Flight from the Incestuous Father plot, as many modern critics have pointed out, even though it does not begin with the threat of incest; Dinshaw argues that the spectre of father–daughter incest haunts the whole of the *Man of Law's Tale*.[49]

Another critical response to the Man of Law's comments takes them as a gibe at his friend and contemporary Gower, who used the Canace story as a cautionary tale about the dangers of Wrath in Book 3 of his *Confessio Amantis*. In Gower's account of the affair between Canace and her brother (derived from Ovid's *Heroides*), the love between the siblings is described quite sympathetically—or at least apparently so, though both here and in the story of Apollonius in Book 8 Gower uses incest to represent love out of control, leading to the breakdown of family life and ultimately of

---

[48] *CT* 2. 77–80. This passage has generated much critical comment; see the notes in the *Riverside Chaucer*. Among more recent criticism see Archibald, 'Flight'; Dinshaw, 'Law of Man'; Goodall, ' "Unkynde Abhomynacions" '; and Scala, 'Canacee'. In the *Legend of Good Women* Chaucer tells many tales from Ovid, but not that of Canace. Was he really shocked by it, or did he think that his audience would be? The use of the term *ensample* here is striking; it usually means an illustrative story or cautionary tale (*exemplum*). Other less loaded words would have been possible here—for instance *story*, *legend*, or even *tale*. This choice might mean that Canace was often invoked as an example of wickedness—or it might be ironic.

[49] See Archibald, 'Flight', and Dinshaw, 'Law of Man'. The heroine of Chaucer's *Squire's Tale* is named Canace; when the tale breaks off, the narrator is promising to tell how her brother Cambalo fought for her. Some critics have seen a hint of an incest plot which is never in fact recounted; see Fyler, 'Domesticating the Exotic', 1–2 and 14; and Scala, 'Canacee'.

the common good.⁵⁰ Machaire and Canace are brought up in close proximity, sharing a bedroom and playing together, and eventually they fall in love. It is Machaire who first feels the pangs and kisses his sister, but after that they are described as mutually 'enchaunted':

> And as the blinde an other ledeth
> And til they falle nothing dredeth,
> Riht so thei hadde non insihte
>
> .   .   .   .   .   .
>
> This yonge folk no peril sihe,
> Bot that was likinge i here yhe . . .   (179–81, 185–6)

(And as the blind lead one another, and fear nothing until they fall, so they felt no concern/had no idea . . . these young people saw no danger, except what in their eyes was pleasure . . .)

The Latin note makes it clear that they fell in love as a result of propinquity during their upbringing, and that the feeling was entirely mutual: 'qui cum ab infancis usque ad pubertatem invicem educati fuerant, Cupido tandem ignito iaculo amborum cordis desideria amorose penetravit' (when they had been brought up from infancy to adolescence together, at length Cupid lovingly penetrated both their passionate hearts with his burning spear). Gower sees such behaviour as typical of the workings of Nature in youth, a time of life

> Whan kinde assaileth the corage
> With love and doth him forto bowe,
> That he no reson can allowe,
> Bot halt the lawes of nature:
> For whom that love hath under cure,
> As he is blind himself, riht so
> He maketh his client blind also.   (154–60)

(when Nature assails the heart with love and makes it bow to her, so that he can accept no reason, but observes the laws of nature; for whomever Love has in charge, as he is blind himself, in just the same way he makes his client blind too.)

Their feelings and actions are controlled by Nature, 'which is Maistresse | In kinde and techeth every lif | Without lawe positif, |

---

⁵⁰ Gower, *Confessio Amantis*, 3. 143–360. For discussion see Benson, 'Incest', 106; Shaw, 'Role'; Spearing, 'Canace'; and Bullón-Fernández, 'Confining the Daughter', and *Fathers and Daughters*, 159–72.

Of which she takth nomaner charge' (170–3: who is Mistress by
nature and teaches every living creature without ecclesiastical
authority, to which she pays no attention). Spearing remarks that
'they are unquestionably victims'; nowhere in Gower's account is
the incest of Canace and Machaire explicitly condemned, though
as Benson points out, 'Genius's failure to condemn Canacee does
not necessarily force the reader to do the same.'[51]

The impossible ambiguity of their relationship is implied by the
oxymorons in Canace's lament (added by Gower to Ovid's
account):

> O thou my sorwe and my gladnesse,
> O thou myn hele and my siknesse,
> O my wanhope and al my trust,
> O my desese and al my lust,
> O thou my wele, o thou my wo,
> O thou my frend, o thou my fo,
> O thou my love, o thou myn hate,
> For thee mot I be ded algate.   (279–86)

(O you who are my sorrow and my joy, O you my well-being and my sick-
ness, O my despair and all my trust, O my distress and all my desire, O you
my happiness, O you my woe, O you my friend, O you my enemy, O you
my love, O you my hate, for you I must certainly die.)

Benson comments that 'Never have these clichés of courtly love
been truer or more fatal', and Spearing makes the same point:
'When the love is incestuous, the paradoxes take on a new edge.'[52]

Machaire departs before Canace's child is born, and no more is
heard of him. The story is told as a warning not against lechery or
incest but against Wrath, here personified in their father Eolus who
is so furious at the discovery of Canace's pregnancy that he sends
her a sword with orders to kill herself, and then has her child
exposed in a wild place where beasts will devour him. There is no
possibility of the survival of the foundling to marry his mother
here. The tragedy of Canace and Machaire is compounded by the
tragedy of their child; in a poignant addition, Gower has the baby
innocently playing in his mother's blood, which is pleasantly warm,
before his cruel grandfather has him taken away to be exposed

---

[51] Spearing, 'Canace', 215; Benson, 'Incest', 102.
[52] Benson, 'Incest', 106; Spearing, 'Canace', 216.

(312–15).[53] The image of the child playing in his mother's blood might be linked to the concept of original sin: the blood they share is tainted by the sinfulness of the fallen world, and perhaps there is also a hint of the heat of illicit passion. I agree with Macaulay's comment that 'In spite of the character of the subject, it must be allowed that Gower tells the story in a very touching manner'; but he goes too far, I think, in arguing that for Gower 'there is nothing naturally immoral about an incestuous marriage', other than the Church's disapproval (note on *CA* 3. 172). It is certainly true that Gower shows no horror or disbelief at the idea of a brother and sister feeling desire for one another. Wetherbee argues that the siblings are presented as 'enfants sauvages' (wild children), and that their passion is 'unmediated by social form', representing 'the horror of a moral void'; he sees it as 'unmeaningness' rather than 'wickedness'.[54] Spearing describes their predicament more sympathetically and, in my view, more accurately: 'As Gower tells the story of "Canace and Machaire", it emphasizes the naturalness of the unnatural: that paradox lies at its center and pervades the whole narrative.'[55] The Confessor tells Amans that 'What nature hath set in hire lawe | Ther mai no mannes miht withdrawe' (355–6: What Nature has set in her law no human strength can remove). This might seem to support Macaulay's view that incest is unacceptable only because it is condemned by the Church, but I think it should be taken rather as an acknowledgement of the dangerous power of love. This does not mean that Gower condones incestuous affairs; but he does feel respect and awe for the power which can create love even between close relations who are well aware of the social taboo. Canace and Machaire behave foolishly, but they are victims, as Spearing argues—first of Nature and then of their irascible father. Their incestuous love is somewhat decentred by the focus on Eolus' wrath, and the placing of this story in a section of the poem devoted to cautionary tales about misplaced anger.[56] Although Chaucer's Man of Law apparently regarded Gower's tale of Canace as a 'wikke ensample' (*CT* 2. 78: a wicked *exemplum*), the modern reader may see it rather as a rare instance of sibling love presented

---

[53] See Spearing's ingenious interpretation of the relationship of this harrowing scene to the Ovidian source, 'Canace', 218–19.

[54] Wetherbee, 'Constance', 67.   [55] Spearing, 'Canace', 214.

[56] See Benson's comments on Genius' heavy criticism of Eolus, which he argues may be ironic ('Incest', 104–5).

in a fairly positive light, as a mutual and genuine passion, though also a fatal one.

Boccaccio does not mention Canace at all in *De casibus*, and Laurent gives only a very brief version of the story focused on Macareus, but Lydgate expands it considerably, using Gower as well as Ovid (*Fall*, 1. 6833–7070).[57] He tells the story of Canace's downfall quite briskly, but then devotes considerable space to her last letter to her brother (6883–7049); it is three times as long as the rest of the narrative, which takes only forty-two lines. Like Gower, but unlike Ovid, Lydgate uses this letter to stress Canace's love for her brother, and the innocence of their child. He remarks that the child born of this unnatural love 'excellid in fauour and fairnesse; | For lik to hym off beute was non other' (6849–50: was outstandingly attractive in appearance; for he had no equal in beauty); this addition to his sources is an interesting piece of evidence that in the Middle Ages incest was not assumed to produce defective children.[58] Like Gower, Lydgate ends the story by emphasizing Eolus' hasty vengeance; unlike Gower, he makes little comment on incest, which is described here as unnatural love, 'ageyn nature' (6839) and 'ageyn kynde' (6845). The beauty of the child, the sincerity of the siblings' love, and the pathos of their plight seem to mitigate the horror of their transgression, which is mostly condemned in the context of their father's reaction:

> For whan ther fadir the maner dede espie
> Off ther werkyng, which was so horrible,
> For ire almost he fill in frenesie,
> Which for tappese was an inpossible;
> For the mater was froward & odible:
> For which, pleynli, deuoid off al pite,
> Upon ther trespas he wolde auenged be.   (6854–60)

(For when their father found out what they were doing, which was so horrible, he almost went mad with anger, and could not be appeased; for the matter was perverse and hateful; and so, to speak plainly, without any pity he was determined to be avenged on their transgression.)

Canace does not blame herself or her brother for her unnatural passion; first she reproaches her father for his cruel punishment and

---

[57] See the comments of Bergen, note on *Fall*, 1. 6736 ff.

[58] Adonis is of course another example; for further discussion see my comments in Ch. 1 and the Conclusion.

implacable anger, and then Cupid, the blind archer, for ruining their reputations (6993–7000). It seems surprising that Canace is allowed to evade responsibility for her actions. As in Gower's version, there is no doubt about the force of the mutual passion—Canace still loves her brother even at the tragic end of her life. Her letter emphasizes that he has made her happy as well as sad; their love is presented as plausible and sincere, wrong but romantic. Macareus' flight is attributed here to fear of the death penalty ordained by his father, whereas in Laurent's version he flees not only in fear of his father's wrath but also out of a sense of sin. Lydgate's version ends not with a moral about mistaken union or unnatural sin, but with criticism of Eolus for being 'to rigerous . . . and to vengable' in allowing pride and anger to overcome mercy (7057–8: too harsh and too vengeful); Gower uses the same conclusion, and is no doubt the model here. As in the case of the Theban story, this ending seems political and public rather than moral and personal; but as far as the sibling incest is concerned, Lydgate's version of the tragedy is fairly sympathetic.

Boccaccio mentions all Ovid's incestuous women apart from Canace in De casibus, but he merely names Byblis and Myrrha; Laurent has more to say about these two, but omits the transformation of Myrrha. Lydgate gives a succinct account of Byblis' love and transformation in four stanzas, without any direct speech, and without any moral; immediately after this he gives rather more space to Myrrha (Bergen notes that he is following Ovid rather than Laurent), but again there is no direct speech and no final moral.[59] Boccaccio does tell the story of Phaedra, but fairly briefly, and only as part of the larger story of Theseus.[60] Boccaccio's conclusion is that after the double blow of Hippolytus' death and Phaedra's suicide, Theseus was deposed by the Athenians and died unhappily in exile; as in the Oedipus story, the incest is subsumed into a larger context of political disaster. Similarly, Lydgate tells the story but ignores the incest in his final comments: Phaedra's death shows that slanderers will be punished (2873–7), and that it is a mistake to make hasty judgements (2881–4: this refers to Theseus). Later Lydgate echoes Boccaccio's criticism of Theseus for his

---

[59] Fall, I. 5678–775. Neither here nor in the story of Phaedra is there any reference to offended gods as instigators of the incestuous passion.

[60] Boccaccio, De casibus, I. x; Lydgate, Fall, I. 2801–84.

credulity; he should have known better than to believe a woman.[61] In none of these versions does the writer draw what one might have expected to be the obvious conclusion: that violent delights—or desires—inevitably have violent ends. This surprising omission is even more striking in medieval texts which give allegorical Christian interpretations of classical incest stories (sometimes offering several apparently incompatible readings of a single text). Since Ovid's incestuous women are so often cited as examples of irrational and wicked lust, it is curious that they rarely seem to have been used as warnings specifically against the sin of incest.

This is especially evident in the *Ovide Moralisé*, where 'polysemous and often contradictory interpretations are the rule' according to Blumenfeld-Kosinski, who notes the innovative and liberating approach of 'the almost unbelievable excess of interpretation practiced by the *Ovide* poet'.[62] A great deal of space is devoted in the *OM* to the story of Byblis and her brother, here called Cadmus rather than the usual Caunus (9. 1997–2762). No doubt the intention was to emphasize the horror of incest by expanding Ovid's version of Byblis' struggle with herself, her approach to her brother, his horrified rejection, her further agonizings, and her wanderings before her metamorphosis into a fountain. The poet makes things much worse for her before he makes them, unexpectedly, much better. Once Cadmus has rejected her, she becomes promiscuous; just as all can drink from a fountain, all could enjoy her favours. But then the interpretation becomes explicitly Christian and much more positive. Byblis lived in a degenerate age when the proper worship of God had been forgotten, and the few saintly and pure people wandered the world combating folly and vanity. The usually virtuous Cadmus here becomes the sinful and ignorant human race, and Byblis becomes divine wisdom, which is sweeter and more desirable than any other drink and so compassionate that she wants to unite herself with the whole human race. Cadmus' rejection of her letter echoes the rejection by the hard-hearted and sinful of the Ten Commandments transcribed by Moses. Her promiscuity represents the fact that divine grace and love are available to all. The fountain is God who cleanses and

---

[61] Boccaccio, *De casibus*, I. XI; Lydgate, *Fall*, I. 4493–6. Lydgate adds that Theseus believed he was being punished for his earlier desertion of Ariadne (4462–6).

[62] *Reading Myth*, 13.

revives the faithful with inexhaustible draughts of grace. The inter-relationship of the fountain, the spring from which it comes, and the stream that runs from it is used to explain the mystery of the Trinity. The poet gets quite carried away in describing the flowers of virtue that spring up round the fountain—humility, patience, chastity, etc. The sins of the lustful Byblis are quite forgotten in this *locus amoenus* of divine love.

Byblis, of course, did not manage to consummate her passion. She may therefore seem a more sympathetic subject than Myrrha, who managed through trickery to sleep with her own father and became pregnant by him (in Ovid's version she sleeps with him many times before he sees her in daylight and recognizes her; the *OM* author gives them only one night together, no doubt feeling that one was quite bad enough). Here too the original story is extended, from 200 lines in Ovid to nearly 900 lines of narrative and 320 of interpretation in the *OM*. Myrrha's monologues and her debate with her nurse make it very clear what a monstrous crime she is contemplating (though the *OM* author does preserve, in slightly altered form, the Ovidian Myrrha's defiant speech about the enviable freedom of animals to mate at will). The first part of the moralization uses the approach of Fulgentius, which was fol-lowed by many later mythographers (3675–747).[63] Cinyras is the sun, and as the sun draws out sap from the tree, so the father unwit-tingly drew out his daughter's desire. Myrrh trees in India glow in the sun's heat; the sun is the father of all life, so Myrrha is said to have fallen in love with her father. Then the tone becomes more moralizing. Adonis represents sweet delight in sexual appetite; the killing of Adonis by the boar is explained as an appropriate end for one who has spent his life in lechery; the anemone which sprang up from his blood represents human sin. But this is fol-lowed by a fully Christian interpretation which is presented as bet-ter and more noteworthy (3748–809). Bitter myrrh represents the Virgin Mary, the daughter and handmaiden of God, who was sought by many men but could only love God, Who loved her too above all others: 'par cele se joint charnelment | Diex a sa fille voirement' (3790: thus truly God united in the flesh with his

---

[63] *The Mythologies*, ch. 8, in *Fulgentius*, 92; for comment see Blumenfeld-Kosinski, *Reading Myth*, 93–8. A brief version of this interpretation is also used by Lydgate in his account in *Fall*.

daughter).[64] This was the conception of Adonis/Christ, the lord and saviour of the world, who removed all reproach and sin from his parents (3799). The boar which killed Adonis represents the Jews; his revival as a flower represents the Resurrection through divine grace. For the OM poet, Myrrha's incest is thus entirely necessary and appropriate, and also unique. Here, as in the Oedipus interpolation, the poet turns a shocking story of human incest into the triumphant story of the Incarnation. Not content with this startling interpretation, however, the poet tries out yet another (3878–954), though it seems almost bathetic after the identification with Mary. Now Myrrha is again an incestuous daughter who conceives by her own father, but the context is Christian: confession and penance could save her as they did Mary Magdalene.[65] In the end Myrrha does show her repentance in weeping and in great suffering, and God shows that he has pardoned her by turning her into a myrrh tree; she is killed by her sin, but anointed with bitter-sweet contrition and satisfaction just as a dead body is anointed with myrrh. Myrrh is available for all dead bodies, just as God's grace is available to all sinners who are killing their souls. The final moral is that it is madness not to repent of one's sins, since God has mercy on every repentant sinner. This interpretation of the Myrrha legend may well have been influenced by the fashion from the late twelfth century on for stories combining incest and contrition (see the following chapters).

Byblis was a standard example for medieval writers of irrational and disastrous passion, yet she could also be presented as the fountain of divine wisdom which offers itself freely to all. Myrrha was widely reviled as an epitome of female lust and deceitfulness; Dante consigned her to the eighth circle of hell among the falsifiers, and bitterly compared her with the Florence that had exiled him.[66] Yet the author of the Ovide Moralisé could read this incestuous daughter both as a contrite sinner and, more startlingly, as the chosen spouse of the Lord. No pagan story was too shocking or too negative for the ingenuity of medieval Christian exegetes.

[64] For discussion of the widespread medieval topos of Mary's 'holy incest', see the final chapter.
[65] Mary Magdalene was identified by medieval readers with the woman taken in adultery and also with St Mary of Egypt; see Karras, 'Holy Harlots'.
[66] Dante, Inferno, 30. 37–41, and Letter VII, quoted by Flinker in 'Cinyras', 62.

Ovid's Innocent Incest Victim

One more Ovidian incest story was widely popular in the Middle Ages: the tragedy of Philomena (medieval writers preferred this spelling to the classical form Philomela), who was raped and mutilated by her brother-in-law and then horrifically avenged by her sister Procne. Here the incest is slightly less shocking in that the participants are related only by marriage, and it is overshadowed by the crimes that follow it: the mutilation of Philomena by Tereus, and the killing and cooking of his son by the outraged Procne. The twelfth-century version found in the *Ovide Moralisé* is often attributed to Chrétien de Troyes, though the attribution is the subject of much debate; it follows Ovid's account in the *Metamorphoses* fairly closely, but there are some significant changes and additions.[67] The French poet remarks that the laws of Thrace permitted incest even between full siblings, so that Tereus was not really committing a crime (219–32), though immediately before this he emphasizes how villainous Tereus was to desire his own wife's sister (215–18); Ovid merely says that the Thracians were particularly passionate. The French Tereus has to work much harder to persuade Pandion to let Philomena visit her sister; Pandion's reluctance to let his daughter leave, and his account of how much he loves her and will miss her, hint at an incestuous love on his part too (344–78).[68] Ovid merely summarizes Philomena's distress just before the rape, but the French poet reports her conversation with Tereus in direct speech. She reproaches him repeatedly: she mentions her sister, but above all she emphasizes his treachery to her father and his perjury in swearing that he would look after her well (807–32). When the French Procne kills her own son, she is spurred on by the thought of Tereus as traitor and perjurer (1320), whereas Ovid's Procne is incensed at her sister's ordeal; Ovid's gory account of the death of the child is considerably shortened here. Unlike his Ovidian counterpart, the French Tereus does feel shame when he sees the mutilated Philomena and when he understands his wife's dreadful

---

[67] *OM* 6. 2183–3840; see also de Boer's separate edition of *Philomena*. Ovid, *Met.* 6. 424–674.

[68] Perhaps this was suggested to the poet by the passage in Ovid where she embraces her father, urging him to let her go, and the besotted Tereus wishes that he were her father and could be so embraced by her; Ovid comments that this desire would have been wicked even in a father (478–82).

revenge, but forgets about it in his desire to punish Procne (1413–27). There is no explicit reference in the French version to incest; the emphasis is on Tereus' treachery in his treatment of his wife and father-in-law as well as his luckless sister-in-law (1450–1).

The story is retold by Gower as an example of Ravine (rape or violent theft), an aspect of Avarice (*CA* 5. 5551–6052). Gower seems to be interested not so much in the incest as in the fact that Tereus is already married, and that Philomena is a virgin (see 5627–50 and 5809–15). The horror is therefore rape of a virgin by a married man which also happens to be incest, rather than incest which also happens to be adultery and rape. When the sisters serve up Ithis to Tereus, Procne reproaches her husband for 'thi tirannye' (5921), and for doing 'shame' to love (5926), but there is no more explicit reference to incest. When Philomena is transformed, she does not mention incest either, but rejoices in her song that 'Thogh I have lost mi Maidenhede | Schal noman se my chekes rede' (5987–8: though I have lost my virginity, no one will see me blushing). When Procne is transformed, she sings of 'Tereus the Spousebreche' (6014: the adulterer), and the falseness of husbands generally. Chaucer makes rather more of the betrayal of Philomena in the *Legend of Good Women* (2228–393): it happens in a cave, and he follows Ovid in comparing Philomena to a lamb mauled by a wolf, or a dove in the claws of an eagle (2318–19). He also omits entirely the second part of the story, the sisters' dreadful revenge and the metamorphosis. Yet his moral is, as throughout the *Legend*, that women should not trust men; again there is no explicit reference to incest.[69]

The moralization of the sad story of Philomena and Procne in the *Ovide Moralisé* also seems to ignore the incest; the tragedy is explained as a sort of fall of man—or in this case woman.[70] Their father Pandion becomes God; Procne is the soul, who is married to the body, Tereus. When Procne yearns to see her sister she becomes human nature, inclined to every villainy. Poor Philomena is worldly love, misguided and open to deception. She is imprisoned by the body (Tereus), and then wrongly freed by the soul (Procne); together the sisters destroy Itys, the good fruit of the virtuous life.

[69] Lydgate mentions the story, but refers interested readers to Chaucer (*Fall*, 1. 1786–1806); he describes it as Tereus' deception of both sisters, and does not comment on the incest.

[70] *OM* 6. 3719–3840; it is not included in de Boer's edition of *Philomena*.

Thus the body brings the soul to destruction in the infernal fire-place! The final transformations are only very briefly mentioned here: the nightingale represents vain and transitory delight; Tereus becomes an owl whose dirty condition mirrors his filthy behaviour. These metamorphoses are presented not as a means of saving the sisters from the vengeance of Tereus and then punishing him, but rather as punishment for the crimes committed by all three. There is no sympathy here for any of the protagonists, except perhaps poor little Itys. All come to a bad end when the soul is corrupted by the body. Philomena seems to be unfairly represented in a very negative way as worldly delight (like Eurydice in moralizations of the Orpheus myth), and is made responsible for her sister's downfall. Procne as soul is the central character in the moral drama here, and the stress is on infanticide rather than incest; it seems that the killing of Itys is the focus of the story for this moralizer, who blames excessive sisterly love (read 'worldly feelings') for such a barbarous rejection of maternal instinct (read 'appropriate and moral love'). The burden of guilt is shifted to women who behave in inappropriate ways; unfeminine behaviour becomes a trope for unchristian behaviour. Modern readers are likely to feel that Tereus the rapist and mutilator gets off disturbingly lightly here, even though we may not consider his rape of his sister-in-law to be incest, as it was for medieval readers.

Semiramis

Semiramis was admired by many classical historians for her achievements as a ruler, a warrior, and a builder. Like many powerful rulers, she was said to be promiscuous; Diodorus Siculus, writing in the first century BC, remarks casually that she used one of her newly constructed pleasure gardens to enjoy handsome young soldiers whom she then had killed, but he makes no moral judgement.[71] The story of Semiramis' incestuous desire for her son, who later murdered her, seems to have appeared first in the reign of Augustus in the universal history of Pompeius Trogus, which survives only in the later epitome of Justinus; the circulation of the

---

[71] *Histories*, 2. 13. 3–4. For a more detailed history of the legend of Semiramis see Samuel's important essay 'Semiramis', and also Archibald, 'Sex and Power'.

story must have been greatly increased by its inclusion in Orosius' very influential *Universal History*, an anti-pagan polemic composed in the early fifth century AD.[72] Orosius paints a savage picture of the shortcomings of Semiramis: according to him, she was not only a bloodthirsty conqueror but also a homicidal nymphomaniac who justified her liaison with her own son by legitimizing parent–child marriages. A barbarian queen with such power as Semiramis would have been particularly horrifying to early Christian writers; the legend of her sexual appetites, combined with her residence in Babylon, would have made her seem a living incarnation of the Whore of Babylon so vividly described in Revelations and depicted in medieval Apocalypse manuscripts.[73]

Not all medieval writers referred to the story of her incest when discussing Semiramis, but it was certainly known to Dante, who put her in the second circle of hell; he does not mention her incest explicitly, but he does allude to her infamous marriage law, assuming that his readers would understand.[74] Boccaccio included her as the second subject in his innovative *De claris mulieribus*, praising her many political achievements, but arguing that they were cancelled out by her incest.[75] He adds the tantalizing story that she invented the chastity belt in order to prevent her court ladies from seducing her son. This surprising claim can be seen as a further sign of Semiramis' monstrous and perverted behaviour, and of her tyrannical abuse of power; these vices led to her murder by her own son, yet another unnatural act. Boccaccio also mentions Semiramis and her infamous law in his misogynist digression in the *De casibus* (1. 8), though modesty forbids him to discuss her sins in detail; his French translator Laurent de Premierfait is much more explicit, and so is Lydgate.[76] Chaucer uses her as the epitome of murderous deceit in his description of the evil old Sultaness who is Constance's first mother-in-law in the *Man of Law's Tale* (CT 2. 359), though elsewhere he mentions her in a less hostile light as a victim of love

[72] See Orosius, *Seven Books*, 1. 4, trans. Deferrari, 22–3.
[73] This important parallel was pointed out to me by Gordon Shrimpton. Augustine mentions her incest in *The City of God*, 18. 2, where Babylon is presented as the antithesis of the city of God.   [74] *Inferno*, 5. 55–60; see Jacoff, 'Transgression'.
[75] *De claris mulieribus*, ch. 2, trans. Guarino, 4–7.
[76] See Lydgate, *Fall*, I. 6631 ff., and Bergen's note.

in the *Parliament of Fowls* (288), and as the founder of Babylon in the *Legend of Good Women* (707).

It was Christine de Pizan who came to the rescue of Semiramis, making her the first stone in her metaphorical city of ladies—a provocative and somewhat scandalous choice.[77] Christine confronts her notorious reputation for incest head-on, arguing that it was not contrary to the laws of the time, that Semiramis would never have done anything wrong or scandalous, and that her motive was not lust but *Realpolitik*. This fits Samuel's argument that in the later Middle Ages and the Renaissance Semiramis' reputation underwent a considerable rehabilitation.[78] From the fourteenth century on she was regularly included in lists of the Nine Worthy Women which were invented to match the well-known male Worthies.[79] Semiramis' claim to fame in these lists consists of her public and political achievements as warrior and city builder which had been celebrated by classical writers; it seems that in the later Middle Ages these pluses cancelled out the minuses of promiscuity, incest, and murder which had previously preoccupied so many Christian writers.

Apollonius of Tyre

As a female barbarian ruler, Semiramis was vulnerable to allegations of tyranny both in the political and the domestic sphere; as we have seen, tyrants are often accused of incest. The popular story of Apollonius of Tyre begins with a tyrannical and incestuous father, and the shadow of incest hangs over the story till the end when Apollonius, his wife, and their long-lost daughter are safely reunited.[80]

---

[77] *Book of the City*, i. 15. 1–2, trans Richards, 38–40. See Quilligan, *Allegory*, 69–70; and Dulac, 'Un mythe'.

[78] Samuel, 'Semiramis', 43. Shakespeare refers to her negatively in the context of promiscuity and lust (*Taming of the Shrew*, Ind. ii. 39; *Titus Andronicus*, ii. i. 22 and ii. iii. 118); but Spenser invokes her as an example of female virtue and success when praising Boadicea (*Faerie Queene*, ii. 10).   [79] See Schroeder, *Der Topos*, 168–202.

[80] I summarize the plot of the standard Latin version, *Historia Apollonii* (*HA*); all references and translations are taken from my own edition. For futher discussion of the medieval reception of the story, see the editions of Kortekaas and Archibald. There is useful discussion of the incest theme in Scanlon, 'Riddle of Incest', though his main focus is Gower's version.

King Antiochus of Antioch, a widower, seduces his only daughter and heiress, and sets a riddle to deter her suitors, on pain of
death for all who fail to solve it. Apollonius of Tyre finds the
answer (that the king and the princess are committing incest), but
is told that he is wrong and given thirty days' grace. He flees to
Tarsus and then is shipwrecked near Cyrene; there he is
befriended by the king, Archestrates, and marries his daughter
(and heiress). When they hear that Antiochus and his daughter
have been killed by a thunderbolt, Apollonius and his pregnant
wife set off to claim the throne of Antioch, but on the way the
princess apparently dies in childbirth, and her coffin is thrown
overboard. It arrives in Ephesus, where she is revived from her
coma by a doctor and becomes a priestess of Diana. Apollonius,
heartbroken, leaves his baby daughter Tarsia with foster-parents
in Tarsus, and goes off to Egypt to be a merchant.

Years later the jealous foster-mother tries to murder Tarsia,
who outshines her own daughter; but in the nick of time Tarsia
is carried off by pirates and sold in Mytilene to a pimp. She manages to preserve her chastity in the brothel under the protection
of the local prince, Athenagoras. Apollonius goes to Tarsus to
collect Tarsia and is told that she is dead. In despair, he sails off
aimlessly and arrives by chance at Mytilene, where the prince
sends Tarsia to try to cheer him up. Apollonius is drawn to the
clever young woman, and solves the series of riddles she sets him;
they discover their relationship. Tarsia is married to the prince;
they sail to Ephesus where Apollonius is reunited with his wife.
They all return to Cyrene where Apollonius inherits the throne,
and begets a son.

Almost every male authority figure in the narrative has a daughter,
including the Ephesian doctor and the prince of Mytilene; indeed,
father–daughter relations are a crucial indicator of moral character
in both the domestic and the political spheres. Antiochus is a bad
father and a bad king; Archestrates is a good father and a good
king. How will Apollonius measure up? He abandons his role as
king when he loses his wife, and abandons his infant daughter too.
Once he has safely negotiated the encounter with his unrecognized
daughter, whom he might have been tempted to seduce, he can
return to his proper status as father, king, and husband.[81] He hastily

[81] See Archibald, *Apollonius*, 15–22; and Schneidegger, 'Pères et filles'.

marries his daughter to prince Athenagoras, her persecutor turned protector; so he distinguishes himself from the villainous Antiochus by not seducing his daughter, and by arranging a conventional marriage for her to a worthy suitor (though without consulting her). Next comes the reunion with his wife, and their return to her father's court; Archestrates bequeaths his kingdom to them, just as Apollonius had made his son-in-law Athenagoras the king of Antioch (or Tyre in some versions). These arrangements can be seen as a welcome return to the normal patriarchal procedure of the exchange of women: the king marries his heiress daughter to a suitable prince, who becomes king in his turn. The triumph of patriarchy in this story is marked, finally, by the birth of a son and heir to Apollonius and his wife; this solves the heiress problem and—by implication—the incest problem too.

The story of Apollonius seems to have been composed in the third century AD, though the earliest extant versions date from the fifth or sixth century. It was extremely popular throughout the Middle Ages and into the Renaissance, though the reasons for this popularity are hard to pin down. The plot in the original Latin and in many later versions is often illogical and problematic. The vogue for 'romans antiques' and chivalric adventures with a strong emphasis on romantic love is usually considered to have begun in the twelfth century. Yet allusions in literary texts show that the story of Apollonius was widely known from the sixth century on; and monastic library catalogues and wills from the eighth century on testify that monks and secular readers alike had access to copies of the *Historia Apollonii*. At least six of the surviving Latin manuscripts were copied before the twelfth century; about a hundred and twenty Latin manuscripts survive from the whole medieval period, plus translations and adaptations in every European language; printed editions in both Latin and vernaculars were frequently produced from 1470 on. Allusions in a wide range of languages and genres indicate that it was a well-known and popular story, recited at social gatherings such as feasts and weddings. It was dramatized by Shakespeare as *Pericles Prince of Tyre*;[82] in the Prologue the narrator, Gower (whose version in the *Confessio Amantis* was one of

[82] There is considerable scholarly debate about the relationship between Shakespeare's *Pericles* and Wilkins' play *The Painefull Adventures of Pericles Prince of Tyre*, and also about the possibility that Shakespeare wrote *Pericles* with a collaborator; see the introductory comments of Hoeniger, from whose Arden edition all references are taken.

Shakespeare's sources), comments on its lasting appeal to high and low:

> It hath been sung at festivals,
> On ember-eves and holy-ales;
> And lords and ladies in their lives
> Have read it for restoratives.
> The purchase is to make men glorious;
> Et bonum quo antiquius eo melius.   (1. Prol. 5–10)

'A good thing is made even better by age': though Ben Jonson, jealous of the success of *Pericles*, famously condemned it as 'a mouldy tale', it was in fact a medieval best-seller, an evergreen which remained popular in the Renaissance too.[83]

The story did attract criticism in some quarters for the very reasons which made it attractive in others. It is sometimes mentioned in lists of texts which are a waste of time and should be replaced by more serious and moral reading material; but elsewhere Apollonius is cited as one of the heroes whose story should be in the repertoire of every jongleur and minstrel. Part of its appeal was clearly the opening incest scene, distressing though many readers found it. In the standard Latin text, the story opens with a brief statement of Antiochus' growing desire for his daughter (some other versions attribute this lust to the devil). He fights against his inappropriate passion for a couple of lines, and the consummation follows in short order. The description is made more shocking by the succinct, matter-of-fact narrative:

Qui cum luctantur cum furore, pugnat cum dolore, vincitur amore; excidit illi pietas, oblitus est se esse patrem et induit coniugem. Sed cum sui pectoris vulnus ferre non posset, quadam die prima luce vigilans inrumpit cubiculum filiae suae. Famulos longe excedere iussit, quasi cum filia secretum conloquium habiturus, et stimulante furore libidinis diu repugnanti filiae suae nodum virginitatis eripuit. Perfectoque scelere evasit cubiculum. Puella vero stans dum miratur scelestis patris impietatem, fluentem sanguinem coepit celare; sed guttae sanguinis in pavimento ceciderunt. (*HA*, ch. 1)

(He struggled with madness, he fought against passion, but he was defeated by love; he lost his sense of moral responsibility, forgot that he was a father, and took on the role of husband. Since he could not endure the wound in his heart, one day when he was awake at dawn he rushed into

---

[83] See Jonson, 'On *The New Inn*', 21–30, in *Ben Jonson*, ed. Donaldson, 502–3.

his daughter's room and ordered the servants to withdraw, as if he
intended to have a private conversation with her. Spurred on by the frenzy
of his lust, he took his daughter's virginity by force, in spite of her lengthy
resistance. When the wicked deed was done he left the bedroom. But the
girl stood astonished at the immorality of her wicked father. She tried to
hide the flow of blood: but drops of blood fell onto the floor.)

When the Man of Law in the *Canterbury Tales* insists that Chaucer
would never tell 'cursed stories' about horrors like incest, he mentions the Apollonius story as an example:

> . . . Or ellis of Tyro Appollonius,
> How that the cursed kyng Antiochus
> Birafte his dogther of hir maydenhede,
> That is so horrible a tale for to rede,
> Whan he hir threw upon the pavement.   (*CT* 2. 81–5)

(. . . Or else of Apollonius of Tyre, how the accursed king Antiochus took
his daughter's virginity, which is such a horrible tale to read, when he threw
her on the floor.)

The detail that Antiochus threw his daughter on the floor does not
occur in any surviving text of the story. Did Chaucer invent this, or
was an even more disturbing version than the ones we know circulating in the later Middle Ages?[84]

The crudity of this opening scene contrasts strikingly with the
crucial scene in which Apollonius encounters his unrecognized
daughter in Mytilene. It is vital that he should pass the morality test
by treating her appropriately, but in the Latin text at least his behaviour hints at the possibility of rape. Schneidegger shows how 'le
rapport père–fille a glissé de l'érotique au discursif, mais il subsiste
quelques traces du déplacement' (the father–daughter relationship
has slipped from the erotic to the discursive, but some traces of the
displacement remain).[85] To rouse Apollonius from his gloom,
Tarsia proposes a riddle contest; Apollonius is impressed by her
intelligence, but after solving the riddles he dismisses her. When she
tries to drag him up to the light, he pushes her so that she falls and
starts bleeding from the nose (the knee in a variant version).
Weeping, she starts to describe her sad history, beginning with her
mother's 'death' at sea. Apollonius realizes who she is, and from

---

[84] It may derive from a misunderstanding of a Latin version; see the note in the
Riverside edition.   [85] Schneidegger, 'Pères et filles', 270; see *HA*, chs. 40–5.

this point on all is well; but his response to her, attraction followed by unwarranted violence, recalls the rape of Antiochus' daughter at the beginning, as does the scenario of a riddle contest involving a nubile girl. The speed with which Apollonius marries Tarsia off to Athenagoras, without consulting her at all, could also be read as conscious or subconscious anxiety to avoid the temptation of incest.[86]

Later versions of the story often downplay the recognition scene, no doubt because it casts Apollonius in such a bad light; Gower's is an exception, and particularly interesting. He emphasizes the strong attraction between the two, which at first seems quite inexplicable to both:

> Bot of hem tuo a man mai liere
> What is to be so sibb of blod:
> Non wiste of other hou it stod,
> And yit the fader ate laste
> His herte upon this maide caste,
> That he hire loveth kindely,
> And yit he wiste nevere why.
>
> .   .   .   .
>
> Fro point to point al sche him tolde,
> That sche hath longe in herte holde,
> And nevere dorste make hir mone
> But only to this lorde al one,
> To whom hire herte can nought hele . . .
>
> (CA 8. 1702–8, 1725–9)

(But from these two a man may learn what blood relationship really means. Neither knew who the other was, and yet the father at last cast his heart upon this girl and felt natural love for her, without knowing why . . . Point by point she told him everything that she had long kept in her heart, and had never dared lament except to this one lord, from whom her heart can hide nothing . . .)

Here Gower suggests that it would be quite natural for an

---

[86] Athenagoras is first introduced as the client willing to pay a lot of money to deflower her; when she wins him over with her tears and her tragic story, he tells her that he has a virginal daughter of the same age, whom a similar fate might befall (chs. 33–4). Though he is filled with sympathy for Tarsia and admires her greatly, he inexplicably leaves her in the brothel, where he is said to watch over her as if she were his own daughter (chs. 35–6); this also hints at incest. Some medieval authors modified the brothel episode considerably.

THE CLASSICAL LEGACY 99

unrecognized father and daughter to feel drawn to each other.[87]
Apollonius does indeed love Thaise 'kindely' or naturally, since he
is her father. He is not described as smitten by inappropriate lust,
like Antiochus, though the possibility of incest is evoked by
Thaise's response a few lines earlier when Apollonius hits her: in
this version she does not bleed, but she says 'Avoi, my lord, I am a
Maide' (1696). The motif of incest averted here is most clearly
emphasized by the startling language used in Shakespeare's *Pericles*
to describe Apollonius' emotions at rediscovering his daughter. In
the standard Latin text, Apollonius embraces Tarsia and cries out
'Iam laetus moriar, quia rediviva spes mihi est reddita' (ch. 44: Now
I shall die happy, for my hope has been reborn and returned to me).
But in *Pericles* it is the royal father himself who is reborn: 'O, come
hither, | Thou that beget'st him that did thee beget' (v. i. 195–6).
This sounds worryingly incestuous—but it is a wonderfully apt
metaphor for his emotional rebirth or resurrection, the reversal of
fortune that returns him to his proper political and domestic status
as king and father, and signals that all's well that ends well.[88]

It would have been easy to omit the opening scene of paternal
rape and invent some other reason for Apollonius' flight and subsequent adventures, and indeed some critics have argued that the Ur-
version of the story did not begin with incest; yet no extant version
omits the sordid opening episode of Antiochus' incest (though
some writers did downplay it as much as possible).[89] Explicit
father–daughter incest was what many people in the Middle Ages
associated most prominently with the story of Apollonius. Some
introductory rubrics mention only Apollonius and some name both
Antiochus and Apollonius, but there are also some which omit
Apollonius entirely, like the one in the fourteenth-century Colmar
text of the popular *Gesta Romanorum*: 'de Antiocho qui filiam

---

[87] Today this phenomenon of intense attraction between long separated siblings, or
parents and children, is well recognized; social workers now warn parents whose children
are to be adopted by different families that there is a significant chance of the siblings
meeting and falling in love later in life. Sibling incest is also a potential hazard of Internet
liaisons, according to a report in the *Globe and Mail* (Toronto), 10 June 2000, R14; a
psychotherapist is quoted as commenting on a report of siblings who discovered that
they had been chatting each other up on-line unawares that this is disgusting, 'but at least
it's not your mom'.

[88] For further comment on this passage, see the final chapter.

[89] *Jourdain de Blaye*, a *chanson de geste* composed in the late 12th or early 13th cent.
which follows the Apollonius plot very closely, does use a different catalyst for the hero's
flight; see Dembowski's edition, and also Archibald, *Apollonius*, 54–5.

propriam cognovit et tantum eam dilexit quod nullus eam in uxorem habere potuit nisi problema ab eo propositum solveret' (of Antiochus who slept with his own daughter and loved her so much that no one could marry her unless he solved his riddle).[90] In Gower's *Confessio Amantis*, a Latin marginal note at the beginning of the tale describes it as 'mirabile exemplum de magno rege Antiocho' (the amazing *exemplum* of the great King Antiochus). Yet versions which introduce the story in this way always give the complete plot; there is no extant text which stops with the death of Antiochus.

Since the story always begins with some version of the incestuous rape, however decorously presented, one might expect that the end would stress the sinfulness of incest, or at least the likelihood that incestuous partners will meet a justifiably violent death, as Antiochus and his daughter do. Yet although the story is often presented as an *exemplum*, it is rare to find an explicit moral at the end; and when there is one, it is often a general admonition about enduring temporal tribulation, rather than a specific comment on incest.[91] In the *Gesta Romanorum*, a collection of hundreds of cautionary tales, the Apollonius *exemplum* is the only one that does not end with a Christian allegorization. Does this mean that the story was supposed to be transparent, to speak for itself? Gower is unusual in ending his version with an explicit moral: he contrasts Apollonius, whose love was honourable in that he got married and had children, with Antiochus, whose pride and unnatural love brought him to grief (*CA* 8. 1993–2008). Just to make the point absolutely clear, the narrator, Confessor, sums up for Amans, the young lover:

> Lo thus, mi Sone, myht thou liere
> What is to love in good manere,
> And what to love in other wise . . .   (2009–11)

(So, my son, in this way you can learn what it is to love properly, and what it is to love in other ways . . .)

Gower makes the story the last in his long series of cautionary tales about love and other dangerous passions in the *Confessio Amantis*; as a good father and husband and also a good king, Apollonius

---

[90] See Archibald, *Apollonius*, 93.   [91] See Archibald, *Apollonius*, 81–106.

represents a sort of mirror for princes as well as a model of appropriate and stable love.

Shakespeare's *Pericles* puts a lot of emphasis on good kingship, and can also be read as a mirror for princes.[92] It is in this very late version of the story, rather than in one written by medieval clerics to explain the dangers of inappropriate love, that a moral is most clearly expressed at the end. The final lines sum up the experiences of all the main characters, starting with the incestuous pair:

> In Antiochus and his daughter you have heard
> Of monstrous lust the due and just reward.
> In Pericles, his queen and daughter, seen
> Although assail'd with fortune fierce and keen,
> Virtue preserv'd from fell destruction's blast,
> Led on by heaven, and crown'd with joy at last.
>
> (v. Epilogue 1–6)

This explicit moral is what we expect, but do not find, in most medieval versions.

The opening incest episode seems to be at least partly responsible for the popularity of the Apollonius story throughout the Middle Ages. Some writers felt it necessary to apologize for it, but they also emphasized that however sordid the story, it did show vice punished and virtue rewarded, and was therefore of moral value to Christian readers. Two writers, one in the late twelfth century and one in the late sixteenth, described its value in terms of the proverb that gold can be found even in a dungheap.[93] In the case of the Apollonius story, as so often in literature, this mixture of gold and dungheap was the recipe for a best-seller.

CONCLUSIONS

Of the many incest stories circulating in the classical world, only a few remained widely known in the Middle Ages, and they were seldom retold as extended narratives; more often the protagonists were cited briefly as examples of tragic love or disastrous lust, or both. Stories of unwitting incest were rare in the classical period; this

---

[92] See Archibald, *Apollonius*, 21–2.
[93] Geoffrey de Vigeois and Markward Welser; see Archibald, *Apollonius*, 205 (V31) and 224 (A16).

category was represented in the Middle Ages only by Oedipus, whose fame derived more from the internecine war of his sons than from his marriage. Of those who yielded knowingly to incestuous desire (and in some cases actually consummated their lust), medieval writers concentrated on a small group of legendary women described by Ovid—Phaedra, Myrrha, Canace, and Byblis—plus the 'historical' Semiramis. Sometimes their incest was ignored and they were presented as tragic figures, betrayed in love; sometimes they were held up as examples of the fate in store for those who give in to lust, though in allegorical treatments they could also take on more positive Christian roles. As for innocent victims of incest, the two best known were Jocasta (pitied more for the loss of her sons than for her fatal marriage) and Philomena. In classical stories mother–son incest seems to be fairly rare, and is always presented as the most shocking relationship, but when it is deliberate on the part of the mother it is regarded as particularly monstrous; it never seems to be initiated knowingly by the son (except in the case of Secundus, who acts out of intellectual curiosity, and has no intention of actually having sex with his mother). Sibling incest may be consensual or unwelcome; Canace loved Macareus deeply (at least according to Ovid), but Caunus fled in horror from the advances of Byblis. Father–daughter incest is almost always initiated by the father— Myrrha is a shocking exception to this rule—and often takes the form of rape. Daughters who have been incestuously raped are likely to kill their offspring in grief or revenge, and sometimes kill themselves too; men who discover that they have unwittingly committed incest never react like this. Incestuous in-laws are rare in classical legend and literature, no doubt because in Greece this did not count as incest; their villainy consists more in treacherously destroying a family than in committing, or attempting, incest. Consummated incest is almost always associated with violence and vengeance, often stretching over several generations. The protagonists generally die, or are metamorphosed, as a direct result of their incest. As for incest stories with happy endings, there were not many to be found in classical myth, legend, and tragedy; but they were more numerous in New Comedy, a genre which may have influenced the late classical 'romances' that survived and flourished in the Middle Ages, the *Historia Apollonii* and the Christian *Clementine Recognitions*. Here the themes of vengeance and violence are subordinated to the more positive theme of family separation and reunion. Incest averted brings material benefits to the protagonists, and there are no unhappy repercussions for later generations; in the *Clementine Recognitions* the benefits are spiritual too, a trend which would continue in the Middle Ages. The Apollonius story is unique in combining scenes of consummated and averted incest; the villain is punished, and the virtuous hero and heroine are rewarded. Perhaps this satisfying combination accounts, at least in part, for its extraordinary popularity and influence throughout the Middle Ages.

Classical writers clearly accepted that incestuous desire was a reality even in civilized societies, and was by no means confined to barbarians and animals. They also found it possible to believe in consensual incest in the tragic story of Canace and Macareus. Some writers, most notably Ovid, were fascinated by the psychology of incest, by the inner struggle of the woman who is afflicted by forbidden desire (men are seldom described as agonizing at any length). But even if the incest was consensual, or was brought about by the intervention of the gods, the protagonists must be punished, either directly or through their families (or both). In classical incest stories there is no concept of sin and/or redemption, no moral lesson to be learned; there are only actions and consequences. The main change introduced by Christian writers is the possibility of contrition and absolution; for them incest is an appalling sin, but through God's grace even the worst sinner can be saved. This change of attitude meant that some classical stories were retold as cautionary tales about the dangers of lust, or as elaborate Christian allegories; it would have been difficult to rewrite the endings of stories as well known as those of Oedipus and Myrrha so that they repent and live happily ever after.[94] Some classical stories were presented as romantic tragedies (Byblis, for instance), but this was not a very popular genre in the Middle Ages, though the medieval versions of the Oedipus story might be described as political tragedies. Another option was to rework the familiar classical incest plots with a change of protagonist, a medieval setting, and a new denouement. In the chapters that follow, we shall see how medieval writers did this, and added some startling new twists.

---

[94] As was noted above, Sophocles' account of Oedipus' death in the classical equivalent of the odour of sanctity was not known in the Middle Ages, but it is possible that some analogous version was circulating orally. Ovid's Myrrha feels guilt and appeals to the gods to remove her from mortal life, and so is turned into a tree; this too could be seen as analogous to the later Christian theme of contrition and penance.

3
Mothers and Sons

RANCE [*to Prentice*]. If you are this child's father my book can
be written in good faith—she *is* the victim of an incestuous
assault!
MRS PRENTICE. And so am I, doctor! My son has a collection
of indecent photographs which prove beyond doubt that he
made free with me in the same hotel—indeed in the same
linen cupboard where his conception took place.
RANCE. Oh, what joy this discovery gives me! Double incest is
more likely to produce a best-seller than murder—and this
is as it should be for love *must* bring greater joy than
violence.

Joe Orton, *What the Butler Saw*, Act 2

IN the course of a rebuttal of the charge of incest so often levelled
by pagans against the early Christians because of their mysterious
love-feasts, Minucius Felix, writing in the late second century,
reminds his pagan interlocutor that classical legends and literature
are full of stories of the promiscuous behaviour of both gods and
mortals:

Merito igitur incestum penes vos saepe deprehenditur, semper admittitur.
Etiam nescientes, miseri, potestis in inlicita proruere: dum Venerem
promisce spargitis, dum passim liberos seritis, dum etiam domi natos
alienae misericordiae frequenter exponitis, necesse est in vestros recurrere,
in filios inerrare. Sic incesti fabulam nectitis, etiam cum conscientiam non
habetis.[1]

(It is no surprise, then, that among you incest is often discovered and is a
constant occurrence. Even without knowing it, you wretches, you can run
headlong into the illicit: while spreading love about in casual affairs, while
making children here, there and everywhere, while you are often exposing

[1] *Octavius*, ch. 31 (my translation, improved by Keith Bradley). In Chs. 1 and 2 I quote
responses of other early Christian apologists to similar charges. For more patristic comments on the practice of exposure and the risk of incest, see Boswell, *Kindness of
Strangers*, 138–79.

even those born at home to the mercy of strangers, it is inevitable that you should come back to your own, that you happen on your own children. Thus you weave a tale of incest without even realizing it.)

From our perspective today, this comment on attitudes to the exposure of children in early Christian Europe is strikingly lacking in family feeling, protective instinct, and reverence for life; it is also an accurate synopsis of an age-old literary plot, in which an exposed child is found, grows up, and unwittingly marries his/her parent.[2] The last sentence of the quotation suggests that the writer was aware of the literary relevance of his argument: 'Sic *incesti fabulam nectitis* (thus you weave a tale of incest).' Mysteries about identity and birth are staples of fiction in all lands and centuries, and so are recognition scenes in which the foundling hero turns out to be the long-lost son of the king or queen.[3] In some stories he has already married his unrecognized mother, and here the recognition scene acts as the peripeteia of the plot, rather than the finale; such stories cannot end, as many quests for identity do, with the happy reunion of the hero and his parents. In the Oedipus story, for instance, the recognition leads to disaster all round: Oedipus' abdication, Jocasta's suicide, the civil war between their sons, and the end of the royal family of Thebes.

Incest stories were doubtless circulating orally in western Europe in the early Middle Ages (and the late Latin *Historia Apollonii* was widely known in written form); but they begin to appear in written texts in increasing numbers from the twelfth century on, when the popular *fabula*, simultaneously shocking and intriguing, was harnessed and put to didactic use. This was not merely because of the growing audience for Latin and vernacular narrative fiction in this period, though of course the 'rise

[2] The father–daughter version is much rarer in medieval literature than the mother–son version; see my comments in the next chapter. Potentially incestuous encounters in brothels between fathers and daughters or siblings are common in classical New Comedy, but very rare in medieval texts.

[3] For analogues of the Oedipus story from all over the world see Edmunds and Dundes (eds.), *Oedipus Casebook*; Johnson and Price-Williams, *Oedipus Ubiquitous*. On recognition scenes see Aristotle, who lists them in five categories of ascending effectiveness (*Poetics*, ch. 16 (1454b–1455a)); and also Cave's magisterial study, *Recognitions*, though it includes little comment on medieval texts. Frye discusses identity as a particularly characteristic and crucial theme for romance in *Secular Scripture*, esp. ch. 4, 'The Bottomless Dream: Themes of Descent', where he considers descent into poverty or despair or madness in relation to the concealment or revelation of descent in the genealogical sense.

of romance', a genre with a strong interest in identity and recognition scenes and in the psychology of love, must have been a contributing factor. Incest was a very topical subject in the twelfth century because of the Church's attempts to define marriage in precise legal terms, and to impose a very elaborate set of rules about who could marry whom (see Chapter 1). There was also a new emphasis in this period on the importance of contrition, inner consciousness of guilt and repentance, and also on the value of confession; the Fourth Lateran Council of 1215 required all Christians to go to confession at least once a year. Incest seems to have been the sin of choice in stories featuring what Payen calls 'le motif du péché monstrueux' (the motif of the monstrous sin); these stories show that even the most heinous behaviour can be forgiven through God's grace if the sinner is truly repentant.[4] As we saw in the previous chapter, the Oedipus story was retold in the Middle Ages, but not as often as might have been expected, given the popularity of incest stories from the twelfth century on. One reason for the comparative neglect of Oedipus may be that for medieval audiences the violent reactions of Oedipus and Jocasta would have been a prime example of *accidia*, one of the Seven Deadly Sins, the fatal despair which turns the victim away from God, from hope and repentance and grace, and leads to death and damnation.[5] The classical setting and tragic ending of the Oedipus story would have emphasized the antiquity of the problem, and the remoteness of the story from the Christian world. It was more advantageous for the Church, and more impressive for medieval audiences, to have the incest theme in a Christian context, and either in a near-contemporary setting (such as the legend of the apocryphal Pope Gregory), or in a pseudo-historical one (such as the legend of Judas). In didactic narratives from the twelfth century on, consummated mother–son incest is usually followed by religious conversion instead of the suicides or metamorphoses found in classical stories (except in the case of irredeemable villains such as Judas); the initial prophecy of disaster may be retained or not,

---

[4] Payen, *Le Motif*, 519 ff., and see also his chapter on Contritionism, 54–75; Archibald, 'Incest'; Dorn, *Der Sündige Heilige*.

[5] As I noted in the previous chapter, Sophocles' ending in *Oedipus at Colonus*, where Oedipus becomes a saint-like figure whose grave will benefit the land where he dies, would not have been widely known in the Middle Ages.

depending on the effect desired.[6] In later vernacular romances, mother–son incest is one of the possible dangers facing the foundling heroes in search of their origins; but the fatal consummation is usually avoided, and there is no explicit moral or religious interpretation. When the incestuous marriage is averted in the nick of time (and the parricide too), the stories are merely titillating and cliff-hanging romances; when mother–son incest does occur, the story becomes an *exemplum* not about the inevitability of fate, but rather about the sinfulness of mankind, the value of contrition and penance, and the possibility of divine forgiveness. The classical combination of prophecy and fate takes a new form, since room has to be left for the good effects of contrition and penance and also for the unpredictable workings of divine grace (the Arthurian legend is an exception which will be discussed in detail in Chapter 5). When the focus is on the mother rather than the son, many conventional elements of the Oedipus pattern are omitted altogether.

In this chapter I do not attempt to survey all the examples of mother–son incest in medieval literature, or to discuss my selected texts in the detail which they deserve. Instead I shall suggest the range of treatments of the theme from the twelfth century to the sixteenth, the various genres in which it appears, the audiences addressed, and the attitudes to incest which are revealed. The texts will all be ones in which mother–son incest is central. Issues to be discussed will include the main focus of each text (the mother or the son), the degree of sympathy for the various protagonists, the extent to which ecclesiastics are involved in the plot, and the presence or absence of explicit moralizing by characters and/or narrator. I shall also consider how different generic conventions affect the use of various traditional motifs.

MEDIEVAL OEDIPUSES: JUDAS, GREGORIUS, AND THEIR LITER-
ARY DESCENDANTS

An early and influential incest narrative which appears to be derived from the Oedipus story is the legend of Judas. Versions in both Latin and the vernaculars circulated widely from the twelfth

---

[6] Propp notes that the prophecy is 'organically linked with the entire plot' in Sophocles, but not in medieval adaptations of the story ('Oedipus', 83).

century, if not earlier; I shall be dealing mainly with Latin narratives. The best-known version of the story is found in the *Legenda
aurea* of Jacobus de Voragine, a thirteenth-century collection of
saints' lives, as part of the story of St Matthias, who replaced Judas
as an apostle.[7] Jacobus begins and ends it with narratorial caveats as
to its apocryphal and implausible nature, but he did decide to
include it in his collection, and in fact it already had a considerable
pedigree.

> Ruben and his wife Ciborea live in Jerusalem. She is woken one
> night by a terrifying dream in which she bears a child so evil that
> he will be the downfall of his race. Nine months later Judas is
> born. Their horror of infanticide is outweighed by fear for their
> people, and they expose the baby at sea in a basket. Judas arrives
> at the island of Iscariot, and is found by the childless queen. She
> presents the boy as her own, then conceives and bears a son her-
> self. Judas mistreats his foster-brother; eventually the truth about
> his origins comes out, and Judas in shame and anger kills the
> younger boy. He flees to Jerusalem, where he takes service with
> Pilate. Pilate takes a fancy to the apples in a neighbouring
> orchard; Judas goes to get them for him, and in a quarrel kills the
> owner, who is in fact his father. Pilate rewards Judas with the
> dead man's land, and also his widow. The unhappy bride
> recounts the various disasters in her life, and Judas realizes that
> he has married his mother. She suggests that Judas do penance
> for his sins, and he goes to Jesus for help. Jesus favours him and
> makes him his purse-bearer. After betraying his new master,
> Judas commits suicide.

Here the incest, and the parricide too, were clearly added to show
what an incorrigible villain Judas was. A man capable of the
supreme sin of betraying Christ was obviously the sort of person
who would have committed other appalling crimes, and in the
twelfth century the worst crimes imaginable (in the context of
didactic literature) were killing one's father and marrying one's
mother, extreme transgressions of the fifth, sixth, and seventh

---

[7] *Legenda aurea*, ed. Graesse, 184–6. For other texts and discussion of the develop-
ment of the legend see *La Leggenda*, ed. d'Ancona; Constans, *La Légende*, 95–103;
Rand, 'Medieval Lives'; Baum, 'Medieval Legend'; Lehmann, 'Judas Iscariot'; Reider,
'Medieval Oedipal Legends'; Edmunds, 'Oedipus in the Middle Ages', esp. 149 ff.;
Axton, 'Interpretations'; Ohly, *Damned*, 1–102.

commandments. This is a good example of Frank Kermode's comment on the development of biblical stories that 'narrative begot character, and character begot narrative'.[8] Baum comments that if there is a connection between Judas and Oedipus, then the Judas story must be a literary creation (probably by a monk) rather than a folk-derivation, since the Oedipus story did not circulate at the popular level.[9] The association of incest with an unpopular figure was quite common in the classical world (see the examples cited in Chapter 1). But the combination of motifs—exposure, prophecy of disaster, parricide, mother–son incest—seems to be beyond the bounds of coincidence or even polygenesis. In the earliest form of the Judas legend (Baum's Type A, found only in one twelfth-century manuscript), there are several further details which suggest a link with Oedipus: Judas' father dreams that his unborn son will grow up to kill him, and the infant Judas' legs are mutilated before he is exposed, creating scars which bring about the recognition scene with his mother.[10]

As we shall see, the combination of parricide and incest is found in various later legends, but generally it has a different thrust, as Edmunds points out: 'Whereas the Judas legend seems to reflect a Pauline sense of human sinfulness, these other legends make a homiletic point: the efficacy of penance and the infinitude of God's mercy.'[11] The sense of human sinfulness in the story of Judas is emphasized by the many biblical echoes. The exposure of the infant Judas and his discovery by the queen of Iscariot recall the story of Moses. The orchard and the illicit desire for apples suggest the Garden of Eden myth, and murder soon follows, as in the Genesis story of Cain and Abel, which is also echoed in Judas' murder of his foster-brother. Judas is doomed by his role in Christian history; though he is absolved by Jesus of his incest and parricide, there can be no redemption or grace for him. Like Oedipus, he cannot escape his destiny, so the story concentrates on the villainy of the betrayer

---

[8] Kermode, *Genesis of Secrecy*, 91, quoted by Axton, 'Interpretations', 179.

[9] Baum, 'Medieval Legend', 615; Axton, 'Interpretations', 182–3. It is hard to assess the possible oral circulation of the Oedipus story, or of analogues; it seems probable that it was popular in oral form in western Europe just as it was in the rest of the world.

[10] It is striking that when his mother discovers Judas' identity, her immediate reaction is to curse the dream which caused her first husband to fear his unborn son and to expose him at birth; rather than simply being horrified at their sin, she makes the crucial connection between exposure and incest, as if it exonerated them, at least in part.

[11] Edmunds, 'Oedipus in the Middle Ages', 149.

of Christ, 'qui malus in ortu, peior in vita, pessimus extitit in fine'
(a man who was bad at birth, worse during his life, and worst of all
at the end), and shows little sympathy for him.[12] Axton argues that
the story evokes no sympathy in any version, and Derek Brewer
considers the Judas legend 'an artistic failure' because of the
impossibility of identifying with the protagonist, the marginal role
of the mother, and the consequent meaninglessness of the 'family
drama'.[13]

But the Judas story represents only the first stage in the medieval-
ization of the incest theme. At the same time that Judas was
credited with an incestuous marriage to his mother, the same sin
was becoming increasingly associated with legendary saints and
ecclesiastics in narratives which were more didactic and also more
optimistic. Some of the earliest medieval mother–son incest stories
occur in hagiographies rather than secular stories, and these lives
often include deliberate as well as unwitting incest.[14] One of the
most startling innovations of medieval writers is this double incest
theme: intercourse between siblings or father and daughter who are
well aware of their relationship is followed by the exposure of their
illegitimate son, who later quite innocently marries his unrecognized mother-aunt-sister (or, much less frequently, a mother and
son who know their relationship produce a daughter who later
marries her father-brother). Such double incest stories do not seem
to appear in classical literature; incest, whether attempted or consummated, may recur in several generations, as in the stories of
Tantalus and Thyestes, but no one commits incest twice with different family members. Rank disapproved of this sensational use of
double incest, and thought these medieval stories 'differ displeasingly from the naive antique traditions in their voluptuous and
torrid fantasies'; he attributes these medieval fantasies to the fact
that 'the great repression of drives expressed in Christianity could
be maintained only at the cost of a fantasy life pouring forth to
the most voluptuous degree'.[15] Other explanations seem more

[12] The quotation is taken from the Type A version printed by Baum, 'Medieval
Legend', 490. This version does show some sympathy for Judas, according to Rand,
'Medieval Lives', 314, and Baum, 'Medieval Legend', 491.
[13] Axton, 'Interpretations', 187; Brewer, *Symbolic Stories*, 61–2.
[14] The brutal father of Beatrice Cenci (d. 1599) is said to have tried to persuade her to
accept his incestuous advances by arguing that the offspring of incestuous liaisons
between fathers and daughters were all saints; see my comments in the next chapter.
[15] Rank, *Incest Theme*, 271.

plausible. Not only does such double incest complicate the tangle of identities and relationships and add to the tension of the recognition scenes, but it also presents a uniquely horrible form of lust, a particularly heinous sin to be confessed, repented, and expiated. As Ohly stresses, 'The real question is not how one gets into guilt but how one gets out of it.'[16] The ability to deal with the guilt induced by such a sin and to avoid despair and damnation after such a lapse represents the extraordinary power of Christian faith and the infinite grace of God. As a further encouragement to the faithful, the heroes of these hagiographic romances are not merely absolved of their sins, but usually end their days in the odour of sanctity as admired and authoritative figures in the Christian community, remarkable examples of the workings of divine grace. In the twelfth century a new type of hagiography emerged in which great emphasis is put on individual contrition and on confession and penance, and in these stories the 'péché monstrueux' (monstrous sin) is often mother–son incest.[17]

The earliest of these stories known to us, and the source, wholly or partially, of many later ones, seems to be the legend of Gregorius. The earliest known texts of this very popular story are not in Latin but in Old French and date from about 1150; probably the best-known version is the German poem derived from them by Hartmann von Aue about 1200 (the source of Thomas Mann's *Holy Sinner*), and it is on this version that I shall base my discussion, since it is one of the most fully imagined treatments of incest in medieval literature.[18]

On his deathbed the widowed Duke of Aquitania commends his young daughter to the care of her brother. The unmarried siblings are devoted to each other, and sleep in the same room. Tempted by the devil, the brother rapes his sister; at first she is upset, but then they enjoy an incestuous affair which is halted only by the discovery that she is pregnant. On the advice of a faithful steward, their baby boy is born in secret and exposed in

---

[16] Ohly, *Damned*, 5.
[17] Payen, *Le Motif*, 54 ff. I know no saint's life from earlier centuries in which the saint-to-be commits incest, with the possible exception of St Metro (see the discussion in the next chapter).
[18] I have used Paul's edition of Hartmann's text ; for the Old French texts see *La Vie du Pape Grégoire*, ed. Sol. On the 'holy sinner' theme see Dorn, *Der Sündige Heilige*, esp. 86–9; and Ohly, *Damned*, esp. 1–61.

a chest in a tiny boat with money, fine fabrics, and a tablet indicating his rank and the circumstances of his birth; the brother sets off on pilgrimage to the Holy Land, where he soon dies. The sister, distraught at the loss of both brother and baby, becomes duchess and devotes herself to good works.

The baby's boat is found by fishermen; their lord, an abbot, makes himself responsible for the child, and baptizes him with his own name. Gregorius is raised by the fisherman; when he enters the monastery school, he excels in his studies. His jealous foster-mother knows that he is a foundling; when Gregorius hits her own son in a quarrel, she maliciously taunts him about his origins. Gregorius goes to the abbot, and insists on being knighted. The abbot shows Gregorius the tablet, and gives him the money that was in his little boat, and clothes made from the rich fabrics. Elated by the discovery that he is of noble birth, but horrified by his conception in such sin, Gregorius sets off to seek his unfortunate parents. Arriving by chance at his mother's city, he finds it under siege by a duke who wishes to marry the duchess. Gregorius defeats the unwelcome suitor in single combat; the barons advise the lady to marry her new young champion, to whom she is strangely attracted. They are very happy, but every day Gregorius emerges weeping from a secret perusal of the tablet which describes his parents' sin. A prying maid brings this to the lady's attention; she finds the tablet, and realizes that she has married her long-lost son. Both are horrified by this revelation. Warning his mother not to abandon herself to despair, as Judas did, Gregorius rules that both must devote themselves to penance, and leaves the country at once.

He arrives after some days at a lonely fisherman's house by a lonely lake, and asks about a suitably remote place to do penance. The fisherman rows him out to a rock, shackles him to it, and throws away the key. In his haste Gregorius loses his precious tablet. He spends seventeen years on the rock in very harsh conditions. At the end of this time, the Pope dies in Rome, and two eminent churchmen dream that his successor is to be a holy man named Gregorius, currently living on a rock in a lonely lake. They eventually come to the fisherman's house; the key to Gregorius' shackles appears miraculously in the fish caught for their dinner, he is freed, and the tablet is miraculously found. On the way to Rome his healing powers are demonstrated, and he becomes an admirable Pope. Gregorius' mother, hearing of his fame but unaware of his identity, decides to go to Rome to seek absolution for her sins. Gregorius recognizes her from her confession; after an enjoyably ambiguous conversation he identifies himself. She enters a convent, and they both live piously in Rome till they die.

From beginning to end, and particularly at the beginning and the end, *Gregorius* is an explicitly didactic Christian poem, though Hartmann von Aue was not a cleric, and was presumably writing for a courtly lay audience.[19] It is, as he repeatedly states, an *exemplum* of the value of repentance and of the importance of resisting despair (see, for example, 44 ff., 162 ff., 3983 ff.). The two main enemies of the protagonists, and of all humankind, are the devil, prompter of the initial incest, and despair, the Deadly Sin against which Hartmann repeatedly warns his readers. Gregory is the name of a series of famous Popes; needless to say, their lives contain no episode remotely analogous to the poem, but the didactic power of the legend is obviously enhanced by the papal aura.

The traditional parricide is omitted here, perhaps to reduce Gregorius' guilt (see below), or perhaps to focus attention on the incest; there is a doubling not only of the incest motif but also of the recognition scene, in a way that emphasizes the shift from secular to religious values, and also the abandoning of the romance pattern. At the end of the poem, the (still unnamed) woman who was first Gregorius' mother and then his wife hears of the reputation of the new Pope and comes to him in complete ignorance as a sinner in search of absolution. He does not recognize her until she tells her terrible tale; then he talks to her of her lost Gregorius, and finally identifies himself as son and husband (3926). But the role in which he is now cast is that of spiritual father: she has done penance, as he instructed her so many years ago, and again he must act as her moral guide.[20] There is one more shift in relationships at the end, when the poet presents the two contrite and innocently reunited

[19] Hartmann also produced a version of Chrétien de Troyes's Arthurian romance *Yvain*, so he clearly had access to a range of French literature, both religious and chivalric; and he wrote another didactic poem, *Der Arme Heinrich*, the story of a man smitten by leprosy and saved by grace.

[20] As Legros points out, Gregorius as Pope is the spiritual father of all Christians, and is also married to the Church, in spiritual terms ('Parenté naturelle', 529). One might add that as a nun, his mother is the bride of Christ.

sinners as children of eternal God (3954). The poem begins with the death of an earthly father who leaves his children vulnerable to mortal sin by failing to arrange marriages for them. It ends with a mother and son who, after passing through a series of unnatural relationships (simultaneously mother–son and aunt– nephew, then also wife–husband), are seen at last as equals, chaste siblings in a spiritual sense under the protection of the heavenly Father (though in terms of status in this world, Gregorius as Pope is clearly well ahead of his anonymous mother in her convent).

Hartmann's poem is a hagiographic romance, not a theological treatise. Christian ethics are everywhere apparent, but there is a notable absence of ecclesiastical advisers at crucial moments, and the protagonists never make formal confessions. It is the faithful steward who gives sound advice to the incestuous siblings about pilgrimage and penance (and about disposing of the baby); and Gregorius himself, driven by his overpowering sense of sin, chooses appropriate penances for his mother and himself without any pro- fessional help. The ambiguous treatment of some of the main theological issues can be judged by the continuing scholarly con- troversy over the distribution of guilt in the *Gregorius*. Was the mother initially at fault in not resisting her brother's advances? Was Gregorius wrong to leave the monastery and pursue worldly ambi- tion? Is ignorance an excuse for incest? Was the newborn Gregorius tainted with his parents' sin? Christians were divided on the prin- ciples underlying this last point. According to Ezekiel 18: 20, 'The son shall not bear the iniquity of the father'; but God declared Himself to Moses to be a jealous god, 'visiting the iniquity of the fathers upon the children unto the third and fouth generation' (Exodus 20: 5). For Tobin the poem reflects an Augustinian pes- simism about original sin: 'since Gregorius falls into the same sin of incest as his parents, it may well be that the story supposes a wide- spread knowledge of the dictum that God punishes those who imi- tate the sins of their fathers'.[21] Mancinelli, on the other hand, thinks that Hartmann was more sympathetic to the Abelardian position that intention is a crucial part of sin; for her, the phrase so frequently used of Gregorius, 'der guote sündaere' (the good

---

[21] Tobin, 'Fallen Man', 92; he reads the poem as the story of fallen man redeemed by divine grace, and stresses the presence of the parable of the Good Samaritan in the Prologue.

sinner), demonstrates Hartmann's belief in his protagonist's inno-cence.[22] Hartmann's signals are ambiguous: at the birth of Gregorius both his mother and the steward's wife agree that he is born in appalling sin (688–90), but the abbot makes no reference to this when Gregorius is found in the sea. When Gregorius learns of the circumstances of his birth, his reaction is divided between dis-tress at the sinfulness of his conception—though he notes that he is not to blame—and delight in his nobility and wealth (1748–55, 1777–84). He is knighted and sets out to find his parents, accepting chivalric adventure on the way; yet later he subjects himself to a penance much more ferocious than would have been required by contemporary ecclesiastical practice.[23] Hartmann's *Gregorius* was translated into Latin by the Benedictine abbot Arnold of Lübeck for William of Lüneburg in the early thirteenth century.[24] He inserted two categorical assurances that the sins of the parents are *not* visited on the children (I. 380 ff. and II. 945 ff.), and in his prologue gives a more encouraging quotation from Romans 5: 20: 'But where sin abounded, grace did much more abound.'[25] In the view of K. C. King, 'Hartmann's purpose is not to criticize the behaviour of either mother or son, nor, particularly, the mode of life which could lead such "good" people into such sin; it is to show that where there is true repentance forgiveness is never impossible.'[26] K. Ruh formulates the same point succinctly and elegantly: 'grosse Sunde—grosse Busse—grosse Gnade' (great sin—great penance—great grace).[27]

---

[22] Mancinelli, 'Der guote sündaere'.

[23] Ohly notes that there is a very ancient tradition of Adam and Eve standing on stones in the Jordan as penance for the Fall, and that in the 10th-cent. *Navigatio Sancti Brendani* the saint meets Judas, who is allowed out of hell at intervals to stand on a rock in the middle of the ocean. These stories may have been models for Gregorius' penance; on the other hand, the Gregorius story may have influenced a later German version of St Brendan's voyage in which he meets a man standing on a rock in the sea as penance for incest with his sister (*Damned*, 49–56).

[24] Arnold von Lübeck, *Gesta Gregorii*, ed. Schilling. Arnold was commissioned to translate Hartmann's poem by William; he seems not to have known any Latin version of the story, or indeed any other version at all. He remarks in his introduction on its value for Christian teaching; this suggests that it had only circulated orally before the 12th cent.

[25] He is, however, more explicit than Hartmann about the status of incest as a sin: in an internal debate before the sibling incest, the sister's Reason reminds her that 'incestus superat omne scelus' (I. 203: incest is the worst of crimes). The poor girl sums up her situation at I. 337 ff.: she feels guilty before God and ashamed before men.

[26] King, 'Mother's Guilt', 93.

[27] Ruh, *Höfische Epik*, 109, quoted by Mertens, *Gregorius Eremita*, 67.

It seems to be assumed that there can only be one Holy Sinner in the story. The focus is on the adventures, reactions, and penance of Gregorius, rather than of his unnamed mother, though she is the one who commits incest twice over; we are told briefly of her good works but never see her in action, and at the end she is over-shadowed by her son the Pope. The world which Hartmann depicts is largely a male world, and initially at least a chivalric world; when Gregorius refuses to become the abbot's successor, he explains that during his years of education he yearned to be a knight, 'sô turnierte mîn gedanc' (1584: I jousted so much in my mind). In making the apparently innocent Gregorius take on such hard penance, Hartmann—and his source—seem to be describing lay reaction to incest (albeit in an extreme and perhaps idealized form), rather than the prescribed theological view. Siegfried Christoph has argued that the *Gregorius* represents the clash of two value systems, the shame culture of a secular and heroic society, and the guilt cul-ture of a religious society; he quotes Hildegard Nobel's view that 'the issue of an incestuous union is burdened with infamy, not sin', and suggests that the incestuous sinners' failure to confess is occa-sioned by a sense of shame and by reluctance to involve outsiders in such a dishonourable family matter.[28] The sojourn on the rock can be seen as a social penance, in that it represents exile from society; the election to the papal throne is, Christoph points out, both a spiritual and a social reinstatement. Simon Gaunt, following Anita Guerreau-Jalabert, argues (with reference to the French version of the story) that the point is to show that lay society is in serious danger because it tends to break the rules about exogamic marriage established by the Church.[29] But Gregorius is quite ignorant of his incest, and by the late twelfth century intention was believed to be crucial to sin.[30]

---

[28] Christoph, 'Guilt, Shame'; for the quotation from Nobel see 212. There may also be some sense of pollution; Mary Douglas comments that 'pollution rules do not corres-pond closely to moral rules' (*Purity*, 130).

[29] See Guerreau-Jalabert, 'Inceste et sainteté', and Gaunt, *Gender and Genre*, 198–212. Gaunt argues that 'the shadow of incest underscores the portrayal of chivalric marriage in romance and once again shows how hagiography contests the values of other vernacular genres' (201). He also thinks that Gregorius' grandfather is ultimately to blame for everything because he failed to marry off his daughter before his own death, and so left her vulnerable to her brother's lust; a similar argument is made by Legros, 'Parenté naturelle', 516.

[30] Abelard uses the example of sleeping with an unrecognized sister to show that intention is crucial to sin: see *Ethics*, ed. and trans. Luscombe, 26–7. See also Herlem-Prey, 'Schuld oder Nichtschuld'.

Nonetheless it is very proper for him to feel the burden of sin; clearly the reader/listener is encouraged to examine his/her conscience and to worry about sin, whether deliberate or unwitting.[31] The 'happy ending' for Gregorius entails 'his rejection of lay social structures and of the lay aristocratic model of masculinity', according to Gaunt.[32] Unlike Oedipus and Jocasta, Gregorius and his mother have no children; it is tempting to see the story at one level as an attack on sex and marriage, and as propaganda for the celibate life. Legros argues that the *Gregorius* condemns all bonds of family kinship, which are an obstacle to saintliness, and emphasizes the superiority of spiritual relationships: 'Grégoire doit, pour atteindre à la perfection, échapper au poids d'une parenté pourtant réduite à des relations de consanguinité ou d'alliances directes: frère/sœur, ses parents, mère/fils, son épouse' (To attain perfection, Gregorius must escape the weight of a kinship which is reduced to consanguinous relationships or actual marriage: his parents are brother and sister, his wife is his mother).[33] The *Gregorius* suggests an alternative set of values for romance narrative, a clash between worldly and spiritual standards and ambitions, just as the invention of the Grail Quest introduced a problematic new value system into the Arthurian world.[34]

If the *Gregorius* contains a mixture of theological and lay attitudes, what can we glean from it about contemporary reactions to incest? It is striking that Hartmann shows considerable sympathy for the young girl raped by her brother; he describes her hesitating between bringing dishonour on her brother by calling for help or sinning with him, an impossible choice between shame and guilt in which vicarious shame wins (385 ff.). But she is not shown simply as a victim of rape; though incest is clearly unacceptable, it is not presented as something which only subhuman barbarians do, nor is it simply a matter of violent sex. Once the affair has begun, Hartmann seems to have no difficulty in imagining that the siblings really do love each other (like Canace and Macareus) in spite of the horror of the situation. When the brother leaves for the Holy Land,

---

[31] Ohly comments (*Damned*, 11): 'The shorter route to grace via absolution is theologically irreproachable, but narratologically weak: the story gives God time to elect those whose penance is not imposed, but chosen freely.'

[32] Gaunt, *Gender and Genre*, 204.

[33] Legros, 'Parenté naturelle', 545; see also 525, and my argument in 'Gold in the Dungheap'.   [34] See Gaunt, *Gender and Genre*, 180–211.

both he and his sister are devastated (639 ff.). When the infant Gregorius is exposed at sea, the poet apologizes for his inability to describe adequately the mother's grief, which he characterizes as triple: she grieves for her sin with her brother and her parting from him, for her frail state after childbirth, and for the exposure of her child (789 ff.).[35] Her brother feels as passionately as she does, for he dies of a broken heart. Hartmann remarks that though women's love is said to be more intense than men's, it is not so, as this example proves (842–4). The mother's meeting years later with her unrecognized son and her growing feeling for him are also sympathetically described. Hartmann explains at some length that it is the practical arguments of the barons which persuade her to marry Gregorius (she needs a champion, like Laudine in Chrétien's *Yvain*, which Hartmann also translated), but they do love each other greatly. Considerable space is given to her anxiety at the news of her lord's secret sorrow, and her horror at the revelation of his origins. Both the mother and Gregorius are allowed to comment on the situation themselves: there is no narratorial moralizing on the sidelines. The devil is given some credit for the attraction between mother and son, and for the lady's decision to marry; and when the tablet reveals the dreadful truth, she laments that God has allowed the devil to trap her yet again. But Hartmann is more interested in maintaining the narrative tension than in delivering fierce moralizing asides about human frailty, and he puts much less emphasis on the role of the devil than does his French source. He includes much dialogue and gives plenty of space to the drama of the recognition scenes (as does the French version). Few later writers spend as much imagination and space on the emotions of the characters, particularly in the recognition scenes, or deal with their lapses so sympathetically.

Though Gregorius' extreme reaction to his unwitting incest seems to emphasize original sin and man's fallen state, the point of the story is not to denounce human weakness and appetite, but to celebrate the power of remorse and penance, and the infinite mercy of God. The double incest certainly represents the lowest depths to which human carnality can sink, depths abhorred by both God and man; but the characters retain their nobility and the reader's

---

[35] In the French version she regrets endangering her brother's soul; this does not seem to worry Hartmann.

sympathy throughout. Gregorius' behaviour up to the time when the incest is discovered and his ignorance of the sin he is committing help to exonerate him, whereas Judas' earlier villainy and violence cancel out his ignorance of his blood relationship with his new wife. The prophecy found in the stories of Oedipus and Judas disappears in the story of Gregorius, who does not kill his father, and whose fate is not explicitly linked to that of his family or people. A further innovation is the happy ending, of course: by renouncing secular life and marriage, and by doing penance, the protagonist is able to achieve social acceptance and ecclesiastical power in the end as a 'holy sinner'. The parricide in the Judas story which reminds us of Oedipus is not present in the *Gregorius*; although the father is removed from the scene early on, he dies of natural causes.

Incest and parricide are both present, together with prophecy and a spiritually happy ending, in a narrative which is clearly a combination of the Judas and Gregorius stories, the legend of St Andreas of Crete.[36]

A merchant receives a prophecy that his wife will bear a son who will kill his father, marry his mother, and rape three hundred nuns. When their son is born they mutilate his body and expose him in a little boat. He is found and raised by a community of nuns; one day, in a fit of lust inspired by the devil, he rapes three hundred of them. He is driven out and arrives in the town of Crete, where he is employed as a watchman by his natural father; neither knows their true relationship. At night his father comes disguised to the vineyard as a test, and is killed by Andreas. Andreas then marries his mother, who subsequently recognizes him because of his scars.

She sends Andreas to a priest, who refuses to absolve him. Andreas kills him, and then two more equally obstinate priests. The Bishop of Crete eventually absolves him, but imposes a severe penance on both mother and son. Andreas is chained at the bottom of a deep cellar; when it is filled with earth to the top, his sins will be forgiven. His mother has a padlock put through her nose; the key is thrown away, and she is ordered to wander through the world praising God until it is found again. After

[36] This legend is preserved in a 17th-cent. folktale collection, but it derives from much earlier legends; see Rank, *Incest Theme*, 279 ff., and Dorn, *Der Sündige Heilige*, 88.

thirty years the key is miraculously found in a fish, and she goes into a convent. Andreas is found sitting on top of his cellar, which has filled up with earth. On the death of the Bishop of Crete Andreas succeeds him, and lives a most holy life.

Baum points out the parallels between this and the story of Judas: both children are of humble birth, both are predestined to commit parricide and incest, both commit violent crimes before fulfilling the prophecy, both discover their unwitting sins through mutual confession of mother and son, both are sent to a holy man to be pardoned.[37] Other parts of the story of Andreas are much more reminiscent of the *Gregorius*: the use of the name of an historical ecclesiastic (there really was a Bishop Andreas of Crete in the seventh century), the penances for both mother and son, their eventual reunion and absolution, and the key miraculously found in a fish. The two story patterns are neatly combined to emphasize both the characteristic violence and sinfulness of man in the extreme examples of mass rape, parricide, and incest, and also the value of Christian penance which leads to absolution and salvation. The prophecy is fulfilled, but this does not preclude a happy ending, in a Christian sense. The message is much the same as that of the *Gregorius*, but its content is more sensational, and the hero's path to redemption much more violent—parricide and the rape of three hundred nuns surely outweigh the taint of sibling incest! Again the spotlight is focused throughout on the male sinner: although the mother does leave her home to carry out her penance, the story does not recount her adventures, and her absolution is not rewarded by any special status.

Parricide and incest are also combined in a thirteenth-century legendary saint's life which is much more heavily dependent on the *Gregorius*, yet contains some striking variations, the story of Saint Albanus, which Baum describes as 'the most horrible, but also, it seems to me, the most moving of all the incest group'.[38]

A widowed emperor in a northern land seduces his daughter, who bears him a son. The child, Albanus, is exposed in Hungary, with a supply of rich clothes and jewels; he is adopted by the

[37] Baum, 'Medieval Legend', 597–8.
[38] Baum, 'Medieval Legend', 598. I cite the text edited by Morvay as Version A in *Die Albanuslegende*, 12–39. See also Constans, *La Légende*, 114–15; Rank, *Incest Theme*, 290–4; and Dorn, *Der Sündige Heilige*, 84–6.

childless King of Hungary, and when grown is married to the daughter of the northern emperor, his unrecognized mother. On his deathbed the King of Hungary tells Albanus how he was found; the princess recognizes the clothes and jewels she left with him, and their incestuous relationship is revealed.

The emperor, the princess, and Albanus are ordered by a hermit to spend seven years wandering separately in penance. At the end of this time they meet again, and on the way to their hermit-adviser are benighted. The emperor cannot resist the presence of his daughter, and relapses into sin. Albanus catches his parents in the act, and kills them both. After another seven years of penance he becomes a hermit. He is killed by robbers who throw his corpse into a river, where miraculous cures subsequently occur.

Here the double-incest-plus-penance pattern apparently first introduced in the *Gregorius* reappears, but in a new form. First, the hero is the product not of siblings whose incest is encouraged by their proximity and orphaned state, but of a deliberate father–daughter liaison. Rank argues that the initial sibling incest of the *Gregorius* did not satisfy the medieval imagination; father–daughter incest was more horrifying, and complicated the relationships still further in that the hero's mother was also his sister.[39] Second, the hero's sins take the form of unwitting incest followed by deliberate parricide, the reverse of the usual Oedipus pattern where the parricide must come first to make the mother available for remarriage; this might seem to make Albanus more culpable. The circumstances of the parricide seem to bear out Edmunds's view: 'Parricide, then, is a morally sensitive episode in the Oedipus-type narrative, and it seems likely that the hero who is to be forgiven ought to commit a justifiable parricide.'[40] Here there is no ominous prophecy, as in the stories of Judas or Andreas; the parricide is an act of righteous anger by a reformed sinner who sees his parents slipping back into their previous sin. Even if not wholly defensible, it seems much less criminal than the thuggish killing of Ruben by Judas (Andreas' killing of his father might be partially justified by his zeal for his new job, and by his father's rashness in coming incognito to test the new guard).[41]

---

[39] Rank, *Incest Theme*, 290.   [40] Edmunds, 'Oedipus in the Middle Ages', 153.

[41] Rank points out the parallels between the stories of Albanus and Julian, whom he calls 'the Catholic Oedipus' (*Incest Theme*, 392 ff.). Julian is warned in a prophecy that

Like the *Gregorius*, the legend of Albanus is an *exemplum* of the value of confession and penance, and the hard road to grace: like Gregorius, Albanus achieves sanctity at the end, and posthumously demonstrates healing powers. The focus here is even more firmly on the hero; his mother-sister does share his penance, but her role is both small and passive, and at the end she is killed by her son for her relapse into sin. This time the father survives almost to the end of the story; his shameful seduction of his own daughter, his failure to reform his ways, and his subsequent death at the hands of his own son serve to emphasize the weakness of the flesh and the difficulty of eradicating human sinfulness, as well as the writer's total rejection of incest. The author of this Latin prose life gives his characters few speeches and little individuality, but often comments himself in strict moral terms. His reaction to the father–daughter incest is typical of his general attitude: 'O humanae libidinis effrenis impietas' (O unrestrained wickedness of human lust). The fact that the story is told in Latin prose suggests that it is designed for a masculine and ecclesiastical audience; this impression is confirmed by the frequent misogynistic references. Phrases such as 'ut mos est mulieribus' (as is characteristic of women) and 'procax mulier' (the impudent woman) indicate the writer's lack of sympathy for the female protagonist of his story, as does his comment that it is better to admire God's justice in making the mother anxious about her new husband's origins than to describe her anxiety. He is not trying to tell an elaborate story of suspense, or to rouse the sympathy of the reader or audience for human weakness, as Hartmann does, but rather to present an explicit *exemplum* in resolutely black and white terms.

These *exempla* are clearly invented to act as propaganda for the value of contrition and penance, but some incest stories purport to be based on real incidents. Such is the legend of Vergogna:[42]

he will kill his parents; he travels far away and marries. His parents search for him and arrive at his house by chance when he is out; his wife realizes who they are, entertains them hospitably, and puts them to sleep in Julian's own bed. When he comes home and sees two figures in his bed, he assumes that his wife has a lover and kills them both, only to discover that they were his devoted parents. He and his wife do penance, and die absolved. Rank suggests that a motive of sexual jealousy, perhaps even incest, has disappeared here. Certainly the pattern of prophecy, murder, penance, and sanctification suggests the Holy Sinner genre to which the stories of Gregorius and Albanus belong, and of which Judas is an antitype; see also Dorn, *Der Sündige Heilige*, 90–102.

[42] See the editions of d'Ancona and Benucci, *La Leggenda*, and also Constans, *La Légende*, 118–20, and Rank, *Incest Theme*, 296.

A baron seduces his daughter. Their son is exposed as a baby, and
arrives in Egypt. The baron goes on a pilgrimage to the Holy
Land and dies there. The daughter refuses all suitors; the neighbouring barons seize her lands, and besiege her in the convent
where her father has installed her. Her son, now grown up, hears
of her plight and comes to rescue her without knowing of their
relationship; then he marries her. Some time after the wedding he
tells her about his birth, and the awful truth is revealed. Together
they go to the Pope, who orders them to do penance separately in
a monastery in Rome; there they die in the odour of sanctity.
They are buried in one tomb, with an inscription indicating their
complex relationship: mother and son, sister and brother, wife
and husband.

The inscription can be seen today in the monastery of Santa
Presidia, says the writer. A number of other such riddling funerary
inscriptions are recorded, including one reputedly seen near
Bourbon:

> Cy-gist la fille, cy-gist le père,
> Cy-gist la sœur, cy-gist le frère,
> Cy-gist la femme et le mary,
> Et si n'y a que deux corps ici.[43]

(Here lies the daughter, here lies the father, here lies the sister, here lies the
brother, here lies the wife and the husband, and there are only two bodies
here.)

It is impossible to say whether such inscriptions are based on real
cases of double incest, or whether they are entirely apocryphal; but
the records of these riddling epitaphs do suggest a popular aspect
of the incest theme, as well as a more literary or didactic one. Even
if the story of Vergogna is based on a real history, the name of the
protagonist, which means Shame, reveals its exemplary aim. The
initial father–daughter incest looks back to Albanus; the rescue of
the beleaguered mother and the role of the Pope recall Gregorius,
and as in the *Gregorius* the hero's father fades from the story early
on (both die in the Holy Land), leaving mother and son to their
spiritually happy ending. No rigorous penance is demanded here; it
is enough that they acknowledge their shame by confessing.

[43] See Constans, *La Légende*, 120–1; Rank, *Incest Theme*, 296–7; and Taylor,
'Riddles', 26–7.

This is also the case in the variant version of the story of Gregorius included in some manuscripts of the very popular collection of exemplary stories known as the *Gesta Romanorum*, where the story is drastically shortened so that it omits the penance, Gregorius' installation as Pope, and the second recognition scene.[44] When Gregorius and his mother discover their incest in this version, they confess and take communion; they hear a voice absolving them, and three days later they die (in the English version they die immediately). The Latin rubric is 'De Gregorio qui matrem duxit in uxorem' (Of Gregorius who married his mother). In the larger group of *Gesta Romanorum* manuscripts edited by Oesterley, the full story is told and the rubric gives away the ending: 'De mirabili divina dispensatione et ortu beati Gregorii papae' (Of the miraculous dispensation of God and the origins of blessed Pope Gregory).[45] In the *Gesta* versions, the story is set in Rome at an unspecified date: the dying father of the opening episode is the emperor. His son is more forceful in raping his sister, and Hartmann's inner monologue in which she has to choose between public and private honour is replaced by her threat that her brother's crime will offend God and cause disorder among men. Her increasing pleasure in the incestuous liaison is also omitted. There is still a surprising lack of ecclesiastical comment on the sibling incest, but the sister and the faithful steward have an interesting quarrel about baptizing the child: she refuses because of its incestuous origins, while the steward urges her not to destroy the child's soul because of her own sin. The tablets put in the baby's boat ask the finder to baptize him.[46] The chivalric aspects of the story are much reduced here. On discovering the circumstances of his birth, Gregorius sets out for the Holy Land in atonement for his parents' sin, but is driven by a storm to his mother's land. There is no suggestion of growing attraction between mother and son; it is at the barons' urgent recommendation that they marry. The first recognition scene and Gregorius' subsequent adventures are much curtailed; there is less of the hostile fisherman and of the arrival of

---

[44] *Gesta Romanorum*, ch. 170, ed. Dick, 148–59 (Latin); *Early English Versions*, ed. Herrtage, 250–63.

[45] *Gesta Romanorum*, ch. 81, ed. Oesterley, 399–409.

[46] This was an important issue in medieval Europe; see Boswell's discussion of foundlings and baptism in *Kindness of Strangers*, 322–5 and 374–5.

the Roman envoys, and the final recognition scene between mother and son is also brief.

Almost a fifth of the story is taken up by the moralization at the end, a characteristic feature of nearly all the stories in the *Gesta Romanorum*; these moralizations tend to be complex and may present a character as playing several apparently incompatible roles. The dying emperor is interpreted here as Christ; his son is man (also the flesh), and his daughter the soul. Their incest represents the corruption of the soul by vice; their incestuous offspring is the human race, born of corrupt parents comparable to Adam and Eve. Gregorius' exposure by sea represents humankind's wanderings on the sea of human misery. His mother's unwelcome suitor is the devil; when Gregorius rescues her he is the Son of God who marries the Church, His Mother. The abbot who rears him is God, the fisherman a prelate. Gregorius' journey to Rome represents his return from the rock of penance to Mother Church, and then he is able to lead his mother, the soul, to the heavenly kingdom. So the story of Gregorius could be interpreted on two levels. It is in itself a cautionary tale with a positive moral: incest is the worst of carnal sins, yet the incestuous sinner can be forgiven, and can even become Pope, after sincere contrition and appropriate penance.[47] But it can also be read as an allegory of the corruption and purification of the soul, and the inevitably sinful state of humankind, which can only be saved by *imitatio Christi* (the imitation of Christ).[48] The story of Albanus is similarly moralized in the *Gesta Romanorum*.[49] Here the incestuous father is man, his daughter is his own evil will, and their offspring is wickedness. Albanus' adopted father is God, who through His death reveals humankind's wickedness and sin. The seven years of penance represent the Seven Deadly Sins. The fatal relapse of Albanus' parents represents evil will again. Finally, the reader is enjoined to turn like Albanus to a hermit-confessor, and to devote his life to penance. Incest here seems to represent original sin.

[47] It may seem surprising that Gregorius never makes a formal confession to a priest. Though in the 12th cent. increasing importance was attributed to contrition, confession, and penance by theologians, it was not usual to confess regularly and frequently until the practice of annual confession was instituted by the Fourth Lateran Council in 1215. For discussion of the literary impact of this change see Baldwin, 'From the Ordeal'.

[48] The notion of *imitatio Christi* in the story of Gregorius is discussed by Mertens, *Gregorius Eremita*, 68–9.

[49] *Gesta Romanorum*, ch. 244, ed. Oesterley, 641–6; it has no rubric and the hero has no name, though it is clearly the story of Albanus.

ROMANCE VERSIONS: INCEST AVERTED

The appeal of the Oedipus plot in its various permutations was not restricted to pious writers trying to improve the morals of the faithful, of course. The story has analogues from around the world which are by no means all exemplary, and in western Europe in the later Middle Ages it also appears in narratives with little or no moral agenda.[50] In the beginning of the thirteenth-century *Prose Tristan*, for instance, the account of the Cornish dynasty to which both Tristan and Mark belong includes the sad story of Apollo l'Aventureus, who is exposed as a baby by the pagan suitor of his mother Chelinde after his father Sador has been thrown overboard by sailors as a murderer who has brought ill-fortune to their ship.[51] Apollo learns of his origins from his adoptive mother, and sets out to find his father. Sador, already mortally wounded, attacks his unrecognized son whom he has mistaken for an enemy; Apollo kills Sador (he also kills his mother's second husband, thus fulfilling the prophecy that caused him to be exposed as an infant); then unwittingly he marries his mother Chelinde. When St Augustine reveals the truth to them, he is sent to the stake by Chelinde, but she is killed by lightning. Apollo is converted to Christianity and marries again, but he and his wife die in tragic circumstances. This story seems intended to show that misfortune dogs the Cornish royal house, leading up to the final tragedy of Tristan, rather as in the classical stories of Oedipus and of the house of Atreus. Although a saint is involved, there is no explicit Christian moral.

It is more common to find romances which adapt the Oedipus plot and defang it, so to speak, making both parricide and incest near-miss, and concluding with an entirely secular happy ending. Such romances include a recognition scene no less exciting for the omission of the incestuous relationship. They usually begin with the exposure of a male baby conceived in a clandestine relationship,

[50] See for instance Johnson and Price-Williams, *Oedipus Ubiquitous*. Since the earliest extant versions of the *Gregorius* are in French and German, it may well be that this and similar stories were circulating orally throughout the earlier Middle Ages, and that it was only in the 12th cent. that they were taken up by writers keen to warn against the dangers of incest and to encourage the practice of contrition and penance.

[51] For the story of Apollo see *Le Roman de Tristan*, ed. Curtis, i. 49–122. It is summarized by Löseth, *Le Roman en prose de Tristan*, 4–15; and by Baumgartner, *Le 'Tristan'*, 1–3. See also Grisward, 'Un schème narratif'; Traxler, 'Observations'; Mickel, 'Tristan's Ancestry'; and Gracia, 'La Prehistoria'.

and they end with a happy reunion of parents and son, released from any danger of incest or scandal and respectably paired off to their own and everyone else's satisfaction. In such stories it may even be the father rather than the son who is the main focus of attention, as in the fourteenth-century Middle English poem *Sir Eglamour*.[52]

Sir Eglamour is set a number of tasks by the hostile father of his beloved, Cristabelle. During this time Eglamour and Cristabelle become lovers, and she becomes pregnant. Eglamour leaves to continue his tasks, and gives Cristabelle a ring for the child. The furious father exiles Cristabelle and her baby in a tiny boat. They arrive at a desert island, where a griffin steals the boy and carries him to Israel; there the king adopts him and names him Degrebelle. Cristabelle arrives in Egypt, where she is protected by the king, her uncle. Eglamour returns to Artois to find her gone. Her father takes refuge in a tower, and Eglamour goes off to the Holy Land for fifteen years.

The King of Egypt offers Cristabelle in marriage to the man who can defeat him at jousting. Degrebelle, now grown up, succeeds, and marries his mother. But his crest, a griffin with a child in its claws, prompts her to inquire about his origins, and their relationship is revealed before the marriage is consummated. Cristabelle is then promised to the man who can defeat Degrebelle in a joust. Eglamour arrives and defeats his unrecognized son, but he too has a crest which provokes Cristabelle's curiosity, a woman and child in a boat. A second recognition scene takes place, and the reunited family returns to France. Cristabelle's father falls out of his tower and breaks his neck, Eglamour marries Cristabelle, and Degrebelle marries a princess previously turned down by his father.

This romance does not conform to the pattern of the Gregorius or Albanus legends, but it contains many characteristic features of mother–son incest stories. There is no initial incest (though the unwillingness of the old king to let his daughter marry may be a trace of an earlier Incestuous Father motif); the exposure of her baby is occasioned by illicit sex and the fear of scandal, the motives for exposures in many other incest stories. Degrebelle is exposed in

---

[52] I cite the edition of Richardson.

a boat, though accompanied by his mother (a motif we shall encounter frequently in the Incestuous Father romances and the Constance group, to be discussed in the next chapter); then he is separated from her and raised by a foster-father. He sets out not to find his parents but to acquire a wife, at the urging of his foster-father; like Gregorius, he wins his mother's hand through his prowess as a knight. In the recognition scene his identity is proved by the clothes found with him as a baby; the ring which Eglamour left for him is never mentioned again, though it may have contributed to the recognition in an early version of the story. But it is the father rather than the son who is the focus of the story (as in the case of Arthur and Mordred discussed below). Eglamour is given a number of chivalric adventures which have nothing to do with his wife or son—hence the princess whom Degrebelle eventually marries—and the story is not complete until he returns to reclaim Cristabelle. The reunion and marriage of these long-separated lovers eclipses the recognition scene between mother and son (both recognitions occur through the rather clumsy repetition of the tell-tale crest). This is a totally chivalric tale, and like most romances it has a happy ending for both generations. No priests are present in this story because there is nothing for the protagonists to confess, except the initial fornication, a very common sin in chivalric romance which does not usually require formal absolution. Cristabelle's hostile father dies at the end, but not at the hand of any of the protagonists; his death is not a deliberate punishment, but merely the deserved removal from the scene of an unpleasant and obstructive character. The near-miss incest is a titillating incident, but the turning-point of the story is the combat of father and son, a frequent theme in medieval narratives (and in many others).[53] We hear little about Cristabelle's feelings. The emphasis throughout the story is on chivalric prowess and its male exponents.

This chivalric emphasis is even more clearly present in the fourteenth-century Middle English *Sir Degaré*, which offers some interesting variations on the familiar theme.[54]

---

[53] See Potter, *Sohrab and Rustum*.

[54] I cite Schleich's edition as corrected by Jacobs, *The Later Versions*, 12–37. Unfortunately the ending of the poem is missing, though a crude version exists in 16th-cent. printed versions, and in an inferior 15th-cent. manuscript; see the comments of Jacobs.

A widowed king does not want his daughter to marry. She is raped in the forest by a fairy knight, who leaves her a sword without a tip for the son she will bear. When she gives birth to a boy she exposes him with a letter round his neck, a large sum of money, and a pair of gloves sent by the fairy knight with the instructions that the boy must marry only the woman who can wear them. He is found and reared by a hermit who names him Degaré [meaning either 'ignorant of himself' or 'lost']. Meanwhile the princess becomes the prize offered to any knight who can defeat her father in battle. When Degaré is 20 he is told that he is a foundling and given the tokens which were left with him; he sets off to find his parents. After some adventures he defeats an old knight in battle, and wins his daughter. They marry in church, but before they sleep together he remembers to make her try on the gloves, and so discovers that she is his mother; the marriage is annulled. Degaré inquires about his father; his mother gives him the fairy knight's sword, and Degaré sets out to find him. He fights an unknown knight who asks about the sword and turns out to have the missing tip; it is his father. His parents are reunited and marry, and Degaré marries a lady he championed in a previous battle.

Here there is a deliberate search for the hero's parents, as in the *Gregorius*, but the motives are social rather than religious. When Degaré and his mother discover their true relationship, the narrator comments that anyone proposing to marry a stranger far from home should always be careful to enquire about the future spouse's family first, in case they turn out to be related (617–24); but overall the story is clearly not intended to be a cautionary tale with an explicit moral about incest. The recognition tokens (one for each parent) are introduced in such a way as to ruin the suspense for the reader by foreshadowing the two recognition scenes. The rapist leaves a sword with his victim for their unborn son, explaining that he is keeping the tip (broken in a fight with a giant) which may help him to recognize his son should they meet in the future (115–32). The princess keeps the sword with her, but when she exposes Degaré she puts in his cradle the gloves sent from fairyland by her attacker, and instructs her son in the accompanying letter that the woman he loves must be able to wear them, adding that they will fit only his mother (215–19). She seems to be anticipating their incest and the saving recognition scene, just as the fairy knight anticipates combat with his son.

As in *Sir Eglamour*, the pattern of events is the reverse of the Oedipus plot: the marriage with the unrecognized mother precedes the battle with the unrecognized father, which is clearly the crucial turning-point. The encounter with his father is Degaré's fourth and final battle; his prowess has increased with each adventure, and proving himself the equal of his father is the final test of his maturity as a knight. The lives of both father and son are incomplete until they find each other. The symbolism of the broken sword tip is striking: the unifying of the sword pieces can be seen as symbolizing not only Degaré's establishment of his identity and reputation, and his sexual maturity, but also the unifying of his family which is necessary to legitimize the erstwhile foundling. The masculine and martial nature of the symbol makes the priorities of the writer crystal clear, as does the fact that the heroine is marginalized once she has had her baby, and spends twenty years as an unclaimed tournament prize before being handed over to an unknown youth who has won her in battle. Although it is a *Bildungsroman* for Degaré, the frame story focuses on his parents, as in *Sir Eglamour*. In both romances the son seems sidelined at the end by the happy reunion of his parents who are now free to marry (the rapist fairy of the beginning seems to have metamorphosed into a respectable mortal knight).

James Simpson comments on *Degaré* that 'a father's incestuous and violent possessiveness of his daughter is the transgression that drives this narrative', and that more near-miss transgression is necessary to reach a happy ending not just for the individual but for the whole kin-group: 'Degaré must nearly kill his grandfather, must nearly sleep with his mother, and must nearly kill his father before proper relations can be established between and within generations.'[55] The near-miss incest and parricide are also muted, though in different ways, in other analogous narratives of this period, such as *Richars li Biaus*.[56] Here another possessive and potentially incestuous king locks his daughter up in a tower, where she is raped by

---

[55] Simpson, 'Violence, Narrative'. See also Kay's interesting discussion of father–son relations in epic and in romance in her chapter on patriarchy in *The Chansons de geste*, 79–115.

[56] *Richars li Biaus*, ed. Holden; it may share a source with *Sir Degaré*. See also Bouché, 'De "l'enfant trouvé" '.

an unknown knight. When Richars is born, his grandfather orders servants to kill the infant, but instead they expose him and he is fostered by a count. When he discovers that he is a foundling and goes off to look for his parents, he defeats an enemy for his unrecognized grandfather, and so meets his mother. They are immediately attracted to one another, but before there is any question of love or marriage she asks him who he is, and recognizes him by means of the cloth with which she had exposed him, and also by his resemblance to his rapist father. Richars then goes off to find his father. He wins a tournament and excuses all his defeated opponents from paying a ransom on condition that they recount the most amazing thing that ever happened to them. His father tells of the rape, and this leads to a recognition scene. Here the potential incest and parricide seem to be deliberately downplayed: there is no danger of incest between Richars and his mother because they discover their relationship so quickly, and the recognition scene with the father is part of a larger episode in which Richars defeats many knights and displays heroic generosity to them all.[57] There is a similar deflecting of the danger of incest and parricide in *Parise la Duchesse*, where the mother recognizes her long-lost son at a very early stage, and the son knows his father's identity while fighting him.[58] The fashion for this type of near-miss mother–son incest, and for a happy ending with a safely exogamous bride provided for the hero, also produced a startling rewriting of the *Gregorius* in the Spanish version published by Timoneda in his *Patrañuelo* of 1576.[59] Here the hero does not consummate his incestuous marriage with his mother, but discovers the truth just in time; she urges him to keep the scandal secret, and on her advice he marries the widow of the faithful steward who had advised on the problems surrounding his birth. The story ends there, shorn of its religious dimension and of its

[57] There is potential incest early on, when Richars is horrified at the suggestion that he marry the woman he thinks of as his sister; this is how he discovers that he is a foundling. The final recognition through story-telling is a secular equivalent of the confessions which trigger recognitions in other incest stories, such as *Gregorius* and the Flight from the Incestuous Father narratives to be discussed in the next chapter. It also occurs in classical New Comedy: see Trenkner, *Greek Novella*, 91. A variant of this motif appears in Apollonius of Tyre in the hero's reunions with both daughter and wife.

[58] I cite the edition of Plouzeau.

[59] Timoneda, *Patrañuelo*, ch. 5, ed. Romera Castillo, 117–22. The editor comments on the last page that it is impossible to tell whether the new ending is the author's own invention; no direct source is known.

propaganda for contrition and penance. In Timoneda's hands it is the tale not of a saint but of a knight, and therefore ends with secular prosperity in the form of a successful and legitimate marriage, rather than retreat from the world and spiritual reward.

We have seen three very different forms of medieval variation on the Oedipus theme. It could be used to blacken further an already accepted villain, as in the Judas story; here the prophecy of disaster comes true, and there can be no rehabilitation for the protagonist, even though his parricide and incest are not deliberate, since he is destined to betray Christ. It could be adapted to show the power of contrition and penance, and the miraculous workings of divine grace, as in the stories of Gregorius, Albanus, and their analogues; when a prophecy is included here, it comes true but does not preclude the repentance and absolution of the protagonist. These stories are comedies in the Christian sense, for although the protagonists abandon the world and may even be martyred, like Albanus, they achieve spiritual success; the incest may be seen as a 'felix culpa', a fortunate crime which leads to salvation.[60] Finally (and this probably was a later development based on the popularity of the exemplary models), it could be used as a rite of passage in chivalric narratives where a noble foundling succeeds in avoiding both incest and parricide, and so proves his maturity and prowess while also discovering his identity and reuniting his long-separated parents. So far the stories under discussion have all been freestanding, unconnected to larger story-cycles. One other variation on the Oedipus plot should be noted here, a version which is neither explicitly exemplary nor titillating in the manner of the romances discussed above. The popularity of the linked motifs of exposure, parricide, and incest is shown by their insertion into some versions of the Arthurian legend. In the early versions of the legend, as recounted by Geoffrey of Monmouth and his followers, Mordred is Arthur's nephew, who betrays the king's trust by usurping his queen and his throne. But in the thirteenth century (if not before) a more elaborate story developed: Mordred is the result of incest between Arthur and his unrecognized half-sister Morgause.[61] His story thus becomes an unusual variation on the stories of Judas and

---

[60] 'Felix culpa' was the phrase used by St Ambrose and many later medieval writers to describe the Fall of Man, an apparent disaster which led to the Incarnation and therefore to the salvation of mankind. Rocher discusses it in relation to *Gregorius* in 'Das Motiv'.

[61] For a full account for the development of the story of Mordred see Ch. 5.

Gregorius, complicated by the particular constraints imposed by the traditional Arthurian frame.[62] Unwitting sibling incest plus a prophecy of disaster lead to the exposure of a child who grows up to attempt quite deliberately to marry his stepmother, and to succeed in quite deliberately killing his father (who simultaneously kills him). Here the tragic ending leaves no room for contrition, confession, penance, or absolution. Mordred is the Judas at the Round Table who betrays his lord (and his father). There is a fatalism about his story which is reminiscent of both Judas and Oedipus; the prophecy of disaster is ineluctable, the monstrous sin cannot be absolved. Neither Mordred's attempted incest nor his successful parricide brings about the sort of peripeteia that we have seen in other medieval stories of mother–son incest, whether consummated or averted. In the Arthurian legend parricide means the end of Arthur, and thus the end of the whole story.

MOTHERS IN *EXEMPLA*: DELIBERATE INCEST

It is a striking aspect of all the stories of mother–son incest discussed so far that the focus has been on the son rather than the mother. In the exemplary stories of Gregorius and Albanus it is the mother who commits incest twice over; we are given some insight into her feelings, especially in Hartmann's *Gregorius*, but it is the contrition and penance of the son which are crucial, and it is he who achieves spiritual greatness at the end. Gregorius' mother, though pious, has no formal status in the Church, and Albanus' mother dies unabsolved. In each case the son is put in a situation towards the end of the story which demonstrates not only his spiritual growth, but also his superiority to his mother and his control over her: Gregorius as Pope absolves his penitent mother and puts her in a convent; Albanus kills his bad mother when she relapses into her old sin, a sin which he has put firmly behind him. In the romances of separated families too, the mother disappears from the story while the son (or the father in *Sir Eglamour*) performs deeds of chivalric prowess. Once she has

---

[62] Arthur must be the hero, and Mordred the villain; Morgause disappears from the story early on, reappearing only to come to a bad end when her sons murder first her and then her young lover.

exposed her illegitimate son, she has no further role to play except to be married, first to her unrecognized son and then to her long-lost lover. She has nothing to repent, and nothing to achieve. I do not know any romances or extended narratives involving mother–son incest, potential or actual, which focus on the mother, or in which the mother initiates the incest.[63] But women do have a central role in a very popular group of short *exempla* in which a mother knowingly commits incest with her adolescent son, a theme which continued to be popular into the Renaissance, and which in some cases offers interesting parallels with the Gregorius/Albanus double incest plot.

In Tubach's *Index Exemplorum* the majority of the entries under *incest* concern mothers and sons: a mother falsely accuses her son of incest because he has rejected her advances, and is subsequently struck dead by a thunderbolt; a mother is denounced by the devil for incest with her son and infanticide, but is saved by the Virgin's intercession; a mother dies of fright when she realizes that she is about to commit incest with her son, who has come home incognito to test her and see if women really are insatiably lustful.[64] These stories usually concern bourgeois women rather than aristocrats, and they are nameless; the sons are also nameless, and play little part in the plots, which emphasize female lust and reluctance to confess (often the spiritual fate of the son remains unknown). The incest is almost always deliberate—or at least there is no uncertainty about identity. The point of the stories is still the value of contrition and confession, but unlike the protagonists of comparable male-centred stories, these women take a long time to acknowledge their sin and cast themselves on God's mercy. Furthermore, they do not usually achieve any special spiritual status at the end; sometimes they die as soon as they have confessed, and the implication is that they are very lucky to have escaped eternal damnation.

[63] Semiramis' affair with her son appears in some collections of *exempla*, but there is no extended medieval account of it (see Ch. 2). In the stories of separated families which focus on the heroine as calumniated wife (the so-called Constance group), the heroine's young son usually stays with her; thus there is no danger of inadvertent incest.

[64] Tubach, *Index Exemplorum*, nos. 2730, 2733–8, 4667. I use Tubach's numbering to refer to the *exempla*, but it should be noted that his survey is not complete; for additional material, see Berlioz and Polo de Beaulieu, *Les Exempla médiévaux*. On misogyny in the *exempla* see Karras, 'Gendered Sin'; on misogyny in confessional literature see Murray, 'Gendered Souls'.

One of the most popular of these *exempla* is the story of the mother who commits incest and sometimes infanticide too, but eventually confesses (Tubach, no. 2730). This type of *exemplum* seems to start in a very simple form; an early version, possibly the earliest, appears in Caesarius of Heisterbach's *Dialogus Miraculorum* (written about 1200), in the section on Contrition.[65]

A woman is overwhelmed by lust for her own son, gets pregnant by him, and bears a son. After consulting a priest she takes the baby to Rome and manages to see the Pope. He orders her to dress as she did to tempt her son; she does so, feeling that shame in this world is trivial compared with shame in the afterlife. The Pope is impressed and absolves her, but a cardinal complains that she should do more penance for such a sin. The Pope invites the devil to enter him if he has made a mistake, or to enter the cardinal if the judgement was just. The devil torments the cardinal, who never again criticizes God's mercy. The novice to whom the stories are being recounted comments that divine grace is amazing, since fifteen years of penance would hardly seem enough in this case.

This version is slightly unusual in that the mother repents so quickly of her sin, but the main point is the standard one, the sincerity of her contrition which so impresses both the Pope and the devil. We are not told what happened to the son, who tends to disappear early on from this type of story, leaving his mother at centre-stage. No mention is made here of her husband; in many versions of this story, the mother is a widow and is passionately attached to her adolescent son. One might compare this situation, which helps to explain her sin without exonerating it, with the popular narrative of the widowed father's desire for his own daughter who resembles his dead wife (discussed in the next chapter).

The *Gesta Romanorum* contains a more elaborate version of the story of the lustful mother under the rubric 'De Amore Inordinato' (About Inappropriate Love).[66]

---

[65] *Dialogue on Miracles*; 2. 11, trans. Scott and Swinton Bland, i. 84–5. On the history of this theme see Cazauran, 'La Trentième Nouvelle', an essay to which I am much indebted.

[66] *Gesta Romanorum*, ch. 13, ed. Oesterley, 291–4; 'inordinato' might also be translated as 'excessive' or 'irregular'. The story appears in many other collections: see Tubach, *Index Exemplorum*, no. 2730.

An emperor's widowed daughter is so attached to her son that she sleeps in his bed until he is eighteen.[67] The devil tempts the son to have intercourse with his mother. When she becomes pregnant, the son travels far away. The mother kills her newborn child by cutting its throat; drops of blood make four ineradicable red circles on her hand, so that she has to cover it permanently with a glove. She is too ashamed to confess, but the Virgin appears to her confessor and tells him that the glove conceals the evidence of the lady's secret sin. He persuades her to remove the glove, and finds four bloody circles on her hand: each contains four letters, four Cs in one, four Ds in the second, four Ms in the third, four Rs in the fourth. Around the circles he sees an inscription: 'Casu Cecidisti Carne Cecata, Demoni Dedisti Dona Donata, Monstrat Manifeste Manus Maculata, Recedit Rubigo Regina Rogata' (You have fallen by misfortune, blinded by the flesh; you have given the gifts you were given to the devil; the stain on your hand shows it clearly; the red mark goes away when the Queen (of Heaven) is invoked). The lady confesses, is absolved, and dies a few days later.

Rank explains this story as the son's wish fantasy, but here again he disappears early on from the story, which focuses on his mother's conscience.[68] The moralization of the *Gesta Romanorum* version explains that the incestuous emperor is Christ, who marries His own daughter, human nature, when He becomes a man. The infanticide represents the soul destroyed by sin and deprived of eternal life. The blood on the lady's hands recalls the recurrent biblical saying 'my life is always in my hands' (see for instance Job 13: 14 and Psalm 119: 109). An alternative moralization explains that the lady is human nature, and conceives through lust when the apple of original sin has been eaten. The first bloody circle is Cogitatio (Resolution) preceding the sin, the second is Delectatio (Delight), the third Consensus (Consent), the fourth Actus Peccati (the Sinful Act). Adam was marked with the same circles when he sinned, says the author, and so are all the rest of us. Here incest is explicitly equated with original sin (though, paradoxically, it also symbolizes

---

[67] The text does not actually say that this is her son by her own father the emperor, but it is assumed in the moralization. I am indebted to students in my 1996 Medieval Studies 210 class at the University of Victoria for pointing this out to me.

[68] Rank, *Incest Theme*, 276.

the mystical marriage of Christ and mankind, as in the moralization of *Gregorius*).

At one level the incest is even more horrifying here than in the
Gregorius and Albanus stories, since it is not unwitting in either
case: father and daughter, mother and son are all well aware of
their relationships. Infanticide was a practical remedy much
employed in contemporary society; it is a frequent theme in *exempla* which involve incest.[69] In the hagiographic romances, of course,
the plot requires that the child of the first incest be exposed but survive to commit incest himself before he repents and is absolved;
exposure was also a common practice in the Middle Ages.[70] The
choice of infanticide rather than exposure in the *exempla* serves to
accumulate sins and thus to emphasize the sinner's need for contrition and the miraculous salvation of the ending; the infanticide
motif also shows how one sin breeds another, as lust leads to violence (for an outstanding example of this, see the discussion of *Dux
Moraud* in Chapter 4). Infanticide also increases the focus on the
guilt and confession of the mother; the feelings and fate of the son
are seldom discussed. The suspense of the story lies in the threat of
eternal damnation for the protagonist; writers of *exempla* felt no
need to tie up all the loose ends and dispose of all the characters in
the manner of romance writers.

This *exemplum* was presumably intended to show that although
women are notoriously weak and sinful and above all lustful, even
they can repent and be saved, so it needed to be accessible to a less
learned audience. It survives in various vernacular versions,
especially in French. 'La Bourjosse de Romme' elaborates plaus-
ibly on the circumstances of the initial incest, and also includes
infanticide.[71]

A rich bourgeois on his deathbed urges his wife to use his money
for charity, and to cherish their infant son. She agrees, and always
sleeps in the same bed as the boy. When he grows up, he realizes
the danger of this practice and asks for a separate bed, to avoid
the sin of lechery. His mother refuses, accusing him of wanting to
run off to loose women. The devil tempts the boy and he gets his
mother pregnant. She dares not confess, strangles her baby, and

[69] See Gravdal, 'Confessing Incests'.   [70] See Boswell, *Kindness of Strangers*.
[71] Jehan de Saint-Quentin, *Dits en quatrains*, ed. Munk Olsen, 39–46; also ed. Jubinal
in *Nouveau recueil*, i. 79–87. See Payen, *Le Motif*, 22–4, and Régnier-Bohler, 'L'Inceste'.

continues to dispense charity and to enjoy an excellent reputation. The devil disguised as a pious doctor denounces her to the emperor (in one version a series of mysterious murders is attributed to her). She is to be burned at the stake, but the Virgin arranges that the Pope himself should hear her confession secretly. The devil is forced to withdraw his accusation, and she becomes a nun devoted to the Virgin.

Here too the emphasis is on confession: no penance is required. The son's responsibility is minimalized; his mother persists in sleeping with him in spite of his protests, and so he gives in to the devil's tempting. No more is heard of him once his mother is pregnant; apparently it is of no interest whether contrition makes him confess or not. This story appears in many collections of miracles of the Virgin, whose role seems particularly appropriate; she is the perfect foil for the incestuous mother, since she herself conceived without sin, and is quite properly the spiritual Bride of her own Son, as well as His Mother.[72]

In a more complex version of this story, the 'Dit du Buef', the writer introduces the story as an example for sinners, and as illustrating a blow we can deal to the devil through confession, but in fact the story is largely about penance.[73]

A widow cherishes her son, who greatly resembles his dead father. She sleeps in his bed, and they have a long affair. When she gets pregnant the devil rejoices, but we are assured that God will save the sinners because of their penitence. The son confesses to the local priest, who sends him to the Pope for absolution. The Pope imposes no penance, but employs the youth as a chamberlain, to keep him from relapsing into sin. The devil tries to persuade the mother to kill the baby she is carrying, but the Virgin helps her at the birth. She confesses to the priest, who tells her to go to Rome, but she does not. Her daughter grows up unaware of her parentage. When she is 12, the Virgin advises her to ask her mother about her father. The mother reveals the secret, and the priest advises the daughter to go to the Pope at Rome. At last the two set off. At Rome the son identifies himself as mother

[72] The relationship of the Virgin with God the Father and God the Son, which is often represented by medieval writers as a sort of 'holy incest', is discussed in the final chapter.
[73] Jehan de Saint-Quentin, *Dits en quatrains*, 216–45; *Nouveau recueil*, i. 42–72. See Régnier-Bohler, 'L'Inceste', *passim*.

and daughter are confessing. The Pope decrees that all three are to be sewn into cowhides which leave only their hands, feet, and heads free; they are to wander through the world separately for seven years, and may not talk if they chance to meet. At the end of this time they are to return to Rome.

After seven years they all arrive on the same night at a village near Rome, and are given lodging in a barn. A series of miracles occurs: an empty pot is found to be full of food for the strangers, and the host's two children, one blind, the other crippled, are cured overnight. A great light shines from the barn: each of the penitents has prayed to God to be taken to heaven that night, and angels come to fetch them. Next morning the Pope is summoned, and is informed by an angel of what has happened. The bodies are too heavy to be moved; each holds a letter with a name and a prayer to the Virgin. The Pope founds a monastery on the spot and buries them in it. Miraculous cures continue to occur there.

Here for once the product of incest is a daughter, who survives to play a crucial part in the story. The shock and horror of Gregorius and Albanus when they discover the identity of their wives is replaced here by the horror of the 12-year-old girl on discovering the identity of her father. We might have expected the son to marry his unrecognized sister-daughter when she arrives in Rome, but the author spares us such double incest (though it does appear in some Renaissance versions which are discussed below). It is the penance that interests him, and here it is a folk variant of the penance of Albanus and his parents; the three sinners must separate and wander the world for a number of years. But what is the significance of the cowhides they wear? The woman who gives them lodging is horrified by their appearance, and thinks that they cannot be Christians: perhaps the implication is that by giving in to animal lust in defiance of social convention and religious prohibition, they have reduced themselves to the level of animals and must be treated as such.[74] Régnier-Bohler suggests that the hides suppress identity and make sexual activity impossible, as a way of redressing the confusion of identities caused by the incest; she argues that this obliteration of identity is a necessary prelude to their spiritual rebirth as

[74] In the Fourth Branch of the *Mabinogion* male siblings are transformed into animals and condemned to mate with each other as a punishment for raping a maiden; see Welsh, 'Doubling and Incest', and my comments in Ch. 5.

absolved Christians at the end.[75] There may be a connection here with the tale of Peau d'Âne, where the animal skin helps the heroine to evade seduction. Possibly there is also an echo of the hair shirts worn as part of penance, or even without penance by devout Christians.[76] Their penance seems to be a combination of the pilgrimage often prescribed as a punishment for incest in the early penitentials, and the social marginalization or scapegoating associated with the shame of breaking a taboo. The 'Dit du Buef' resembles the story of Albanus in that the family separates to do penance by wandering in the world, and that they all die at the end of the penance (though in very different circumstances). Again the emphasis is on the value of contrition and, in this case, rigorous penance as prescribed by an ecclesiastical authority. But here the whole family is absolved; the focus is not on the son alone as in the pious romances, nor on the mother as in analogous *exempla*. One might argue that in both cases a family is destroyed by incest, but here the moral seems to be that the family that repents sincerely together also goes to heaven together. The absolved sinners are only named at the very end (the son's name is missing in the manuscript); the story does not seem to be linked to an existing saint's cult, but rather to be purely exemplary.

In the 'Bourjosse de Romme' and the 'Dit du Buef', as in 'De Amore Inordinato', there is no question of unwitting incest; the transgression seems to be largely attributable to obsessive maternal love (and perhaps the frustrations of widowhood).[77] The son in these *exempla* bears little responsibility; he simply gives in to temptation when his mother provides the opportunity. The writers often attribute the incest to the influence of the devil; clearly the son is not actually raped, but very little is said about his feelings (there is no profound passion as in the sibling incest in *Gregorius*). As Cazauran shows, variants on this theme of the knowingly incestuous mother and her eventual repentance were very popular throughout the later Middle Ages, and into the Renaissance. I want to discuss three Renaissance versions all written about 1540–50 because, although strictly speaking they are outside the period of this study, they include some important plot twists which seem to

[75] Régnier-Bohler, 'L'Inceste', 291.
[76] See the comments of Kleist, *Die erzählende französische Dit-Literaturen*, 56 ff.
[77] This kind of incest is undoubtedly present in our own society, but is not widely publicized or discussed.

be borrowed from the Gregorius/Albanus pattern of double incest. This variant appears in Bandello's influential collection of *novelle*, in Luther's commentary on Genesis, and in Marguerite de Navarre's *Heptaméron*.[78] Here is the basic plot; I will comment on the variations in each of the three stories in turn.

> A maidservant complains to her mistress, a noble widow, that the son of the house is propositioning her. The mother hides in his bed to verify the story, and succumbs to his lust without revealing her identity. She conceives that night; overcome by guilt and shame, she finds excuses to send away both the maid and her son. The daughter who is subsequently born is reared in another house. She grows up to be very beautiful; her father/brother falls in love with her and marries her—neither knows their true relationship. The mother is horrified. The young couple remain married in blissful ignorance.

Here we have double incest comparable to that in the *Gregorius*. The mother knows who her son is when she sleeps with him, but the second incest is entirely unwitting on both sides. The main innovation here, however, is that the lady's children never discover the truth, and are allowed to remain married. Only the mother suffers the physical and emotional consequences of her lapse into sin, a lapse which is emphasized by the unexpectedly determined virtuousness of the maid at the beginning.

In Bandello's version, the mother is presented as somewhat worldly. The narrator gives several possible explanations for her incest: she may have secretly desired her son, or just wanted to embarrass him, or there may have been some other reason. She is still relatively young, and responds enthusiastically to his embrace; he on the other hand is a virgin, and cannot distinguish a maiden from an experienced woman. A cousin raises the baby at first, but then the mother takes her in, apparently as an act of charity, before sending her off to the court of Navarre. When the mother hears that her son has married his sister/daughter, she becomes mortally ill, confesses to the bishop, and dies. This ending recalls the earlier *exempla* in which the mother resists confession for many years, and

---

[78] Bandello, *Le Novelle*, 2.35, ed. Brognoligo, iii. 243–7; Luther, *Lectures on Genesis, Chapters 31–37*, trans. Paul, 291–300; Marguerite de Navarre, *Heptaméron*, ch. 30, ed. François, 229–33, trans. Chilton, 317–23. See also the comments of Cazauran, 'La Trentième Nouvelle', *passim*.

then dies as soon as she has confessed. The bishop and the Queen of Navarre decide that the newly-weds must never know the truth, so the cover-up is both theologically and socially sanctioned.

Luther tells his version as part of his commentary on Genesis 36: 14 (written between 1535 and 1545), which mentions Esau's wife Oholibamah: according to one Jewish tradition she was the daughter of Anah who was born of incest between Zibeon and his step-mother, but according to another she herself committed incest with her father-in-law Anah. Luther comments that there is no historical record of the incest of Anah and Oholibamah, and so it should remain hidden, like the secrets of the confessional. Although Luther was opposed to the corrupt system of indulgences, he saw psychological value in confession as a means of consolation for sinners, and as an example tells this story of double incest which he says was recounted in the confessional to a colleague of his at Erfurt. In his version the child of the first incest is raised incognita in her mother's house, and it is there that the son falls in love with her; because of their mother's opposition the young lovers marry secretly. The mother is so desperate that she contemplates suicide, but eventually confesses to a priest. He consults expert theologians, who rule that since the couple are ignorant of their relationship and are very happily married, they should not be separated or told the truth; the mother is absolved. Luther approves this judgement, and offers the story as a reminder to keen young priests that good pastors 'do not burden or involve consciences but liberate, encourage, and heal the consciences which the devil has driven mad and enmeshed in his snares' (300).

Marguerite de Navarre's version in the *Heptaméron* offers further variations, and an intriguing and unexpected moral. Here the mother is a particularly pious young widow who rejects all worldliness. As soon as the incest is committed she feels deep remorse, but her pride is such that she thinks she can resist future sin without help from God (the narrator stresses this point). She sends her son away to the wars; when he wants to return, she forbids him until he can bring a well-born wife whom he loves deeply, whether or not she is rich. This stipulation seems to function like the gloves in *Sir Degaré*, virtually guaranteeing that he will eventually meet and fall in love with his daughter/sister. The girl is sent to the court of Navarre, where she has many admirers, but because she is poor no one wants to marry her. Her father/brother arrives one day and falls in love with her; he marries her and writes to his mother that he has fulfilled her condition. The mother realizes the truth and is in despair, but confesses to the Legate at Avignon. He consults theologians, who advise that the couple must be told nothing but the lady must do penance secretly for the rest of her life.

This story is told by a man, Hircan, and occurs in the series of tales 'Des dames qui en leur amytié n'ont cerché nulle fin que l'honnesteté, et de l'hypocrisye et mechanceté des religieux' (Of ladies who in love have sought no goal but goodness, and of the hypocrisy and wickedness of monks). The storyteller specifically addresses the ladies in his audience when he comments at the end of his tale: 'Voylà, mes dames, comme il en prent à celles qui cuydent par leurs forces et vertu vaincre amour et nature avecq toutes les puissances que Dieu y a mises' (233: There, Ladies, that is what becomes of those women who presume by their own strength and virtue to overcome love and nature and all the powers that God has placed therein). A lady, Longarine, remarks that the moral is that no woman should share a bed with a male relative of any kind, 'car le feu auprès des estouppes n'est point seur' (234: for it is not safe to set a naked flame near tinder). Ennasuite comments cattily that the lady must have been convinced by the Franciscans that she was incapable of sin, and Longarine explains that the Franciscans deliberately subject themselves to sexual temptation. The general conclusion seems to be that the human inclination to carnality is pandemic, and should never be underestimated. Although the lady does confess, there is no happy ending for her; she must do penance and live with her awful secret for the rest of her life, while her children live happily in their transgressive marriage. In a way, this is the most misogynistic of all the versions of the theme of the mother who knowingly sleeps with her son, though here it is her pride rather than her lust that is attacked. By comparison, the medieval versions seem much more sympathetic to the incestuous mother. And in all these stories the son seems to get away scot-free, whether or not he marries his sister.[79]

---

[79] The only example I know of mother–son incest where the focus is on the son and his confession is a post-medieval ballad which probably had medieval antecedents, 'Brown Robyn's Confession': see *English and Scottish Popular Ballads*, 57, ed. Child, ii. 13–16. Here Robyn confesses during a storm at sea that he has had two children by his mother and five by his sister, and so his men throw him overboard; but because he has confessed, the Virgin gives him the choice of returning to his ship or going to heaven, and he chooses heaven.

The conclusion of this *exemplum* seems far removed from the twelfth-century view that the infant Gregorius is tainted at birth by his parents' incest, and that once he has himself committed incest, albeit unwittingly, he is no longer fit for human society till he has paid for his sin with many years of extreme suffering. There was certainly a substantial change in thinking about incest in the early modern period, partly as a result of the Reformation.[80] The most common and also the most serious form of incest problem in Elizabethan and Jacobean plays seems to be falling in love with one's sister. The most extreme example is Ford's *'Tis Pity She's a Whore* (1633), where the male protagonist feels no shame in defying social convention and ecclesiastical advice, and is prepared to die rather than deny his love. At the end of his valuable article on incest in folksongs, Brewster concludes that songs of brother–sister incest outnumber all others, and that songs of a mother's desire for her son are rare.[81] The situation in medieval literature appears to be just the opposite, though of course many of the longer mother–son incest stories are about unwitting incest; it is mostly in the brief *exempla* that mothers knowingly sleep with their sons.[82] Didactic tales that begin with sibling or father–daughter incest often continue with mother–son incest (for instance *Gregorius*). In those that begin with mother–son incest, there is usually no such sequel (for instance, the 'Bourjosse de Romme' and the 'Dit du Buef'); mother–son incest is a sufficient sin for the subsequent moral about confession and penance. For the Middle Ages, the most serious form of incest, deliberate or not, was incest between son and mother.

[80] See McCabe, *Incest, Drama*, and Boehrer, *Monarchy and Incest*, and my comments in the final chapter.

[81] Brewster, *Incest Theme*, 25; I comment further on his conclusion in Ch. 5.

[82] There is an example of deliberate (and multiple) mother–son incest in the legendary history of Britain, according to a narrative found in both Latin and Anglo-Norman and often attached to French prose *Bruts*, and sometimes to Geoffrey of Monmouth's *Historia*: see *Des Granz Geanz*, ed. Brereton, trans. Régnier-Bohler in *Le Cœur mangé*, 281–92, and for discussion and recent bibliography, Lesley Johnson, 'Return to Albion', in *Arthurian Literature*, 13 (1995), 19–40. The thirty (or fifty) daughters of a Greek king are set adrift after murdering their husbands. They come to an uninhabited island which they name Albion after the eldest, Albina. Sexually frustrated, they sleep first with incubi, and then with the giant sons produced by this intercourse. When Brutus and the Trojans arrive, they kill all the giants except Gogmagog, who tells the story of his origins. This strange episode may be a sort of parody of Gen. 6: 1–5, where the sons of God sleep with the daughters of men and beget a race who behave so badly that God devises the Flood.

4
Fathers and Daughters

When fathers love daughters and daughters love fathers, it's
like tying up into a knot the thread that runs into the future,
it's like a stream wanting to flow backwards.

Simone de Beauvoir, *The Mandarins*

JUST as sons do not knowingly seduce their mothers in medieval
incest stories, daughters do not knowingly seduce their fathers;
though Myrrha was well known in the Middle Ages, she seems to
have had no literary descendants. Some medieval incest narratives
describe at length the growth of mutual affection between sons and
their unrecognized mothers (e.g. Gregorius), and between brothers
and sisters (e.g. Gregorius' parents, or Canace and Machaire); but
no such developing mutual love is attributed to fathers and daughters.[1] This may be because there is almost never any doubt about
their close relationship, and the father is clearly in control of the situation. It is a typical polemical strategy to accuse an unpopular ruler
of incest; a man who behaves immorally in one area of his life is
assumed to be corrupt in others too, and as a king is the father of
his people, his family can be seen as the microcosm of his kingdom:

. . . in a social formation that ascribes rank, wealth, and identity genealogic-
ally, family structure is always already macropolitical; to write or rewrite
the family is to write or rewrite the state . . . the deep interconnectedness
of royal family and royal state results from the fact that they are socially
and conceptually the same thing . . .[2]

As Boehrer points out, endogamy as a deliberate strategy is likely
to be of greater appeal at the highest levels of society, where there

[1] In many Incestuous Father stories the father is presented as falling gradually in love
with his daughter, and in some cases he fights hard against this forbidden desire (see
below); but the daughter is almost never attracted in the same way to her father (for a
startling exception, see the end of this chapter).
[2] Boehrer, *Monarchy and Incest*, 4; he is writing here about the Renaissance, but his
comments apply equally well to the Middle Ages. See also McCabe, *Incest, Drama*,
120–1.

is more to be gained in terms of wealth, land, status, and power.[3] Tyrannical rulers may also be drawn to incest (and to other outrageous behaviour) as a demonstration of their freedom from the moral and legal constraints which bind their subjects. In medieval stories the father is generally cast as the villain and as the initiator of the incest, while his daughter is presented as an innocent victim (though she may subsequently accept and even enjoy the liaison). If there is any question of contrition and penance, it is usually on the part of father rather than daughter. It is interesting that such contrition usually occurs in stories of unconsummated incest, and more often in romances than in *exempla*. On the whole fathers who actually seduce their daughters seem to be regarded as a lost cause, and are punished for their unacceptable behaviour by death.

Father–daughter incest stories in the Middle Ages can be divided into two main groups: those in which the incest is consummated, and those in which it is avoided. When it is consummated, it is almost always initiated by the father in the full knowledge of his relationship to his daughter. Unwitting incest with a daughter is a highly unusual motif, though the threat of it may hang over a story, as in the *Historia Apollonii*; it does occur in some late versions of the incestuous mother *exemplum* where the son marries his unrecognized daughter/sister, but the focus in this narrative is on the mother and her sin. Stories of consummated father–daughter incest do not usually constitute the main plot, but appear as minor episodes embedded in larger narratives. There is seldom any mention of children born of the forbidden liaison. Sometimes the daughter kills them at birth, but it seems that often the consequence of such an unnatural union is also unnatural: the father keeps his daughter for himself, but she does not provide him with an heir (the great majority of literary incestuous fathers are rulers). When the incest is not consummated, the story focuses on the daughter's rejection of her father's advances, her flight or banishment, and her subsequent adventures; the father is absent from the narrative after the opening incest episode, though sometimes he reappears at the end to repent and be reconciled with her (and to attest her noble birth).

From the early Middle Ages on, the *Historia Apollonii* (Apollonius of Tyre) with its shocking opening episode of violently consummated father–daughter incest was widely popular.[4] Here the function of the incest motif seems to be exemplary: the wicked father and his submissive daughter are killed by a divine thunderbolt, and the hero later resists the opportunity for incest offered by his meeting with his own unrecognized daughter. But in the later Middle Ages consummated father–daughter incest is rare in exemplary literature.[5] Unconsummated father–daughter incest seems to have been much the more popular form, judging by the many versions of the Flight from the Incestuous Father narrative, which first appears in the thirteenth century. This is the most popular and widespread type of incest plot circulating as an extended narrative in the later Middle Ages. I shall begin by discussing this Flight from Incest plot which appears as *exemplum* and as romance, in chronicles and in saints' lives, throughout the later Middle Ages; then I shall move on to some examples of consummated father–daughter incest.

UNCONSUMMATED INCEST—THE FLIGHT FROM THE INCESTUOUS FATHER

There are plenty of incestuous fathers in classical mythology and literature, but the story of the flight of the innocent daughter from her father's unwelcome advances seems to be a medieval innovation, with possible folkloric roots (versions of the Cinderella story). It combines the widely known motifs of the woman set adrift or exposed, the Accused Queen or Calumniated Wife who is unjustly driven from her home, and the father who wants to marry his own daughter, plus in some cases the Maiden without Hands.[6] Schlauch

---

[4] For references and discussion see Ch. 2.

[5] Of the twelve entries under *incest* in Tubach's *Index Exemplorum*, only four concern father–daughter incest (and three of them are effectively the same plot); mother–son incest is much more frequent in exemplary collections.

[6] See motifs 706 and 712 in Aarne, *Types*, 240–2 and 247–8. On the woman adrift see Reinhard, 'Setting Adrift'; Kolve's richly illustrated discussion of the *Man of Law's Tale* in *Chaucer*, 297–358; and Hares-Stryker, 'Adrift'. On the Accused Queen theme see Schlauch, *Chaucer's Constance*; Micha, 'La Femme'; and Roussel, *Conter de geste*, esp. 21–221. I read Roussel's wide-ranging and learned study of the Flight from Incest theme at a late stage in my own research; we discuss many of the same texts and have arrived independently at many similar conclusions, but I am also indebted to him for some valuable insights and references. Two recent essays focused on specific texts contain many useful comments and arguments that are applicable to other incest narratives: see Putter, 'Narrative Logic', and Scanlon, 'Riddle of Incest'.

believed that though the incest motif was undoubtedly very ancient, its use as catalyst for the heroine's wanderings cannot have belonged to the original Accused Queen story because it is omitted in so many versions (in her view the Exchanged Letter was the unifying factor in this group of stories). I have argued in detail elsewhere that the use of incest as the catalyst for the flight and misadventures of the protagonist, and the combination of incest and mutilation, are in fact much older than Schlauch acknowledges, going back to the story of Apollonius of Tyre and to the *Clementine Recognitions*, two late classical texts which retained their popularity throughout the Middle Ages.[7] Apollonius of Tyre offered the greater number of narrative building blocks: a series of royal fathers each of whom has only one child, a daughter; the hero's horrified flight after his discovery of the incestuous liaison of his prospective bride and her father; the abandonment of his new wife at sea after childbirth; the ordeals of their daughter at the hands first of her jealous stepmother and then of a series of hostile or aggressive men; the intervention of a deity; and a two-part family reunion, the second part caused by a sort of confession in a temple. The *Clementine Recognitions* offered some variations and additions on the same theme: flight of an innocent woman from the unwanted approaches of her brother-in-law; separation of mother and children; mutilated hands; and a multiple family reunion through the agency of St Peter, the first Bishop of Rome, including a sort of confession by the father. Of course the Flight from the Incestuous Father story may have been circulating in oral forms throughout the first millennium AD; it has survived as a folktale to the present day.[8] It would seem that the fully-fledged medieval version of the story was developed (or at least first committed to writing), like the legend of Gregorius, in the twelfth to thirteenth centuries. This was the period which saw not only the rise of romance, with its increased interest in the psychology of love and

---

[7] Archibald, 'Flight'; and see Ch. 2 above. Marijane Osborn has tried to link what she calls the 'Castaway Queen' plot to ancient goddess worship and especially to the cult of Isis, but her argument is highly speculative; see ch. 3 of *Romancing the Goddess*.

[8] See Bernier, *La Fille*, who records versions told in Quebec in this century. It has long been a popular theme in other parts of the world: see Johnson and Price-Willliams, *Oedipus Ubiquitous*. Ramanujan confirms that it is widespread in India ('Indian Oedipus', 248 and 250): 'The most ancient myths bear witness to a father's desire for his daughter' and 'Dozens of tales open with the flight of the daughter from the lecherous father-figure'. On fairytales see also Warner, *From the Beast*, esp. chs. 19 and 20.

adventure stories about women, but also great anxiety among clerics about the definition of marriage, the consanguinity laws, and the incest taboo, and great emphasis by clerical writers on contrition, confession, and penance.

A remarkable number of versions of the Flight from the Incestuous Father have survived.[9] The earliest seems to be in the English *Vitae Duorum Offarum* attributed to Matthew Paris, written about 1250; the life of St Dympna, written about 1240, is clearly an analogue, but lacks several parts of the standard plot. At about the same time Beaumanoir's *La Manekine* was composed in France, and *Yde et Olive* followed at the end of the thirteenth century; in Germany the same period produced *Mai und Beaflor* and Enikel's *Der König von Reussen*. From the fourteenth century we have in Latin the *Ystoria Regis Franchorum et Filie in qua Adulterium Comitere Voluit*, and the elaborate seven-act drama *Comedia sine nomine* (also known as *Columpnarium*); in English from the end of the century *Emaré*; in French *La Belle Hélène de Constantinople*, Jean Maillart's *Le Roman du Comte d'Anjou*, *Lion de Bourges*, and *Le Miracle de la fille du roy de Hongrie*; in Catalan *La Istoria de la Fiyla del Rey d'Ungria*; and in Italian the *Novella della Figlia del Re di Dacia*. The fifteenth century offers in Latin Fazio's version in his *De origine inter Gallos et Britannos belli historia*; in French *De Alixandre, Roy de Hongrie, qui voulut espouser sa fille*, and Wauquelin's prose versions of *La Belle Hélène* and *La Manekine*; in German *Die Königstochter von Frankreich* by von Bühel (also known as der Büheler), and a prose version of Enikel's *Der König von Reussen*; in Catalan *La Istoria de la Filla de l'Emperador Contasti*; in Spanish the version in Gutierre Diez de Games's chronicle *El Victorial*; and in Italian the play *Rappresentazione di Santa Uliva* and a poem about the same saint. In the early sixteenth century, my cut-off point, Lord Berners translated *Yde et Olive* into English.[10] These are all fairly elaborate and lengthy narratives; shorter versions of the story also exist in exemplary collections

[9] Brief plot summaries of the texts discussed in this chapter (apart from *La Manekine*) are given in the Appendix; see also the more extended descriptions provided by Roussel in *Conter de geste*, 73–140. Here I list the versions by century and then by language, beginning with Latin; in the Appendix they are arranged in chronological order, in so far as this can be established.

[10] Various versions of the theme continued to appear in later centuries, some apparently influenced by oral accounts too. Basile's *Pentamerone* (early 17th-cent.) includes

such as the *Scala coeli* of Jean Gobi (or Johannes Gobius), an anthology of Marian miracles begun in the late thirteenth century and completed about 1330. I shall discuss the implications of the contexts in which the story appears later in this chapter.

The earliest extant version of the Flight from the Incestuous Father plot appears in the life of Offa I as told in the mid-thirteenth-century *Vitae Duorum Offarum*; it differs in some significant respects from the later and better known vernacular versions of the story.[11] I want to begin with this Latin text produced in England in order to show how it, or some similar version, may have contributed to the fashion for retelling this grim story in more elaborate ways according to the conventions of the newly popular genres of romance and *exemplum*.

The young and unmarried King Offa is out hunting one day when he hears the sound of weeping and finds a young woman alone and unhappy. She tells him that her father, the King of York, was overcome with incestuous love for her. When she resisted his bribes and threats, preferring to risk any human danger rather than offend against God, he had her exposed in a wilderness. The servants to whom this task was entrusted were moved by her beauty and did not mutilate her, but left her without food. Offa takes her home and has her suitably looked after in his household. Some years later, his lords press him to marry, and he remembers his protégée, who is much loved and admired. He marries her and she bears him several sons and daughters.

Some years later Offa is summoned to the aid of the King of Northumberland, who is being attacked by the Scots and by his own men. The messenger bringing back news of Offa's victories happens to stay a night with the King of York, who knows of his daughter's marriage. Maliciously he forges a letter from Offa reporting that he has been defeated and most of his lords killed; that he realizes that this disaster must be the result of his

---

the story of a princess who evades her father's advances by putting a magic stick in her mouth which turns her into a bear (2. 6), and also the story of Penta the Handless, who has the usual round of adventures when she flees from her incestuous brother (3. 2). A lurid variation on the traditional plot is told in Straparola's *Le Piacevoli Notti* of 1556 (1. 4).

[11] The text is printed by Furnivall in *Sources and Analogues*, 73–84, and by Chambers in *Beowulf*, 227–35. For a defence of the authorship of Matthew Paris, and an important discussion of the shape of the story, see Vaughan, *Matthew Paris*, 42–8 and 190 ff.

sin in marrying a witch without the consent of his people; and that she is to be exposed in a lonely place with her children, and her hands and feet are to be cut off so that she dies. Offa's lords are amazed by this order, but they send the queen and her children away. The servants in charge spare the queen because of her beauty, but mutilate the children. A hermit hears the queen lamenting and finds her in a deep swoon and the children lifeless; through his prayers they are all revived and the children's limbs are restored. They live with the hermit.

Offa returns home and is horrified to learn what has happened. After some time his lords suggest a hunting trip to cheer him up. He happens on the hermit's hut, remembers how he met his wife, and tells the hermit the sad story. The hermit reveals that his wife and children are all alive, and there is a happy family reunion. The narrative ends with the hermit's advice to both king and queen to thank God for their good fortune, and to found a monastery which their children too should endow and protect.

This story is part of a larger history of the origins of the monastery of St Albans, which the first Offa supposedly promised to build in the fourth century, though it was actually founded by his namesake Offa II in the eighth century. We cannot know at what point the story of the abandoned girl who becomes queen only to be unjustly cast out again was inserted into Offa's biography, or how well known such stories were at the time. The decision to include it may have been partly influenced, as Vaughan suggests, by the story that Offa himself was born dumb and blind and was subsequently healed by a miracle; the revival of the queen and the restoration of the mutilated hands and feet of the children could be seen as providing symmetry (the repetitions in the plot are also very obvious: two hunting scenes, two exposures in the wilderness when the heroine narrowly escapes the mutilation ordered by her malevolent father, two rescues). The story provides an important role for the hermit and foregrounds the royal intention to found the monastery as thanks for divine favours. It is striking that in this version Offa is the protagonist, and the hermit also has an important part: his prayers for the revival of the queen and her children and his injunction to Offa are given in direct speech at some length. In contrast, the queen is a shadowy character who rarely speaks; the story begins with Offa, not with her, and when he finds her in the wood, the story of her harassment by her father is reported indirectly, rather than in her own words. Though her children are mutilated, she herself is not; the writer does not seem interested in milking her story for as much pathos as possible. At the end she is marginalized by the final speech of the hermit which is addressed primarily to the king, though she does receive some advice too. There is a strong religious tone to the ending of the story, but no explicit moralizing: it is striking that there is no reference here to the fate of the incestuous King of York, who does not seem to be punished in any way.

It is not clear whether this particular story circulated widely enough, in Latin or in vernacular forms now lost, to have influenced the spate of more elaborate versions of the same plot which followed in the next decades. Perhaps the life of Offa is simply one literary reworking of a traditional story which had long circulated orally. But it is a very suggestive story; it is easy to see how it, or its source, could have been taken up and expanded to fit two different and very popular genres in the thirteenth century: romance and *exemplum*.[12] A romance needs considerable emphasis on emotion and psychology, both in narrative and direct speech, and also on details of courtly life and behaviour; it ends when the protagonist achieves or retrieves status, fame, and worldly happiness. An *exemplum* needs explicitly Christian motivation and activity, and also moral commentary (often allegorical); it may or may not finish happily in worldly terms, but there is a clearly Christian message at the end. Later versions of the story explain how the widowed king came to desire his daughter and plan to marry her, often after a long struggle with himself; and they also describe in detail the daughter's horrified reactions. Much more space is given to her misery each time she is exposed, and her prayers (often to the Virgin). Sometimes the incestuous father reappears at the end, contrite and in search of absolution from the Pope; the recognition scene(s) may be preceded by the confession of husband and/or father. The happy ending, often presided over by the Pope or a saint, is expanded to describe the reactions of all the main characters, the celebrations, and the return home of the reunited family; and there is sometimes a moralizing epilogue.

---

[12] The Gregorius story seems to have circulated first in French and German, and then was translated into Latin when its exemplary value became apparent; see my comments in Ch. 3.

There are a number of variants in the plots of these texts, and no single version can be taken as representative, but all the motifs most relevant to this study are included in the mid-thirteenth-century French poem *La Manekine* by Beaumanoir; if one accepts recent arguments that it is the work of Beaumanoir *père* rather than *fils* and was written about 1240, it is the earliest extant vernacular version of this plot.[13] I shall discuss it in some detail as my base text, and shall then go on to consider some of the more important variants in other versions.

The King of Hungary marries the heiress to the kingdom of Armenia and has one daughter, Joie. When his queen is dying, she makes him promise not to remarry; but if the barons insist on a male heir, he is only to marry a woman who looks just like her. The barons do urge him to remarry and search for a suitable wife, but can find none. Then they notice that Joie is the image of her mother, and encourage the king to marry her; at first he demurs, but then agrees, and feels increasing desire for her. Joie is horrified; she cuts off her left hand, which is thrown out of the window and swallowed by a fish; then she tells the king that a cripple cannot be queen. The furious king orders that she be burned, but a kind seneschal sets her adrift in a little boat instead.

She arrives in Scotland, where the local king falls in love with her and marries her, though no one knows her name or her origins. Leaving her pregnant, he goes off to tournaments. She gives birth to a son, and sends a messenger to her husband; but the messenger lodges with the jealous queen-mother, who alters the letter to say that Joie has borne a monster. The king is distressed, but writes back that mother and baby should be kept safe till his return. Again the messenger lodges with the queen-mother, who alters the letter to say that Joie and her baby are to be burned. The kind provost takes pity on them and burns replicas instead; once more Joie is set adrift, with her son. She arrives in Rome and is taken in by a rich senator, a widower living with his two unmarried daughters.

---

[13] References are taken from the recent edition by Sargent-Baur. See also the useful commentary in the editions by Suchier and Gnarra and the translation by Marchello-Nizia. Among the many critical studies, see Fenster, 'Beaumanoir's *La Manekine*'; Roussel, 'Chanson de geste' and *Conter de geste*; and Castellani, *Du conte populaire*.

The King of Scotland returns home; when he learns what has happened he immures his mother and sets out in search of his wife. Seven years later he comes to Rome and happens to lodge with the senator who is protecting her. He sees a boy playing with a wedding ring which he recognizes as belonging to his lost wife, and so they are reunited. Meanwhile the King of Hungary has come to Rome to do penance for his incestuous lust, and makes a public confession. Joie hears it and forgives him. Soon afterwards her severed hand is found in a pail of water, and the sturgeon which had swallowed it in a nearby fountain: the Pope reattaches the hand, and the sturgeon furnishes the celebratory banquet. The Armenians remind Joie that she has inherited their country from her mother, and invite her to visit them. She goes there with her husband, father, and son; her husband restores peace to the land and receives the homage of the lords, who hail her son as their future ruler. They then return to Scotland, and more children are born to Joie.

Beaumanoir introduces this disturbing story as one which will please everyone, and also do good to those who can understand it (1–48), but he does not specify here what the moral will be (unlike Hartmann von Aue at the beginning of his *Gregorius*, for instance). The ending of the main narrative of *La Manekine* is secular and conventionally pious: we are told that the happy couple have numerous children for whom God arranges the enviable fate that the girls all become queens and never cease to love Him, and the boys become kings, respecting divine law all their lives. Then the poet adds an epilogue (8529–90) in which he explains to the reader at considerable length that one should never despair, but rather should trust in God like Manekine; despair is tantamount to believing that God cannot relieve unhappiness or suffering—for this reason God hates despair more than anything else. This is the same moral as Hartmann's in *Gregorius*; like Hartmann, Beaumanoir says nothing at all about the sin of incestuous lust which was the cause of his heroine's need to trust so devotedly in God. But Gregorius' penance is self-inflicted out of his guilt about his unintentional sin, whereas Joie has committed no sin and does not seek penance; it is her father who tries, unsuccessfully, to commit incest, and he who initiates the long series of ordeals for his innocent daughter.

La Manekine is narrated in an elaborate and leisurely style for its 8590 lines, with a much greater emphasis on pathos than the *Vitae*

Duorum Offarum version of the story. In the French poem the main characters are given lengthy and emotional monologues and dialogues at every stage in which to express their hopes, desires, and fears; considerable space is given to minor characters and to scenes which could have been summarized briefly, such as the forging of the letters, the reactions of the courtiers who are charged with burning Joie, and her dealings with the senator who protects her at Rome. This is all typical of the romance mode; but religious elements are also very marked in *La Manekine*.[14] A number of critics have commented on the hagiographic aspects of the story; Legros calls Joie's life a model of lay sanctity.[15] Shepherd argues that she has Marian aspects in that she mediates between God and sinful mankind, and also Christ-like aspects in that she redeems her father: 'Change in *La Manekine* derives not from the protagonists' achievement of purely emotional maturity, but from their progress towards God.'[16] Throughout her adventures Joie prays to God and and to the Virgin (for instance, she is given long prayers each time she is set adrift, at 1095–1160 and 4601–738), and is sustained by them. Castellani has explored in great detail the significance of water in *La Manekine*: she argues that it is the symbol of life and also of death, the locus for the test of faith, the place of disequilibrium where everything is decided, and where the main characters can be reborn.[17] Each of Joie's voyages in her rudderless boat brings her through exposure and the threat of death to a new life, from the feudal world of Hungary to the courtly world of Scotland and finally to the Christian world of Rome; her husband's seven-year quest for her offers him too a new beginning, which culminates most appropriately in his arrival in Rome during Lent (the same is true for the contrite father). The chronology of the story is strongly Christian throughout, as many critics have noted: crises take place

---

[14] See Roussel, *Conter de geste*, 83–5; in the 'Postface' to her translation Marchello-Nizia calls it 'ce roman tout impregné de christianisme' (259: this romance completely impregnated with Christianity). [15] Legros, 'Parenté naturelle', 538.

[16] Shepherd, *Tradition and Recreation*, 22 and 42; she notes that at 409–11 the innocent Joie is said to pay for the sins of others. Shepherd speculates that the model of St. Elizabeth of Hungary may account for the setting in the liminal lands of Hungary and Scotland, frontiers of the civilized world (49); see also Legros, 'Parenté', 523, and *Manekine*, ed. Sargent-Baur, 106–8. Conversion is an important theme in some analogues of the story, for instance *La Belle Hélène*, and also in the related story of Constance told by Trivet, Chaucer (*The Man of Law's Tale*), and Gower.

[17] Castellani, 'L'Eau'. See Kolve's discussion of the rudderless boat motif as a common allegory for the soul and also for the Church (*Chaucer*, 297–358).

in Lent, and happy events at Easter and Pentecost. All journeys seem to lead in the end to Rome, where the Pope presides over the family reunion; the 'coincidence' of this reunion is trumped by the miracle of the discovery of the heroine's lost hand together with the fish which had swallowed it and its reattachment to her arm by the pontiff. Before he attempts to reattach the hand, he explains that Joie has been protected by God, and invokes the Virgin (7501–40); when he succeeds, a voice from heaven informs the assembled company that it was the Virgin who preserved the hand of her devotee (7587–620).

Critics differ in their assessment of Joie's role in her adventures— or rather vicissitudes, since her challenge is to survive unharmed, rather than to carry out specific tasks. In a Freudian reading of the poem Fenster suggests that 'Joie is the vehicle through which the childish sexual desire for the parent of the opposite sex is lived out and punished', but there is no hint of such desire in the text (or in any of the other versions), apart from her blushing early on when her father enters her room, before he reveals his desire (*Manekine*, 384–6).[18] Shepherd seizes on this blushing as a guilty awareness of her attraction to her father: 'Manekine must learn to overcome her own guilty impulses, undergoing a process of re-education through confrontation with images of family life and, with the Senator, the ambiguity of her role as daughter and wife is made explicit . . . Manekine's resistance to the Senator's love represents her release from the spell of her father' (123–4). In the final reunion, according to Shepherd, 'Manekine achieves the correct division of paternal and husbandly love and represents with her husband and child the recovery of the ideal family' (27). But the senator makes no explicit declaration of love; he offers to protect Manekine and to raise her child as she desires, and she makes it very clear in accepting his protection that she is married and is not interested in any dishonourable relationship with him (*Manekine*, 5117–93). Shepherd's comments suggest that Joie has made mistakes and has had to learn from them. I see no sign of this in the text, where Beaumanoir goes to great lengths to stress Joie's very proper horror at her father's

---

[18] Fenster, 'Beaumanoir's *La Manekine*', 45–6. A similar, though to me unconvincing, argument has been made about the heroine of the *Roman du Comte d'Anjou*, claiming that her success in putting her father in check during a game of chess reveals her responsibility for his incestuous desire, and questioning whether this heroine should be seen as saint or whore: see Foehr-Janssens, 'Quand la manchote'.

incestuous proposal, and the undeserved nature of her suffering; both these elements are typical of all the medieval versions of this story. Beaumanoir stresses at the end that the story is an *exemplum* of the importance of not giving in to despair. In this case despair would not be likely to be aroused by the heroine's sense of her own incorrigible sinfulness, as in the Gregorius story, but rather by the seemingly endless series of disasters heaped on her innocent head, reminiscent of the undeserved ordeals of Job.

Several recent critics have argued that the heroines of analogous texts do in fact have considerable control over their own destinies, but this seems to me implausible in the *Manekine* and also in other versions of the Flight from Incest.[19] While I agree with Osborn that the Flight from Incest story is 'above all a tale about family dysfunction expressed in violence' in both the heroine's and the hero's families, I do not share her view that it is also about 'a brave woman's self-possessed effectiveness despite the violence', and that 'cleverly bringing all parties together . . . the heroine succeeds in reintegrating her ruptured family'.[20] It is true that in some of the medieval versions it is the heroine who orchestrates the family reunion, recognizing first her husband and then her father, and sending her son to talk to them; but in others she shrinks from encountering them for fear of further harassment (for instance in *La Belle Hélène*). Hares-Stryker makes the astute comment that the fate of heroines set adrift is very different from that of infants or male heroes. For men, this apparently disastrous exposure turns out in fact to be 'a promise of forthcoming greatness'; for women, on the other hand, it is 'stark and unnatural, for it signals the expulsion of stability and virtue', and in these stories it is also linked in very particular ways to sexual sin.[21] Sexual transgression can also be the catalyst for the exposure in some stories of male heroes, of course, but it is usually transgression by the parents in conceiving their son, and the hero is usually exposed as an infant. Hares-Stryker emphasizes the very different tone of the two sets of story-types:

Generally speaking, then, the setting adrift motif in plots surrounding heroines symbolizes not adventure or heroism, but the ugliness and fearful

---

[19] See Robson, 'Cloaking Desire', and Osborn, *Romancing the Goddess*, 23–6.
[20] Osborn, *Romancing the Goddess*, 28–9; see also Hares-Stryker, 'Adrift', 92–5.
[21] Hares-Stryker, 'Adrift', 92.

unnaturalness that occur when the family, the basic human unit, is corrupted or broken. . . . Clearly the image of a woman afloat is far more than
ornamental; it complicates and darkens the text. It suggests that instead of
the often externalized, impersonal violence confronted by heroes—giants,
warriors, aggressive nations—the heroine faces violence of an internalized
and very personal nature—fathers, mothers, and brothers.[22]

The helplessness of the heroine, and the dominance and frequent
cruelty of patriarchy, are strongly emphasized in this plot; I think
that Chaucer highlights this emphasis very deliberately in the version he gives to the Man of Law in the *Canterbury Tales*.[23] Here the
heroine, Custance, laments as she is sent off by her father to marry
an unknown heathen king that 'Women are born to thraldom and
penance, | And to been under mannes governance' (*CT* 2. 286–7:
Women are born to servitude and suffering, and to be under the
control of men). Chaucer's narrator digresses frequently to stress
that although Custance seems absolutely defenceless, she is protected and provided for by God. This is, as Kolve remarks, 'the
nature of power at its most mysterious, when what may appear to
be weakness, passivity, defeat or even death emerges victorious
through its perfect alliance with God's will—in Christian terms, the
only true source of power'.[24] The same could be said of the many
Incestuous Father narratives too, whether or not they are presented
explicitly as Christian *exempla*.

   Though we may find it hard to read these stories in the twenty-
first century without anachronistic thoughts of dysfunctional family behaviour and the problem of healing the damage it causes,
medieval writers and readers do not seem to have been interested in
these aspects of the plot—witness the surprising lack of reference
to incest and its consequences in the epilogue of *La Manekine* and
its analogues. Once again incest is used by medieval writers as the
'péché monstrueux', the worst possible form of sexual sin—but as
it is not consummated, its main function here is as a catalyst for
the subsequent adventures of the heroine. In all these texts the
widowed father's incestuous desire for his daughter is presented as

---

22   Hares-Stryker, 'Adrift', 92–3.
    [23] Although in Chaucer's version there is no incestuous father to motivate the hero-
ine's departure from her home, the Man of Law's disapproving comments on incest in
the prologue to the tale clearly link it to the Flight from the Incestuous Father group of
stories. See Archibald, 'Flight' and 'Contextualizing Chaucer's Constance'; and Dinshaw,
'Law of Man'.   [24] Kolve, *Chaucer*, 305.

psychologically plausible but, of course, morally unacceptable. This is emphasized in some texts by his anguished deliberations as he first recognizes his forbidden desire, and in all versions by his daughter's horror and unequivocal rejection of his proposition. However, it is the daughter who is apparently punished, in spite of her innocence, by a series of undeserved vicissitudes lasting for years, and sometimes by physical mutilation too. If the mother–son incest theme in medieval literature depicts spiritual disorder in individuals, with incest standing for original sin which is inevitably transmitted from parents to children, the father–daughter theme can be seen as representing social disorder which may originate in a small family group, but affects the larger community too in terms of anxiety about the continuation of the royal or ruling line. Although the father sometimes repents at the end, contrition and penance are not crucial to the plot here, as they are in the mother–son stories.

The Flight from the Incestuous Father plot can be read as an important social and personal rite of passage gone horribly wrong. In chivalric romance, and to some extent in medieval society too, a standard male rite of passage marking the transition from adolescence to maturity, and from obscurity to fame, requires the protagonist to win his spurs on a quest or at a tournament, discover his identity (literally in the form of finding his parents, or metaphorically in terms of establishing his heroism), and receive his final reward in the form of a lady's love and the acclaim of the court. What could a female rite of passage consist of? Women's adventures have to be passive—much may happen to them, but they cannot demonstrate heroism through action. They cannot go out on lone quests or fight in tournaments to prove their strength and maturity; success for them in the eyes of the world means possession of outstanding beauty, nobility, and virtue (the first two are qualities which cannot be augmented by personal effort), and then a prestigious marriage and many children, preferably male.[25] In the Incestuous Father plot, instead of arranging a suitable exogamic marriage for his daughter in terms of social and political advantage, the besotted father claims her for himself; in some versions both his lords and the Church connive at this flagrant breach of the

---

[25] For further discussion of women's roles in romance see Marchalonis, 'Above Rubies', and Archibald, 'Women and Romance'.

consanguinity laws.[26] When she leaves his court, the heroine does not journey to her new home with an entourage provided by father or bridegroom, but wanders alone and ignominiously, rejected by her only surviving parent, with no protection against the many dangers of sea and land, and no means of subsistence. Osborn describes this disparity of male and female 'quests' very clearly in her discussion of the 'Castaway Queen' stories: 'Although these stories share with the male romance the theme of a journey into the wilderness, there is no quest as such and no dragon to be slain. Instead, the heroine is buffeted by the whims of fate and the whims of any man along the way who is attracted to her.'[27]

The marriage which Joie and her literary sisters eventually make is highly irregular (and indeed implausible): the heroine is without family, inheritance, or dowry, and attracts her royal husband by her beauty and goodness alone—her name, parentage, and social status remain unknown. When she produces a male heir in his absence, an occasion which should be joyful, her enemy (usually her mother-in-law) reports to the absent king that she has given birth to a monster, and her husband's puzzled but generous response is perverted by forgery into a sentence of exile (or death in some texts).[28] So at the moment when she succeeds in her marital role by becoming a mother and producing a son, she loses husband and home, and in some versions is separated from her child(ren) too. She finds other protectors on her travels, but it is left to divine providence to bring about the final recognition scene and reunion which restore her identity and her social status. Many male-centred romances involve the hero's quest for his family or his true identity, and in some cases he also has to win back his throne or rightful inheritance. The heroines of the Flight from Incest plot, on the other hand, deliberately suppress their identities and accept long years of exile, often in menial conditions, because they fear the

---

[26] See Rubin, 'Traffic in Women', and Boose, 'Father's House'. Boose critiques the Lévi-Straussian view of the patriarchal marriage economy based on the exchange of daughters (30): 'By giving too little weight to what we might call an "emotional economics", the anthropological construction of family ends up producing a narrative of disinterested fathers that is quite at odds with the picture drawn by most Western myth and literature, where the father most often appears as a blocking figure bent on retaining, not exchanging, his daughter.'   [27] Osborn, *Romancing the Goddess*, 18.

[28] Dinshaw has suggested that the mother-in-law's hatred of the heroine is fuelled by an incestuous obsession with her son, a desire which balances that of the incestuous father at the beginning ('Law of Man').

consequences of return to the fathers or husbands who have treated them so brutally. From a modern feminist point of view the Flight from the Incestuous Father plot can be read as a searing indictment of patriarchy, which has such unlimited power over women (not least by assessing their marriageability and controlling their marriages), and which abuses and harasses them in so many ways.[29] This is the 'thraldom' of which Chaucer's Custance complains.

Variations on the Flight from Incest Theme

In order to discuss further aspects of the Flight from Incest theme, it is now necessary to introduce some of the variations found in the many analogues of *Manekine*. For the purposes of this study, there are four significant areas of variation: first, the presentation of the father's desire and the reactions of his court; second, the circumstances of the heroine's departure into exile and, in some versions, the mutilation of her hand(s); third, the ultimate fate of the father; and lastly, the tone of the ending and of the narrative as a whole, and the context in which it appears.

An interesting depiction of a modern-day incestuous father appears in Alice Walker's prize-winning novel *The Color Purple*; her plot has been compared with the Patient Griselda story, but it has not been noticed that it is also a modern-day version of the Flight from Incest and Accused Queen themes.[30] It begins with what both the heroine Celie and the reader take to be father–daughter incest (in the form of rape), though it later turns out that the aggressor is in fact her stepfather; the resulting babies are taken away and exposed to die, as Celie believes; she leaves home unwillingly for a marriage

---

[29] Scanlon calls it 'insidious patriarchal logic' that the daughter should suffer more than the father ('Riddle of Incest', 121). An unusual version of this plot which functions, at least for the modern reader, as an additional indicator of the power of patriarchy and the helplessness of women is found in *Yde et Olive*, part of the 13th-cent. French *Huon of Bordeaux* cycle which was translated into English by Lord Berners in the early 16th cent. The heroine, Yde, flees in male clothing from her father's court, makes a reputation as a soldier, marries the Emperor of Rome's daughter, and is miraculously metamorphosed into a man. Roussel comments that the 'virilisation' (masculinization) of the heroine, first self-determined and then made permanent by God, functions as protection against male lust; see his 'Aspects du père', 56. It is a depressing comment on female vulnerability that to be safe the heroine has to become a man, quite literally. See also Archibald, 'The *Ide and Olive* Episode', and Watt, 'Behaving like a Man?'

[30] On the Griselda parallel see Ellis, '*Color Purple*'.

in which she is for many years a Calumniated Wife, though her persecutors are her husband and stepchildren, not her mother-in-law,
and she is not driven away; and the novel ends with a family reunion,
the recovery of her children and also of her long-lost sister. When
Celie's 'father' rapes her at the beginning of the book, her mother is
alive but recovering with difficulty from the recent birth of yet another
child; rejected by his wife, the frustrated Fonsus says to his supposed
daughter, 'You gonna do what your mammy wouldn't.' When plain
and naive Celie has borne him two children, he begins to turn his
attention to her prettier younger sister. This is probably an all too realistic scenario, both in the past and the present.[31] But in the medieval
Flight from Incest plot the king has only one child, a beautiful daughter, and his beloved wife is dead.

   The circumstances which lead the king to propose marriage to
his daughter vary, making him more or less responsible for this
crime. Sometimes he is already a widower at the opening of the
story; sometimes it begins with the death of the queen, and the
promise she extracts from her husband in relation to possible
remarriage. In *La Manekine*, and also in *Lion de Bourges, La Filla
de l'Emperador Contasti*, and the *Comedia sine nomine*, the king
promises his dying wife not to marry again unless he finds a
woman who looks just like her or else is just as beautiful, a rash
promise which must inevitably lead either to incest or to celibacy.
In *La Manekine* it is the barons who notice the princess' resemblance to her mother and suggest that the king should marry her.
He is horrified at first, but when he is persuaded he suddenly sees
as if with new eyes how very beautiful Joie is, and falls in love
with her. It might be argued that the blame is somewhat displaced
from the king, but the detailed account of his inner battle between
'folie' (madness) and 'raison' (reason), a passage typical of
romance interest in psychological processes connected to love,
makes it clear that in the end the decision is based on his own

---

[31] In the 14th-cent. English romance *Sir Degaré*, the heroine worries when she
becomes pregnant by a fairy knight that people may think she has been seduced by her
father, as she has never loved any other man (151–4). It is impossible to judge whether
this is an indication of the popularity of Incestuous Father romances, or the frequency
of father–daughter incest in medieval households. Roussel discusses a comic reference to
it in one 13th-cent. romance (see *Conter de geste*, 183–5): when Cristal comes to his
beloved Clarie's room at night her suspicious father, alerted by a dream, knocks at the
door, but Clarie refuses to let him in on the grounds that his intentions may not be honourable (*Cristal et Clarie*, 8781 ff., ed. Breuer).

desire rather than pure political expediency (see 431 ff.). In *Lion de Bourges*, a text closely related to *La Manekine*, it is also the barons who suggest that King Herpin should marry his daughter Joieuse, and in this case he accepts enthusiastically.[32] In the Catalan *La Filla de l'Emperador Contasti* too, the dying empress makes the emperor swear only to marry a woman who resembles her, and adds the stipulation that the new bride must be able to wear her glove.[33] The barons search in vain for a suitable candidate, and eventually suggest the princess. The emperor is not particularly horrified, but asks for time to think over their suggestion; when the princess passes by, he is struck by her beauty and makes her try on the glove, which of course fits perfectly. She agrees very reluctantly to the wedding on the understanding that he will not have intercourse with her, and they are actually married (a unique variant); but he cannot endure this celibate life, and tells her that it will be her fault if he dies of sorrow.

In the Latin play *Comedia sine nomine*, it is the nurse who innocently comments to the king that the princess is the image of her dead mother, thus triggering his lust. Many scenes of the play are devoted to the king's struggle with his inappropriate feelings. At first he seeks a wife abroad, sending the court painters to make portraits of possible candidates. He is given many monologues in which to agonize over his inappropriate passion; he calls himself a second Oedipus, and complains that the queen's demand has put him in an impossible position (II. i). But later his resolve becomes firmer, and in a conversation with the nurse he justifies his planned marriage by the example of Adam in the early days of the world, when it was not yet wrong for fathers to sleep with daughters or brothers with sisters; he declares 'Nullum necessitas nefas parit' (III. i: the product of necessity cannot be a crime), claiming that his

---

[32] In *Der König von Reussen* too the suggestion comes from the barons; there is no promise here to the dying queen. In *Yde et Olive* the barons are delighted to hear that the king thinks of marrying again, but are horrified when he announces that the bride will be his own daughter (it is he who draws attention to her likeness to her mother).

[33] This is also a common feature of the Catskin group of Cinderella analogues, where the mother leaves a ring or sometimes gloves as a test of her replacement; see Cox, *Cinderella*, and Rooth, *Cinderella Cycle*. Compare *Sir Degaré* (see Ch. 3 above), where the mother who exposes her newborn son leaves with him a pair of gloves which will fit only his future wife; inevitably he marries his unrecognized mother, though they discover the truth (by means of the gloves) in time to avoid consummating their union.

line will die out if he does not marry his daughter.[34] By 'Adam' the playwright presumably means the earliest humans and the biblical patriarchs; I think he is drawing on the well-known Augustinian argument, much quoted by theologians and canon lawyers, that when the population of the world was very small, nuclear family incest was acceptable.[35] In the Middle English *Emaré* the emperor Artus' lust for his daughter seems to be prompted by an object, a present which he receives from the King of Sicily (72 ff.): it is a cloth richly embroidered with jewels and with images of four pairs of lovers. Artus has a wedding dress made for his daughter out of this cloth; she is wearing it when she is exposed at sea and at other critical moments in the story, and it seems to enhance her attractiveness in a supernatural way, though curiously it does not act as a recognition token at her reunion with her father, as one might have expected.[36] The lack of explicit linking of the cloth with the desire of the emperor and other men in the story has led Amanda Hopkins to argue recently that in fact it is not meant to be the fatal trigger, but clearly magical dresses did play a part in some early version of the plot which survives in many analogues of the Cinderella story.[37]

It is striking that in *La Manekine* the prelates at court undertake to obtain the Pope's consent to the marriage; the pontiff himself is represented as giving permission in several other Incestuous Father stories.[38] This must be a reflection, if not a criticism, of the

[34] Roy emends the manuscript reading 'parit' (gives birth to) to 'parat' (prepares); 'parit' seems to me to make much better sense here. The same excuse was given by medieval theologians for Lot's incestuous daughters (see Ch. 1).

[35] Augustine's argument in *The City of God* is quoted by Gratian in his discussion of incest laws, and by many later writers; see my comments in Ch. 1.

[36] See Donovan, 'Middle English *Emaré*'.

[37] Hopkins, 'Veiling the Text', and Putter, 'Narrative Logic', 174–8. In *Der König von Reussen* the heroine is exposed by her father with her wedding dress, though it plays no further part in the plot. In the Catskin variant of the Cinderella story, the daughter asks her incestuous father for three dresses decorated respectively with gold, silver, and stars (or in some cases chimes); these are the dresses that she wears to the balls where the prince falls in love with her. Anne Savage sees the dress as a sign of 'the divorce from worldliness, from the stains and ugliness of sin'; see 'Clothing Paternal Incest', 353–4.

[38] For instance the English *Emaré* and the German *Der König von Reussen*; in von Bühel's *Die Königstochter*, however, the Pope refuses to sanction the marriage. See Kelly, 'Canonical Implications'; various Popes were requested to give dispensations for royal or aristocratic marriages well within the prohibited degrees of consanguinity, including one case of brother and sister, but I do not know of any request for a dispensation for a father and daughter.

Church's notorious leniency in sanctioning aristocratic marriages within the prohibited degrees of kinship. This detail also appears in *La Belle Hélène de Constantinople*, where political expediency is again a factor, though in a somewhat different form. Antoine, the Emperor of Constantinople, is summoned by the Pope to defend Rome against the Saracens; in reward he receives the Pope's niece in marriage, but she dies in giving birth to their first child, Hélène. Antoine loves his daughter deeply; but the devil turns his love to lust. When the Pope summons him to ward off a second attack, he demands as his reward permission to marry his own daughter; the Pope is shocked, but eventually agrees, encouraged by a celestial voice which assures him that Antoine will never be able to carry out his wicked desire. The devil is implicated as the instigator of the father's unnatural lust in several other narratives, including the *Figlia del Re di Dacia* and the *Roman du Comte d'Anjou*. This might seem an obvious explanation for such a heinous crime (it is used in some Apollonius texts, and for the brother–sister incest in *Gregorius*); yet it is striking that in the majority of versions the writers see no need to invoke diabolical influence, but consider incestuous lust quite plausible, though of course unacceptable.

Not only is the king in these stories prepared to marry his daughter publicly, but often his barons accept this marriage, and indeed sometimes suggest it themselves in their anxiety to see their king produce a male heir. Margaret Schlauch has proposed that this is a vestige of the widespread ancient tradition of matriliny according to which sovereignty is vested in the woman.[39] This matrilineal tradition would, she argues, explain the reluctance of royal fathers to allow their daughters to marry (a familiar theme in classical legend and in the Apollonius story, where all suitors who fail to answer Antiochus' riddle are beheaded); it would also explain why kings should plan publicly to marry their own daughters. But matriliny was so long outmoded in Europe by the time of the composition of the Flight from Incest stories that her argument seems very doubtful. It is true that in *La Manekine* Joie's mother is described as the heiress to Armenia (53); at the end of

---

[39] Schlauch, *Chaucer's Constance*, 40–7. Zipes quotes approvingly the view of Heide Göttner-Abendroth that European folktales have undergone 'patriarchalization' from an original matriarchal form, so that by the Middle Ages 'matrilineal marriage and family ties became patrilineal' (*Fairy Tales*, 7). But Roussel considers this approach too reductive (*Conter de geste*, 143).

the story, after the joyful family reunion, the barons of Armenia send a messenger to Joie reminding her that she has inherited their land through her mother, and inviting her to come and visit them (8013–42). But although the Armenians receive Joie enthusiastically as their queen, they do homage for their fiefs to her husband, who resolves conflicts and establishes peace in the land, and they also hail her son as their future king; any suggestion of matriliny is thus firmly replaced by patriliny.

In the Incestuous Father stories the dying queen tries to prevent her husband from remarrying, as if to safeguard the rights of her daughter; but she worries that the barons may urge a second marriage in the hope of producing a male heir, who would clearly take precedence over the princess. So as a fall-back position she imposes the provision that any new wife must strongly resemble the dead one, which of course points very clearly to the daughter as the only candidate. Roussel suggests that the promise exacted by the dying queen and the daughter's extraordinary resemblance to her mother serve to exonerate the incestuous father; he also argues that the curious publicity which the father gives to his intention of marrying his daughter is possible precisely because the incestuous desire is never realized.[40] It is also true that in many versions of the story the court makes no objection to his plan; indeed it is often the barons who suggest it (though in *Yde et Olive* they are shocked, and warn him that such a marriage is worse than heresy). But any good—or less dishonourable—impression which may be made by the plight of the widowed father is soon dispelled by his daughter's horrified reaction to his proposal, his response to her refusal, and the circumstances of her departure from his court. This is my second area of variation.

In most texts the incestuous father is furious when his daughter refuses to marry him. Sometimes he banishes her; sometimes he condemns her to death, but a kind courtier helps her to escape. Often she is put to sea in a small boat: this could be seen as comparable to the exposure of the infant protagonist in the Judas and Gregorius legends (indeed in the prose version of the *König von Reussen* the hostile mother-in-law refers to the heroine contemptuously as a 'vindelkint' or foundling), and it is also a kind of living death comparable to the burial at sea of the comatose queen in the

---

[40] Roussel, 'Aspects du père', 53–4.

Apollonius story. This paternal rejection marginalizes the heroine socially as well as geographically: she no longer has the protection of her father and he takes no steps to hand her over to a husband in the conventional way. In some texts, on the other hand, she runs away of her own accord, showing her very proper horror at her father's incestuous proposal: this happens in *Mai und Beaflor*, and also in the *Ystoria Regis Franchorum* and *Yde et Olive*, where she takes the further precaution of dressing as a man. Sometimes she is accompanied, at least initially, by her nurse or governess, and in *Lion de Bourges* by a squire. In the *Comedia sine nomine* the nurse remains with her until her second exile, and plays a crucial part in the plot right up to the end, but this is most unusual: usually the heroine must endure her trials quite alone except for her infant child(ren).

In a number of Flight from the Incestuous Father narratives, including *La Manekine*, the heroine's banishment or flight is preceded by mutilation of one or both of her hands; later in the story she is miraculously healed. This strange but popular motif requires extended discussion.[41] In the earliest known version of the story, the life of Offa, the heroine is condemned to have her hands and feet cut off not when she is first exposed by her father for refusing to marry him, but in the letter that he later forges which causes her second exposure; in fact she is not mutilated, though her children are.[42] In *La Belle Hélène* too, she does not lose her hand until she is about to be burned on account of the forged letter; the kindly seneschal cuts off her hand instead, and then sets her and her children adrift. But more frequently the mutilation occurs near the beginning of the narrative when the father proposes the incestuous marriage, and the heroine herself is responsible for it. In *La Manekine* Joie cuts off her left hand, and tells her father that she cannot marry him because a king cannot have a wife who is missing

---

[41] On the general popularity of the Maiden without Hands motif (Aarne–Thompson, 706), see Bernier, *La Fille*, and Roussel, *Conter de geste*, 207–16. It does not seem to have been used in classical literature, apart from the late *Clementine Recognitions*, where the mother, who has run away from the advances of her brother-in-law and has then been separated from all her children, gnaws her hands to the bone in her grief; though she recovers all her family through the agency of St Peter, she does not regain the use of her hands (see Ch. 2).

[42] The servants who take her to the wilderness to die pity her and so do not mutilate her; this may be taken to indicate that mutilation was in fact part of her first sentence in the source.

a limb. In *Lion de Bourges* Joieuse also mutilates herself, but in this case she tells her father that now she no longer resembles her mother. In the *Istoria del Rey d'Ungria*, *Alixandre*, *El Victorial*, and the Uliva stories, the heroine cuts off her hand(s), or has a servant do it, because her father loves her hands especially or has kissed them. In *La Figlia del Re di Dacia* she is told in a vision to cut off the hand with which her father forced her to touch him 'nel disonesto luogo' (in the shameful place); this is the only version which suggests any sexual contact between father and daughter. In *La Manekine* and *Lion de Bourges* the severed hand is thrown out of a window and swallowed by a fish; in *La Figlia del Re di Dacia* the heroine buries it; in *La Belle Hélène* it is carried by one of the heroine's twin sons till he is reunited with his mother. In *El Victorial* and the Uliva stories, the heroine takes her hand with her when she is exposed.

There is similar variation in accounts of the restoration of the heroine's hand, which is usually depicted as a miracle performed through the agency of the Pope or a saint, or the Virgin in the Uliva stories. The timing of the miraculous healing depends on what happened to the hands after the mutilation. *El Victorial* is unusual in introducing the healing very early on: when the heroine is exposed at sea with her hands in a basin, the Virgin soon comes to her in a vision and heals her. The Virgin performs the same miracle in the Uliva play when Uliva has taken refuge in a nunnery after her initial exposure. In *La Figlia del Re di Dacia* it happens just a little later, when the heroine is about to marry the Duke of Austria. But more frequently the restoration is connected to the recognition and reunion scene at the end of the story. In *La Manekine* the hand is found at Rome in a fountain; the Pope is able to reattach it, and the miracle is celebrated by a banquet in which they eat the fish which had swallowed it, which has also miraculously arrived at Rome. In *Lion de Bourges* the hand is found in a fish which the cook is already preparing for dinner.[43] In *La Belle Hélène* one of the heroine's sons, the future St Martin, restores the hand, which had been carried around for many years by his brother. In *Alixandre* the heroine is healed by a miracle, without any human agency: God restores her hands when she tries unsuccessfully to help the priest

---

[43] Both versions recall the famous classical story of Polycrates' ring, which appeared in various forms in medieval stories (including the Gregorius legend).

performing the mass in the convent where she has found refuge (just after this she is reunited with her husband). In every case the healing is associated with Christian power, whether the agent is human or divine; this final miracle shows the fruits of chastity and faith in divine providence, and cancels out the sinful attempt at incest at the beginning.

Why should the mutilation of the heroine be a feature of so many medieval Incestuous Father stories?[44] It is certainly not common in other medieval narratives of adventure, and I only know one example of the mutilation of a male protagonist which is at all comparable.[45] Mutilation in the Flight from Incest stories could be seen as a kind of secular martyrdom, a torture which does not lead to death and which proves to be reversible through a miracle; Roussel notes that St Anastasia had her hands and feet cut off.[46] It could also be seen as the equivalent of the rigorous penance performed by the hero in some stories of mother–son incest. Gregorius undergoes a much more painful penance than his mother, although no more guilty than she; the Flight from Incest heroine suffers much more than her villainous father, even though she is entirely innocent. Penance for Gregorius and Albanus involves leaving the world of their own free will, but the Flight from Incest heroine has to remain very much part of it; her mutilation is not always voluntary, and she has even less to feel guilty about than those who unknowingly commit incest. In many versions the mutilation is explained as the daughter's method of deterring her father by getting rid of the hands with which he fell in love, or by destroying her exact resemblance to her mother, or

---

[44] Mutilation of the hands, which was a common form of judicial punishment in the Middle Ages, does occur in a number of Accused Queen folktales mentioned by Schlauch, in some of which the heroine's persecutor is a stepmother or sister-in-law (*Chaucer's Constance*, 26–32), and also in Basile's story of Penta who was propositioned by her brother; but it seems to be most persistently associated with the Incestuous Father theme. The circumstances of the mutilation are interestingly different in the German folktale 'The Girl Without Hands', where the father is foolish but innocent (see *Grimm's Tales*, trans. Mannheim, 113–18). Here the father has inadvertently promised his daughter to the devil, who is foiled in his attempt to collect her by the girl's purity; the devil orders the reluctant father to cut off his daughter's hands, but the stumps are washed clean by her tears and so the devil loses his claim to her.

[45] It occurs in *Tristan de Nanteuil* (ed. Sinclair); here the man in question is in fact the transgendered heroine Blanchandin(e) whose hand, cut off in battle by a pagan, is miraculously restored later by her son, the future St Gilles.

[46] Roussel, *Conter de geste*, 61.

by making herself unfit to be queen.[47] The logic of this move is questionable; the king or noble who later falls in love with the fair stranger and marries her is not deterred by her deformity.[48] Indeed it is not mentioned in the context of her marriage either by the king's lords, who might have been expected to worry about it, or by the jealous mother-in-law, who is concerned about the unknown origins and social status of her son's bride, rather than her deformity. I know only one version in which the forged letter reports that the newborn child has no hands (*Alixandre*), though this seems an obvious charge to make.

Some critics have suggested that the heroine's self-mutilation is a punishment for her suppressed incestuous desire. Otto Rank, an early Freudian, saw it as punishment for masturbation as a substitute for sex with the father, though there is of course no explicit (or even implicit) suggestion of this in the texts; Fenster argues that in *La Manekine* mutilation represents a form of castration, 'a self-inflicted punishment for forbidden desire'.[49] Several other interpretations seem to me equally plausible and less anachronistic. From a feminist perspective, the mutilation could be seen as a triumph for paternal tyranny in that although the heroine's hymen remains intact, her father's incestuous desire does make her bleed and causes her to lose a precious part of her body (though it is not irreplaceable, as the hymen is). The heroine is not actually raped, but she is symbolically and also physically violated. The image of her bleeding wrist could be seen as comparable to the image in the opening of the Apollonius story when Antiochus rapes his daughter

[47] In *Der König von Reussen* she cuts off her hair instead. Roussel notes that St Lucy and St Bridget are both said to have presented their eyes to a suitor who had admired them (*Conter de geste*, 209).

[48] Fenster makes this point in 'Beaumanoir's *La Manekine*', 51 n. 17. In this text the king does wonder whether Joie has lost her hand as a punishment for some crime, but quickly rejects this explanation (1550–3). What appear to us to be failures of logic are often turned into positive features in stories of this kind: in Basile's story of Penta, the handless heroine becomes maid of honour to a queen and uses her feet to thread needles and brush her mistress' hair!

[49] Rank, *Incest Theme*, 317 and 322; the closest that the medieval texts come to a directly sexual explanation is the vision in *La Figlia del Re di Dacia*, in which the heroine is ordered to cut off the hand with which she had been forced to touch her father 'in the shameful place'. See also Fenster, 'Beaumanoir's *La Manekine*', 50. Comparing the stories of Cinderella and King Lear, Dundes argues that in the original story the daughter wants to eliminate and replace her mother, but that since the desire to marry her father is taboo, the story is reworked with the father as the initiator of the incest ('"To Love My Father All"', 236).

and leaves her dripping blood onto her bedroom floor (*HA*, ch. 1). Mutilation may also be seen as representing the heroine's forced alienation from the society in which she has grown up. If she gives in to her father, she will become a queen, but will be spiritually mutilated, as she herself recognizes. His desire to keep her for himself mutilates her socially by denying her a conventional exogamic marriage. Her refusal to yield to him (or to give him her hand— Dundes detects a macabre pun here) mutilates her in a different way: she cannot remain at court, a witness to his illicit desire and his failure to fulfil it, so she is deprived of status and home. Whether she is exiled or whether she takes refuge in flight, it is her fate to wander about unprotected, a very unusual and dangerous situation for an unmarried noblewoman. Physical violence is frequently associated with incest stories. When the incestuous relationship is consummated and a child is born, it is often killed or exposed (and sometimes mutilated before the exposure, like Oedipus). Roussel points out that in *exempla* the sequence of incest followed by infanticide, parricide,m or attempted suicide shows how deeply the sinner is mired in sin.[50] But in the Flight from Incest stories the violence serves to emphasize the innocence and purity of the heroine.[51]

Schlauch comments that in fairy tales a mutilation frequently has the function of providing evidence that the victim really has been put to death (as in the Offa version of the story, the earliest known literary account in medieval Europe), and argues that this is the source of the Maiden without Hands motif; the idea that the beauty of the heroine's hands makes her father fall in love with her is very late, in Schlauch's view.[52] Though the Maiden without Hands plot does not appear in classical literary sources apart from the *Clementine Recognitions*, so far as I am aware, there is a very suggestive incident involving incest and mutilation of hands in

---

[50] Roussel, 'Aspects du père', 49–50. *Dux Moraud* (discussed later in this chapter) is a striking example of this pattern of incest followed by other kinds of violence.

[51] As Wesselofsky pointed out long ago, there is a sly subversion of the convention of the virginal or chaste heroine in Boccaccio's story of Alatiel (*Decameron*, 2. 7), who undergoes a lengthy and sensational series of adventures during which she sleeps with many men, but at the end manages to persuade the bridegroom to whom she was journeying at the beginning of her ordeals that she is still a virgin. See his introduction to *Novella della Figlia del Re di Dacia*, XCII (repr. as 'La Favola della Fanciulla Perseguitata', in Veselovskij-Sade, *La Fanciulla Perseguitata*, ed. Avalle, 100–1).

[52] Schlauch, *Chaucer's Constance*, 17.

Herodotus' account of Egypt.[53] King Mykerinus, son of Cheops the pyramid builder and generally an admirable ruler himself, seduced his own daughter; when she killed herself out of grief, he had her buried in a sarcophagus shaped like a golden cow. His wife is said to have ordered the hands of all the maids who acted as accomplices to be cut off, but Herodotus finds this tale unconvincing; he suggests that it arose because the statues of female companion figures in the tomb of Mykerinus' daughter had lost their arms.[54] It seems unlikely that broken statuary could have been the source of the theme which later became so widespread in folklore and in literature too, but this early tale of father–daughter incest does suggest that mutilation of the hands may originally have been a punishment (whether of the victim or of accomplices), or perhaps a threat.[55] If this is so, the *Clementine Recognitions* might represent a second phase of the tradition, in which the mutilation is performed by the victim herself out of grief for the tragedies she has experienced, even though she did not yield to her incestuous persecutor. Later still, in the thirteenth-century Flight from an Incestuous Father narratives in which incest is threatened but not actually consummated, explanations for the mutilation were ingeniously multiplied, as we have seen.[56] A link between incest and mutilation continues into modern times: young female incest victims often mutilate themselves in some way, out of a sense of guilt or as a sign of disgust with their own bodies or their sexuality.[57] Medieval

[53] Herodotus, *Histories*, 2. 129–31.

[54] Rank mentions this passage, and remarks that it is curious that the mother should have been the instigator of the mutilation (*Incest Theme*, 372); this is not the case in any of the medieval versions. Rooth mentions the story too, and notes that the sarcophagus in which Mykerinus interred his daughter could be equated with the wooden hiding-box (or wooden dress) which occurs in many Cinderella stories (*Cinderella Cycle*, 118–19). Roussel associates the wooden cow with the animal skin worn by the heroine in folktales like 'Peau d'Âne', but he is especially struck by the antiquity of the link between father–daughter incest and mutilation (*Conter de Geste*, 146).

[55] In classical myth Philomela's tongue was cut out by her brother-in-law Tereus to prevent her revealing that he had raped her; in a similar episode in Shakespeare's *Titus Andronicus* the villainous rapists cut off their luckless victim's hands as well as her tongue.

[56] In *La Belle Hélène* the mutilation is no longer linked to the attempted incest, but instead is a consequence of the mother-in-law's hostility to the heroine, as Suard notes in 'Chanson de geste', 368–9.

[57] See for instance Shapiro, 'Self-Mutilation'. In a recent novel, *The Handless Maiden* by Loranne Brown, an incest victim accidentally shoots herself in the hand as she struggles with her abusive grandfather, and the hand has to be amputated. The rest of the

writers do not seem to have been interested in this sort of psychological response to threatened or consummated incest, but one may
wonder if the widespread literary linking of the Maiden without
Hands and Flight from Incest motifs did in fact have some basis in
real life.

The third important variable element in this group of narratives
is the fate of the Incestuous Father. In the *Ystoria Regis
Franchorum* he is never mentioned again after his daughter's flight;
in the *Vitae Duorum Offarum* he is never mentioned again after he
has forged the letter ordering her death. In some versions he dies
early on in the story; in *Le Comte d'Anjou* he starves himself to
death. In *Yde et Olive* he becomes ill from chagrin after his daughter's flight, but does meet the transformed Yde before he dies and is
reconciled with her.[58] In many texts, however, the father not only
regrets the lust which drove his daughter away, but also seeks formal
absolution for his sin. In *Alixandre* his repentance is expressed
quite early on, when his new son-in-law arrives to ask if the shocking story told by his bride can be true;[59] Alixandre tells his court
that he is unwilling to give a feast because he can never be happy, as
a result of the wrong he has done his daughter. At the end of the
story he comes to visit the reunited couple, hands over his kingdom
to them, and enters religious life, but he makes no public confession. More commonly, however, the repentant father goes to Rome
to seek the Pope's forgiveness, and inevitably this happens at the
very moment when the heroine's husband also comes to Rome,
where she already is, so that there is a general family reunion (as in
La Manekine).

In the story of Apollonius and in the *Clementine Recognitions* it
is the husband's public confession or his recital of his past history
that brings about the reunion with his wife, and thus with his
child(ren). In the medieval Flight from Incest stories, in contrast, it
is often the father's public confession that brings about reunion
with his daughter and her new family. In *La Manekine* it is striking
that it is only after the reunion with her father that Joie regains her

novel is largely concerned with the effect of this amputation on her emotional and pro-
fessional life; this was not the concern of medieval writers.

[58] This detail does not appear in the 13th-cent. French poem, but is included in an
early printed French text and in the 16th-cent. English translation.

[59] This is an extremely unusual detail: in most versions the heroine refuses to identify
herself to her new husband or to explain her distressed circumstances.

hand; Fenster suggests that the presence of her father is necessary for the establishing of her identity, which has been a mystery throughout her travels.[60] It is also possible that reconciliation with her father represents the re-establishment of the proper social order, and that this in turn is symbolized by the restoration of her hand.[61] In the normal course of events her father would have arranged her marriage (Apollonius does this as soon as he redis-covers his lost daughter); so his meeting with his son-in-law and grandchild is a sort of retroactive validation of his daughter's mar-riage, and also of her status as his heiress. In *La Filla de l'Emperador Contasti* it is only after the heroine has revealed her-self to her father that he starts to do penance. But in *La Belle Hélène* Antoine repents long before the reconciliation with his daughter, and indeed becomes a sort of missionary for good pater-nal behaviour. In his search for Hélène he happens to go to Bavaria, where the pagan king is in love with his own daughter and has been advised by a demonic idol to marry her; Antoine destroys the idol and converts the country to Christianity. This determined rejection of his old sin suggests that he is already absolved long before he is reunited with his daughter. In some versions the reunion is precipi-tated by the unwitting encounter of grandfather and grandson (in many cases a repetition of the child's role in his mother's reunion with her husband). In *Emaré* when the heroine's repentant father comes to Rome to seek absolution, he feels strangely drawn to his unrecognized grandson. Here kin attraction is legitimate; it may recall Artus' previous attraction to his daughter, the boy's mother, but this time there is no question of any sexual advances. The plot repetition does not lead to a vicious circle, but rather to the happy ending of appropriate family interaction and proper patrilineal dynastic succession. One might feel that these fathers are lucky to have been prevented from committing incest, and to have been allowed to live to the end of the story and obtain absolution for their lust. It does seem surprising that in none of these versions is there any comment or moral at the end about the incestuous pater-nal desire which set the whole plot in motion.

This brings me to the fourth significant element of variation, the question of context and tone, particularly in relation to the ending.

---

[60] Fenster, 'Beaumanoir's *La Manekine*', 55–6.

[61] It must be noted, however, that in a number of texts which include the mutilation, the healing occurs without the presence of the father.

It is true that there is always a happy ending in these stories: the heroine is reunited with her husband and restored to her proper status, and her innocence and virtue are affirmed. The secular nature of this ending is emphasized by the circumstances of the recognition scene; although the Pope (or some other male religious figure) is often present, he seldom actually controls the process of recognition.[62] In *Alixandre* the husband happens to see his child playing in the convent, and wonders who his mother can be; he is then told the story of the mutilated stranger, and recognizes her as his lost wife. Sometimes the heroine recognizes her husband first, and uses her son to make her presence known to him: this scenario is used in *Emaré* and the *Ystoria Regis Franchorum* (and by Chaucer in *The Man of Law's Tale*).[63] In some versions the husband recognizes the wedding ring with which the child is playing, as for instance in *La Manekine* and *Lion de Bourges*. These two motifs are very cleverly combined in *La Filla de l'Emperador Contasti*: the heroine recognizes her husband when he comes to Rome and sends her son to him with her wedding ring, the twin of the one her husband wears. The use of both the child and the wedding ring emphasizes secular family values; there is no question of the protagonists here abandoning the world for religious life. Even when miracles occur and a religious figure comments on them, in this story a happy ending means the resumption of family life and secular power and status.[64] It also signals a return to the proper workings of patriarchy and patriliny, in that the husband is reunited with his heir (and so is the once-incestuous father, if he is present). And of course this heir is always male; as in the Apollonius story, a male heir assures return

---

[62] An unusual exception to this rule is the version in Gobi's *Scala coeli*, in which the Bishop, who himself turns out to be the heroine's long-lost brother, is the first to guess the relationship between husband and wife and so brings about the reunion.

[63] This is one of the elements which makes some critics argue that the heroines are not merely passive, but take control of their own fates (see n. 19 above); it seems to me a very minor detail, and does not occur in many versions.

[64] Chaucer's *Man of Law's Tale* is unusual in this respect. His heroine is not at all happy at first about being reunited with her husband and father; when her husband dies a year later she returns with apparent relief to her father, who makes no effort to find another husband for her, and they devote the rest of their lives to virtuous activities such as almsgiving. I think Chaucer is commenting here on the patriarchal and misogynistic conventions of romance: see my 'Contextualizing Chaucer's Constance'. Bullón-Fernández shows how differently Gower and Chaucer treat the relationship of Constance and her father, and how Gower suggests a more incestuous link between them, though she sees this as a metaphor for Church–State relations: see her 'Engendering Authority'. See also Scanlon, 'Riddle of Incest', 134–41.

to normal (patriarchal) life and allows the dynasty to continue without risk of the incest that threatened to disrupt the social order at the beginning of the story, when the widowed father had no heir but his daughter.[65] As Evelyn Birge Vitz remarks about another medieval story of the ordeals of an innocent heroine, *La Fille du Comte de Pontieu*, 'the family is, more than any individual protagonist, the real Subject here'.[66]

The exemplary potential of the Incestuous Father story was spotted early by medieval writers. In the *Scala coeli* of Gobi, produced in the 1330s, the story appears under the rubric 'De Castitate' (about chastity). Beaumanoir had already presented his Joie/Manekine as a sort of Job who resists despair as her faith is tested over and over again in spite of her absolute innocence. Trust in divine providence seems to be a feature of many of the versions, though it is rare for this to be an explicit moral at the end, as it is in *La Manekine*; Christian charity is also stressed in Maillart's *Roman du Comte d'Anjou*. In many other versions the presence of the Pope or some other religious figure (St Martin, a hermit) at the final reunion lends an exemplary aspect to the ending and to the whole story—but it is not always clear what the point of the *exemplum* might be. As we have seen, the incestuous father sometimes reappears, contrite, at the end to obtain absolution from the Pope; but in none of these versions is there an explicit moral about the dangers of incestuous lust, and in a number of them the father dies before the end, leaving the emphasis on the reunion of husband and wife. Sometimes the husband comes to Rome in search of absolution too—for the presumed drowning of his wife in *Emaré*, or for

---

[65]   The importance of a male heir is emphasized when the heroine is falsely accused of bearing a monster. In most versions, including *La Manekine*, the heroine has one boy, but in *La Belle Hélène* and the *Ystoria Regis Franchorum* she has two (in *Lion de Bourges*, unusually, she has a boy and a girl). As Schlauch points out, twins might easily have provoked a charge of adultery—witness the mother's fear at the birth of twins in Marie de France's *Lai le Fresne*—but the wicked mother-in-law's accusation is almost always that she has produced a monster (*Chaucer's Constance*, 21 ff. and 77 ff.). Schlauch argues that the charge of animal birth is the oldest and the closest to folklore; later comes the charge of infidelity based on the birth of more than one child, and the simple charge of infidelity is relatively modern. Fenster claims that animal birth was thought to be a consequence of incest, and argues that the heroine of *La Manekine* is accused as if she had committed incest ('Beaumanoir's *La Manekine*', 53–4). However, she gives only one medieval example of this view, and I have found very little evidence for it in literary and historical sources, though it may in fact have been quite widespread (see my comments in Ch. 1).

[66]   Vitz, *Medieval Narrative*, 102.

killing his mother in *La Filla de l'Emperador Contasti*. But as he is not responsible for his wife's death, and his mother richly deserved hers, this hardly represents a significant moral. The author of the *Comedia sine nomine* went to all the trouble of relocating the plot in an entirely classical pagan setting, only to conclude with a comparison between the theatre and the Christian comedy of human life: he stresses that at the end of life, God alone can take off the masks and reveal the truth that the rich man is really poor, the strong weak, the wise foolish, the lord a slave, etc. Here again the moral contains no explicit comment on incest.

The Flight from Incest stories are presented in a clearly Christian context, apart from the *Comedia sine nomine*; faith and divine providence sustain the heroine through her many ordeals, and there is a strong Marian element in some versions.[67] This plot does twice appear as a saint's life, though in one case it is only the opening episode which is used to emphasize the virtue of the saint and the villainy of her father and murderer. According to a life written in the mid-thirteenth century, the Irish saint Dympna fled from the incestuous advances of her pagan father, accompanied by a faithful priest, and lived as a hermit near Antwerp; her furious father followed her there and killed her with his own hands.[68] In a later Italian legend, however, St. Uliva is given the full story with all the usual journeys and persecutions, considerably embellished with minor characters and scenes. This version was composed at the end of the Middle Ages when a married woman with children could aspire to sanctity, though in fact Uliva does little to deserve the title of saint, and the plot is very similar to non-hagiographic versions.[69] But these stories are also secular family romances, a popular medieval genre; they centre on a noble or royal family of three generations, beginning with a cautionary tale of abnormal

[67] The heroines of some versions have symbolic names such as Emaré (generally interpreted as 'afflicted', 'troubled', though Rickert thinks it means 'pure' or 'refined'), and Joie or Joieuse ('joy', 'joyful'—during her travels Joieuse, the heroine of *Lion de Bourges*, calls herself Tristouse, 'sad'); but they do not explicitly represent Christian virtues. In the *Man of Law's Tale* Chaucer does not call his heroine Constance, as Trivet and Gower do in the analogues, but rather Custance; he seems to draw back from explicit personification of the virtue.

[68] This legend is apparently based on stories circulating after the discovery of Dympna's corpse in the 1230s; a cult grew up based on miraculous cures for lunatics and epileptics.

[69] As d'Ancona points out in his introduction to the play (VII), it is not really a saint's life at all, but simply another witness to the fashion for stories of persecuted maidens.

family relations which leads to separation and ordeals, and ending with a happy family reunion and return to courtly life for the long-suffering heroine. Thus the Flight from Incest plot can be treated as *exemplum* and as romance, as miracle story and as family saga.

One of the most significant variables among the versions is the context in which they appear and the generic conventions they display. The plot is used relatively rarely as an explicit moral *exemplum*; it appears more frequently as a kind of romance, is sometimes subsumed into a larger series of romance or epic adventures, and is even found in several chronicles. In one version, *La Belle Hélène*, the adventures of all the main characters are repeated and multiplied with ridiculous frequency so that it becomes a very complex family narrative with numerous protagonists and plot strands including many journeys, wars, crises, and triumphs which are not present in other versions, plus many elaborate subplots involving minor characters encountered by the protagonists during their endless travels and adventures. The timespan is also unusual here; by the time Hélène is restored to her family, her twin sons are adults, and one has married and begotten her grandson, the future St Brice. Roussel considers that *La Belle Hélène* belongs more to the epic than the romance tradition; he notes that the usual emphasis on the individual piety of the heroine is completely overshadowed by an emphasis on saints and sanctuaries and on militant crusading and conversion, an emphasis which is much more typical of *chanson de geste* than of romance.[70] The incestuous father reforms himself early on and converts the pagan King of Bavaria who was about to marry his own daughter; one of Hélène's sons is St Martin and the other is the father of St Brice. Hélène often seems quite a marginal character in the midst of all the hectic activity by the other characters. *Yde et Olive* is also part of a larger cycle, for it is one of the continuations of *Huon of Bordeaux*: Yde is Huon's granddaughter; her incestuous father is the spotless hero of the previous romance in the sequence, *La Chanson de Clarisse et Florent*, which describes his courtship and marriage; and the series continues with the adventures of Croissant, the son begotten by Yde after her miraculous sex change. Perhaps the most startling integration of an Incestuous Father romance into a larger text is *Lion de Bourges*.

---

[70] Roussel, 'Chanson de geste', 571.

The account of Joieuse's ordeals closely resembles *La Manekine*, but it is interwoven with a very complicated *chanson de geste* narrative, and the familiar episodes of the Incestuous Father plot are constantly interrupted by the complex chivalric adventures and love stories developed during the twenty-seven thousand lines before Herpin de Chypre, a character who has already been introduced and has behaved admirably thus far, is suddenly transformed into an incestuous father.[71] The Incestuous Father plot ends when Herpin and his son-in-law Olivier go to Rome and are reunited with Joieuse, whose hand is found by the cook at her hostel and reattached by the Pope, just as in *La Manekine*; but this is not the end of the entire narrative, for other male characters continue to have martial adventures. Of course the focus on the suffering heroine is greatly diminished by this treatment; one wonders why the incest plot was introduced at all. Like *Yde et Olive*, this text bears witness, if more were needed, to the popularity of the Incestuous Father theme, which could be inserted in the middle of chivalric narratives of love and adventure.

In a number of versions the Flight from Incest story is associated with England, starting with the life of Offa, and some critics have argued for an English origin for the story, though it seems likely that an oral version had long been widely known before the extant versions were written down.[72] In three fifteenth-century narratives it is associated with the historical rivalry between England and France. In von Bühel's *Königstochter von Frankreich*, the French heroine flees from the unwelcome advances of her royal father to London, where she marries the King of England. After the usual vicissitudes and reunion scene with husband and father at Rome, she returns to London, and soon inherits the throne of France on her father's death. Her husband and son are summoned away to war, and she dies. Another king takes over France, and her husband fights for his son's rights, winning Calais and two other towns (Calais was for centuries a bone of contention between England and France); the poem ends with the comment that now the readers/audience know how the Hundred Years War began. The

---

[71] On the relationship between *La Manekine* and *Lion de Bourges* see Fenster, 'Joie mêlée', and Suard, 'Chanson de geste'.

[72] See for instance Rickert, 'Old English Offa'. D'Ancona suggested long ago that Beaumanoir might have first encountered the story at the English court: see his introduction to the Uliva story, *Rappresentazione*, XXVII n. 4.

German poem has all the usual episodes except the mutilation of the heroine's hands. A more abbreviated account is given in the Spanish *El Victorial*, where the heroine is the daughter of the Duke of Guienne and a French princess. She also marries the King of England, and then receives the news that the King of France has died without an heir. She and her husband demand her father's dukedom, which had been left to the King of France. This is the cause of the war which is still in progress, says the writer.[73] The Spanish version includes the mutilation of the heroine's hands (by a servant at her own request), but omits the usual Calumniated Wife section of the story: there is no wicked mother-in-law, no second exposure, and no reunion with her husband. A much more elaborate version including all the standard episodes is told by Bartolomeo Fazio in his *De origine inter Gallos et Britannos belli historia*; the level of detail is appropriate to a romance narrative, but as in the German and Spanish versions, the Incestuous Father story is used to explain a political situation, the traditional hostility between France and England which reached a peak during the Hundred Years War. The French throne is presented as rightfully due to England by virtue of the marriage of a French princess to an English king, an argument frequently made by the English in the later Middle Ages. But it is not clear why Spanish, German, and Italian writers should support this argument, and bolster it by condemning the French king as an incestuous father.

For medieval authors and readers, the main value and the interest of the Flight from Incest stories seem to have been the series of vicissitudes endured by the heroine, rather than the specific incident which motivates her flight or exile, the incestuous proposition from her father. Stories of separated families of various kinds were very popular in the later Middle Ages; there seems to be an interesting gender distinction in the forms that they generally took.[74] When the protagonists have a child who must be exposed because of illegitimate birth, the child is almost always male, and the subsequent

---

[73] The choice of Guienne as a setting is not a random one; it was a part of Aquitaine which was controlled alternately by the French and the English during the High Middle Ages. Louis IX gave it to Henry III of England in 1259; the French retook it in the early years of the Hundred Years War; it was ceded to England in 1360 by the Treaty of Bretigny, but reclaimed by the French in the following century, and was formally united with the French crown in 1472.

[74] For further discussion see Archibald, 'Contextualizing Chaucer's Constance'.

adventures centre on his development as a knight and his reunion with his parents (for instance *Sir Eglamour*). The mother may seem a major character at the beginning of the narrative, but subsequently she plays only a small part, overshadowed by the chivalric exploits of her son and her lover, whose duel and recognition scene constitute the climax of the story. If the narrative is to focus on the heroine, her child is legitimate and stays with her. He—for it is always a boy—also stays young; he cannot grow up during the course of the story and rival her by having independent adventures.[75] Heroines cannot have adventures that involve significant action initiated by them; they can only endure various kinds of ordeals, often involving unwanted suitors, and they are often slandered and misunderstood. What could be the catalyst for the lone wanderings of a noble and innocent young woman? If she is already married, she can be rejected, unjustly, by a husband who thinks himself wronged, or by a wicked mother-in-law; if she is not married, she can reject, or be rejected by, the widowed father who has tried to marry her (some texts combine these two motifs). Both these forms proved extremely popular—alarmingly popular, we might think, in terms of medieval tolerance for descriptions of the victimization of innocent women who have committed no fault, and who learn nothing from their experiences except how cruel the world can be, and how faith in God and the Virgin can preserve them through any kind of trouble. We may read these romances today as an indictment of patriarchy, but that is not why they were written or why they were so popular in the later Middle Ages.

One of the reasons for their success may be that this plot offers a way to focus the story on a woman. She cannot play an active role, and must remain virtuous; flight from incest keeps her at centre stage without requiring her to do anything but suffer and endure. Much of what happens in these stories of persecuted maidens is very similar to the adventures of the heroines of the Hellenistic romances of late antiquity; in fact the Greek romances far outdo the medieval ones in the accumulation of disasters which beset the separated lovers or newly-weds.[76] But the focus in these classical

---

[75] *La Belle Hélène* might be regarded as an exception to these rules, since the heroine's twins are separated from her very early on; but the narrative does not stay focused on her, as we have seen.

[76] For a useful survey of these romances which includes discussion of their circulation and influence in the post-classical period see Hägg, *Novel*.

texts is always on a couple; once away from home and separated, both become the playthings of a cruel Fortune which constantly flips them out of the frying pan into the fire and keeps them apart until the very end of the story. In the Greek romances the heroes as well as the heroines may be sold as slaves, bullied, humiliated, tortured, and generally mistreated, and sometimes they too have to struggle to preserve their chastity (not always successfully). In contrast, the medieval Flight from Incest stories can hardly be said to have heroes, for the role of the heroine's husband is small and far from heroic; and the heroine's adventures are generally restricted to two or three unprovoked crises involving sexuality, with long periods of inaction in between.

This type of story seems to have a good deal in common with what Braswell has called 'The Man Tried by Fate', the type of story to which the Eustace and Isumbras legends belong (another female version is the Griselda story); the fashion for this sort of story may well have been influenced by the ever-popular Apollonius of Tyre story, which was similarly adapted to fit the conventions of both *exemplum* and romance.[77] These stories seem to have satisfied a widespread medieval desire to hear about the caprices of Fortune and the human ability to endure, Job-like, till the evildoers are sated or destroyed, and the protagonist's family is reunited and restored to prosperity. Chaucer's *Man of Law's Tale* seems to me to be a shrewd comment on the implications for women of this kind of plot. It emphasizes the pointless suffering inflicted on women by men, repeatedly draws attention to the divine protection afforded the saint-like Custance, and rejects the feel-good happy ending of most versions for a bleaker view of women's lives and human existence in general. As Kolve has shown, the helpless heroine adrift at sea was often understood allegorically in the Middle Ages as the Christian soul, beset by trials but sustained by faith. This interpretation may have occurred to medieval readers of the Flight from Incest narratives, but it is rarely made explicit in the texts. A taste for stories of persecuted but innocent maidens seems to have been widespread in the Middle Ages, as indeed in later centuries and up to the present day; Avalle argues that there was a continuous tradition of

---

[77] See Braswell, ' "Sir Isumbras" ', 133 and Hornstein, 'Eustace-Constance-Florence-Griselda'. Both Apollonius and Griselda are compared with Job in medieval texts.

Persecuted Maiden stories from the Middle Ages to the novels of the Marquis de Sade.[78] In the introduction to *Justine*, Sade dismisses as banal the usual mode of romance, the triumph of virtue over vice; he boasts that he will show instead the triumph of vice, though he hopes that the end result will still be to make the reader cry 'Ô combien ces tableaux du crime me rendent fière d'aimer la vertu! Comme elle est sublime dans les larmes! Commes les malheurs l'embellissent!' (Oh, how these renderings of crime make me proud of my love for Virtue! How sublime does it appear through tears! How 'tis embellished by misfortunes!)[79] Medieval readers too seem to have enjoyed descriptions of Virtue embellished by misfortunes, but of course these medieval heroines endure their series of crises and disasters less abjectly than Sade's luckless victims. Joie and the others are sustained by Christian faith and fortitude, and by occasional miracles; the threats to their chastity (never more than threats) are brief and occur at infrequent intervals, and retribution usually strikes down their assailants sooner or later unless they see the error of their ways (as some of the incestuous fathers eventually do). In *Justine*, on the other hand, it is the poor heroine who is killed by lightning; her wicked sister interprets this fate allegorically as an awful warning, and retreats immediately to a convent. Surprisingly, perhaps, the medieval tradition prefers the conventional happy ending in which the long-suffering heroine is restored, like Job, to prosperity and blissful family life.

CONSUMMATED INCEST

When Beatrice Cenci was tried in the late 1590s for the murder of her father, it was reported that he had attempted to seduce her by arguing that it was well known that all children born of father–daughter liaisons became saints.[80] Ironically, he seems to have ignored the fact that saints born of incest sometimes kill their

---

[78] See his introduction to Veselovskij-Sade, *La Fanciulla Perseguitata*.

[79] *Justine*, ed. Delon, ii. 129–30; trans. Seaver and Wainhouse, 455–6.

[80] This detail is included in Shelley's own translation of a contemporary account of the death of the Cenci family (*Cenci*, ed. Woodberry, 133): 'He tried to persuade the poor girl, by an enormous heresy, that children born of the commerce of a father with his daughter were all saints, and that the saints who obtained the highest places in Paradise had been thus born.'

fathers (see the discussion of St Albanus in the previous chapter). One wonders which stories he did have in mind, for in fact father–daughter incest is fairly rare in medieval hagiography. In the Albanus legend it is merely the curtain-raiser, necessary to the story, but only as a prologue, like the sibling incest in *Gregorius*; in both these legends it is the discovery of the unwitting marriage of mother and son which is the peripeteia and the cause of contrition and penance for the whole family, and of ultimate sanctity for the male protagonist. Contrition for incest with a daughter does not seem to have been considered grounds for sanctity (nor indeed was contrition for incest with a father), except in the doubtful case of St Metro. The *Vita* by Bishop Ratherius of Verona (*c*.962) refers to unspecified sins for which this saint performed a rigorous penance not unlike that of Gregorius, but the specific charge of unwitting incest with a daughter appears only in a late source which may well have been influenced by the popular lives of Gregorius and Albanus.[81]

In the stories of the births of saints which do include father–daughter incest, the father is well aware of what he is doing. Unwitting father–daughter incest is extremely rare in medieval literature, it seems, though it cannot have been so rare in real life (Minucius Felix's main criticism of the practice of exposing unwanted babies, quoted at the beginning of the previous chapter, was the danger of unwitting incest with an unrecognized child later in life). Father–daughter incest does occur in some late versions of the *exemplum* of the mother who is reluctant to confess having had intercourse with her son (see the discussion in Chapter 3); but the fact that the extra twist in which her son later unwittingly marries his daughter/sister only appears in a few late versions of the story suggests that this second incest may have been added on the model of popular hagiographic texts such as the stories of Albanus and Gregorius. This version of the *exemplum* is unique among medieval incest stories in that the father and daughter never discover their relationship and are not separated, so they never do penance; there seem to be no disastrous consequences apart from the agony of the mother, who is all too aware of their true relationship and of her responsibility for their situation.

---

[81] See *AASS* Maii II, 306; Dorn, *Der Sündige Heilige*, 80–3; Mölk, 'Zur Vorgeschichte'. Several Irish saints were said to be the product of father–daughter incest, for instance St Cuimmin.

The only other example known to me of unwitting
father–daughter incest is equally unconventional in its outcome: it
is part of the saga of a Norse hero, Hrólf.[82] The story begins two
generations before his birth:

> Queen Olof of Germany is raped by an enemy, King Helgi, in
> revenge for a previous dishonour; she names the daughter she
> bears Yrsa after a dog and gives her to peasants to rear, since she
> feels no affection for her. One day Yrsa encounters her natural
> father who is disguised as a beggar; he falls in love with her, car-
> ries her off against her will, and marries her (neither knows her
> true parentage). Olof hears what has happened but does nothing
> to stop the marriage. Yrsa and her father are happy together, and
> their son Hrólf becomes a famous hero. Olof, irritated by the
> fame of father and son, visits them, and when Yrsa enquires
> about her parentage, the Queen maliciously reveals the awful
> truth. Yrsa is horrified and returns to her mother, and later mar-
> ries again; but Helgi is distraught at losing her and anxious to
> maintain the marriage. He is killed when he tries to retrieve Yrsa
> from her new husband.

Infant girls are very rarely exposed in medieval literature, and this
is a unique motive for the exposure.[83] The story dates from a pre-
Christian era. There is no question of contrition or penance here,
and the very different reactions of father and daughter suggest considerable ambivalence about the incest taboo. Although Helgi's
death is in a sense the result of his incestuous marriage, there is no
explicit comment that he deserved his fate. No stigma is attached to
Hrólf, and unlike Gregorius he feels no responsibility for the sins of
his parents. The rest of the saga is concerned with his secular
adventures, not his spiritual progress.

The absence of narratives about potential or actual incest between
unrecognized fathers and daughters is striking.[84] Such stories would

---

[82] *Hrólfs Saga Kraka*, chs. 6–12, trans. Jones, 234–50. This saga describes events in the
6th cent., though it was probably composed in the late Middle Ages and is preserved in
a 17th-cent. manuscript. I am indebted for knowledge of this text to Boswell, *Kindness
of Strangers*, 387.

[83] In Marie de France's *Lai le Fresne* the heroine is exposed at birth because she is a
twin; I discuss this story in relation to the Middle English adaptation in my '*Lai le
Freine*'.

[84] They are rare in folktale too; see Johnson and Price-Williams, *Oedipus Ubiquitous*,
59–61. This is surprising; the plot works very effectively in Max Frisch's tragic novel,
Homo Faber.

have offered oppportunities for mutual attraction such as Gower
describes in his version of the Apollonius story, when the despairing
Apollonius encounters his daughter Thaise (Tarsia), whom he has
not seen since her birth and believes to be dead (*CA* 8. 1702–3; see
discussion in Chapter 2, pp. 98–9):

> Bot of hem tuo a man mai liere
> What is to be so sibb of blod.

Here Gower suggests that it would be quite natural for an unrecognized father and daughter to feel drawn to each other. Apollonius
does indeed love Thaise 'kindely' or naturally, since he is her father;
he is not described as smitten by inappropriate lust. But much more
common is the scenario of the tyrannical father who forces his
daughter into an incestuous affair, which appears both as an *exemplum* and as a subplot in chronicles and romances.[85] These fathers
are villains who sometimes repent of their misdeeds in *exempla*, but
never in romance. In most father–daughter incest stories there is no
doubt about the identity of father and daughter, and there is every
indication that the daughter's feelings are not consulted. At the
beginning of the Apollonius story, Antiochus knows that his daughter is out of bounds, but as Gower's narrator remarks, 'whanne a
man hath welthe at wille, | The fleissh is frele and falleth ofte'
(288–9: When a man has riches to command, the flesh is frail and
often falls). Antiochus' rape of his daughter is brutally depicted: he
leaves her bleeding and so horrified by what has happened that she
determines to kill herself, until her nurse persuades her that she
should yield to her father. Her spirit is totally cowed; she is like a
subject nation, enslaved and abused. Antiochus' private immorality
is mirrored in his public behaviour. He displays similar violence
towards his daughter's many suitors: whether they solve his riddle
or not, they are decapitated, and their heads are impaled over the
gate as a warning to others. He persecutes Apollonius quite
unjustly, and his offer of a reward for the young man, dead or alive,
corrupts even his friends. I showed in an earlier chapter how the

---

[85] One of the earliest medieval examples of consummated father–daughter incest
associated with bad kingship (apart from the *Historia Apollonii*) occurs in the pseudo-
historical *Historia Britonum* attributed to Nennius and probably composed about 830,
when St. Germanus confronts Vortigern over his incest with his daughter, and calls down
fire from heaven to destroy the impenitent king; see *Historia Britonum*, chs. 39–45, ed.
Faral, iii. 30–5.

plot of the Apollonius story introduces a series of fathers who are also kings, and compares their treatment of their daughters and of their subjects. No other medieval text is so rich in incestuous fathers, actual and potential; but there are some other ways of drawing attention to paternal tyranny.

One way is to attribute incestuous behaviour to giants, who are well known for two characteristics: lust and violence. The two are combined in an episode at the beginning of the *Prose Tristan*, as part of the story of Tristan's ancestor Apollo l'Aventureus (a foundling who unwittingly kills his father and marries his mother—see the discussion in Chapter 3).[86] During the very complicated adventures of Apollo's parents, they find refuge in a forest with a giant who puts a riddle to his visitors: he had a fruit tree that he loved very much, but after taking the flower he came to despise the fruit and ate it eagerly. Sador, Apollo's father, solves the riddle: the giant loved his wife very much, loved their daughter even more, seduced her and later killed and ate her (a second riddle solved by Pélias reveals that the giant had eaten his mother too, though apparently he did not seduce her).[87] It is striking to find this story of father–daughter incest combined with a riddle involving eating, as in the Apollonius story (though the prize here is not the giant's daughter in marriage). Furthermore this episode occurs in the middle of the story of the foundling Apollo who later kills his father and marries his mother. It seems that almost all the possible motifs of medieval incest stories are combined here. Another giant who has a child by his own daughter appears in *Doon de Mayence*; he is excommunicated for seven years.[88] But these giants, and Antiochus, are all tyrannical fathers who show no sign of contrition for their sin. The father of Albanus, who is not a tyrant, willingly does penance for seven years to pay for his incest, but as soon as he is reunited with his daughter, they relapse into their old sin and are immediately killed by their son.

In all these stories the daughters remain extremely shadowy. Very little is said about their reactions to the incest, and they do not seem

---

[86] *Le Roman de Tristan*, ed. Curtis, i. 75–84. Synopses of the relevant section are given by Löseth in *Le Roman en prose de Tristan*, 7–10; and by Baumgartner, *Le 'Tristan'*, 2. See also Ménard, *Le Rire*, 510–13; Traxler, 'Observations'; Mickel, 'Tristan's Ancestry'; and Gracia, 'La Preistoria'.

[87] Cannibalism is another characteristic of giants; in classical legend it is often associated with incest (see Ch. 2).   [88] *Doon de Mayence*, 3246–57, ed. Pey.

to have the gumption to defy their fathers or run away. The result is that they usually die violently, often at the same time as their fathers. One very striking exception proves the general rule that stories of consummated father–daughter incest focus on the fathers, who never repent successfully. It is a story popular in exemplary collections and also preserved in the early fifteenth-century English dramatic fragment *Dux Moraud*.[89]

A man seduces his daughter, and the affair continues for several years. When her mother catches them *in flagrante delicto*, the daughter cuts her throat and buries her; she also kills the two children whom she conceives by her father. When he grows old and repents, she cuts his throat too, and then travels far away and lives as a prostitute. Eventually a sermon (in one version by St Augustine) moves her to confess. She dies immediately afterwards. In some versions the people feel she does not deserve Christian burial; but miraculously, roses come out of her mouth, bearing Latin inscriptions testifying to her salvation, and warning that her detractors too must face judgement. In another version, when the priest who has heard her confession asks the congregation to pray for her, a voice from heaven tells him that he and the people should rather ask her to pray for them.

An incestuous daughter who takes the initiative in this alarming way is possible in an *exemplum* because she is intended to be a larger-than-life cautionary tale of vice run wild. This bizarre story of a victimized daughter who turns into a worse monster than her father could be taken as indicative of a widespread medieval attitude towards women, as well as towards incest: carnal desires, to which women are notoriously prone, lead the daughter to a series of horribly violent crimes.[90] Incest is the primary sin which underlies all the later transgressions, each bad enough in itself: matricide, infanticide, parricide, prostitution. On the other hand, this daughter does eventually confess her sins. The story of the repentant prostitute was

---

[89] My synopsis here is a conflation of various versions; *Dux Moraud* consists only of the father's part (ed. Davis). Five analogous *exempla* (including one from the English version of the *Gesta Romanorum*) are printed and discussed by Heuser, '*Dux Moraud*'; see also Homan, 'Two *Exempla*'. As all the exemplary versions end with the daughter's confession and salvation, it is assumed that the play did too.

[90] On the representation of women in exemplary literature see Karras, 'Gendered Sin' and Murray, 'Gendered Souls', and my discussion of knowingly incestuous mothers in Ch. 3.

always popular in the Middle Ages (other well-known examples are Thais, St Mary of Egypt, and Mary Magdalene):[91] but how much more effective it is when the prostitute has also committed the same terrible crimes as Judas and Albanus, with infanticide thrown in too! None of the medieval incestuous heroes behaves quite as badly as the protagonist of *Dux Moraud* and the analogous *exempla*—it is hard to think of any parallel for such violent behaviour until Giovanni in Ford's *'Tis Pity She's a Whore* (1633). The male protagonists of incest stories are often foundlings ignorant of their true identities who marry their mothers (and in some cases kill their fathers) unintentionally; they are allowed to survive for years to do penance, and to be rewarded for it by sanctity. It is striking that like some other women in exemplary incest stories who commit incest knowingly, the daughter in *Dux Moraud* dies as soon as she has confessed, without time to perform some rigorous penance and achieve sanctity; the implication is that she is lucky to have been saved at all, given her monstrous crimes. It may seem surprising that it is a priest or male saint rather than the Virgin who brings this hardened sinner to confession. Perhaps this is further propaganda for the Church, and evidence of pervasive misogyny: however wicked the woman, she is no match for an educated male ecclesiastic.

The incestuous father in *Dux Moraud* is very unusual in that he does repent and confess before his death. It seems surprising that in the Flight from the Incestuous Father stories in which the incest is not consummated, the fathers should (in some cases at least) repent and obtain absolution, as well as reconciliation with their daughters; yet fathers in stories of consummated incest practically never feel the prick of conscience, even though they have so much more to confess. Does this imply that father–daughter incest was perceived by medieval writers as worse than mother–son, or that men are more obdurate sinners? If so, why is father–daughter incest not used as the peripeteia in saints' lives? Is the reappearance of the contrite fathers in some Incestuous Father narratives perhaps typical of the romance desire for a happy ending and a family reunion (here combined in the form of validation and continuation of the royal lineage)? If so, these stories could be seen as comparable to *Sir Eglamour* and *Sir Degaré* with their near-miss mother–son incest and final reunion with the long-lost husband/father—although the foundling heroes in these romances have a very easy time in comparison with the vicissitudes and suffering of the heroines of Incestuous Father stories.

Whether consummated or merely threatened, father–daughter incest seems to have been the most common literary form of incest in the later Middle Ages, at least in extended narratives; mother–son incest is the most common form in brief *exempla*. Today father–daughter incest is generally perceived as the most common form, and like medieval writers we tend to see incestuous fathers as domestic tyrants. For us the charge of child abuse is a very serious one: modern incestuous fathers are unlikely to make a pilgrimage to Rome, but they are often referred to psychiatrists, the modern confessors, and sometimes they are even driven by guilt to commit suicide. In our twenty-first-century view, the problem of incest is frequently entwined with social and psychological issues such as living conditions, marital problems, violence in parents (usually male) as a response to abuse in their own childhoods, and silent acquiescence from mothers who may themselves have been incest victims. Although many of the medieval romances begin with a plausible psychological explanation for the father's incestuous infatuation with his daughter (his wife's death and the strong resemblance between dead mother and beautiful daughter), clearly the main issue is not what makes a man try to seduce his daughter or what effect this may have on the daughter in later life. The heroines never retreat permanently to nunneries; although they are not always eager to marry, the implicit assumption is that they are happy with their husbands, and that the final reunion which returns them to normal family life really is a happy ending. The opening episode of flight from incest is merely the catalyst for the subsequent adventures, though it sets the tone in presenting a vulnerable heroine in a world of powerful men, and in introducing a story about the moral and social disorder which results from abnormal parent–child relationships (excessive paternal, and later also maternal, devotion). In the Shakespearean adaptation of the Apollonius story, *Pericles Prince of Tyre*, Antiochus' liaison with his daughter is succinctly summed up by Gower, the Chorus, as 'Bad child, worse father' (I. i. 27). In medieval stories of consummated incest the moral target is definitely the 'worse father'; often incest is only one aspect of his tyrannical behaviour. Most daughters in these stories are bad only in that they do not seem to have the courage to run away; they are minor characters, anonymous and silent for the most part. The striking exception is of course the ferocious daughter in *Dux Moraud*. But she, like so many women in medieval literature, seems to represent the worst fears of male writers: sexually voracious, murderess of her parents and her children, she is a perfect vehicle for Church misogyny as well as contritionist propaganda. She is not a flesh and blood woman, just as the roses bearing Latin inscriptions which come out of the mouth of her corpse are not real roses.

5
Siblings and Other Relatives

GIOVANNI: Shall then, for that I am her brother born,
  My joys be ever banished from her bed?
  No, Father; in your eyes I see the change
  Of pity and compassion: from your age,
  As from a sacred oracle, distils
  The life of counsel. Tell me, holy man,
  What cure shall give me ease in these extremes?
FRIAR: Repentance, son, and sorrow for this sin —
  For thou hast moved a Majesty above
  With thy unrangèd almost blasphemy.

John Ford, *'Tis Pity She's a Whore*, i. i. 36–44

THE main focus in this chapter will be on the addition of incest to the Arthurian legend in the story of Mordred's birth, though a number of non-Arthurian texts will also be discussed. Sibling incest seems to have been regarded as considerably less heinous than parent–child incest; it is usually a sub-plot rather than a central theme, and often involves minor characters rather than the protagonists.[1] It is therefore harder to detect a pattern of development in the stories I shall be discussing here than in stories of parent–child incest, and this chapter may seem more fragmented than the previous ones. It will end with a brief survey of stories of incest outside the nuclear family in various forms: between more distant blood relatives, between affines (relatives by marriage rather than blood), and between spiritual relatives (persons linked by baptismal sponsorship, priests and their parishioners, and any persons who have entered religious life). Incest outside the nuclear family is fairly rare in medieval literature; I shall speculate on possible reasons for this neglect of an area which so preoccupied the Church in the later Middle Ages.

---

[1] The story of Canace and Macareus, a rare instance of an extended and sympathetic treatment of sibling incest, is discussed in Ch. 2 as part of the classical legacy; I do not repeat those comments here.

Siblings

According to Brewster's survey of early modern ballads and folksongs, 'songs in which there is brother–sister incest outnumber all
others'; he is mostly concerned with materials from the Balkans, and
the siblings have usually been long separated.[2] There are a number of
examples of sibling incest in the English and Scottish ballads col-
lected by Child; the siblings are often unaware that they are related
('Babylon', 'The Bonny Hind'), but there are also instances where
they do know the truth ('Sheath and Knife', 'Brown Robyn's
Confession').[3] If these ballads are an accurate reflection of the degree
of interest in various kinds of incest in oral tradition in the early
modern period, it seems surprising that the sibling motif plays such
a small part in medieval literature. Medieval writers often alluded to
the stories of Byblis and Canace which they knew from Ovid and the
mythographers, but very few chose to retell these stories at any
length, and even fewer invented new narratives focusing on
brother/sister incest (see my comments in Chapter 2). Whether writers
wanted to titillate their readers or to encourage them to confess their
sins, stories of sibling liaisons were apparently less shocking, and
therefore less effective, than the stories about liaisons between parents and children which were so popular in the later Middle Ages.
When sibling incest is present in medieval narratives, it generally
appears as a sub-plot. In saints' lives and *exempla* it is usually overshadowed by the much more serious sin of parent–child incest; in
romances it tends to involve very minor characters. But the modern
reader may be surprised by the medieval fashion for attaching sibling
incest stories to some of the great hero cycles, most notably those of
Charlemagne, Arthur, and Siegfried; possible reasons are suggested
later in this chapter. Stories of sibling incest usually include consummation; even when this is avoided, there may be a violent ending
for at least one protagonist (as in the story of the Questing Beast).
Plots in which unrecognized siblings are saved from committing
incest were quite common in the New Comedy of Greece and Rome,
but medieval examples are few and far between.[4]

---

[2] Brewster, *Incest Theme*, 25; see also Krappe, 'Über die Sagen'.
[3] *English and Scottish Popular Ballads*, nos. 14, 16, 50, and 57, ed. Child, i. 170–7,
185–7, 444–7, and ii. 13–16.
[4] One example appears in the *Decameron* (5. 5): two young men are rivals for the
love of a mysterious young woman, but when it emerges that she is the long-lost sister of

Exempla

Tubach has only one entry for sibling incest, and mentions only one *exemplum* (a version of the Gregorius story), though there are in fact more.⁵ The English version of the *Gesta Romanorum* includes as chapter LXXI a story not found in the Latin versions in which a brother seduces his sister, runs away with her when she becomes pregnant, and then kills her for no apparent reason as soon as she has given birth to their child; after marrying the widow of a rich merchant and making a prosperous life for himself, he finally confesses on his deathbed.⁶ Here as in *Dux Moraud* incest leads to murder, and here too the point of the story is the importance of repentance. Very little detail is given to substantiate the story; it is never clear why the brother kills the sister and the child. His confession is not given verbatim, and there is no reference to incest in the final part of the story. When he dies, a supernatural voice is heard to say 'syn criste deyed, was never soule so slely wonne and savyd, blessyd be gode!' (since Christ died, no soul was ever so cleverly won and saved, blessed be God!) The main moral of the story is that confession leads to salvation, rather than that incest is to be avoided.

In some exemplary narratives involving double incest (both inter- and intra-generational), sibling incest is used as the curtain-raiser, and can be treated quite sympathetically. In the story of Gregorius, for instance, Hartmann gives considerable attention to the mutual devotion of the orphaned siblings, the real love which grows between them once the reluctant sister has submitted to her brother's incestuous desire, and their panic over her pregnancy (see my comments in Chapter 3). Once Gregorius is born, however, the sibling plot is no longer interesting or relevant. The brother dies almost immediately, and although the sister grieves for him, it is her subsequent relationship with her son that dominates the story. Her loves and losses are only a minor part of the plot; although she is

one of them he abandons his suit, and the girl lives happily ever after with his rival. This type of plot reappears in Renaissance drama, no doubt borrowed from Greek and Roman plays.

⁵ Tubach, *Index Exemplorum*, no. 2728; for additions to Tubach's material, see Berlioz and Polo de Beaulieu, *Les Exempla médiévaux*.

⁶ *Early English Versions*, 388–90; the text is taken from BL Add. 9066 (a variant version appears in Harley 2316).

allowed to reappear at the end to seek absolution for her sins from her son the Pope, her narrative is summarized briefly in indirect speech. She has no name; the focus is squarely on Gregorius and his extraordinary destiny. In the stories of Albanus and of Vergogna, the protagonist and his mother are also brother and sister, but very little is made of this; again, it is the idea of a son sleeping with the mother who bore him that dominates the plot and causes the peripeteia. In some versions of the popular *exemplum* of the incestuous mother, her son unwittingly marries his own sister/daughter; the horrified mother is advised to leave them in blissful ignorance (see the discussion of the versions by Bandello, Luther, and Marguerite de Navarre in Chapter 3). But this twist, the equivalent of the mother–son incest in the hagiographic tradition of double incest stories, only seems to occur in a few late versions of the plot; in these too it is the mother–son incest which dominates the story and which must be expiated, if not by public penance then by private contrition.

Romance

I know no romance text in which the main plot centres on a brother's desire for his sister, as in *'Tis Pity She's a Whore*. In romances which begin with the heroine's flight from incest, the aggressor is almost always her father.[7] Where the motif of sibling incest does appear in romances, it is usually a sub-plot, and often very brief. If the protagonist is involved, the incest is not likely to be consummated (though Charlemagne and Arthur are striking exceptions, as we shall see). Near the end of Chrétien de Troyes' *Conte du Graal* (*Perceval*), Gawain visits a chateau where the ladies in charge turn out to be his grandmother, mother, and sister; Gawain's mother does not recognize her own son and expresses the hope that the glamorous newcomer will marry her daughter (his sister), but no incestuous liaison ensues.[8] In the thirteenth-century *Richars li*

---

[7] Penta flees from her incestuous brother in a later analogue of the Flight from the Incestuous Father stories in the 17th-cent. *Pentamerone* of Basile (3. 2), but I know no medieval example. In some cases the persecutor is the brother-in-law; see the end of this chapter.

[8] *Le Conte du Graal*, 8771–99, ed. Lecoy; ironically, in expressing this wish for their marriage she uses the phrase 'qu'il soient come frere et suer' (8790: that they may be like

Biaus, the hero is horrified to be offered as a bride the woman he believes to be his sister; this leads to his discovery that he is in fact a foundling, and his quest to find his parents.[9] In Froissart's *Meliador* the hero's sister Phénonée has a tremendous crush on her brother. She manages to avoid the fate of Byblis, however: at a crucial point she mistakenly identifies as her beloved brother another knight, Agamanor, who is desperately in love with her, and it is Agamanor whom she ends up marrying.[10]

Another sister who desired her own brother was less fortunate than Phénonée; her story explains the origin of the Beste Glatissant, better known to English readers as the Questing Beast. This story, reminiscent of the tragedy of Phaedra and Hippolytus, and also of the transformation of Scylla in Ovid's *Metamorphoses* (14. 59 ff.), appears at the very beginning of the so-called Post-Vulgate Cycle or *Romance of the Grail* in the *Suite du Merlin*.[11] The Beast is the monstrous result of thwarted sibling incest. A king's daughter falls desperately in love with her brother, a pious and chaste young man. When he rejects her she plans to commit suicide, but the devil appears to her in the shape of a handsome youth and offers to help her, if she will obey him. On his advice she accuses her brother of raping her; their horrified father condemns the innocent boy to be eaten by hounds. Before he dies he prophesies that God will avenge him, and that his sister will bear a diabolical child in the shape of a monster with yelping hounds in its belly, to commemorate his unjust death ('glatissant' and 'questing' are medieval hunting terms for the baying of hounds when game is sighted). His

---

brother and sister). The poem was left unfinished by Chrétien, so we never see the recognition scene. On the importance of hidden incest for the Grail world see Roubaud, 'Généalogie morale'; Bloch, *Etymologies*, 209–12; and Méla, 'Oedipe'.

⁹ See nn. 56 and 57 in Ch. 3.

¹⁰ For Phénonée's comments on her forbidden passion see Froissart, *Meliador*, 8689–96, 19246–7, and 19317–18, ed. Longnon.

¹¹ There is no complete text of the Post-Vulgate Cycle, which was written *c*.1235–40; some of the extant parts are in French, some in Portuguese and Spanish. As Fanni Bogdanow's edition of the whole cycle for SATF is not yet complete, references to the *Suite* will be taken from the edition of Paris and Ulrich, published as *Merlin*, but cited here as *Suite* to avoid confusion with the prose *Merlin* attributed to Robert de Boron (ed. Micha); references to all other sections of this cycle will be taken from the translation in *Lancelot-Grail*, ed. Lacy (hereafter *L-G*). For the Questing Beast episode see *Suite*, i. 149; and *L-G*, iv. 167–8, v. 276–8, and v. 283–5. For discussion see Muir, 'Questing Beast'; Bozóky, 'La "Bête glatissant"'; Bogdanow, *Romance*, 124–6, and 'L'Amour illicite'; and Furtado, 'Questing Beast'.

prophecy comes true; eventually the daughter confesses to her father, and is killed. According to Merlin in the *Suite*, the pursuit of the Beast constitutes a Grail adventure, and Arthur will learn the truth about it from a knight not yet living, who will be a virgin born of a virgin. This seems to be Perceval, but in the account of the birth of the beast in the Post-Vulgate *Queste* the dying brother declares that the Good Knight Galahad will be the one to hunt and kill it.[12] In fact the Beast is eventually killed by Palamedes, who is on the Grail Quest with Galahad and Perceval; it sinks into a lake which then seethes and burns as if full of devils. Nothing is said during the various quests for the Beast about its connection with incest; but it is highly significant that in the *Suite* Arthur encounters this diabolical symbol of extreme sexual sin just after his fatal night with his unrecognized sister Morgause.[13] He is not aware of the origin and symbolic significance of the Beast, but readers and audiences were presumably intended to remember the explanatory incest story given at the very beginning of the narrative, and to make the connection with Arthur's sin.

The Questing Beast appears in earlier Arthurian texts, but without any account of its origins; in some it is a positive Christian symbol, and has no connection with incest. It is characteristic of the Post-Vulgate Cycle to give it a history with a strong moral emphasis; this is also the version of the legend which makes the most of Arthur's incest and links it explicitly to the final disasters. Paloma Gracia notes that in *Amadis de Gaula* a dragon is the result of father–daughter incest.[14] The tradition of metamorphosis as a punishment for incest, and of the connection between transgressive sex and animals, is an ancient one found in classical legend and literature. An indication of possible Celtic sources or analogues is

---

[12] *L-G*, v. 285.

[13] *Suite*, i. 147–53; *L-G*, iv. 167 ff. Arthur's incest is discussed in more detail later in this chapter. The same sequence occurs in Malory, but without any explanation of the history of the Beast—perhaps he did not want to add diabolical implications to Arthur's sin (Malory, 41–3 (I. 19–20)). References to Malory are taken from Vinaver's three-volume edition, revised by Field (no volume numbers are given since pagination is continuous); Caxton's divisions by book and chapter are also given in parentheses for the convenience of those using other editions. Furtado points out that medieval readers might well have associated the Questing Beast with the seven-headed beast of Revelations, thus adding eschatological implications to its part in the story of Arthur ('Questing Beast', 40).

[14] Gracia, *Las Señales*, 73 ff.; the first part of this useful study deals with incest in a wide range of medieval texts.

given by a strange story in the Fourth Branch of the *Mabinogion*.[15] Two brothers, Gwydion and Gilfaethwy, are punished by Math for the rape of a virgin at his court by being turned into animals, a different kind each year for three years (stag and hind, boar and sow, and male and female wolves); they alternate genders, and they mate with each other, bringing their young to Math's court. Here sibling incest is imposed as a punishment for another sexual crime—or perhaps their behaviour as beasts is intended as an extreme reflection of their promiscuity as humans.

In the story of the Questing Beast, it is the sister who pursues her horrified brother, but in other romance contexts sibling incest is often presented as a form of male tyranny, like father–daughter incest. In such situations (usually involving minor characters), the incest may actually be consummated; it is then punished, and so forms a cautionary tale, an *exemplum* within the romance context. In the French *Queste del Saint Graal*, for instance, the three Grail knights, Galahad, Perceval, and Bors, enter the Chateau Carcelois, where they are attacked by armed men whom they succeed in killing. An old man then appears, congratulates them, and reveals that the three sons of the lord of the castle fell in love with their beautiful sister, raped her, and killed her when she complained to their father, whom they threw into prison.[16] This sordid tale has no significance for the main plot, but it is interesting that the evil presented as a contrast to the virtue of the Grail knights and a target for their prowess should be incest, which as we have seen is sometimes represented as an image of original sin. This contrast of sexual vice and virtue is also present in the prophecy that the Questing Beast is destined to be killed by Galahad.

Galahad is named again as a saviour in the context of incest in a curious episode in the late thirteenth- or early fourteenth-century French *Erec en prose*.[17] The hero faces a terrible dilemma: should he break his oath to a certain damsel to do anything that she may ask him, or should he keep it by obeying her order to kill his own sister? He maintains his reputation for integrity by killing his sister, albeit very reluctantly. Soon afterwards he comes to a fountain called the Fontaine de la Vierge, and is told how it got its name.

---

[15] See *Mabinogion*, trans. Jones and Jones, 59–63; and Welsh, 'Doubling and Incest', 359–60.

[16] *Queste*, ed. Pauphilet, 229–33. The story is abbreviated in Malory, 996–8 (XVII. 8).

[17] *Erec*, ed. Pickford, 184–94.

A prince who had lost his way in the forest came to the fountain and met the devil disguised as an old man. The devil complained that the prince's sister was in fact his own daughter, substituted at birth for the real princess whose mother murdered her to avoid a prophecy of disaster. He offered to help the prince out of the forest, demanding as a reward that the prince return with his supposed sister and hand her over to her 'real' father. The prince was reluctant, but eventually agreed. When he came back with his sister, he was suddenly overcome with desire for her, killed her attendant, and threw her to the ground in order to rape her. She prayed for help, and her brother fell down dead. To commemorate her brother's sin of lechery she put an enchantment on the fountain: any knight who comes there and who is not a virgin will lose the power to move until released by a woman. This enchantment can only be undone by the Bon Chevalier (Galahad), who will undo all the enchantments in Logres.

It is curious that the brother's desire for his sister is only awakened at a very late stage in the story; the devil's long account of her parentage seems an unnecessarily elaborate preamble, especially in comparison with a story like Apollonius of Tyre, where Antiochus' passion for his daughter is often attributed to the devil's prompting, without further elaboration (or a personal appearance and narrative by Satan). It is not clear if the devil's participation is supposed to show that the brother would never have thought of such a thing himself, or if it merely highlights the deviousness and blarney of the devil. The maidens who tell Erec this story then reproach him for the murder of his sister. The juxtaposition suggests that the two crimes are to be seen as equally heinous. As so often in medieval literature, incestuous desire leads to violence.

Charlemagne and Arthur

It would be wrong, however, to conclude from the lack of *exempla* and romances focused on sibling incest that the motif was of negligible literary interest or moral shock-value in the eyes of medieval writers and their readers, for incest with a sister was inserted into the legends of two of the most famous and admired kings in medieval literature, Charlemagne and Arthur. The motivation for the addition in both cases seems to have been religious and exemplary, though as we shall see the moral was not always explicitly developed. In the case of Arthur it is particularly interesting to see how the patterns well known from stories about the exposure of a child born of incest, such as the legends of Gregorius and Judas, had to be adapted to fit the traditional mould of the Arthurian legend.

From the ninth century on a wide range of texts contain allusions to Charlemagne refusing for a long time to confess some serious but unspecified sin, but finally acknowledging it and receiving absolution.[18] This story is particularly connected with St Gilles (or Aegidius). In the *Vita Aegidii* (probably tenth-century), Charlemagne asks the saint to pray for him in connection with a shameful sin which he has never dared to confess; the following Sunday during Mass, an angel places on the altar a parchment which contains details of the sin, and also the assurance that it is forgiven because of the saint's prayers, as long as the king repents and never repeats it.[19] This story was widely copied and retold, in Latin and in the vernaculars. In some versions the sin remains a secret, but in others it is declared to be deliberate incest with his sister Gillen, resulting in the birth of Roland. Martinet notes that the standards of sexual behaviour at Charlemagne's court were so notoriously loose that the secret sin cannot have been mere adultery; Roncaglia argues at length that there must have been some historical basis for the legend, and adduces evidence to suggest that Charlemagne's sister Gisla was in fact committed to a convent rather young because of a sexual scandal.[20] It should also be noted that rumours of incest were associated with Charlemagne because he was so attached to his daughters that he refused to let any of them marry; several of them had illegitimate children.[21]

The earliest explicit account of Charlemagne's incest is in the Old Norse *Karlamagnús Saga* (1230–50).

King Karlamagnús went to Eiss, and there he found Gilem, his sister. He led her into his sleeping hall, and slept next to her, so that he felt love for

---

[18] For discussion of the legend and useful surveys of critical material, see Lejeune, 'Le Péché'; Meslier, 'Le Thème', 17–336; Martinet, 'Le Péché', 9–16; and Roncaglia, 'Roland'.   [19] *AASS* Sept. I. 299–314.

[20] Martinet, 'Le Péché', 10–11. Roncaglia's evidence includes the letters sent to Gisla in her convent by Alcuin, which can be interpreted as implying that she should devote her love to her spiritual spouse, the heavenly king, rather than to her brother, the earthly king.

[21] See Einhard, *Life of Charlemagne*, 3. 19, trans. Thorpe, 74–5; also Martinet, 'Le Péché', 10–11.

her, and they lay together. Afterwards he went to church, and confessed to Egidius all his sins except this one; Egidius blessed him and went to Mass. And as he sang low Mass, Gabriel, God's angel, came, and laid a letter on the paten. On it was written that King Karlamagnús had not confessed all his sins: 'He has lain with his sister, and she shall give birth to a son who shall be named Rollant. And he shall give her in marriage to Milon of Angler; she shall be delivered seven months after they shared a bed; and he shall know that he is both his son and his nephew, and he should see that the boy is well looked after, for he has need of him.' Egidius took the letter from the paten and at once he went, in his vestments, to King Karlamagnús and read it before him. He confessed, and fell before his feet begging forgiveness, promising that he would never again commit that sin. He was shriven, and did all that the letter had ordered: he gave his sister to Milon, and made him duke of Brettania. The boy was born seven months later.[22]

Charlemagne is well aware of what he is doing when he sleeps with his sister. No particular motivation is given for his sudden lust, not even the promptings of the devil, and they sleep together only once. Absolutely nothing is said about his sister's feelings or reactions. The point of the story is the scenes that follow, first between the saint and the angel and then between the saint and the king, which stress the importance of contrition and confession (though not penance). On the other hand, in this version the angel's revelation follows immediately after the incest: there is no long period of obstinate silence. This may perhaps be attributed to a desire to present Charlemagne in as good a light as possible.

Allusions to Charlemagne's incest are also found in later texts, though the whole story is not told. In a *chanson de geste* written in the thirteenth century, *Tristan de Nanteuil*, St Gilles persuades the hero to confess his sin, which is that many years before he had slept with his cousin and begotten a son; this is compared with the horrible sin of Charlemagne.[23] In the fragmentary late fourteenth-century Occitan poem *Roncesvalles*, Charlemagne actually reveals to his 'nephew' that he is the result of a great sin committed by the king with his own sister: Charlemagne is both uncle and father, and Roland both nephew and son.[24] References in various thirteenth- and fourteenth-century texts to Roland as both nephew and son of

---

[22] *Karlamagnús Saga*, i. 36, trans. Hieatt, i. 116–7.
[23] *Tristan de Nanteuil*, 22869 ff. Tristan's son fulfils the prophecy that he will kill his father; in this respect the story resembles that of Oedipus or Judas, rather than the Charlemagne legend.
[24] *Roncesvalles*, 1323–6, ed. Roques; there is no mention here of St Gilles.

the king suggest that the writers assumed widespread knowledge of the story of Charlemagne's incest. Indeed, Roncaglia argues that it is hinted at much earlier, in the Oxford manuscript of the *Chanson de Roland*.[25]

Why should Charlemagne's heroic standing as one of the three Christian Worthies have been sullied by this very serious blot? Several possible reasons come to mind. An incestuous birth story might have been considered an appropriate beginning for the tragic story of Roland's death. Charlemagne's grief at the loss of his favourite champion is obviously even more poignant if Roland is his own son, and if the death of this splendid son is the price that the King has to pay for redemption from his long-ago sin.[26] Although the legend of a dreadful and unconfessed sin seems to have begun very shortly after his own lifetime, it may be that it was identified as incest only in the eleventh or twelfth century, when incest stories were becoming popular (or at least being recorded more often), and when the contritionist movement was finding stories of monstrous sins to be very useful ammunition. Although no prophecy of disaster is included in the angelic revelation to St Gilles, the implied link between Charlemagne's sin and Roland's death could only add strength to the moral value of the story. From an exemplary point of view, Charlemagne's incest, silence, and eventual confession constituted a powerful propaganda weapon for the Church.

Incest as the focus of a trial of strength between a king and a saint also occurs in the story of Vortigern and St Germanus, where the saint's prayers bring punishment in the form of death by fire, rather than absolution (see my comments in Chapter 4). Churchmen were frequently cast in this confrontational role in real life in relation to inappropriate liaisons or marriages among the nobility, though the incest was not always so shocking. Duby has chronicled the battles between the French kings in the eleventh and twelfth centuries and the clerics who condemned them for

---

[25] Roncaglia, 'Roland', 315–20.

[26] Bloch discusses the very close relationship of Charlemagne and Roland in 'Roland', though his main subject is the relationship between Roland and his stepfather Ganelon. Morgan, discussing an early 14th-cent. Franco-Italian version of the life of Charlemagne's mother Berta, argues that her deformed foot made her a 'marked woman', and that she transmitted her misfortune and suffering to her son so that 'in biblical terms, her evil is visited upon the second generation' in the form of Charlemagne's incest ('*Berta*', esp. 40–5).

marriages within the permitted degrees of consanguinity.[27] Arthur is also presented as coming off badly in a confrontation with a saint in several early Welsh hagiographies, but the issue there is not incest, which does not seem to have been added to his legend until relatively late. When the story of his encounter with his unrecognized sister is first introduced (apparently in the thirteenth century), moral comment is curiously lacking. It could have been the ultimate cautionary tale—but Arthurian writers seem to have shied away from making much of it, at least until the composition of the Post-Vulgate *Romance of the Grail*. Geoffrey of Monmouth, who wrote the first birth-to-death 'biography' of Arthur about 1135, gives him one sister, Anna, mother of Gawain and Mordred; but in later accounts he acquires several half-sisters, daughters of Ygraine and Gorlois.[28] They include Morgan la Fée, the enchantress who is constantly hostile to Arthur but eventually carries him off to Avalon to cure his fatal wound, and Morgause, Queen of Orkney and mother not only of Gawain and Mordred but also of Gareth, Gaheris, and Agravain. In Geoffrey's account and in many derived from it, such as the *Bruts* of Wace and Layamon, and the Alliterative *Morte Arthure*, Mordred is presented as Arthur's nephew. But in a number of later medieval Arthurian narratives, Mordred is the result of Arthur's unwitting incest with his half-sister Morgause.[29]

This disastrous episode in Arthur's otherwise stellar career seems to appear first in the French prose Vulgate Cycle (also known as *Lancelot-Graal*) which was composed by various hands in the first third of the thirteenth century.[30] The two earliest references to

[27] See Duby, *Medieval Marriage* and *Knight*; and my discussion in Ch. 1.

[28] *Historia*, chs. 152 and 176 ff., ed. Wright, 106–7 and 129 ff.; *History*, chs. 9. 9 and 10. 13 ff., trans. Thorpe, 221 and 237 ff. See also Blaess, 'Arthur's Sisters'.

[29] It should be noted, however, that the story of Mordred's incestuous birth is not mentioned by many medieval writers who discuss Arthur, for instance Dante and Boccaccio. Some Scottish writers argued that since Arthur was illegitimate, Mordred, as Lot's son, was the rightful heir to the British throne: see Alexander, 'Late Medieval Scottish Attitudes'.

[30] Edited by Sommer as *Vulgate*; trans. as *Lancelot-Grail*, ed. Lacy (L-G). Where the constituent parts have been edited separately and more recently, references are taken from the following editions, and cited by title only: *Lancelot*, ed. Micha; *Queste*, ed. Pauphilet; *Mort*, ed. Frappier. Micha's edition of the prose *Merlin* attributed to Robert de Boron, which is very close to the Vulgate *Estoire de Merlin*, will also be cited (as *Merlin*). For discussion of the chronology see Bruce, 'Composition' and 'Mordred's Incestuous Birth'; Micha, 'Deux source's; Frappier, *Étude*, 31 ff., and also the introduction to his

Mordred's conception in it are both rather cryptic, one in the section of the *Lancelot* known as the *Agravain*, and one in the final part of the Vulgate Cycle, the *Mort Artu*. It is not clear which was composed first, and it might be argued that each writer was unaware of the work of the other. In the *Agravain* Mordred and Lancelot meet a hermit who tells them that they are the two most unfortunate knights in the world: Mordred is destined to destroy the Round Table and to kill his father, the best man in the world, who will also kill him.[31] Mordred replies that his father is dead, but the hermit insists that he is not the son of King Lot, who is indeed dead, but rather of a great man who is still alive. He says that Mordred's natural father had a prophetic dream that a snake would come out of his belly and destroy his land and himself, though he would also kill the snake; to commemorate this dream he had a snake painted in the cathedral at Camelot, which can still be seen. The hermit adds that according to the prophecy, he himself will also be killed by Mordred. On hearing this, the scornful Mordred says that he will fulfil at least one part of the prophecy, and kills the hermit. In the scroll which the hermit was holding Lancelot finds the prophecy repeated, with further details about the fatal combat of father and son; Arthur and the Queen of Orkney are named as Mordred's parents, but there is no mention of incest. Later Lancelot sees the painting of the snake in the cathedral at Camelot, and feels depressed; he tells Guinevere of the prophecy about Arthur's death, but out of delicacy conceals Mordred's true parentage.

In the *Lancelot* when the Orkney brothers are described, Mordred is characterized as envious, deceitful, and generally evil, but nothing is said of his incestuous birth; the writer notes that he will cause the death of Arthur and many other knights, but there is no hint that he actually kills the king himself.[32] But in the *Mort Artu*, the final section of the Vulgate Cycle, Mordred's incestuous birth is discussed on three separate occasions, all near the end of

---

edition of the *Mort*, xvi–xvii; Archibald, 'Arthur and Mordred'; and Guerin, *Fall*, esp. 1–17. Guerin argues that the story of Mordred's incestuous birth was already known to Geoffrey of Monmouth, but that he chose not to discuss it explicitly; this forms an interesting parallel to Roncaglia's argument about the early date of the legend of Charlemagne's begetting of Roland.

[31] *Lancelot*, v. 219–24 and vi. 19–21; *Vulgate*, v. 284–5, 329, and 334 (this section is not included in the *L-G* translation).

[32] *Lancelot*, ii. 411; *Vulgate*, iv. 359; *L-G*, iii. 108–9.

the narrative. First, when Mordred forges letters announcing Arthur's death in France and his own succession to the throne, he attributes to Arthur the comment 'Mordret que ge tenoie a neveu— mes il ne l'est pas—' (Mordred whom I treat as a nephew—but he is not); presumably this detail is intended as a justification of his choice as successor.[33] Later Guinevere reveals to the faithful knight Labors that Arthur is Mordred's father as if it has long been known to her, but says nothing of Mordred's mother or of incest.[34] Finally, when the news of Mordred's treachery reaches Arthur in France, he recalls his dream of the snake, identifies it as Mordred, identifies Mordred as his son, and swears to kill him (though he does not name Morgause, or refer to the painted snake); his lords are amazed, so apparently the story was not common knowledge.[35]

Perhaps the writers of these two texts were drawing on information that was already available to their readers, as Guerin believes, and so they saw no need to expand on it. Or perhaps they invented the prophecy of parricide without having fully considered the implications and potential of Mordred's incestuous birth. The writer of the *Estoire de Merlin*, a section of the Vulgate Cycle which was written after the *Agravain* and the *Mort Artu* but precedes them in Arthurian chronology, gives conflicting information on the subject of Arthur's relationship to Mordred. At one point Mordred is identified as one of King Lot's sons;[36] but later Arthur is told by Merlin that he has fathered one of Lot's children, though he is not told which.[37] Later still in the *Estoire* a fuller explanation is offered, with the comment that people might think less of Arthur if they did not know the truth about what happened:[38]

When the barons of Logres gather to elect a successor to Uther Pendragon, King Loth of Orkney comes to court with his wife, Arthur's half-sister. Arthur, still a humble squire, is attracted to her, not knowing that they are related; he creeps into her bed one night when her husband is away and begets Mordred. She takes him for her husband, and it is only the next day that Arthur reveals what he has done. The queen is embarrassed, but she does

---

[33] *Mort*, 172; *L-G*, iv. 135.   [34] *Mort*, 176; *L-G*, iv. 136.
[35] *Mort*, 211; *L-G*, iv. 145.   [36] *Merlin*, 244; *Vulgate*, ii. 73; *L-G*, i. 207.
[37] *Vulgate*, ii. 96–7; *L-G*, i. 220 (the prose *Merlin* edited by Micha ends before this point).   [38] *Vulgate*, ii. 128–9; *L-G*, i. 237.

not learn until after Mordred's birth that Arthur is Uther's son, and therefore her half-brother. Secretly she loves Arthur more than her husband.

Rosemary Morris has suggested that this account contains deliberate parallels with the story of Arthur's conception by Uther, disguised as Ygraine's husband Gorlois.[39] Nothing more is said in the *Estoire* about Mordred's birth and upbringing, though one incident suggests that Mordred was raised at Lot's court; there is no reference to persecution by Arthur.[40]

The first coherent account of Mordred's conception, exposure, and miraculous survival seems to have been written down (and perhaps invented) by the author of the *Suite du Merlin*, the first part of the Post-Vulgate Cycle. Fanni Bogdanow has shown how this writer made Arthur's incest a central theme of his narrative, and how this approach was continued by the other authors of this cycle, so that the final disasters are explicitly linked to Arthur's initial sin not only by the narrator but also by Arthur himself.[41]

The Queen of Orkney comes to court with her four sons; neither she nor the recently crowned Arthur knows of their relationship. Arthur is attracted to her, keeps her at court for a month, sleeps with her, and begets Mordred. After her departure he has a disturbing dream in which a dragon and griffins ravage England. He manages to destroy the dragon, which has killed all his men, but is fatally wounded himself. Next day Merlin reveals that Arthur has committed a terrible sin by sleeping with his own sister, and that their child will do great harm to England. They discuss the ethics of killing the child: Arthur argues that England must be saved, but Merlin is worried about jeopardizing his own soul. Eventually he reveals that the child will be born in May, though he will not say where.

As the first of May draws near, Arthur orders that all newborn children be sent to him. Lot sends Mordred down from Scotland by sea; as he is being put into a splendid cradle, he hits his head

[39] Morris, *Character*, 96–7, and 'Uther'.
[40] *Vulgate*, ii. 201–5; *L-G*, i. 277–9. During the Saxon wars Lot and his wife are riding south with the infant Mordred to make peace with Arthur when they are attacked; the squire carrying Mordred's cradle flees, but is later found and escorted back to his party by Gawain. There is no reference here to Arthur's demand that all newborn babies be sent to him.
[41] *Suite*, i. 147–60, and ii. 203–12. See Bogdanow, *Romance*, esp. 138–55.

and receives a permanent scar. The boat is wrecked, but Mordred survives and is found by a fisherman who hands him over to the local lord, Nabur, to be reared with his son Sagremor. Meanwhile Arthur intends to immure all the other babies in a tower, but a dream persuades him to dispatch them in a boat with no steersman. They arrive near Amalvi and are found by King Oriant, who lodges them in a special castle. The barons are angry at the loss of their sons, but Merlin explains the threat to the realm, and assures them that their children are all safe.

Much has been added here: Merlin's explanation of Arthur's parentage; the detailed account of the ominous dream (though the painted snake of the *Agravain* is missing), and Merlin's interpretation of it; the exposure and rescue of Mordred; the attempted mass infanticide, and its political consequences for Arthur (Lot, believing himself to be Mordred's father, becomes very hostile). The writer seems to have several aims in developing this story, and on the whole they are not favourable to Arthur. Of course the prophecy that Arthur will be killed by his own son lends extra tragedy to the ending of Arthur's story. But he is also presented as bringing this fate on himself by his lust: he certainly knows that the Queen of Orkney is married, so he is committing adultery, even though he does not realize that he is committing incest too. Furthermore the debate with Merlin shows him as ruthless, a second Herod, even if his plan to murder the newborn Mordred stems from his desire to save England; curiously it is Merlin, devil's son and enchanter, who worries about the spiritual consequences.[42] It was this version of Mordred's birth in the *Suite du Merlin* which was taken over by Malory, though he condensed it considerably, and also made some significant changes.[43] In his version the Queen of Orkney comes as a spy to Arthur's court; Merlin advises Arthur to kill all children born on May Day, without any ethical discussion; Mordred is in the same boat as the other babies, and he alone survives the subsequent shipwreck. The barons are angry at the loss of their children, but blame Merlin rather than Arthur. Mordred is found by a 'good man' who rears him till he is 14 and eventually brings him to court; Malory seems to indicate that he will recount

---

[42] I am grateful to Jill Mann for pointing out this paradox to me.
[43] Malory, 41–56 (I. 19–27).

this arrival, but does not in fact do so, perhaps because it was not in his sources.[44]

It seems very likely that whoever invented this episode knew the stories of Judas and Gregorius (and probably the Oedipus legend too). The *Suite* account echoes the Judas story in its use of a prophecy of unavoidable disaster, and in making an exposed child later commit parricide (though in the Judas story the parricide is not part of the prophecy). Three details in the *Suite* account suggest that the writer borrowed motifs from other incest stories. There are two sets of recognition tokens: the splendid cloths put in Mordred's cradle when he is sent south to Arthur, and the scar he receives when he is being put into the cradle. Similar rich materials are mentioned in the exposure stories of Gregorius, Albanus, and also Gawain (though in this last case there is no incestuous encounter), and are crucial to the later recognition scenes; scars bring about the recognition in one version of the Judas story, and in the legend of Andreas.[45] These unnecessary details—or rather details which are never exploited—seem to have been included by the writer as a 'Pavlovian' reaction, even though the Arthurian context means that this story will not culminate in mother–son incest and a dramatic recognition scene; there is no reunion for Mordred with either of his parents in any extant text. A third detail supports this interpretation: when Merlin reveals to Arthur that Mordred is not dead, he also prophesies that Mordred will kill his foster-brother.[46] Again, the quarrel with a foster-brother or playmate which reveals to the hero that he is not the child of the couple raising

---

[44] P. J. C. Field has argued in 'Malory's Mordred' that in referring to a recognition scene between Mordred and Arthur, Malory may have been following a now lost version of the Alliterative *Morte Arthure*.

[45] For the Gawain birth-legend see *De Ortu*, ed. and trans. Day, and also the comments of Thompson, 'Gawain', who detects traces of an earlier story of incest and parricide in the *De Ortu*, though Morris dismisses his argument (*Character*, 110). Loomis argued that the placing of rich materials in the cradle of an exposed child was a Celtic motif, and that the Mordred story was 'unadulterated Celtic tradition'; see *Celtic Myth*, 331–43. But tokens were very common in classical stories of foundlings too, though Aristotle considered their use in recognition scenes to be inartistic (*Poetics*, 16 (1454[b]–1455[a])).

[46] See *Suite*, ii. 139; *L-G*, iv. 245. When Merlin tells Arthur this, he also remarks that the boy is being raised far away by one of Arthur's barons, but no further details of Mordred's childhood and education are given, here or in any other extant source. The prophecy is repeated to Mordred's foster-father later in the *Suite*, and the foster-brother is named as Sagremor (*Suite*, i. 275; *L-G*, iv. 202); Mordred does kill Sagremor in the final battle on Salisbury Plain, though there is no comment there on the prophecy (*L-G*, v. 302).

him is a feature of earlier incest stories (Oedipus, Judas, Gregorius).[47] It can also be an indication of character: Judas, the future betrayer of Christ, actually kills his foster-brother, whereas Gregorius, the future Pope, merely hits his. Mordred, like Judas, is a treacherous bully; in the *Agravain* he kills the hermit who tells him the truth about his birth, in a comparable display of brutality.

What could have motivated the insertion of the dubious story of Mordred's conception and infancy into the Arthurian legend? Mordred may be destined to be a villain, the cause of Arthur's fall, but he is born because of Arthur's sin, and as an innocent baby narrowly escapes the horrible death arranged for him by Arthur. The legend of Charlemagne's unconfessed sin may have prompted the decision to credit—or rather debit—Arthur too with a charge of incest, as some critics have argued.[48] But it offers no solid parallel to the tale of Mordred's incestuous birth: Charlemagne does not try to kill the infant Roland nor does Roland kill Charlemagne, and confession is not an issue for Arthur in any of the texts which include the incest. Some critics think that incest was seen as the fatal flaw which proved Arthur to be human and explained the downfall of his kingdom, including Helen Adolf, who offers several possible explanations.[49] The first is that incest made Arthur 'typical of the human condition', not because it is characteristically human to commit incest, but because incest is the worst kind of lust, and therefore symbolizes original sin. The exemplary stories discussed in the previous chapters, and particularly some of the moralizations in the *Gesta Romanorum*, would support this theory. Her second suggestion is that the incest charge showed Arthur to be 'blatantly human' at a time when 'he threatened to become a national and political saint'. Morris disagrees, arguing that 'no French prose author could consider Arthur any kind of saint', and that the English were quite undeterred in their admiration by the incest charge.[50]

Adolf also suggests that '[Arthur's] irregular birth called for

---

[47] *Suite*, ii. 139; *L-G*, iv. 244; and see Bogdanow, *Romance*, 139–41. On the frequency of this topos see Potter, *Sohrab and Rustum*, 106.

[48] The *Karlamagnús Saga* in which the first explicit reference appears was written after the Vulgate Cycle, but if Roncaglia is right that the story of Charlemagne's incest was already circulating soon after his lifetime, it could have been known to Arthurian writers in the early 13th cent.—and even to Geoffrey, as Guerin argues.

[49] Adolf, 'Concept'.   [50] Morris, *Character*, 107.

some kind of irregular union', and she is not alone in this view. Morris has noted that there seems to be a pattern linking the adultery of Uther Pendragon, which produced Arthur, with the incest of Arthur, which produced Mordred, although incest is a more serious sin than adultery, and to be the child of incest is a greater handicap than to be the child of adultery.[51] Of course illegitimacy has never been a bar to future success for legendary heroes.[52] But the shift from adultery to incest has very serious moral implications. Geoffrey of Monmouth characterized many of the kings of Britain in terms of their moral failings, especially sensuality and indulgence. It would be a great irony if this writer, who was almost single-handedly responsible for the boom in Arthurian literature in the later Middle Ages, deliberately suppressed such a major moral flaw in his hero, as Guerin suggests. It is certainly a tragic irony of the post-Geoffrey incest episode in its more developed form that Uther's deceitful lust (taking on the shape of Gorlois in order to seduce his wife) results in the magnificent Arthur and glory for England, whereas the lapse of the youthful Arthur, who is quite ignorant of both his own and his sister's identity, results in the monstrous Mordred and disaster for England. A further parallel can be drawn with Lancelot's unwitting begetting of Galahad on Elaine as a result of his lust for Guinevere; Lancelot's lapse, like Uther's, is a sort of 'felix culpa' (fortunate crime), since it produces the saintly 'Bon Chevalier' who will achieve the Grail Quest, whereas Arthur literally sows the seed of his own destruction.[53]

The story of Arthur and Mordred has much in common with the popular stories of Judas and Gregorius and their literary descendants, but the familiar motifs are mixed and deployed in unexpected ways; sometimes the effect is a mirror image, or a backwards version of a familiar plot. I have listed and discussed the discrepancies between the Mordred story and its probable models in considerable detail elsewhere; here I shall give a slightly revised account of my conclusions.[54] The first discrepancy is that Mordred is not the result of deliberate incest, as Gregorius and Albanus are. Arthur at least is unaware of his relationship to Morgause when they sleep

---

[51] Adolf, 'Concept', 29, and Morris, 'Uther'.

[52] As Rank shows in his classic study, *Myth*, illegitimacy or some other form of transgression associated with the birth story has been a standard motif in hero tales all round the world for thousands of years.   [53] This idea was suggested to me by Jill Mann.

[54] See Archibald, 'Arthur and Mordred'.

together, and in some versions she is too.[55] Presumably the writer(s) made this decision in order to protect Arthur: uncontrollable lust is bad enough, but deliberate incest would have been an insurmountable handicap.

The second discrepancy is that Mordred's mother plays such a small part in the story. It is Arthur who requires the exposure of the baby (whom he has not yet identified), and his order is based not on shame but on fear of the prophecy that this child will grow up to destroy him (though he seems to forget or repress the prophecy during the war against Lancelot when he makes Mordred a knight of the Round Table, and later regent). Boswell notes that in classical exposure stories 'a male figure orders the abandonment, to the regret of the mother', for political reasons; but in medieval stories it is usually the mother who acts alone, out of shame or guilt (the Judas story, where the parents share the decision, is an exception).[56] The Arthurian legend combines two popular story patterns, exposure by the mother because of incestuous birth and exposure by the father because of an ominous prophecy about the political succession. We never see a recognition scene between Mordred and his mother, and we know nothing about their reactions to each other. Morgause is ignored till her dramatic death at the hand of another of her sons, Gaheris. When the Orkney brothers set on her lover Lamorak, it is Mordred who administers the fatal blow, according to Malory—but there is no suggestion that Mordred in particular was jealous of his mother's lover.[57]

---

[55] Bogdanow notes that in the Cambridge manuscript of the *Suite* the Queen of Orkney has heard rumours that Arthur is her brother, and decides to go to his court to find out the truth. Bogdanow comments that it is absurd that she then willingly sleeps with him, but argues that the *Suite* author is keen to make the incest theme as prominent as possible (*Romance*, 34): 'The Cambridge MS . . . starts off the *Suite* proper with the incest, to prevent it from being lost in a mass of other material, as in the Vulgate.' The author might have made more of the queen's responsibility for the consequences of her curiosity; but this is not a story about guilt and confession, and she disappears from view very soon.

[56] Boswell, *Kindness of Strangers*, 76. Redford notes in 'Literary Motif' that in ancient Near Eastern legends (including classical myths) he found no examples of children exposed because they were the result of incest. See also Propp, 'Oedipus', 87–8.

[57] Malory, 699 (x. 58); Vinaver notes that in a comparable passage in a prose *Tristan* text in BN. fr. 103, it is Gawain who kills Lamorak. Modern Arthurian novelists often represent the devotion of the Orkney princes to their mother in more complex psychological terms, sometimes hinting at a quasi-incestuous obsession; see for instance Mary Stewart's *Wicked Day*.

The third point of difference is the mass exposure of babies, which is unprecedented in medieval incest stories, or indeed classical ones. At this stage, as Morris points out, Mordred is presented as an innocent victim, even though he is destined to destroy the Arthurian world.[58] It is clearly difficult to exonerate Arthur; the parallel with Herod is inescapable. The *Suite* author, who insists on the king's incestuous guilt, also makes him argue vigorously in favour of sacrificing one child in order to save England, but allows the other babies to be saved by the benevolent King of Amalvi. Malory is harsher in letting all the other babies drown, which makes Mordred's survival all the more miraculous; but he protects Arthur by omitting his debate with Merlin, and by deflecting the responsibility for the massacre entirely onto the magician, as well as the anger of the barons. Such political consequences do not arise in other medieval incest stories, where the child is usually exposed alone and in secret.

Up to this point, nevertheless, Mordred's story runs recognizably parallel to the popular medieval incest stories: incest, prophecy of disaster, exposure at sea. But the exposure episode includes a fourth discrepancy which underlines the unusual nature of the whole account. Mordred's birth-story is described very briefly (in some Arthurian texts) in the course of the lengthy history of Arthur and his court; the protagonist of this history is not Mordred but Arthur. It is Arthur's reactions to the incest and the prophecy and Arthur's subsequent fate which are the focus of interest. Although Mordred starts life with a birth-story so often associated with heroes, he is destined from birth (indeed, from conception) to be the villain. This is true of Judas too, of course, but in his story there is no rival protagonist and no digression from the account of his adventures; and Judas commits both parricide and incest entirely unawares. In Mordred's case, it is only his conception, his escape from the 'Massacre of the Innocents', and later his fatal intrigues against his father which are of interest; the rest of his story is omitted. There is no account of his growing up and discovering his true identity, no arrival at Arthur's court, no recognition scene, no

---

[58] *Character*, 107–8; she notes that the *Suite* author does not assume that Mordred is wicked just because he is the result of incest, and she argues that the infanticide episode is intended to demonstrate that 'it is wrong to visit the sins of the fathers upon the children'. Helen Cooper comments that 'Malory's redrafting of his source rewrites it as if to make Judas the only survivor of the Massacre of the Innocents' ('Counter-Romance', 153).

acknowledgement by Arthur of his paternity; perhaps medieval writers avoided these topics as too embarrassing for Arthur (and also for Guinevere), though many modern novelists and film-makers have felt the need to supply them.[59]

Most medieval double incest stories focusing on a male protagonist begin with deliberate incest for his conception and use unintentional incest (usually mother–son) as the prelude to the recognition scene, thus keeping the protagonist as innocent as possible. The fifth discrepancy in the story of Mordred is that this conventional order is reversed, for it begins with unintentional sibling incest, thus reducing Arthur's guilt. The deliberate incest is left to Mordred, the villain. His pursuit of Guinevere in the final stages of the Arthurian legend is usually presented as the blackest treachery to his king at a political level, but it is also incestuous, of course, and so it completes the Gregorius pattern of incest, exposure, and more incest, though in reverse order. Mordred, born of unintentional incest, desires the woman he knows to be his father's wife (though not his natural mother). In the narratives in which Mordred is Arthur's nephew, Guinevere does yield to his advances, and in some texts even bears his children; but in the stories in which Mordred is Arthur's son and she is Lancelot's lover, she makes every effort to escape him, presumably out of loyalty to Lancelot as much as to Arthur. Thus the attempted (step)mother–(step)son incest is obscured because it is not consummated, and because of the stress on the love affair of Guinevere and Lancelot, and on Mordred's treachery towards Arthur.[60] Mordred's story is not about a son's emotional relationship with his mother, but rather about his political relationship with his father. There is a recognition scene here, but it does not concern identity and parentage: instead it focuses on the shocking discovery that the son has deliberately betrayed his father. Very little attention is paid to Guinevere's emotions in most versions, though Wace does describe her as feeling guilty both about her adultery and about the forbidden relationship with her

[59] See Field, 'Malory's Mordred', and also my concluding comments in 'Comedy and Tragedy'. It might be argued that some of these traditional scenes are transferred to Galahad, whose arrival and parentage cause a great stir at Camelot at the beginning of the Grail Quest in the Vulgate Cycle and in Malory.

[60] Mordred behaves treacherously towards Lancelot too; it is he and Agravain who force Arthur to have Lancelot caught in the Queen's chamber. At one point towards the end of the story, Malory puts the blame for the fall of Camelot squarely on Mordred and Agravain (1161 (XX. 1)).

husband's nephew.[61] In the fourteenth-century Stanzaic *Morte Arthur*, the Archbishop of Canterbury reproaches Mordred for his attempt to marry his father's wife; Malory makes the Archbishop threaten Mordred with bell, book, and candle.[62] But in all these versions much more is made of the treachery than of the incest (as in the Tristan legend, discussed later in this chapter).

In some medieval incest stories, including those where the hero is the product of a legitimate marriage, the mother–son incest is preceded by parricide, so that the mother is free to become a wife again (for instance in the stories of Judas and Andreas). The sixth discrepancy in the Mordred story concerns the ordering and significance of these episodes. Far from innocently accepting a widowed queen and a rulerless kingdom as a reward for prowess, and then discovering with horror his true relationship to the queen and his responsibility for her widowhood, Mordred cold-bloodedly sets out to deprive his living father of both wife and kingdom, and finally of his life. Parricide usually introduces some kind of crisis in incest narratives: in the stories of Oedipus, Judas, and Andreas it leads to marriage with the unrecognized mother and thus to discovery of the hero's identity; in the story of Albanus it comes later and leads directly to contrition, penance, and sanctity. But in the Arthurian legend the crisis when Mordred's treachery is revealed precedes the parricide. Parricide means the end of Arthur, and thus an irreversible 'Finis' to the whole story.

Arthur's dream comes true: he kills the snake which emerges from his belly and threatens his country, but it kills him too. Here is the seventh discrepancy, parricide combined with the entirely new motif of filicide. In Geoffrey of Monmouth and in versions derived from his account, Arthur and Mordred both die in the battle of Camlann, but it is not specified who kills either of them. In the description of the Orkney brothers in the *Lancelot*, where Mordred is so negatively characterized, it is said that he caused the death of his uncle Arthur and many other knights, but there is no hint that he actually kills the king himself.[63] The *Agravain* and the *Mort Artu*, apparently the first Arthurian texts to introduce the incest theme, also introduce the prophecy that father and son

---

[61] Wace, *Roman de Brut*, 13201–22, ed. Weiss.

[62] *Morte Arthur*, 3006–7, ed. Hissiger; Malory, 1227–8 (XXI.I).

[63] *Lancelot*, ii. 411; *Vulgate*, iv. 358–62 (a variant reading in which Arthur is not described as Mordred's uncle); *L-G*, iii. 108–9.

will eventually kill each other, and its fulfilment: when Arthur discovers his son's treachery, he swears to kill him and does so, though he dies himself at Mordred's hand. The combination of parricide and filicide, deliberate and simultaneous, seems to be very unusual indeed. Morris has suggested that in earlier versions of the story it would have been inappropriate for Arthur to be killed by his treacherous nephew, 'as if Ganelon killed Roland'; but once Mordred is known to be Arthur's son, and also to have been conceived in incest, the final combat takes on a quite different significance.[64]

The peculiarity of the ending of Mordred's story is threefold: the son deliberately betrays his father; he does not subsequently inherit his father's throne or marry his father's wife, nor does he repent and turn to religious life; father and son kill each other deliberately and simultaneously. All the children in the ancient legends discussed by Redford who are exposed because of prophecies that they will usurp the throne of male relatives do eventually fulfil their destinies and take over the kingdoms of their fathers or grandfathers. In the *Sohrab and Rustem* story type, which culminates in father–son combat, one or the other survives to mourn his fatal ignorance of his opponent's identity. In twelfth- and thirteenth-century exemplary narratives, the hero who has committed parricide and incest usually turns away from the world and from secular power once he discovers his identity and his sin, and after long penance achieves great religious distinction (Judas is of course the chief exception to this pattern). In romances, such as the Middle English *Sir Degaré* and *Sir Eglamour*, the mother–son incest tends to be discovered just in time for consummation to be averted, and the hero and his father both survive their combat to enjoy the family reunion. In contrast, the simultaneous deaths of Arthur and Mordred make an unusually bleak ending.

The eighth and last discrepancy concerns the tone of the story. The Judas legend is obviously a polemic against a villain whose known wickedness is confirmed by the additional crimes of parricide and incest, but the villain is allowed some moral sensibility,

---

[64] Morris, *Character*, 131–2. In a later article she makes an interesting point in relation to the parallels between the conceptions of Arthur and Alexander (see 'Uther', 75). Alexander fulfils a prophecy by killing his unrecognized biological father Nectanebus; Arthur is conceived through a magical trick, rather like Alexander, but instead of killing his father he is killed by his own son. Morris suggests that in the Arthurian legend the motif of vengeance on the father skipped a generation.

some consciousness of sin, and is in fact absolved before he betrays Jesus. The Gregorius legend is an explicit *exemplum* of the value of contrition and penance and the miraculous workings of grace, and so are many of its derivatives. In the story of Arthur and Mordred there is no demonstration of contrition, no place for penance, no possibility of the absolution which Charlemagne found through the prayers of St Gilles. No priest ever comments on the king's sin, no angel reveals the truth: the person from whom Arthur learns that he has committed incest, and the only person with whom he discusses his sin (or rather its political consequences), is Merlin, a devil's child with magical powers. In the *Suite* the enchanter tells Arthur that he has committed a fatal error and also a grievous sin, and Malory repeats this in a compressed form: 'ye have done a thynge late that God ys displesed with you . . . hit ys Goddis wylle that youre body sholde be punysshed for your fowle dedis' (you have recently done something that has made God displeased with you . . . it is God's will that your body should be punished for your foul deeds).[65] But Arthur does not inflict severe physical penance upon himself, as Gregorius does; the punishment of his body will come only at the very end of the story, in the form of the fatal wound given him by his son Mordred. In the more moralizing Post-Vulgate Cycle, in which the initial incest is presented explicitly as the key to his downfall, Arthur remains conscious of his guilt throughout and reproaches himself for his incest at various points during the story.[66] But the Arthurian legend is essentially a secular drama; here the price paid for incest is the destruction of a kingdom and the death of a king, not the mortification of a body or the damnation of a soul. Although the story of Mordred's incestuous birth borrows many motifs from the exemplary incest stories popular from the twelfth century on, in tone and in outcome it is fatalistic and more reminiscent of classical legends such as the Oedipus story. The prophecy of disaster is ineluctable, as in the case of Judas; the monstrous sin cannot be absolved, the 'culpa' (crime) is not 'felix' (fortunate), and the story of Arthur ends with unredeemed and unredeemable personal and political catastrophe.

It is not clear whether the consequences of Arthur's incest were fully apparent to the writer(s) who inserted this episode into the Arthurian legend. Bruce believed that they were:

---

[65] *Suite*, i. 154; Malory, 44 (I. 20).   [66] See Bogdanow, *Romance*, 148 ff.

This writer [of the *Mort Artu*] was endowed with a dramatic sense beyond any other in the whole domain of medieval romance and he endeavoured to intensify the tragedy of Arthur's downfall by representing the chief agent in this catastrophe as being the offspring of the monarch's incestuous relations with his sister. [67]

In Bogdanow's view too, 'the theme of Mordred's incestuous birth seems to serve mainly to heighten the horror of the final tragedy'; but Morris disagrees, pointing out that the author of the *Mort Artu* did not make explicit use of the incest as an explanation of Arthur's fall or of Mordred's wickedness.[68] I find Morris' argument convincing; furthermore, it seems hard to justify Bruce's admiration for the terse comments in the *Mort Artu* when nothing is said there of the circumstances of Mordred's birth, the identity of his mother, or the incestuous nature of the liaison, and there is only a brief reference to Arthur's prophetic dream. Frappier's argument that the incest was first introduced in the *Agravain* also raises problems: although the hermit's letter names the Queen of Orkney as Mordred's mother, there is no comment on her relationship to Arthur, and this episode seems to have had very little influence on the *Mort Artu*. This argument of Frappier's marks a change of heart; his earlier view was that the writer of the *Mort Artu* only thought of making Mordred Arthur's son towards the end of his work, to compound the tragedy, and this is certainly one possible way of making sense of the cryptic references and also of the omissions.[69] Another explanation would hinge on Guerin's argument that the story of Arthur's incest was already well known in the thirteenth century—but then one would still have to account for the strange terseness of the references in the *Agravain* and *Mort Artu* and the discrepancies between them, which suggest that the writers were uncertain of the details, or hesitant to develop them.

There can be no conclusive answer to the question why the incest story was inserted into the Arthurian legend. The writer(s) may have wanted to make Arthur commit a sexual sin which would provide a moral explanation for the collapse of his world, and may have had Charlemagne in mind as a model; but as we have seen, Arthur's incest differs from Charlemagne's in a number of

---

[67] Bruce, 'Mordred's Incestuous Birth', 197–8.

[68] Bogdanow, *Romance*, 143; Morris, *Character*, 107.

[69] See Frappier, *Étude*, 31 ff.; and the introduction to his edition of the *Mort Artu*, xvi–xvii.

important ways. From a different moral viewpoint, it may be that Mordred was seen as the Judas of the Arthurian world, and so was given a similar history of exposure, attempted incest (albeit with his stepmother), and parricide; but this would not explain why Arthur's reputation was sullied not only by Mordred's incestuous conception but also by the attempted Massacre of the Innocents. Perhaps Mordred's incestuous liaison with his uncle's wife in Geoffrey of Monmouth's influential account suggested to thirteenth-century ecclesiastical writers the idea of expanding the story according to the pattern of double incest and parricide which was so popular in exemplary literature at the time. Another possible influence is the legend of Gawain's early adventures recounted in the *De Ortu Waluuanii*, in which Thompson has detected traces of an earlier story of incest and parricide.[70] It may be that the story of Gawain's illegitimate birth, abandonment, and later recognition by his parents was transferred to his brother Mordred, and that because he was already the traditional betrayer of Arthur, it was adapted in accordance with current literary fashion to include a form of double incest and parricide. The final motif of simultaneous parricide and filicide, an unusual variation on traditional story patterns, may have been introduced to make the collapse of the Arthurian world a domestic tragedy as well as a political one.[71]

These speculations must remain tentative, but it is certain that moralizing incest stories were in vogue in the twelfth and thirteenth centuries, stories which offer far more parallels with the account of Mordred's incestuous birth than the Charlemagne legend. From ancient times the same motifs were traditionally used as building blocks for 'birth of the hero' legends: prophetic dreams, incest (or some other form of transgressive conception), exposure, rescue and fostering, discovery of origins, parricide, recognition scenes. The Gregorius and Judas legends and their offshoots offered both old and new motifs, and a great variety of patterns in which they could be combined. Arthurian writers clearly knew and borrowed from this kind of plot, including details such as the recognition tokens of

[70] See his 'Gawain', and n. 45 above.
[71] One of the earliest Arthurian texts to develop these two aspects in terms of Arthur's complex attitude to Mordred is Thomas Hughes' play *The Misfortunes of Arthur* (1588), where Arthur is torn between love for his son, guilt at the circumstances of his birth, and determination to crush his rebellion; see Corrigan's edition of the play, and also Archibald, '"Price of Guilt"', and Fuwa, 'Metaphors'.

cloths and scars; but as the story of Mordred was apparently developed piecemeal by different Arthurian writers, the popular sequence of motifs was rewritten back to front, and the focus and tone completely changed, to produce a unique variant. This mirror image of the popular stories omits three elements crucial to the exemplary tradition: the unwitting mother–son incest, the recognition scene, and the religious ending of contrition, penance, and absolution. Contrition and penance are useless in the Arthurian legend, since everyone already knows the end of the story, that Mordred will betray Arthur's trust and that both will die in the civil war which follows. Arthur's incest could not have been an *exemplum* of the workings of grace unless the writer had been brave enough to rewrite the end of the story, and the legend was too strongly established for that; for the same reason it could not really become a cautionary tale in which the unrepentant sinner deservedly goes to hell. The story of Arthur's incest and Mordred's birth developed in such an idiosyncratic form because of the peculiar constraints imposed by the well-established Arthurian legend, and above all because of the necessity of casting the incestuous father who exposes his child as the hero whose death we dread and mourn, and the would-be incestuous son who survives exposure to fulfil the prophecy and kill his father as the villain. In *The Wandering Fire*, the second part of Guy Gavriel Kay's fantasy trilogy *The Fionavar Tapestry*, the secret name by which Arthur can be summoned is revealed to be 'Childslayer'; but in the Middle Ages he was not reviled as a second Herod, or criticized frequently for his incest. It is significant that even in the moralizing Post-Vulgate version which stresses Arthur's sin more heavily than any other, the only person to express sympathy for Mordred is Ganelon, Roland's betrayer, who makes a surprise appearance after the final battle on Salisbury Plain. He considers the display of Mordred's head on a tower on the battlefield to be 'an affront and a warning to all the traitors in the world' and cuts it down secretly at night.[72]

Volsunga Saga

Neither Charlemagne nor Arthur plans to commit incest with a sister as part of a deliberate strategy; in both cases it seems to have

---

[72] *L-G*, v. 303.

been an unconsidered act of lust with tragic consquences. Charlemagne begets a great but doomed hero; Arthur begets a treacherous rival destined to destroy his kingdom. A different pattern is found in another influential royal epic from northern Europe, the Volsunga saga.[73] In the Old Norse version, probably composed in Iceland in the mid-thirteenth century, Signy wants to punish her husband Siggeir for killing her father Volsung and all her brothers except Sigmund, now in hiding in the woods. Her sons by Siggeir prove too weak, so Sigmund kills them. Signy then changes shapes with an enchantress; the enchantress sleeps with Siggeir, and Signy goes to her brother Sigmund and asks for shelter. Sigmund does not recognize her; finding her attractive, he asks her to sleep with him, and she agrees without revealing who she is. The son she bears Sigmund, Sinfjotli, turns out to be a worthy avenger of the family wrongs, though he is reared as Siggeir's son and does not know the truth about his birth. When he and his biological father Sigmund set fire to Siggeir's hall, Signy reveals the truth about his parentage, adding that 'His immense vigour comes from being King Volsung's grandson on his father's as well as his mother's side' (13–14). But at this moment of supreme triumph, she chooses to die with the husband she despises, on the grounds that 'I have done so much to achieve vengeance that to go on living is out of the question' (14). It seems to be her treachery to her husband (which includes bringing about the deaths of all their sons) that makes her feel guilty, rather than the incest specifically. There is no reference in the text to an incest taboo, nor to any overwhelming incestuous lust on her part. Signy's comments make clear her confidence that doubling the Volsung genes would be beneficial, rather than dangerous. No supernatural prompting leads her to the decision to commit incest deliberately, but her story recalls Thyestes' seduction of his daughter in order to beget an avenger, which was inspired by an oracle (see Chapter 2). This grim tale of incest as an instrument of revenge is not a plot motif that one would expect to find in an explicitly Christian text.

---

[73] *Saga of the Volsungs*, 8. 2–8, ed. and trans. Finch, 3–14.

OTHER RELATIVES

The incest regulations in the Middle Ages were aimed just as much at the extended family as at the nuclear family; such court records as exist suggest that most of the cases that were publicly discussed did not concern liaisons within the nuclear family, but rather intercourse or marriage between cousins, affines, and persons linked by spiritual relationships, or by the *copula carnalis*. Yet these types of non-nuclear family incest rarely occur in the literature of the period. I offer some possible reasons at the end of this chapter, but first I discuss very briefly some of the few examples known to me.

Stories of incestuous stepmothers seem to be very rare in medieval literature. One example is the Middle English *Generides*, in which a young prince, the illegitimate son of the King of India, flees his father's court to escape his lustful stepmother who has falsely accused him of rape.[74] This is the Phaedra plot, but his fate is happier than that of Hippolytus. At the end of the story his stepmother confesses and asks him to kill her; when he refuses to do so, she soon dies of grief. In *Fingal Rónáin*, an Irish tale preserved in a twelfth-century manuscript, the parallels with the classical Phaedra plot are closer: the king's son (a hunter, like Hippolytus) is unjustly killed by his father because of his spurned stepmother's false accusation; in revenge his foster-brothers kill her father.[75]

The sad story of Philomela's rape and mutilation by her brother-in-law Tereus was well known from Ovid's account in the *Metamorphoses*, and was retold by various medieval authors (see the discussion in Chapter 2). Incestuous brothers-in-law do occur as persecutors in some versions of the Accused Queen plot, both romance and *exemplum*; the oldest known is the twelfth-century *Crescentia*, which may have been influenced by the *Clementine Recognitions*.[76] Typically a queen rejects the advances of her brother-in-law, who then abandons her in a forest, or brings false charges against her so that she is exiled by her credulous husband.

---

[74] I cite the edition of Wright.   [75] See Meyer, '*Fingal Rónáin*'.

[76] Wallensköld discusses the possible origins of this theme and surveys medieval versions in many languages in *Le Conte*; see also Schlauch's section on 'The Brother-in-Law as Accuser' in *Chaucer's Constance*, 108–13. The earliest version of the story of Crescentia was inserted into the German *Kaiserchronik* in the mid-12th cent.; see Wallensköld and Schlauch, and also Baasch, *Die Crescentialegende*. On the *Clementine Recognitions*, see my comments in Ch. 2.

She is further persecuted by unwanted admirers, and is sometimes accused of killing a child in her charge, or the wife of her protector. Sometimes the Virgin, or St Peter, gives her the power to heal lepers and she duly heals her persecutors, including the lustful brother-in-law, when they confess. Eventually she is reunited with her husband and cleared of all accusations. This story appears in both exemplary and (later) more secularized versions. The version of the story in which the heroine is protected by the Virgin was very popular; it is found in influential works by Vincent of Beauvais, John of Garland, and Gautier de Coincy, in Gobi's *Scala coeli* collection of *exempla*, and in the *Vies des Pères*.[77] It is also included in the *Gesta Romanorum*, where the moralization interprets the wronged heroine as the soul which is faithful to its spouse, God, and which has to withstand the temptations of the flesh.[78] Here again, as in the moralizations of other stories in the collection, incest stands for sin in general. The best-known romance version is *Le Bone Florence de Rome*, preserved in a thirteenth-century French version and a fourteenth-century English version. The popularity of this plot may owe something to the plausibility of the initial premises. No doubt it was not uncommon for a man to covet the young wife of his elder brother, out of lust or ambition or a mixture of the two; no doubt some wives resisted virtuously, while others succumbed. Historical fact and literary representation are most famously linked in Dante's tragic story of Paolo and Francesca, who died because of their forbidden love.[79]

I do not know any accounts in fictional narratives of incest between father-in-law and daughter-in-law, but the possibility of incestuous mothers-in-law is raised in exemplary texts. Etienne de Besançon's *Alphabetum Narrationum*, later translated into English as *An Alphabet of Tales*, includes the disturbing story of a woman so fond of her son-in-law, who lives in her house, that people begin to gossip about them.[80] Out of fear of slander the woman kills the young man, and then confesses to a priest, who spreads the news. When the parents of the dead man find out, they take her to court

---

[77] For references see Wallensköld, *Le Conte*.
[78] *Gesta Romanorum*, ch. 249, ed. Oesterley, 648–54, and *Early English Versions*, ch. 69, 311–22.   [79] See *Inferno*, 5. 73–6. 3.
[80] There is no edition of the French text; for the English version see *Alphabet*, ch. 466, ed. Banks, 317–18.

and she is sentenced to be burned, but she prays to the Virgin and the fire does not burn her. She is sent home, and dies three days later. This story may be derived from the popular incestuous mother *exemplum* (discussed in Chapter 3).

There seem to be few stories of liaisons between uncles and nieces or aunts and nephews in which incest is explicitly mentioned, apart from an *exemplum* of a woman who kills her three children by her uncle and is saved from suicide by the aid of the Virgin.[81] Tristan is the nephew by marriage of Isolde, but their affair is always presented as adultery and treason rather than incest, and this is also the case in most of the accounts of the liaison between Mordred and Guinevere which are derived from Geoffrey of Monmouth.[82] In Chrétien's *Cligès*, a romance deliberately conceived as an anti-Tristan love story, the hero becomes the lover and eventually the husband of his uncle's wife Fénice; technically this is not incest, however, since Fénice's marriage has not been consummated, thanks to a magic drug which preserves her virginity while giving her husband the illusion of sexual satisfaction.[83] As in the story of Tristan, the explicit emphasis is on the problem of feudal loyalty and on adultery, but nonetheless the shadow of incest must have hung over the story for audiences and readers in the late twelfth century. The same could be said of the anonymous lai of *Guingamor*, an analogue of the *Lanval* story in which the hero is the nephew of Arthur, and thus also of the Queen, who propositions him.[84] It has been argued that the relationship between Pandarus and Criseyde in Chaucer's *Troilus* has incestuous overtones, especially when Pandarus comes to Criseyde's bedside the morning after the consummation scene in Book 3; but like a number of other critics, I am not persuaded either of the plausibility or of the usefulness of this reading.[85]

---

[81] Payen, *Le Motif*, 519–22; Tubach, *Index Exemplorum*, no. 4667. The story is found in various collections; for details and for a recent edition of a version in verse see Jehan de Saint-Quentin, *Dits*, 135–40 (it is striking that the rubric mentions the infanticide but not the incest).

[82] See my comments on Mordred earlier in this chapter. André de Mandach is one of the few to draw attention to the incest in the Tristan stories ('L'Inceste'); he also argues that Tristan was the son of sibling incest between Mark and his sister.

[83] Chrétien, *Cligès*, ed. Micha.

[84] *Guingamor*, ed. Tobin in *Les Lais anonymes* 127–55.

[85] See for instance apRoberts, 'Contribution', and Kelly, 'Shades of Incest'.

In the mid-twelfth-century Latin *Ysengrimus*, the trickster fox addresses the wolf as uncle, though they are not really related.[86] The fox rapes the wife of the wolf while she is wedged into the entrance to a burrow, to her apparent pleasure. He comments that in her immobile condition someone else would take advantage of her if he did not; better he who is both friend and relative than some passing stranger. The narrator comments 'et mechum patruum zelotipase suum' (818.18: so the adulterer cuckolded his uncle); there is no reference here to incest. The lack of further comment is not really surprising: beast fables tend to combine the moral commentary of the fable tradition with the more satirical and amoral approach of the beast epic. Fabliau is also an amoral genre, and there is a similar lack of seriousness in a French fabliau where a wife confesses that she has committed incest with her nephew, who was disguised as her husband at the time; this is a double sin, but since the confessor is in fact her husband disguised as a priest, the story emphasizes cunning and tit-for-tat revenge rather than morality.[87] In other texts, however, this type of incest is taken rather more seriously. In the thirteenth-century *Roman de Lanvin* Jaspin falls in love with his aunt by marriage and becomes ill; when she innocently comes to visit him, he dies of excitement, and his mother accuses the aunt of seducing him and strangling him to keep the secret.[88]

The motif of incest between cousins is found in several French *chansons de geste*, but is not usually central to the plot.[89] In the late twelfth- or early thirteenth-century *Aiol*, the hero realizes with relief that he has narrowly missed committing incest with his unrecognized cousin (2143 ff.).[90] In *Garin le Loherain* the archbishop bans

[86] *Ysengrimus*, 5. 813–818.18, ed. and trans. Mann; there is no reference to their relationship in the comparable passage of the French *Roman de Renart*. In the French text, however, the fox is godfather to the wolf's children; I discuss the references to incest in this text later in this chapter.

[87] 'Le Chevalier qui fit sa feme confessé', no. 16 in *Recueil*, ed. Montaiglon and Reynaud, i. 178–87.   [88] *Roman de Lanvin*, ed. Thorpe.

[89] Kullman notes that the writers of *chansons de geste* lagged somewhat behind theologians in paying attention to current marriage regulations, and points out an interesting paradox ('Le Rôle', 184). The earlier texts, though apparently ignorant of Church doctrine, do frequently involve clerical characters in decisions about marriages; but texts from the later 12th cent. on are notably free of such clerical intervention, although they assume considerable knowledge of the complex rules about who could marry whom. See also Kullmann, *Verwandtschaft*, a study of kinship in Old French *chansons de geste* and romances.   [90] *Aiol*, 2143 ff., ed. Normand and Paris.

a marriage when two monks confirm that the future spouses are cousins in the second degree, but the eponymous hero of *Tristan de Nanteuil* (fourteenth-century) is not so fortunate; he sleeps unwittingly with his cousin Clarisse and is eventually killed by their son, thus fulfilling the prophecy of St Gilles.[91] This fatalistic combination of incest and parricide is strongly reminiscent of the stories of Oedipus and also of Mordred; there is no possibility of redemption here, as there is in the hagiographical treatments of the Oedipus theme. St Gilles is himself the child of first cousins, but, as Pinto-Mathieu points out, he is an anti-Oedipus, a holy man with healing power (it is to him that Charlemagne confesses his own incest).

The fiftieth story in the fifteenth-century collection *Les Cent Nouvelles Nouvelles* is a case of grandmother–grandson incest which is clearly not intended to be taken at all seriously.[92] A young man who has spent ten years away from home returns, to great family rejoicing, and is put to share a bed with his grandmother. When he climbs on top of her, she screams, and the father drives his degenerate son away. Some time later, the father finds the son in a street and they fight. When an onlooker asks why the father wants to kill his son, the boy replies that he is quite innocent: 'Il me veult tou le mal du monde pour une pouvre foiz que j'ay voulu ronciner sa mere; il aronciné la mienne plus de cinq cens foiz, et je n'en parlay oncques ung seul mot!' (He wishes me all the ill in the world, just because of the one time I wanted to mount his mother. He's done the same to mine, and more than five hundred times at that, and I've never said a word about it.) Here the incest is merely a vehicle for the unexpected dénouement of false logic, and is intended to evoke laughter rather than horror.

In medieval thinking, a single incident of sexual intercourse constituted a *copula carnalis* or bond of flesh between the partners, regardless of their marital status; a person was therefore forbidden to marry any relative of a previous sexual partner.[93] The court records suggest that this rule often created problems in real life, but it is rarely invoked in literature. One well-known example is Marie de France's *Lai le Fresne*, in which the foundling heroine falls in love with a nobleman, Gurun, and lives as his concubine until he rejects

---

[91] *Garin le Loheren*, ed. Vallerie, 5877–85; *Tristan de Nanteuil*, 9482–10353 and 22869 ff. On *Tristan* see Pinto-Mathieu, 'Adultère'.

[92] *Les Cent Nouvelles Nouvelles*, ed. Sweetser, 324–6, trans. Diner, 199–200.

[93] For fuller discussion see Ch. 1.

her in order to marry a suitably noble bride; but before the consummation of this marriage it is discovered that the bride is the
heroine's twin sister, Le Codre.[94] When Le Fresne's identity and
social status are revealed, Gurun's wedding to Le Codre is annulled
and he marries Le Fresne. Although there is no specific reference to
the *copula carnalis* in the text, medieval readers would have been
well aware that Gurun's marriage to his lover's sister would have
constituted a sin against the laws of the Church as well as the laws
of love.

   The Church was also very concerned with spiritual incest, which
occurred if a godparent married or slept with his/her godchild or
with close relatives of the godchild, and vice versa for the godchild.
This theme does crop up occasionally in medieval literature,
though not nearly as much as one might expect given the anxiety
about it demonstrated by the Church. In *Orson de Beauvais*, a
twelfth-century *chanson de geste*, the villain insists on marrying the
heroine (whose husband is a prisoner of the Saracens) even though
he is godfather to her son; she is able to prevent consummation of
this forbidden union by means of a magic drug, and eventually she
is rescued by her husband and son who take vengeance on her persecutor.[95] In *Elie de Saint Gille*, a late twelfth-century *chanson de
geste*, the hero is prevented from marrying his beloved because he
has helped to baptize her and is therefore technically her godfather.[96] There is an *exemplum* about consummated godfather–
goddaughter incest in the Anglo-Norman *Manuel des Pechiez* of
William of Wadington, which was translated into English by
Robert Mannyng of Brunne as *Handlyng Synne*.[97] A bourgeois
invites his goddaughter to spend Easter with him, and seduces her.
After debating whether to confess or to stay away from church and
risk being criticized, he decides to go to church; as there are no
repercussions, he believes that God has forgiven or forgotten him.
But after seven days he dies, and a foul-smelling fire ignites in his

[94] Marie de France, *Lais*, ed. Ewert. For comment on this potential incest in the context of the Middle English version of Marie's *lai*, see my '*Lai le Freine*'. For an interesting discussion of more recent literary examples of this sort of incest, see Héritier, *Les
Deux Sœurs*.
   [95] *Orson de Beauvais*, 291 ff., ed. Paris. For comments on this and other examples of
spiritual kinship in French romances and *chansons de geste* see Collomp, 'Le Parrainage'.
   [96] *Elie de Saint Gille*, 2658–81, ed. Raynaud de Lage.
   [97] See 7163–218 in the French text and 9701–86 in the English version; they are printed
side by side in Furnivall's edition, 304–6.

grave and destroys his body. This fire is clearly the equivalent of the thunderbolt which destroys incestuous sinners in both classical and medieval stories, and is also intended to evoke the fires of hell which will burn his damned soul eternally.

But it seems that many people regarded the prohibition against spiritual incest as irrelevant. In the irreverent and satirical *Roman de Renart*, the voluminous French version of the trickster fox story (based in part on the Latin *Ysengrimus*) written by twelfth- and thirteenth-century clerics, the fox is presented as godfather to the children of the wolf.[98] When he calls on the wolf's wife Hersent, she reproaches him for failing to visit them: 'Je ne sais rien de tel conpere | qui sa conmere ne revide' (2. 1072–3: I don't know of a godfather who does not visit the mother of his godchildren). She professes herself eager to take Renart as her lover, and he obliges at once; a little later he is able to take her again while she is stuck halfway into a burrow, apparently giving her great pleasure. The aggrieved husband complains to the king that Renart flouts all the laws of marriage: 'Renars ne dote mariage, | Ne parenté ne cosin-nage; | Il est pire que ne puis dire' (5a. 327–9: Renart does not respect marriage or the ties of kinship or cousinhood; he is worse than I can say).[99] Here the wife is presented as undisturbed by her transgression of the rule against sex with spiritual kin, while her jealous husband is shocked by it. Though Renart is the only one to be openly criticized, this episode may of course be a salvo in the long-standing literary tradition of clerical misogyny; women are so insatiably lustful and eager for lovers that they even flout the incest taboo!

A further clue that many people did not fear committing spiritual incest is offered by two stories in Boccaccio's *Decameron*.[100] In the third story of the seventh day, Rinaldo arranges to become god-father to the child of a pregnant neighbour with whom he has fallen in love, so as to gain access to her. He becomes a friar, but is still filled with lust for her, and propositions her. She claims to be

---

[98] *Roman de Renart*, 2. 1027 ff., ed. Dufournet and Méline, i. 260 ff.; 5. 5705 ff., ed. Roques, ii. 6 ff. The two editions vary slightly in phrasing; I quote from Dufournet, with variants from Roques. See the comments of Salvatore D'Onofrio on this passage, and on spiritual incest, in 'La Parentela'.

[99] Roques' text gives an interesting variant at line 28: 'ne loiautez ne conparage' (nor loyalty, nor spiritual kinship [through baptismal sponsorship]).

[100] *Decameron*, 7. 3 and 7. 10, ed. Branca, iv. 599–605 and 657–6, trans. McWilliam, 532–7 and 579–83. For discussion see Haas, 'Boccaccio'.

shocked: 'Voi siete mio compare: come si farebbe questo? Egli sarebbe troppo gran male, e io ho molte volte udito che egli è troppo gran peccato: e per certo, se ciò no fosse, io farei ciò che voi voleste' (You are my child's godfather; how could you suggest such a thing? It would be awfully wicked; in fact I was always told it was one of the worst sins anyone could commit, otherwise I would be only too willing to do as you suggest). Rinaldo persuades her to yield by a twofold argument: first he declares that though it is indeed a sin, God shows mercy to much worse sinners as long as they repent; then he persuades her that since she goes to bed with her husband, who is much more closely related to her, she can surely go to bed with the godfather of her child. She is easily convinced by this specious logic to do what she clearly wants to do in any case. In the tenth story of the same day, two close friends, Tingoccio and Meuccio, pledge that whichever of them dies first will come back to inform the other about the joys and torments of the afterlife. They both fall in love with the same married woman. Tingoccio, who is godfather to her son, has more opportunity to visit her, and in spite of his qualms of conscience he manages to seduce her, to the chagrin of his friend Meuccio. Exhausted by his affair, Tingoccio contracts a fever and dies; three days later, his ghost appears to Meuccio as promised, recounting how he is being punished for his sins, and asking Meuccio to have masses said for him. At the end of their conversation Meuccio asks what punishment is allotted for having an affair with the mother of one's godchild. Tingoccio replies that his guilt at this sin caused laughter in hell, where one sinner told him 'qua non si tiene ragione alcuna delle comari!' (there's nothing special down here about the mother of a godchild!) When Tingoccio's ghost disappears, Meuccio's reaction is 'far beffe della sua sciocchezza, per ciò che già parecchie n'avea risparmiate' (to laugh at his own stupidity for having in the past spared several such ladies from his attentions). Had Friar Rinaldo known what Meuccio knew, the narrator concludes, he would not have needed to have recourse to such ridiculous logic.

Another definition of spiritual incest was sex with any person who had taken religious vows. Much emphasis was put on this aspect of incest in confessors' manuals and treatises on the vices, yet I have not found any examples in fictional narratives. There are plenty of stories about lecherous priests, monks, and nuns, but they are not usually accused explicitly of incest. No doubt clerics who

were responsible for hearing confession and absolving the incestuous among the laity were reluctant to attribute the same failings
publicly to their brothers and sisters in Christ.

CONCLUSION

It remains somewhat puzzling that although sibling incest is not a
major motif in medieval literature, it is so common in early modern
ballads and folktales. Incest outside the nuclear family does not
seem to have been of much interest either to medieval writers or to
composers of ballads. The lack of interest in the Middle Ages is the
more surprising, since the elaborate and wide-ranging rules forbidding incestuous liaisons (whether through consanguinity or affinity) were constantly reiterated in church councils and decrees, and
cases involving relatives outside the nuclear family are frequently
mentioned in court records. It may be that such transgressions, and
even cases of sibling incest too, were more openly discussed than
parent–child incest, and were not regarded as serious moral lapses.
It may also be that oral tradition, which was less likely to be influenced by contemporary church rulings, had little to say about incest
outside the nuclear family. In either case, stories of incest between
siblings or other more distant relatives seem to have been generally
perceived as less shocking or titillating than parent–child incest,
and thus were less useful as moral propaganda and less exciting as
chivalric adventures.

Conclusion: Sex, Sin, and Salvation

> Then commanded and spake to me
>   He who framed all things that be;
> And my Maker entered through me,
>   In my tent His rest took He.
> Lo! He standeth, Spouse and Brother,
>   I to him, and He to me,
> Who upraised me where my mother
>   Fell, beneath the apple-tree.
>
>   Francis Thompson, 'Assumpta Maria'

PARADOXES abound in medieval incest stories. Incest may further the protagonist's career in some unexpected way, as in the case of Gregorius, or it may lead to the destruction of his life's work, as in the case of Arthur. Medieval writers sometimes used incest as the epitome of original sin, yet they constantly referred to the Virgin Mary as the mother of her own Creator, and the bride and daughter of her own Son. I shall return to this unique example of 'holy incest' later in this chapter. First I want to emphasize that there was nothing ambivalent or paradoxical about the view of both secular and religious writers that for sinful mortals it was very hard to avoid what Our Ford in Huxley's *Brave New World* called 'the appalling dangers of family life'.[1] Thomas Aquinas would have agreed with Ford and Mustapha Mond about these dangers, though his solutions were very different: he argued that incest taboos are necessary to restrain lusts which can be dangerously inflamed by living at close quarters (the 'nothing propinks like propinquity' principle).[2] The sad experience of the late twentieth century has been that incest, in the modern sense of sexual intercourse within the nuclear family, is much more widespread than had been supposed. There seems every reason to believe that in the Middle Ages it was just as widespread, if not more so: birth control was minimal,

---

[1] For this and other criticisms of old-fashioned family life, see *Brave New World*, ch. 3.
[2] Aquinas, *Summa Theologiae*, 2a2ae.154, 9; see the discussion in Ch. 1.

wives were constantly pregnant, and it was quite normal for family members and also friends to share beds. The literature of the period also suggests that incest occurred quite frequently. If it had been extremely rare, it would have been bad propaganda for the Church to make a showpiece of the contrition of incestuous sinners. Cautionary tales could be sensational, but they could not be completely implausible. Although for medieval theologians incest with an unrecognized parent or sibling was a less serious sin than deliberately contrived incest, many of the stories I have been discussing do use the motif of unwitting incest to drive home the importance of contrition and penance even when there has been no intention to sin. But there are also many stories which assume that incestuous desire is not an incredible perversion found only among barbarians, pagans, heretics, or power-mad tyrants (as well as among animals), but rather an overwhelming emotion that may strike quite normal and respectable Christians, even some previously notable for their heroism and virtue. Although in some texts the devil is blamed for such shocking lust, this apparently easy explanation was by no means standard.

Staying at home is certainly dangerous for the young in medieval narratives. A boy may be tempted to seduce his sister, or to share a bed with his doting widowed mother. An orphaned girl may be seduced by her brother. If she does have a father, he may try to seduce or even marry her, causing her to run away from home, or to be exiled for refusing him. If she stays and tolerates the incest, she may get pregnant; if she exposes the child, she may later find herself married to him. If she kills the baby, she is guilty of infanticide and destined for hell. Her father may murder her after seducing her, or she may die with him when he is struck by a thunderbolt. But separation from one's family has its perils too. A male foundling may unknowingly marry his mother, and also kill his father; a female foundling may marry her unrecognized father and have children by him.[3] It is not quite a case of 'Damned if you do, damned if you don't!', however, for even the most horrifying accumulation

---

[3] It is interesting that, unlike Oedipus, male foundlings who unwittingly marry their mothers in medieval stories do not seem to have children; but when a widowed mother deliberately seduces her adolescent son, she always gets pregnant (and sometimes kills the child at birth). Could it be that medieval writers wanted to protect incestuous men destined to become Popes and saints from excessive sin, but felt no qualms about letting women who initiate incest compound their sins with a child?

of these sins of lust and violence can be absolved through sincere contrition and divine grace. Rank argued that the double incest stories which seem to be a medieval invention, and 'which differ displeasingly from the naive antique traditions in their voluptuous and torrid fantasies', were a response to ascetic Christian attitudes to sex:

If we were dealing simply with the assimilation of existing traditions and their extension to the passive Christian heroes—the saints—there would be no explanation for the burning sensuality with which incestuous crimes were aligned one upon the other, approaching the limits of the humanly conceivable. Based on this excess, we must assume that the great repression of drives expressed in Christianity could be maintained only at the cost of a fantasy life pouring forth to the most voluptuous degree; here the repressed drives found a place where they could be played out.[4]

It seems just as plausible to argue that double incest stories were developed by the Church as a valuable propaganda weapon: they emphasized the innate and incorrigible sinfulness of mankind, but also the infinite mercy of God. It is also the case that, as Shelley remarked, incest is 'a very poetical circumstance'.[5] The theme has been used for thousands of years in many literary genres, sophisticated and unsophisticated, written and oral, in cultures all over the world, and its popularity shows no signs of abating. It appealed not only to Christian clerics composing edifying texts, but also to writers of romance, one of the dominant literary genres of the later Middle Ages; medieval romance, like the later novel, made much use of the themes of identity, separation, and reunion, and also of coincidence. Repetition is a frequent technique in the structure of romance; doubling the incest allowed for the doubling of emotional speeches, painful separations, and shocking recognition scenes, all vital elements in these stories of repeated incest (as well as in other narratives about children separated from their families).[6]

Brewster comments that although incest was often condoned among the ruling class, it was regarded with horror by the population in general.[7] We have seen that charges of incest were used in antiquity and the Middle Ages to discredit controversial or unpopular rulers and politicians, though they did sometimes get away

---

[4] Rank, *Incest Theme*, 271.   [5] See Introduction, n. 14.
[6] On the characteristic themes of romance (both medieval and modern) see Frye, *Secular Scripture*.   [7] *Incest Theme*, 3.

with serious transgressions of the taboos. In one of the many medieval Incestuous Father stories, when the widowed king declares that he is going to marry his only daughter, one of his horrified courtiers comments that incest is 'worse then bogery [heresy]', and indeed heretics were often accused of incest too.[8] But was abhorrence of incest really so 'deeply rooted in the minds of all peoples' as Brewster claims? In medieval literature, incestuous desire is certainly not confined to the ruling classes, though the social status of the protagonists is largely determined by the genre of each narrative (romances are concerned only with the aristocracy, whereas *exempla* are more wide-ranging in their cast of characters). Indeed, the fact that incest is interpreted in some *exempla* as original sin suggests strongly that all humans are potentially incestuous sinners, regardless of class or status. And as I argued above, incest is presented as a very plausible sin, though a horrifying one.

One of the shocking discoveries of the late twentieth century was that incest is found among all social and economic groups, and is not merely a by-product of poverty and overcrowding. This would not have come as a surprise to classical and medieval writers. Today we tend to blame aggressive patriarchy for the disturbing prevalence of incest in our society, but in classical and medieval stories it is not always tyrannical fathers and brothers who initiate incestuous advances, and their partners are not always downtrodden victims. Medieval writers followed their classical sources in depicting the love of the siblings Canace and Macareus as consensual and deeply felt. In Hartmann von Aue's poem, Gregorius' mother is initially raped by her brother, but comes to love him so much that she greatly mourns first his departure and then his sudden death. Medieval writers had no difficulty in imagining a mother who loved her adolescent son so much that she became pregnant by him. There is no indication that the son in this very popular *exemplum* was forcibly seduced; the incest seems to have been consensual, even if the mother is represented as more obsessed, and later more contrite. Dux Moraud's daughter kills her mother in order to continue her affair with her father, and then kills her father when he

[8] Lord Berners, *Ide and Olive*, 693–4. In an essay on the various versions of this story, Diane Watt discusses the connotations of the French term *bougrenie* and the English *bogery* ('Behaving like a Man', 270–1).

repents; she may be a victim in the beginning, but she soon becomes the dominant partner in the affair. As these examples show, and as I pointed out at the beginning of this study, medieval writers were surprisingly gender-blind in their incest stories. Although there are certainly plenty of cases in which the incestuous initiative is taken by the father (or sometimes by a brother), there are also many in which the sinner in the spotlight is the mother, and one or two in which a daughter or sister makes the first move. Of course, medieval ecclesiastics wanted to stress that all humans are inevitably sinners; and it was perhaps easier for misogynistic clerics in the Middle Ages than it is for us in the age of feminism to invent, and repeat, stories of monstrous mothers who love their sons too much. But we should note that the initial misogyny in these stories is balanced by a surprisingly positive ending. The incestuous mothers almost always repent and die saved, whereas incestuous fathers who actually commit incest very rarely repent, and often meet violent deaths (for instance by thunderbolt). I know of no saint's life in which the protagonist is a reformed incestuous father;[9] on the other hand, no woman who has actually committed incest becomes a saint. Gregorius' unnamed mother becomes an abbess in some versions of the story, but is eclipsed by the greatness of her son the Pope. Albanus' mother relapses into sin and is killed by her own son. The mother in the 'Dit du Buef' dies in a saintly manner and her burial place is associated with miracles, but she is never given a name. St Dympna escapes the incestuous advances of her father, though he does kill her in revenge for her refusal to marry him.

Incestuous sons do not meet such violent deaths as incestuous fathers; perhaps this is because they never force their unwilling mothers. There are two possibilities in their stories: if the son is the central character (e.g. Gregorius or Albanus), he commits incest unknowingly, repents, and eventually achieves spiritual greatness. If the mother is the central character and it is she who deliberately brings about a situation where they sleep together in full awareness of their relationship, then little or nothing is said of the son's complicity; he usually disappears rapidly from the story, though occasionally he does penance like his mother (and in the exceptional twist recounted by Bandello, Luther, and Marguerite de Navarre he

---

[9] One possible exception is St Metro; see my comments in Ch. 4, and Mölk, 'Zur Vorgeschichte'.

lives happily ever after as the husband of his unrecognized sister/daughter). Generally incestuous daughters meet violent ends—in some cases they are killed and even eaten by their own fathers—though a few do repent, as for example in *Dux Moraud*. Stories of unconsummated incest have happier endings, of course. A foundling who grows up to be a knight (e.g. Eglamour or Degaré) discovers just in time that his new bride is in fact his mother; he then has a reunion with his father, and achieves full chivalric status and honour. A daughter who rejects the proposition of her incestuous father and is forced to leave home unprotected (e.g. Joie or Emaré) must undergo many ordeals, but in the end she too is restored to her proper status as wife, mother, and (very often) queen.

The main characteristics of medieval incest stories become very clear when they are compared with what came after them in the Renaissance. Space does not permit me to discuss in any detail the changes in social context and literary fashion which took place in the sixteenth and seventeenth centuries, so I shall simply comment briefly on the use of the incest motif in Renaissance English drama, where it was very popular.[10] Of the many important changes which took place in this period, two of the most influential for the incest theme were the Protestant Reformation and the new humanist interest in classical literature and culture. Classical literature was generally fatalistic; no amount of contrition could bring its protagonists grace or salvation. The Protestant Reformation was also fatalistic in a different way, in terms of an apocalyptic vision, since Protestants in the Calvinist tradition believed that the elect are predetermined; their doctrine of justification by faith alone reduced the need for charity and good works and the patronage of the saints, and meant that confession and penance were no longer central to religious life. In commenting on Genesis, Calvin 'labours the doctrine of human depravity, employing sexual deviance as an index of universal corruption. As the supreme example of such behaviour, incest enforces the point that, left to his own devices, man cannot obey even the natural law.'[11] Medieval writers also emphasized human depravity, but insisted that there was always hope of salvation, and that despair was the worst sin. In

---

[10] For detailed discussion see Bueler, 'Structural Uses', Boehrer, *Monarchy and Incest*, and McCabe, *Incest, Drama*.   [11] McCabe, *Incest, Drama*, 58.

Renaissance incest plays the focus is no longer on individual souls but on society more generally.

Incest is a frequent motif in English drama of the sixteenth and seventeenth centuries. It can be combined with a happy ending, as in medieval quest-for-identity romances. Borrowing from Greek and Roman models, the writers of Renaissance comedies made much of incest narrowly averted by a recognition scene, or of the threat of incest removed when would-be lovers discover that they are not in fact siblings (for instance in Lyly's *Mother Bombie*, and in Beaumont and Fletcher's *A King and No King*). In Shakespeare's *Pericles*, the combination of incest consummated and incest averted proved very popular. Here the incest theme is intertwined with the theme of good and bad kingship, and this is also true of many of the tragedies which include incest. It often functions as 'an index of social confusion', as McCabe puts it (293), a symbol of 'something rotten in the state'. In medieval texts the fact that a king is incestuous does not necessarily mean that his whole family and kingdom are tainted and must be destroyed; indeed little is usually said about his kingdom, for it is the fate of his soul, and that of his partner in incest, that is important. In Renaissance drama the incestuous protagonists tend to drag everyone else down with them, as for instance in Ford's *'Tis Pity She's a Whore* and Middleton's *Women Beware Women*. There can be no recovery from consummated incest in these plays; villains and victims alike must die. It is not just incest that destroys them, but other sins too; incest is merely one manifestation of an evil character. Renaissance writers were much more interested than medieval ones in possible motives for committing incest, which might be pure lust but might also include revenge, envy, hatred, and greed. The overall effect is pessimistic, as McCabe notes:

The incestuous and all they represent are effectively abandoned to a deterministic psychosis that may be termed 'sin' only in the sense, as Malefort argues in *The Unnatural Combat*, that the absence of grace is sin. The most challenging plays of Massinger, Webster and Ford confront the stark truth that aberration is integral to human nature, that moral distortion is woven into the pattern of history.[12]

In these plays, as in medieval texts, incest and violence are

---

[12] McCabe, *Incest, Drama*, 294.

inextricably linked. But in the plays human tragedies cannot be resolved as Christian comedies, with a happy ending in spiritual terms. We are meant to count the bodies lying on the stage, to be shocked at the wickedness of those responsible, and to be saddened at the waste, the death of relatively innocent bystanders, and the destruction of entire families. In a medieval incest story, on the other hand, we can discount the number of dead bodies at the end if the protagonist's soul is saved, as in the exemplary *Dux Moraud* and its analogues, which focus on the contrition and salvation of the heroine rather than the large number of family members she has murdered.

One aspect of incest which is much discussed today is strikingly missing from medieval incest stories: the dangerous genetic effects of inbreeding. This argument, so often invoked in modern discussions of incest, seems to have been almost totally ignored as a justification for the incest taboo in the Middle Ages, though there is some evidence for belief in the linking of deformity and incest (see my comments in the Introduction and Chapter 1). I suspect that any physical or mental deformities in children of close kin would have been viewed as divine punishment, rather than as a predictable biological consequence. It might be argued that moral deformity is present in a product of incest such as Mordred, but this is almost never explicitly stated, though there is an interesting comment on Oedipus' sons in the fifteenth-century prose epitome of Lydgate's *Siege of Thebes*: 'Fore hit preved well there of theym two, that weren so horribly gotten ayenst all nature and ordenaunce, for as clerkes seyn, blode to touche blode, bringeth forth corrupt frute' (For it was clearly shown in the case of these two, who were so horribly conceived against all nature and law; for as clerics say, when blood touches blood [when blood-relatives have intercourse], the resulting fruit is corrupt).[13] On the other hand, classical and medieval incest stories offer some striking examples of what might be called positive inbreeding, or eugenics, who can be grouped in three categories: the beautiful, the virtuous, and the heroic. Adonis, the epitome of human beauty and beloved of Venus herself, was the result of father–daughter incest; and according to Lydgate at least, the short-lived son of Canace and Macareus was also notably beautiful.[14] Father Cenci had some

---

[13] *Sege of Thebes*, ed. Brie, 269, quoted by Cooper, 'Counter-Romance', 147.
[14] See the discussion of Canace in Ch. 2.

justification for his claim that the children of incest grew up to be saints: legendary holy men conceived through incestuous relationships include Gregorius, Albanus, and in the Irish tradition St Cuimmin. Cuchulain, Hrólf, and Siegfried are examples of heroes produced by incestuous liaisons. The notion that a special child is born as the result of some form of sexual transgression is found in myths and legends all over the world.[15] Rudhardt draws attention to a Greek tradition that Zeus not only slept with his sister Demeter but also with their daughter Persephone, and that the result of this father–daughter incest was Dionysus.[16] In some accounts, the infant Dionysus was killed and eaten by the Titans, but his heart was preserved and so Zeus was able to make him be born a second time. The Titans were destroyed by thunderbolts and humankind was born of their ashes; thus something of the murdered god passed into humans. This story offers suggestive parallels with the story of Christ, another example of the belief that unorthodox conception produces extraordinary heroes.[17]

THE IMMACULATE EXCEPTION TO THE RULE

Tertullian pointed out in a tone of invincible superiority that unlike the gods of Greek and Roman myth, Christ was born without any taint of incest or adultery.[18] In fact incest was associated with the birth of Christ throughout the Middle Ages, but far from being a source of reproach, it was a matter for celebration: 'the description of the Virgin Mary as being both mother and daughter of Jesus Christ, the so-called *mater et filia* topos, is one of the oldest of the

---

[15] See Rank, *Myth*. Lisa Bitel notes that in Irish legend 'in sagas and saints' lives . . . women coupled with their fathers or brothers—sometimes more than one—to produce kingly heroes and holy men' (*Land of Women*, 60).

[16] Rudhardt, 'De l'inceste', 759–60.

[17] Origen draws attention to the parallel between Christ and Dionysus only to deny it (*Contra Celsum*, 4. 17, trans. Chadwick). Earlier in this book, in reply to pagan criticism that Jesus was the product of an adulterous relationship between Mary and a soldier, Origen argues that a man destined to do such great deeds would never have had an illegitimate and dishonourable birth (*Contra Celsum*, 1. 32).

[18] *Apologeticus*, 9. 16; this claim was made by other early Christian writers too, including Origen. Warner notes an early rumour circulating in Alexandria that Jesus was Mary's son by her own brother (*Alone*, 35).

paradoxes applied to her.'[19] This topos was easily available to later medieval writers in the work of St Augustine, but it was not Augustine's invention, nor was it merely metaphorical; Breeze notes that the doctrine that Christ was both the father and the son of the Virgin was officially declared at the Eleventh Council of Toledo in 675. From the twelfth century on it was increasingly common to interpret the Bride of the *Song of Songs* as Mary.[20] The *mater et filia* topos continued to be widely used all over Europe, though its popularity seems to have varied somewhat from one country and language group to another; it is used in many Marian lyrics, though apparently less in Middle English than in other languages.[21] Chaucer makes his Second Nun quote the famous phrase with which Dante's St Bernard begins his prayer to the Virgin, 'Vergine madre, figlia del tuo figlio' (*Paradiso*, 33. 1: Virgin mother, daughter of your son), when she describes Mary as 'thou Mayde and Mooder, doghter of thy Sone' (*CT*, 8. 36). The topos also occurs in the well-known antiphon *Alma redemptoris mater* which got the diminutive hero of the *Prioress's Tale* into so much trouble: 'tu que genuisti | Natura mirante tuum sanctum genitorem | Virgo prius ac posterius' (You who, to nature's astonishment, gave birth to your holy father, virgin before and afterwards).[22] The importance and familiarity of this topos is emphasized by the addition of father–daughter incest to the legend of Antichrist in the thirteenth century (if not earlier). In a grotesque parody of the Christian story which also draws on the notion of incest as original sin, Antichrist is said in Berengier's *De l'avenement Antecrist* to be 'born in Babylon from an incestuous relationship between the devil and his whorish daughter'.[23]

[19] Breeze, 'Virgin Mary', 267; see also Mayer, 'Mater et Filia'; Kristeva, 'Stabat Mater'; Méla, 'Oedipe', esp. 31–6; Shell, 'Want of Incest', esp. 627–30; Philippart, 'Le Récit miraculaire marial', esp. 581–5; and Newman, 'Intimate Pieties'.

[20] See Astell, *Song of Songs*.

[21] See Woolf, *English Religious Lyric*, 132–4; it seems to have been much more popular in Celtic literature (Breeze, 'Virgin Mary').

[22] Quoted by Woolf, *English Religious Lyric*, 130–1. Newman cites a number of similar Latin examples, and remarks on their riddling quality: see 'Intimate Pieties', 79.

[23] See Emmerson, *Antichrist*, 82–3. He notes that Gower in the *Mirour de l'Omme* makes the devil and his daughter Sin give birth to Death, who then mates with his mother to produce the Seven Deadly Sins (205–37). Noam Flinker has argued in 'Cinyras, Myrrha' that the story of Myrrha and her father was the source for Milton's allegory of Death as the product of Satan's incest with his daughter Sin, and of Death's subsequent rape of his own mother (*Paradise Lost*, 2. 746–814). But it seems more likely

As far as I know, Mary's conception of Christ is not described explicitly as incest by medieval writers, nor Mary herself as incestuous; clearly her complex relationship with God the Father and God the Son was understood to be in a very different category from the forbidden liaisons of the fictional characters discussed in this study. Nevertheless, it is striking that allusions to Mary's 'holy incest' are also found in more secular contexts; this suggests that the topos really was a household concept, so to speak.[24] In Chrétien de Troyes's *Chevalier de la Charrete* (*Lancelot*) a knight defeated by Lancelot appeals for mercy in the name of 'ce Deu qui est filz et pere | et qui de celi fist sa mere | qui estoit sa fille et s'ancele' (God who is both Father and Son, and who caused His daughter and handmaiden to become His mother).[25] A similar example occurs at the end of the same author's *Conte du Graal* (or *Perceval*), when Gawain is staying at the castle of two queens who are in fact his grandmother and mother, though neither they nor Gawain have yet realized this. The queens wish their unrecognized guest a day full of joy, adding piously 'Ce doint icil glorïeus pere | qui de sa fille fist sa mere' (8045–6: May this be granted by the glorious Father who made His daughter into His mother).[26] Another romance hero, Partonopeu in *Partonopeu de Blois*, prays to Mary in terms very reminiscent of the lyrics which celebrate her paradoxical relationship to God: 'Sainte Marie, virge mère, | Ki conceus en toi ton Pere, | Et enfantas contre nature | Ton creator, tu, creature' (St Mary, virgin mother, who conceived in your body your own Father, and against nature gave birth to your Creator, you, [his] creature).[27] Not everyone seems to have been familiar with the topos, however. In the thirteenth-century romance *Perlesvaus* King Arthur visits a chapel where he has a vision of Mary with her infant son Jesus.[28] She addresses her baby as 'mes pere, e mes filz, e mes sire' (my

that Milton was aware of these late medieval legends and that, like the medieval inventors of the Antichrist legend, he was deliberately creating an evil parody of the Christian story.

[24] My examples are all taken from Old French literature; I have not searched for analogues in other languages, though it seems likely that they exist.

[25] *Chevalier de la Charrete*, 2821–3, ed. Roques.

[26] This is particularly ironic given that a little later on Gawain's mother, not recognizing her own son, expresses the hope that he and her daughter will soon be 'come frere et suer' (8790: like brother and sister), by which she means that they should marry.

[27] *Partonopeu de Blois*, 5405–8, ed. Gildea.

[28] *Perlesvaus*, ed. Nitze and Jenkins, i. 35.

father, and my son, and my lord); Arthur is astonished both by the vision and by this form of address, but no more is said about it.

In a fascinating essay on the representation of the Holy Family in the later Middle Ages, Barbara Newman compares the Oedipus myth with the Christian topos of Mary as the mother, bride, and daughter of God, and argues that for Christians 'incestuous familial love symbolizes not the primal sin but the final reward'.[29] This might not have been obvious to all, Newman admits: 'But to those who aimed at exceptional devotion, the incestuous complexity of Mary's relations with God made her the emblem not of transgression, but of a total intimacy that could not be symbolized save by the compression and fusion of all earthly ties.' Among the mystics who aspired to such intimacy was Margery Kempe: Christ told her that she was His daughter, mother, sister, wife, and spouse, and when she reluctantly underwent a mystic marriage with God the Father, He addressed her as daughter as well as wife: 'I take the, Margery, for my weddyd wyfe . . . For, dowtyr, ther was neuyr childe so buxom to the modyr as I xal be to the' (I take you, Margery, for my wedded wife . . . For, daughter, there was never a child so kind to its mother as I shall be to you).[30] I agree with Newman's view that medieval writers can hardly have failed to notice the full implications of their descriptions of Mary's multiple relationship to God.[31] Newman rightly notes that medieval poets would have read in the schoolroom classical incest stories about Oedipus, Myrrha, Canace, Phaedra, and Byblis; but she does not mention the comments of patristic writers on the incestuous liaisons of the classical gods, or the allegorical treatment of classical incest stories by medieval writers. The early Church fathers frequently criticized pagan stories of the incestuous behaviour of both gods and men; yet in some later allegorizations, such as the *Ovide Moralisé*, Oedipus and Myrrha are interpreted allegorically as types of Christ and Mary respectively (see my discussion in Chapter 2). Since the topos of Mary's 'incest' occurs so widely in both Latin and

---

[29] Newman, 'Intimate Pieties', 93.

[30] *Book of Margery Kempe*, chs. 14 and 35, ed. Meech and Allen, 31 and 87; trans. Windeatt, 66 and 123. I have normalized thorn.

[31] This is no doubt why the Virgin intervenes in many *exempla* of mother–son incest to save the repentant mother; and why she also appears in a number of Incestuous Father stories to protect the heroine on her travels and to reattach her missing hand. She does not save any incestuous men in medieval narratives, though she does in the later ballad 'Brown Robyn's Confession' (see Ch. 3, n. 79).

vernacular writings in the later Middle Ages, such allegorizations would presumably have been much less startling to medieval readers than they may seem to us.[32] The stories of Oedipus and Myrrha would have seemed particularly shocking in that they focus on parent–child incest, indubitably the worst kind in medieval terms. But they would also naturally have prompted thoughts of the one occasion when it was entirely appropriate, indeed absolutely necessary from a theological perspective, for the Father to impregnate His daughter and for the Son to marry His own mother.

Since accusations of incest were bandied back and forth so freely by early Christian writers and their pagan opponents, it seems possible that the topos of Mary's 'incest', not transgressive but absolutely necessary and glorious, was developed at least in part as a response to and also a trumping of pagan mythology.[33] In Greek and Roman cosmogonies, as in many others, it was necessary for the first-created deities to have intercourse with each other at the beginning of the world. In the new Christian mythology, Mary is not part of a cosmogony but a late addition to the divine family. Zeus/Jupiter has many wives, mistresses, and offspring, but the Christian God has only one Bride and only one Son. Zeus was nearly destroyed at birth by his jealous father; he survived only by meeting violence with violence and castrating Cronus. But Mary's Son is an essential part of the Triune Godhead, born in human time yet also Himself the eternal Creator; He submits to death in obedience to His Father, and then they reign together. Zeus slept with his sister Demeter and also with their daughter Persephone; Mary is the Bride of both the Father and the Son, but this represents two different aspects of the same relationship (as in the case of Margery

---

[32] Méla implies that for medieval exegetes who loved word-play, the name Myrrha, 'la mirre amere' (bitter myrrh), might have suggested an association with Mary, who was traditionally described as 'mare amarum' or 'mer amere' (bitter sea); see his comments in 'Oedipe', 25 and 36. Woolf quotes from a 13th-cent. French lyric in which the paradox of Mary's relationship to God is illustrated as fruit planting the tree from which it grows, and a fountain emerging from a stream (*English Religious Lyric*, 132); the fountain/stream example recalls the passage in the story of Byblis in the *Ovide Moralisé* where her transformation into a fountain is used to illustrate the doctrine of the unity of the Trinity (*OM*, 9. 2652 ff.—see my comments in Ch. 2).

[33] Shell argues that the Christian Holy Family is based on the first Jewish family of Abraham, Sarah and Isaac ('Want of Incest', 627–8): Christianity responded to Sarah's dual role as both wife and sister to Abraham by making Mary 'fully affined to God as God's fourfold kin'. Méla mentions the story of the birth of Dionysus, and also argues for the influence of the Isis cult ('Oedipe', 24, 31, 36).

Kempe's relations with God the Father and with Christ). Unlike the jealous and vengeful Hera, who constantly asserted her superiority as the wife of the supreme Olympian, Mary remained humble and indeed virginal during her lifetime; she is celebrated as the human mother of Christ just as much as the immortal Queen of Heaven. Christians took over pagan festivals and sacred sites; it seems very possible that they deliberately took over the pagan myths of divine incest (and perhaps especially the story of the two births of Dionysus) and transformed them from something sordid and much repeated into something unique and triumphant.[34] An intriguing, if tantalizing, piece of evidence to support this theory is offered by Gower, who in the *Confessio Amantis* presents Cupid not only as the offspring of the incest of Jupiter and Venus, but also as the lover of his own mother.[35] Georgiana Donavin has argued persuasively that in the *Confessio* Cupid and Venus, the King and Queen of Love, 'are exposed as a gross parody of Mary and Jesus, their literal incest a perverted substitute for the spiritual relationship cultivated by the Christian Mother and Son'.[36] Gower's point is that the Lover to whom his narrative is addressed, and all good Christians too, should choose the court of heavenly love rather than the court of worldly love.

For medieval Christian writers, humankind was mired in sin. Both men and women were all too inclined, in spite of the frequently reiterated incest prohibitions, to 'taken wher thei take may' (take wherever they can) since, as Gower points out in his version of

---

[34] Mary Douglas argues that 'religions often sacralise the very unclean things which have been rejected with abhorrence', and that 'Within the ritual frame the abomination is then handled as a source of tremendous power' (*Purity and Danger*, 160 and 166). It is tempting to see Mary's 'holy incest' as an example of this tendency, perhaps prompted by the charges of incest made against early Christians (see Ch. 1), though the Church's obsession with the enforcement of the incest taboo developed gradually over the first millennium AD, and the Marian 'incest' topos dates back to the early centuries of Christianity.

[35] *CA*, 5. 1404–20. It is not clear where Gower got the story of Cupid's incest with Venus, though it seems likely to be a medieval invention to denigrate erotic love, perhaps in response to classical images of mother and son embracing. The story also seems to have been current in the Renaissance; McCabe uses as the cover illustration of his *Incest, Drama* Bronzino's very suggestive painting of Cupid caressing the naked Venus, *Allegory with Venus and Cupid*. McCabe says little about it (see 28), but Panofsky, commenting on the same painting, notes that Pierre Bersuire in his *Ovidius Moralizatus* (c.1340) interprets the embrace of Venus and Cupid as an allegory of excessive displays of affection between blood-relatives caused by lust ('Father Time', 88 n. 72). This could well have been Gower's source too.   [36] Donavin, *Incest Narratives*, 25.

the Apollonius story, 'the flesh is frail and falleth oft' (*CA* 8. 152 and 289). At the end of Shakespeare's version of the evergreen Apollonius story the hero (here named Pericles), who has abandoned himself to despair, is reunited with his long-lost daughter Marina and hails her as 'Thou that beget'st him that did thee beget' (v. i. 196). This riddling phrase with its incestuous implications is an ingenious expression of his sense of being restored to life. It is also strikingly close to the traditional phrases used to describe Mary's relationship to Christ, such as 'tu quae genuisti . . . tuum sanctum genitorem' (you who gave birth to your holy father). Shakespeare must have been drawing on medieval Marian rhetoric here, deliberately or not; his father was a Catholic, the Reformation was only half a century old, and he was clearly well read in a wide range of earlier literature.[37] The immaculate 'incest' of Mary and her Father/Brother/Son is the salvation of mankind, the solution to the problem of original sin which was created by the Fall of Adam and Eve. Medieval writers sometimes interpreted incest as representing original sin; Thompson's linking of incest and the apple tree in his poem on the Virgin quoted at the beginning of this chapter is peculiarly apt. But Mary's immaculate 'incest' is also the exception that proves the rule. Medieval narratives make it very clear that although it is not unusual for postlapsarian men and women to feel desire for a close relative, incest is indeed 'worse then bogery', but it is also 'a very poetical circumstance'.

---

[37] Philip Edwards calls the Marian topos 'the ancient paradox of Christianity', and claims that this line 'is the key to the play, and perhaps to the whole group of Shakespeare's late Romances'; see the note on v. i. 196 in his edition of *Pericles*.

Appendix:
Synopses of Flight from Incestuous Father Stories

This appendix includes the stories discussed in Chapter 4 (except the versions in the *Vitae Duorum Offarum* and *La Manekine*), arranged in approximately chronological order, with the editor of the text I have used; where one is printed as part of a larger narrative or collection, I give the title of the source text too. Full bibliographical details are given in the Bibliography, where they are listed by author or, if the text is anonymous, by title. For fuller descriptions and discussion of these texts (and of some other versions) see Roussel, *Conter de geste*, 73–140.

Thirteenth Century

Pierre de Saint-Aubert, *Vita Sanctae Dympnae*, in *AASS* [Latin prose, 1238–47]
A pagan Irish ruler and his wife are childless for many years. The queen secretly becomes a Christian, and gives birth to a daughter, baptized Dympna. When the queen dies, the king will only consider marrying someone just like her; no such woman can be found, so his counsellors advise him to marry Dympna. The king begins to desire her, but Dympna, a Christian, is horrified. She obtains forty days' respite, and flees with Gereburnus, an elderly Christian convert, and also the court jester and his wife. They arrive in Antwerp and travel on to Gheel, where they live near an oratory of St Martin. The king tracks her down; he still wants to marry her, but she still refuses. The king himself beheads Dympna, and his men kill Gereburnus. They are buried side by side, and miracles are associated with the tomb.

Yde et Olive, ed. Schweigel in *Esclarmonde* (= *Huon of Bordeaux* cycle) [French verse, 13th cent.]
(See also the sixteenth-century version by Lord Berners, *Ide and Olive*. One synopsis is given for the two versions; English forms of names appear in parentheses.)
The widowed King Florens (Florence) of Aragon announces his intention of marrying the only woman who resembles his dead wife—his daughter Yde (Ide). She runs away in male clothing, lives as a soldier, and becomes the favourite of the Emperor of Rome, who insists that s/he marry his only

child Olive. The embarrassed Yde tells her secret to her bride, who is quite prepared to accept the situation; but a spy informs the emperor of Yde's disguise. He threatens to burn Yde if a public bath reveals that she is a woman, but a voice from heaven warns him not to touch her: God will change her into a man as a reward for her virtue. Yde is transformed, and that night her son Croissant is conceived. A few days later the emperor dies. (In a late printed French text, and in the English version, Florens becomes ill from chagrin some years later, and is reconciled with Yde before he dies.)

Mai und Beaflor, ed. anon. [German verse, c.1260]

The widowed King of Rome falls in love with his daughter Beaflor. She flees by boat, helped by her tutor Roboal and his wife Benigna, and arrives in Mailand (Greece), where she marries the young Count Mai. When her son is born, his mother forges letters declaring that Beaflor is an adulteress and has borne a monster, and that she should be killed. Beaflor is set adrift with her baby and arrives back in Rome, where she lodges with the faithful servants who had helped her escape; she is afraid of her father. After eight years Mai is so miserable that his anxious people suggest a pilgrimage to Rome. He too lodges with Roboal, who promises to reunite him with Beaflor, and duly organizes a recognition scene at dinner. Meanwhile Beaflor's contrite father confesses and abdicates; he becomes a hermit.

Jansen Enikel, *Der König von Reussen*, 26677–7356 in his *Weltchronik*, ed. Strauch [German verse, late 13th cent.]
(There is also a 15th-cent. prose version, ed. anon. in *Mai und Beaflor*.)

The widowed King of Russia gets the Pope's permission to marry his daughter, but she refuses; she scratches her face till she is 'like the devil' and cuts her hair off. The furious king sets her adrift in a barrel with a special wedding dress. She arrives in Greece, where the king marries her. When her baby is born the hostile mother-in-law reports that it is a devil; the king orders mother and child to be returned to wherever they came from (there is no second forgery). They drift to Rome, where an old nobleman finds them and has the child baptized by the Pope. When the King of Greece discovers what has happened, he has his mother walled up, and comes to Rome for absolution for his sin of wrongly condemning his wife; the King of Russia, also contrite, arrives at the same time. The Pope hears their confessions, realizes who the mysterious woman is, and brings about a general reunion.

Fourteenth Century

Jean Gobi, 'The Daughter of the Count of Poitou', ch. 180 in *Scala coeli*, ed. Polo de Beaulieu [Latin prose, 1325–30]

The Count of Poitou has a son and a daughter. The son goes to study in Bologna. When the count's wife dies, he falls in love with his daughter. She flees, and later marries the son of the King of Arles. When she has a son, her mother-in-law forges letters saying that the baby has a dog's head. She is taken to the forest to be killed, but the assassins spare her when the baby smiles at them, and order her to go far away. She arrives as a beggar in Bologna, where her brother is now bishop; a holy man sees her begging and asks the bishop to provide for her. Her husband searches for her, dressed as a beggar himself, and comes to Bologna. The bishop questions him and reunites him with his wife, who turns out to be the bishop's sister.

Jean Maillart, *Le Roman du Comte d'Anjou*, ed. Roques [French verse, early 14th cent.]

The devil makes the widowed Count of Anjou fall in love with his own beautiful and talented daughter. She flees with her nurse; they take refuge with a poor woman in Orléans, and earn their living by marvellous embroidery. The count, horrified by his crime and by his daughter's flight, soon dies. A young man sees and desires the heroine, so she and the nurse flee again and find work in the castle of Lorris, teaching embroidery to the lord's daughters. The lord's young and passionate overlord, the Count of Bourges, comes to visit, and marries the heroine. He is away when she gives birth; his aunt forges a letter announcing the birth of a monster, and a reply ordering mother and child to be killed. Disarmed by the baby's smile, the assassins let the heroine go. Destitute and still recovering from childbirth, she makes her way to Estampes and on to Orléans, where the bishop is her uncle, and there finds refuge in the hospital. The count comes home and discovers the plot. Disguised as a vagabond, he searches for his wife among the poor and finds the trail to Orléans, where he is reunited with his wife whose identity is revealed through the bishop. The wicked countess is burned.

La Belle Hélène de Constantinople, ed. Roussel [French verse, mid-14th cent.]
(Also a prose version of 1448 by Jean Wauquelin, trans. de Crécy.)

Antoine, Emperor of Constantinople, helps the Romans during a Saracen siege and is rewarded with the hand of the emperor's daughter; she dies giving birth to their daughter Hélène. Antoine falls in love with his daughter; when the Pope again asks for help against the Saracens, Antoine asks in return for permission to marry Hélène. The Pope agrees, reluctantly; he is very anxious when Antoine claims his reward, but a voice from heaven announces that Antoine will never be able to fulfil his impious desire. Antoine returns to Constantinople and tells Hélène that they will be married the next day. She escapes by boat, arrives in Flanders, and lives in a convent. Alarmed by the local king's interest in her, she sets off again in her boat, but is captured by pirates. The captain makes advances to her, but her prayers bring a storm in which all but she are drowned. She floats ashore on a plank near Newcastle in northern England and meets King Henry, who marries her, to the dismay of his mother.

Rome is attacked again: Antoine is away looking for his daughter, so the Pope asks for help from Henry, who agrees and entrusts his pregnant wife to the care of the Duke of Gloucester. In Rome Henry sees portraits of his wife which had been painted on the columns of the papal palace at Antoine's orders; the Pope tells him the story. Hélène gives birth to twin sons; her mother-in-law forges a letter announcing the birth of two monsters, and a reply ordering the burning of the queen and her children. Instead the Duke of Gloucester cuts off one of her hands, attaches it to one of the twins, and exposes them all in a boat which arrives at an island called Constance. While Hélène is dozing a wolf carries off the baby with the hand, who is then raised by a hermit. A lion takes the other baby, and eventually the hermit finds it too: he names the twins Brac and Lion. Henry defeats the Saracens and returns to England. Antoine arrives in Bavaria, where he stops a pagan king from marrying his own daughter, and converts the country to Christianity. Henry discovers his mother's treachery, and has her burned. The two kings meet in Boulogne, confer, and set out in search of Hélène.

The twins learn something of their history, and set out to find their mother, meeting on the way the Duke of Gloucester and the Archbishop of Tours; the latter baptizes them Brice and Martin. Hélène has been living in Nantes but moves to Tours, where her sons give her charity without recognizing her. Henry and Antoine meet the hermit, and conquer and convert the King of Bordeaux. Henry comes to Tours where Hélène recognizes him but is too frightened to speak. Henry and Antoine meet the twins and see the miraculously preserved hand, which leads to a recognition scene. The two kings, plus the King of Bordeaux, go on a crusade to Jerusalem and have adventures there. Hearing a rumour that they have been killed, Hélène becomes a beggar; she goes to Rome but does not reveal herself to her great-uncle the Pope, nor to the two kings when they return. The Saracens attack yet again: Hélène flees to Tours, leaving letters for her father and husband. Henry is captured in Flanders but freed by the twins; in Scotland Antoine and Brice are captured, then freed by a Saracen princess who falls in love with Brice, converts to Christianity, and marries him (their son becomes St Brice). The kings travel to Tours, and eventually find the terrified Hélène; her hand is miraculously reattached through the agency of Martin, the future saint. All return to Rome, where the converted King of Bordeaux is made king; Henry and Hélène die and are buried in St Peter's; Antoine abdicates in favour of Brice; Martin becomes Archbishop of Tours; the Duke of Gloucester becomes King of England.

Lion de Bourges, ed. Kibler *et al.* [French verse, mid-14th cent.]
(The Flight from Incest/Accused Queen episode begins at 27778; it is preceded by numerous martial adventures.)

Herpin, King of Cyprus, promises his dying wife not to marry again unless he finds a woman just like her. His barons urge him to remarry, but cannot find a suitable bride until they notice the resemblance between the Princess Joieuse and her dead mother; they tell the king to marry her (having already obtained the Pope's permission). Herpin agrees: he is already in love with her. Joieuse cuts off her left hand and throws it into the river, where it is swallowed by a sturgeon; she explains to the king that now she no longer resembles her mother. Herpin orders that she be burned, but is persuaded by the barons to exile her by sea with the squire Thierry. They eventually arrive in Spain, where Joyeuse calls herself Tristouse. (Here the story turns to the adventures of Olivier, future husband of Joieuse, and of his brother Guillaume.) Olivier takes in Joieuse and Thierry; Joieuse explains that she lost her hand in a struggle with pirates. He has a golden hand made for her and marries her, over the objections of his foster-mother Béatris. He leaves her pregnant in order to help his brother. (Adventures of Olivier and his father Lion.)

 Joieuse/Tristouse gives birth to twins, a boy and a girl. Béatris uses a clerk she has seduced to forge a message ordering the burning of the queen and her children. The king's castellan spares them (he burns some animals instead) and exposes them again at sea. They arrive at Rome and are taken in by a rich senator and his wife; Joieuse/Tristouse tells them that during a pilgrimage robbers killed her husband and cut off her hand. (Further adventures of Lion and his sons. Olivier invites them back to Caffaut to meet his wife.) Olivier is baffled by the disappearance of his wife and the forged letter, but suspects Béatris. The treacherous clerk confesses; he is hanged and Béatris is locked in a tower. Olivier goes to Sicily with his father and brother; there he meets the King of Cyprus who talks about his wife's death and his treatment of his daughter. Olivier realizes that this is his father-in-law. The two kings go to Rome and lodge in the house where Joieuse lives. She is too afraid of them to appear, but at dinner Olivier sees his son Herpin playing with her wedding ring, which he recognizes; this leads to a reunion. The cook finds Joieuse's hand in a fish he is preparing, and the Pope is miraculously able to reattach it. Olivier and Joieuse return to Burgos, Herpin to Cyprus. (Further martial adventures of the male protagonists.)

Comedia sine nomine (also known as *Columpnarium*), ed. Roy [Latin prose drama, late 14th cent.]

The Queen of Thrace dies after making her husband Eumolphus promise only to marry a woman who is her living image; no such woman can be found. Urged by his people to remarry, the king falls in love with his daughter Hermionides. Horrified, she flees with her nurse; they find refuge with Sophia in Phocis, where the local king, Orestes, falls in love with Hermionides and marries her. When she bears a son, the hostile queen mother Olicomesta forges letters announcing that the baby is an Ethiopian monster, and that mother and child are to be killed. A faithful seneschal exposes the baby in a splendid basket with money and jewels, and sends Hermionides into exile. The baby is found by a fisherman, who wants to adopt him, but first decides to consult the oracle of Apollo on Mount Parnassus. As he discusses this plan with a friend, he is overheard by Orestes and his counsellor Regulus, who are returning to Phocis because they are suspicious of the news that has reached them about the queen. The faithful seneschal is also suspicious, discovers the forgery of the letters, and tells the king. Meanwhile Hermionides, wandering on Parnassus, meets a shepherd who urges her to consult the oracle there. All the main characters make for the oracle. Hermionides meets the fisherman, hears his story, and manages to recover her baby. The nurse, Orestes, and the seneschal overhear their conversation, and so Orestes and his wife are reunited. News arrives that the queen mother has killed herself, and also that Eumolphus has died, leaving his kingdom to Hermionides.

La Istoria de la Fiyla del Rey d'Ungria, ed. Aramon i Serra [Catalan prose, mid-14th cent.]

The widowed King of Hungary is urged by his barons to marry; when they cannot find a woman who fits his specification of resemblance to his dead wife, they suggest his daughter. After initial reluctance, he is persuaded by the devil to marry her. The night before the wedding he tells her how much he admires her hands; she makes her servants cut them off. The furious king exposes her in a boat, and she arrives at Marseilles; there the Count of Provence falls in love with her and marries her secretly. They have a son who is notable for his charity to other children. After some years the count goes to Hungary to verify his wife's story, and to announce that she is alive. He sends a letter home confirming her identity, but the messenger stops at the home of the count's hostile mother, who forges the message that the countess is low-born and has been mutilated for theft and sent into exile; she and her son are now to be burned. The messenger tells the people the truth, but they are confused, and expose the countess and her son in a boat. They find lodging at a convent where the countess lives piously. Five years later, she feels a fervent wish to help the priest at Mass, and suddenly sees two hands in front of her, which miraculously affix themselves to her stumps. Meantime the count has come home and discovered what has happened. He sets out to find his wife, and after seven years arrives at the abbey where she acts as porter. She looks like his wife, but he is baffled by the fact that she has hands. The miracle is explained to him; the couple is reunited, and four more children are born.

Miracle de la fille du roy de Hongrie, no. 19 in *Miracles de Nostre Dame par personnages*, ed. Paris and Robert   [French verse drama, 1340–80]
(Adaptation of *Manekine*, but with strong Marian emphasis and many variations on names, e.g. Bethequine for Manekine. See also in the same collection nos. 32, *Du roy Thierry*, and 37, *De la fille d'un roy qui se parti d'avec son pere pour ce que il la vouloit espouser*.)
The King of Hungary refuses to marry any woman who does not closely resemble his dead wife; no such woman can be found. He decides to marry his daughter and gets the Pope's permission. His daughter, horrified, cuts off her hand. She is condemned to be burned, but her executioners expose her in a boat instead. She arrives in Scotland and marries the king, to the anger of his mother. When she gives birth, the mother-in-law forges a slanderous letter and then a cruel response. The heroine and her baby are exposed at sea; helped by the Virgin, they arrive at Rome and find refuge with a senator. The King of Scotland returns, discovers what has happened, and punishes his mother; then he goes to Rome to pray and to look for his wife. At the same time the King of Hungary decides to go to Rome to be absolved. There is a family reunion in the house of the senator, brought about by the child playing with the wedding ring. The missing hand is found in the river and miraculously reattached by the Pope.

Ystoria Regis Franchorum et Filie in qua Adulterium Comitere Voluit, ed. Suchier   [Latin prose, 1370]
The King of France propositions his own daughter. Eventually she yields, but asks for four days' respite and flees, briefly disguised as a man. In a neighbouring town she learns embroidery. The local count marries her, to the horror of his mother who lives in a convent. While the count is away the countess has twin boys. The count's enthusiastic response to the news in a letter is changed by his mother to cruel threats. Alarmed, the young countess flees with her babies; she arrives by boat in Rome, where she works as an embroiderer. A cardinal oversees the education of the twins. The count comes to Rome for a great feast given by the Pope, and stays with his old friend the cardinal. The countess happens to see him; she sends for her sons, and goes to the cardinal's house to greet her husband and explain her flight. The count learns of his mother's trick and has her

burned. When the King of England dies, one twin inherits his throne, while the other succeeds his father as count.

Novella della figlia del re di Dacia, ed. Wesselofsky [Italian prose, probably 14th cent., though the manuscript is 15th cent.]

The story is presented as a miracle performed by Pope Benedict (1012–24). The devil makes the widowed King of Dacia fall in love with his daughter Elisa. One day when she kisses him innocently, he kisses her back and makes her touch him intimately. When he propositions her, she puts him off and prays to Christ and the Virgin. Acting on instructions imparted in a vision, she cuts off the hand with which she touched her father and buries it, telling him that it happened in her sleep as divine justice. Her nurse helps her to flee secretly and they arrive in Rome, where a kind widow takes them in. Apardo, Duke of Austria, marries her, to his mother's displeasure; her hand is miraculously restored during the blessing of the marriage.

When their child is born the hostile mother-in-law forges letters reporting that it is a monster with multiple heads and limbs, and condemning the young mother to death. A poor woman is burnt instead of Elisa, who sends her child to be fostered in secret and herself returns to the widow at Rome, where she becomes nurse to the child of Count Marco. On their way to his home in Germany, they pass through Apardo's lands; Elisa collects her son, and the two children are raised together. Apardo goes to Rome and visits the widow in his search for Elisa. By chance he comes to Marco's city; he and Elisa recognize each other at a feast. When their stories are told, messengers are sent to Elisa's father. He repents, writes to them, is reunited with them, and makes them his heirs. He goes to do penance at Rome, and dies.

Emaré, ed. Rickert [English verse, *c.*1400]

The Emperor Artus' wife dies young, leaving a beautiful daughter, Emaré. The Emperor of Sicily comes to visit and gives Artus a splendid cloth embroidered in each corner by the daughter of a heathen emir with images of pairs of lovers. At a feast soon afterwards Artus falls in love with his own daughter and decides to marry her; the Pope's permission is obtained. Artus has a robe made for Emaré from the cloth, and tells her his intentions; she is horrified. Furious, he exposes her with the robe in a boat, though he soon repents and tries in vain to find her. Emaré arrives in Galys (Wales) and is found by the king's steward. When the king sees her in her beautiful dress he falls in love with her and marries her, although his mother declares the stranger a fiend.

Emaré gives birth to a son, Sagramour; the mother-in-law substitutes news of the birth of a devil with three animal heads, and forges a response ordering the queen and her child to be exposed at sea. They arrive at Rome, and find refuge with a rich merchant. When the king hears what has happened he wants to burn his mother, but is persuaded to exile her. After seven years he goes to Rome to do penance for his wife's presumed drowning, and lodges in the house where Emaré lives. Emaré sends Sagramour to serve his father; the king is charmed and wants to raise him. Emaré tells Sagramour to bring the king to her, and they are reunited. Then Artus arrives to do penance too. Emaré asks her husband to introduce her to Artus, and instructs Sagramour to bring the old emperor to her. There is a further reunion; later Sagramour succeeds his grandfather.

Fifteenth Century

Hans von Bühel (der Büheler), *Die Königstochter von Frankreich*, ed. Merzdorf [German verse, 1401]

The widowed King of France decides to marry his daughter, though the Pope refuses him permission. She flees in horror to England, and lives at first with peasants, looking after animals. She becomes known for her expert embroidery. In London the royal marshal and his wife take her in, and the king marries her. He is away fighting when their son is born; the mother-in-law forges two letters accusing her of sorcery and of bearing a monster, and ordering her to be burned. The marshal burns a cow and a calf instead, and exposes her again with her baby in her boat. She arrives in Rome, and finds refuge with a rich citizen. The child becomes the Pope's favourite. When the king finds out what has happened, he burns his mother. The Kings of France and England arrive in Rome to do penance. The boy serves them; when the mother is summoned, the King of England and his marshal both recognize her. The King of France makes a public confession which leads to a further reunion. The reunited couple go to Paris and then to London. On the death of the King of France the princess inherits the throne. Her husband and son are away at war when she dies; another king takes over France. Her husband fights for his son's rights, winning Calais and other towns: the poet comments that this was the beginning of the Hundred Years War.

De Alixandre, Roy de Hongrie, qui voulut espouser sa fille, ed. Langlois [French prose, mid-15th cent.]

The widowed King of Hungary falls in love with his 15-year-old daughter Fleurie, and passes a law that Hungarian kings can marry their daughters. She discovers that her father especially loves her hands, so she makes a servant cut them off and sends them to him. The furious king wants to burn her, but his counsellors persuade him to expose her and her maid at sea. They arrive at Marseilles, where Count Varron of Provence marries

Fleurie, to his mother's displeasure. Leaving her pregnant, Varron goes to Hungary to check the story she has told him about her identity and troubles. The king, now ashamed, confirms it all.

The count's mother forges a letter announcing that Fleurie has born a monster with no hands and a dog's muzzle, and then also the reply that mother and baby are to be exposed at sea. They find refuge in a convent. When Varron returns and discovers the truth from his mother, he condemns her to a shameful death and swears to search till he finds his wife. After long and vain journeys he is returning by sea when he hears the convent bells and stops there. When Fleurie tries to help the priest at Mass, God is pleased and restores her hands. Her son plays at his father's feet and the count, charmed, wonders who his mother can be. When the abbess explains about their handless guest, the count is reunited with his wife and son, and takes them back to Provence. The old King of Hungary hands over his throne to them and retires into religious life.

Bartolomeo Fazio, *De origine inter Gallos et Britannos belli historia*, ed. Camusat, repr. Roy [Latin, *c*.1470]

The King of Britain promises his dying wife that he will only marry a woman who is her equal; when no suitable bride can be found, the devil prompts him to desire his own daughter. She is horrified at his proposal to marry her, but pretending to give in, she asks him to obtain the Pope's permission; before the messengers return with forged papal letters (as instructed by the king), she escapes with the help of her uncle, John Duke of Lancaster. She takes refuge under a pseudonym in a convent in Vienne, where the Dauphin sees her and marries her, to his mother's fury. When the King of France dies the Dauphin goes to Paris, leaving his pregnant wife behind. The queen mother sends forged letters to the king announcing that the queen has committed adultery and other shameful acts; she also forges his reply ordering that the young queen be killed, but the guards send her and her infant son secretly to Rome, where she lodges in another convent and becomes wet-nurse to the empress' new baby. The new King of France returns to Vienne; suspecting a plot by his mother, he besieges her city and orders her death.

Some years later he feels contrite, and is persuaded to go to Rome to seek absolution. He is graciously received by the emperor and the Pope, and absolved by the latter. At an imperial feast the king is especially charmed by his own unrecognized son, and asks the emperor to give him the youth. The emperor consults the boy's mother, who reveals her secret; the King of France is reunited with his wife and son. The King of Britain has recently died without a male heir, leaving his kingdom to his daughter if she is still alive. The Duke of Lancaster makes public the circumstances of her flight; when uncle and niece meet by chance, the King of France discovers his wife's parentage. Another son is born to the happy couple. The King of France leaves France to his older son and Britain to the younger; but to show the unity of the two kingdoms, he orders that every Christmas the King of Britain and his sons shall serve wine to the king of France at a public banquet. This custom is continued for many generations, but eventually the British abandon it. The French king, offended, declares war (the Hundred Years War).

Rappresentazione di Santa Uliva, ed. d'Ancona [a play with musical interludes preserved in a printed text of 1568 but based on a 15th-cent. Italian poem]

The Emperor Giuliano promises his dying wife only to marry a woman as noble and gracious as her. His daughter Uliva alone fits this description: he plans to ask the Pope for permission to marry her. When he informs Uliva, praising her hands in particular, she is horrified. With a prayer to the Virgin, she cuts off her hands and has them taken to her father. He is furious, and dispatches her to Brittany with two assassins. The assassins pity her and leave her in a wood, where she is found by the king's huntsmen. Both king and queen think her charming, and make her nurse to their baby son. A baron in love with her pulls at her arm so that she drops the baby, who is killed. She is again exposed in a wood. The Virgin appears to her and restores her hands. She finds refuge in a nearby monastery, but the priest feels so tempted by her that he hides a supposedly stolen chalice in her cell. The nuns decide to expose her at sea in a chest. She is found by two Castilian sailors and taken to the royal court, where the king marries her; his furious mother retires to a convent.

While the king is away at war, the queen mother forges letters announcing that Uliva's new baby is neither man nor beast, and that she is to be burned. The merciful Viceroy decides to burn a wooden image and to expose Uliva and the baby at sea. Uliva arrives near Rome and is taken in by two old women. Meanwhile the King of Castile comes home, is horrified by the news, and burns his mother's convent. Twelve years later he decides to confess to the bishop, who orders him to Rome to be absolved by the Pope. Uliva tells her son who the king is and asks him to make contact with his father; the boy is anxious to reunite his parents. The next day Uliva herself comes to court and identifies herself to her father and husband, reproaching them for their cruelty. The emperor acknowledges his grandson as his heir. The king and Uliva are married a second time; the Pope absolves and blesses the king. The king and queen go home and distribute rewards and alms. An angel tells the audience to learn from the example of this 'santa piena di prudenzia' (saint full of wisdom).

Gutierre Diez de Games, *El Victorial—Crónica de Don Pero Niño*, ch. 57, ed. de Mata Carriazo [Spanish, *c*.1435]

The widowed Duke of Guienne falls in love with his daughter, who greatly resembles her dead mother (a French princess). When the duke kisses her hands, she tells a servant to cut them off. Her father wants to kill her, but his counsellors persuade him to put her in a ship with some provisions and set her adrift, with her hands in a basin of blood. The Virgin appears to her in a dream, and in response to her prayers her hands are healed and the wind blows. She meets the English fleet under the command of the king's brother, who marries her. When her father dies, they claim the dukedom, which her father has left to the King of France. This is why there is still a war between France and England.

La Istoria de la Filla de l'Emperador Contasti, ed. Suchier [Catalan, 15th cent.]

Contasti [Constantine], Emperor of Rome, promises his dying wife to marry only a woman as beautiful as her who can also wear her glove. His barons urge him to marry again and produce a male heir; no sufficiently beautiful woman can be found except his 12-year-old daughter, so they suggest her. The glove fits her perfectly; after long resistance she agrees to marry him, but only on condition that they do not have sexual relations. The king finds this unbearable; he threatens to die if she does not give in. She still refuses to sin with him, so he orders servants to take her to a desert and kill her. They pity her and put her on a ship on its way to Spain. She refuses to tell the captain who she is or why she is there, and is put ashore at Cadiz, where she is adopted by a rich childless couple. The King of Spain marries her; when she gives birth, his hostile mother forges letters saying that her baby is black as a Saracen, and that mother and child are to be burned. A kind seneschal puts her on a boat to Rome, where the emperor notices her when he is distributing alms. Meanwhile the King of Spain has learned the truth and burned his mother. He falls ill and promises to go to Rome for absolution if he recovers. At Rome he tells his story to the emperor, and is overheard by the heroine. She sends her son to him with her wedding ring, and all are reunited.

Sixteenth Century

Lord Berners, *Ide and Olive*, ed. Lee [English prose version of *Yde et Olive*, *c*.1515]

See the plot summary for *Yde et Olive* (13th cent.).

Bibliography

Loeb Classical Library editions of classical texts are not included in this bibliography. Anonymous texts are cited by title (or by cross-references to the editor if they appear in a collection). Some modern critical texts include editions of primary texts; I have generally listed such books under Primary Sources. When several editions of a text are given, an asterisk marks the one from which my references are taken.

PRIMARY SOURCES

ABELARD, PETER, *Ethics*, ed. and trans. D. Luscombe (Oxford, 1971).

Aiol, ed. Jacques Normand and Gaston Paris (Paris, 1877).

ALAIN DE LILLE, *Liber Poenitentialis*, ed. Jean Longère, 2 vols. in 1 (Louvain, 1965).

De Alixandre, Roy de Hongrie, qui voulut espouser sa fille, ed. Roy, in *Études sur le théâtre*, 275–9.

*—— ed. E. Langlois in *Nouvelles françaises inédites du XVe siècle* (Paris, 1908), 61–7.

An Alphabet of Tales, ed. M. M. Banks, EETS OS 126 (London, 1904).

AMBROSE, St, *Epistolae*, PL 16: 914–1342.

ANDREAS CAPELLANUS, *Andreas Capellanus on Love*, ed. and trans. P. G. Walsh (London, 1982).

AQUINAS, St THOMAS, *Summa Theologiae*, gen. ed. and trans. Thomas Gilby, OP, 61 vols., Blackfriars edn. (London, 1964–81).

ARNOLD VON LÜBECK, *Gesta Gregorii Peccatoris*, ed. Johannes Schilling, Palaestra, 280 (Göttingen, 1986).

ARTEMIDORUS, *The Interpretation of Dreams*, trans. Robert J. White (Park Ridge, NJ, 1975).

AUGUSTINE, St, *De bono coniugali*, ed. J. Zycha, Corpus Scriptorum Ecclesiasticorum Latinorum, 42 (Vienna, 1900), 185–231.

—— *De nuptiis et concupiscentiis*, ed. C. F. Urba and J. Zycha, Corpus Scriptorum Ecclesiasticorum Latinorum, 41 (Vienna, 1902), 209–319.

BANDELLO, MATTEO, *Le Novelle*, ed. G. Brognoligo, 5 vols. (Bari, 1910–12).

BARTHOLOMEW OF EXETER, *Liber Poenitentialis*, ed. Dom Adrian Morey, in *Bartholomew of Exeter, Bishop and Canonist: A Study in the Twelfth Century. With the Text of Bartholomew's Penitential from the Cotton MS Vitellius A.XII* (Cambridge, 1973), 163–300.

BASILE, *Il Pentamerone*, ed. and trans. A. Burani and R. Guarini as *Il Racconto dei Racconti* (Milan, 1994).

BAUM, PAULL F., 'The Medieval Legend of Judas Iscariot', *PMLA* 31 (1916), 481–632.

BEAUMANOIR, PHILIPPE DE, *La Manekine*, ed. H. Suchier, *Œuvres Poétiques de Philippe de Rémi, Sieur de Beaumanoir*, SATF (Paris, 1884–5), vol. i.

—— *La Manekine: Roman du XIIIe siècle*, trans. C. Marchello-Nizia (Paris, 1980).

—— *Philippe de Rémi's 'La Manekine': Text, Translation, Commentary*, ed. Irene Gnarra (New York, 1988).

*—— *Le Roman de la Manekine*, ed. and trans. Barbara Sargent-Baur, with contributions by Alison Stones and Roger Middleton (Amsterdam and Atlanta, Ga., 1999).

BEAUVOIR, SIMONE DE, *The Mandarins*, trans. L. Friedman (Cleveland and New York, 1956).

BEDE, *Bede's Ecclesiastical History of the English People*, ed. B. Colgrave and R. A. B. Mynors (Oxford, 1969; repr. 1991).

La Belle Hélène de Constantinople, chanson de geste du XIVe siècle, ed. Claude Roussel, TLF (Geneva, 1995). *See also* Wauquelin.

BERNERS, LORD, *Ide and Olive*, in *The Boke of Duke Huon of Burdeux*, ed. S. L. Lee, 2 vols., EETS ES 40, 41, 43, 50 (London, 1882–7; repr. New York, 1975), ii. 690–737.

BLAMIRES, ALCUIN, with KAREN PRATT and C. W. MARX (eds.), *Woman Defamed and Woman Defended: An Anthology of Medieval Texts* (Oxford, 1992).

BOCCACCIO, GIOVANNI, *De casibus virorum illustrium*, ed. P. G. Ricci and V. Zaccaria, in *Tutte le opere*, ed. V. Branca, vol. ix (Milan, 1983).

—— *De claris mulieribus*, ed. V. Zaccaria, in *Tutte le opere*, vol. x (Milan, 1967).

—— *Concerning Famous Women*, trans. Guido A. Guarino (New Brunswick, NJ, 1963).

—— *Decameron*, ed. V. Branca, in *Tutte le opere*, vol. iv (1976).

—— *The Decameron*, trans. G. H. McWilliam (Harmondsworth, 1972).

Le Bone Florence de Rome, ed. A. Wallensköld (Paris, 1907).

Le Bone Florence of Rome, ed. Carol Heffernan (Manchester, 1976).

The Book of Vices and Virtues, ed. W. Nelson Francis, EETS OS 217 (London, 1942).

BROWN, LORANNE, *The Handless Maiden* (Toronto, 1998).

BÜHEL, HANS VON [DER BÜHELER], *Die Königstochter von Frankreich*, ed. J. F. L. Merzdorf (Oldenburg, 1867).

BURTON, ROBERT, *The Anatomy of Melancholy*, ed. Thomas C. Faulkner, Nicholas K. Kiessling, and Rhonda L. Blake, 3 vols. (Oxford, 1989–94).

CAESARIUS OF HEISTERBACH, *The Dialogue on Miracles*, trans. H. von E. Scott and C. C. Swinton Bland, 2 vols. (London, 1929).

Calendar of Entries in the Papal Register relating to Great Britain and Ireland: Papal Letters Vol. 3, 1342–1362, ed. W. H. Bliss and C. Johnson (London, 1897).

The Canons of the Church of England (London, 1969).

Les Cent Nouvelles Nouvelles, ed. Franklin P. Sweetser (Geneva, 1966).

——— trans. Judith B. Diner as *The One Hundred True Tales* (New York, 1990).

CHAUCER, GEOFFREY, *The Riverside Chaucer*, ed. Larry D. Benson *et al.*, 3rd edn. (Boston, Mass., 1987).

CHILD, F. J. (ed.), *English and Scottish Popular Ballads*, 5 vols. (Boston and New York, 1882–94).

CHRÉTIEN DE TROYES, *Le Chevalier de la Charrete*, ed. Mario Roques, CFMA (Paris, 1963).

——— *Cligès*, ed. A. Micha, CFMA (Paris, 1957).

——— *Le Conte du Graal*, ed. Félix Lecoy, 2 vols. (Paris, 1975).

CHRISTINE DE PIZAN, *The Book of the City of Ladies*, trans. Earl Jeffrey Richards (New York, 1982).

CHRYSOSTOM. *See* John Chrysostom, St.

Clementine Recognitions. See *Die Pseudoklementinen*.

CLOGAN, PAUL, 'The *Planctus* of Oedipus: Text and Comment', *Medievalia et Humanistica*, NS I (1970), 233–9.

The Code of Canon Law: A Text and Commentary, ed. James A. Coriden, Thomas J. Green, and Donald E. Heintschel (London, 1985).

Codex Theodosianus, ed. T. Mommsen and P. M. Meyer as *Theodosiani libri XVI cum constitutionibus Sirmondianis et leges novellae ad Theodosianum pertinentes*, 2nd edn., 2 vols. in 3 (Berlin, 1954), i. 2.

Comedia sine nomine [*Columpnarium*], ed. Émile Roy, in *Études sur le théâtre français du XIVe et du XVe siècle. La Comédie sans titre publiée pour la première fois d'après le manuscrit latin 8163 de la Bibliothèque nationale et les Miracles de Notre Dame par personnages* (Paris, 1902).

The Commentaries of Pius II, Books IV and V, trans. Florence A. Gragg, Smith College Studies in History, XXX (Northampton, Mass., 1947).

CONSTANS, L., *La Légende d'Œdipe* (Paris, 1881).

Constitutiones Concilii quarti Lateranensis una cum Commentariis glossatorum, ed. Antonius García y García, Monumenta iuris canonici (Città del Vaticano, 1981).

Cristal et Clarie, ed. Hermann Breuer (Dresden, 1915).

DANTE, *Commedia*, ed. and trans. Charles Singleton, 3 vols. (Princeton, 1970–7).

De Ortu Waluuanii, in *Historia Meriadoci and De Ortu Waluuanii*, ed. J. D. Bruce (Göttingen, 1913).

De Ortu Waluuanii, ed. and trans. Mildred Leake Day as *The Rise of Gawain, Nephew of Arthur (De Ortu Waluuanii Nepotis Arturi)* (New York, 1984).

Des Granz Geanz, ed. Georgina E. Brereton (Oxford, 1937).

DIEZ DE GAMES, GUTIERRE, *El Victorial—Crónica de Don Pero Niño*, ed. Juan de Mata Carriazo (Madrid, 1940).

Doon de Mayence, ed. M. A. Pey (Paris, 1859).

Dux Moraud, in *Non-Cycle Plays and Fragments*, ed. N. Davis, EETS SS 1 (London, 1970), 106–13.

Dympnae, Vita Sanctae. See Pierre de Saint-Aubert.

The Early English Versions of the Gesta Romanorum, ed. S. J. H. Herrtage, EETS ES 33 (London, 1879).

EINHARD, *Life of Charlemagne*, trans. Lewis Thorpe (Harmondsworth, 1969).

Elie de Saint Gille, ed. G. Raynaud de Lage, SATF (Paris, 1879).

Emaré, ed. Edith Rickert, EETS ES 99 (London, 1908; repr. 1958).

ENIKEL, JANSEN, *Der König von Reussen*, in *Weltchronik*, ed. P. Strauch, in *Deutsche Chroniken* III, MGH 30 (Hanover, 1891).

Erec. Roman arthurien en prose, ed. Cedric E. Pickford, TLF (Geneva, 1968).

FAZIO, BARTOLOMEO, *De origine inter Gallos et Britannos belli historia*, ed. D. Camusat (Paris, 1731); *repr. Roy, in *Études sur le théâtre*, 262–74.

La Istoria de la La Fiyla del Rey d'Ungria, ed. R. Aramon i Serra, in *Novel·letes Exemplars* (Barcelona, 1934), 29–60.

FORD, JOHN, *'Tis Pity She's a Whore*, ed. Marion Lomax, in *'Tis Pity She's a Whore and Other Plays* (Oxford, 1995), 165–239.

FROISSART, JEAN, *Meliador*, ed. A. Longnon, 3 vols., SATF (Paris, 1895).

FULGENTIUS, *Fulgentius the Mythographer*, trans. Leslie Whitbread (Columbus, Oh., 1974).

FURNIVALL, F. J. (ed.), *Sources and Analogues of Chaucer's Canterbury Tales* (London, 1888).

GAIUS, *The Institutes of Gaius*, ed. E. Seckel and W. Kuebler, trans. W. M. Gordon and O. F. Robinson (London, 1988).

Garin le Loheren, According to Manuscript A (Bibliothèque de l'Arsenal 2983), ed. Josephine E. Vallerie (New York, 1947).

Generides, ed. W. A. Wright, 2 vols., EETS OS 55 and 70 (London, 1873–8).

GEOFFREY OF MONMOUTH, *The Historia Regum Britannie of Geoffrey of Monmouth, I: Bern Burgerbibliothek, MS 568*, ed. Neil Wright (Cambridge, 1985).

—— *The History of the Kings of Britain*, trans. Lewis Thorpe (Harmondsworth, 1966).

GERALD OF WALES [GIRALDUS CAMBRENSIS], *The History and Topography of Ireland*, trans. John O'Meara, revised edn. (Harmondsworth, 1982).

Gesta Romanorum, ed. H. Oesterley (Berlin, 1872).

Die Gesta Romanorum nach der Innsbrucker Handschrift vom Jahre 1342 und vier Münchener Hss, ed. W. Dick (Erlangen and Leipzig, 1890; repr. Amsterdam, 1970).

Gesta Romanorum. See also *Early English Versions of the Gesta Romanorum*.

GOBI, JEAN, *Scala coeli*, ed. Marie-Anne Polo de Beaulieu (Paris, 1991).

GOTTFRIED VON STRASSBURG, *Tristan*, ed. F. Ranke, revised and trans. Rüdiger Krohn, 3 vols. (Stuttgart, 1980).

—— *Tristan*, trans. A. T. Hatto (Harmondsworth, 1960).

GOWER, JOHN, *Confessio Amantis*, ed. G. C Macaulay as *The English Works of John Gower*, 2 vols., EETS ES 81–2 (Oxford, 1900–1).

—— *Mirour de l'Omme*, ed. G. C. Macaulay in *The Complete Works of John Gower*, vol. i: *The French Works* (Oxford, 1899), 1–334.

—— *Mirour de l'Homme*, trans. William Burton Wilson (East Lansing, 1992).

GRATIAN, *Decretum Magistri Gratiani*, ed. E. Friedberg, in *Corpus iuris canonici*, 2 vols. (Leipzig, 1879; repr. Graz, 1959).

GRIMM, JACOB, *Grimm's Tales for Young and Old*, trans. Ralph Mannheim (New York, 1977).

Guingamor, ed. Prudence Tobin, in *Les Lais anonymes des XIIe and XIIIe siècles* (Geneva, 1976), 127–55.

HARRISON, KATHRYN, *The Kiss* (London, 1997).

HARTMANN VON AUE, *Gregorius*, ed. Hermann Paul, 14th edn. revised by B. Wachinger (Tübingen, 1992).

HEUSER, W., '*Dux Moraud*, Einzelrolle aus einem verlorenen Drama das 14. Jahrhunderts', *Anglia*, 30 (1907), 180–208.

Historia Apollonii Regis Tyri, ed. G. A. A. Kortekaas, Medievalia Groningana, III (Groningen, 1984).

*—— in Elizabeth Archibald, *Apollonius of Tyre, Medieval and Renaissance Themes and Variations, Including the Test of the* Historia Apollonii Regis Tyri *with an English Translation* (Cambridge, 1991).

Historia Britonum [Nennius], in *La Légende Arthurienne*, ed. E. Faral, 3 vols. (Paris, 1929; repr. 1983), iii. 1–62.

Hrólfs Saga Kraka, trans. Gwyn Jones as *King Hrolf and His Champions* in *Eirik the Red and Other Icelandic Sagas* (London, 1961), 221–318.

HUGHES, THOMAS, *The Misfortunes of Arthur: A Critical, Old-Spelling Edition*, ed. Brian Jay Corrigan (New York and London, 1992).

HUXLEY, ALDOUS, *Brave New World* (London, 1977).

HYGINUS, *Fabulae*, ed. Peter K. Marshall (Stuttgart, 1993).

ISIDORE OF SEVILLE, *Etymologiarum libri XX*, ed. W. M. Lindsay, 2 vols. (Oxford, 1911; repr. 1969).

La Istoria de la Filla de l'Emperador Contasti, ed. H. Suchier, in 'La Fille Sans Mains', *Romania*, 30 (1901), 519–38.

—— ed. R. Aramon i Serra, in *Novel·letes Exemplars* (Barcelona, 1934), 61–99.

IVO OF CHARTRES, *Decretum*, PL 161: 47–1036.

JACOBUS DE VORAGINE, *Legenda aurea*, ed. J. G. Th. Graesse, 2nd edn. (Dresden and Leipzig, 1850).

—— *The Golden Legend: Readings on the Saints*, trans. W. G. Ryan (Princeton, 1993).

JEHAN DE SAINT-QUENTIN, *Dits en quatrains d'alexandrins monorimes de Jehan de Saint-Quentin*, ed. B. Munk Olsen, SATF (Paris, 1978).

JOHN CHRYSOSTOM, St, *Homilies on Genesis 18–45*, trans. Robert C. Hill, The Fathers of the Church, 82 (Washington, DC, 1990).

JONSON, BEN, *Ben Jonson*, ed. Ian Donaldson (Oxford, 1985).

Jourdain de Blaye, ed. Peter F. Dembowski, CFMA (Paris, 1991).

JUSTINIAN, *Codex Justinianus*, ed. P. Krueger in *Corpus Iuris Civilis*, ed. P. Krueger and T. Mommsen, vol. ii (Berlin, 1954).

—— *Digest of Justinian*, ed. T. Mommsen with P. Krueger, trans. Alan Watson, 4 vols. (Philadelphia, 1985).

JUSTINUS, *M. Iuniani Iustini Epitoma Historiarum Philippicarum Pompei Trogi*, ed. Otto Seel (Stuttgart, 1972).

The Karlamagnús Saga, trans. Constance B. Hieatt, 3 vols. (Toronto, 1975–80).

KAY, GUY GAVRIEL, *The Wandering Fire*, vol. ii of *The Fionavar Tapestry*, 3 vols. (Don Mills, Ont., 1986).

KEMPE, MARGERY, *The Book of Margery Kempe*, ed. Sanford B. Meech and Hope Emily Allen, EETS OS 212 (London, 1940).

—— *The Book of Margery Kempe*, trans. B. Windeatt (Harmondsworth, 1985).

Der König von Reussen [prose version], ed. anon. in *Mai und Beaflor*, Dichtungen des deutschen Mittelalters, VII (Leipzig, 1848; repr. Hildesheim, 1974), pp. ix–xv.

LACTANTIUS, *Lactantii Placidi in Statii Thebaidi commentum*, ed. R. D. Sweeney, vol. i (Stuttgart, 1997).

Lancelot, roman en prose du XIIIe siècle, ed. A. Micha, 9 vols., TLF (Geneva, 1978–83).

Lancelot-Grail: The Old French Arthurian Vulgate and Post-Vulgate in Translation, ed. Norris J. Lacy, 5 vols. (New York, 1992–6).

The Laws of Æthelred, ed. and trans. A. J. Robertson in *The Laws of the Kings of England from Edmund to Henry I* (Cambridge, 1925), 45–133.

Leges Langobardorum, ed. F. Bluhme in *MGH*, LL IV (Hanover, 1868), 96–175.

—— trans. Katharine Fischer Drew as *The Lombard Laws* (Philadelphia, 1973).

Leges Visigothorum, ed. K. Zeumer in *MGH*, LL I. 1 (Hanover, 1902; repr. 1973), 33–456.

La Leggenda di Vergogna, ed. Alessandro d'Ancona in *La Leggenda di Vergogna, testi del buon secolo in prosa e verso, e la leggenda di Giuda, testo italiano antico in prosa e francese antico in verso* (Bologna, 1869; repr. 1968).

—— ed. Elisabetta Benucci (Rome, 1992).

Lion de Bourges, poème épique du XIVe siècle, ed. W. Kibler, J. L. G. Picherit, and Thelma Fenster, 2 vols., TLF (Geneva, 1980).

LUTHER, MARTIN, *The Babylonian Captivity of the Church*, trans. A. T. W. Steinhäuser, revised F. C. Ahrens and A. R. Wentz, in *Word and Sacrament*, vol. xxxvi of *Luther's Works*, ed. Jaroslav Pelikan and Helmut T. Lehmann (Philadelphia, 1959), 92–105.

—— *Lectures on Genesis, Chapters 31–37*, trans. Paul D. Paul, vol. vi of *Luther's Works*, ed. J. Pelikan (St Louis, 1970).

LYDGATE, JOHN, *Fall of Princes*, ed. H. Bergen, 4 vols., EETS ES 121–4 (London, 1924–7).

—— *Lydgate's Siege of Thebes*, ed. A. Erdman and E. Ekwall, 2 vols., EETS ES 108, 125 (London, 1911 and 1930). *See also Sege of Thebes.*

LYSIAS, *Discours*, ed. and trans. Louis Gernet and Marcel Bizos, 2 vols. (Paris, 1967).

The Mabinogion, trans. Gwyn Jones and Thomas Jones (London, 1949).

MCNEILL, JOHN T., and GAMER, HELENA, *Medieval Handbooks of Penance: A Translation of the Principal 'Libri Poenitentiales' and Selections from Related Documents* (New York, 1938; repr. 1990).

Mai und Beaflor, ed. anon., Dichtungen des deutschen Mittelalters, VII (Leipzig, 1848; repr. Hildesheim, 1974).

MAILLART, JEHAN, *Le Roman du Comte d'Anjou*, ed. M. Roques, CFMA (Paris, 1931).

MALORY, Sir THOMAS, *The Works of Sir Thomas Malory*, ed. Eugene Vinaver, 3rd edn. revised by P. J. C. Field, 3 vols. (Oxford, 1990).

MANNYNG, ROBERT OF BRUNNE, *Robert of Brunne's 'Handlyng Synne' and its French Original*, ed. F. J. Furnivall, 2 vols., EETS OS 119, 123 (London, 1901, 1903; repr. as 1 vol., 1973).

MANSI, GIOVANNI DOMENICO, *Sacrorum conciliorum nova et amplissima collectio*, 60 vols. (Paris, 1901–27).

MARGUERITE DE NAVARRE, *Heptaméron*, ed. M. François (Paris, 1963).

—— *The Heptameron*, trans. P. A. Chilton (Harmondsworth, 1984).

MARIE DE FRANCE, *Lais*, ed. Alfred Ewert (Oxford, 1944).

Merlin, roman du XIIIe siècle, ed. A. Micha, TLF (Geneva, 1979).

MEYER, KUNO, 'Fingal Rónáin', *Revue Celtique*, 13 (1892), 368–97.

Miracle de la fille du roy de Hongrie, ed. G. Paris and U. Robert in *Miracles de Nostre Dame par personnages*, 8 vols., SATF (Paris, 1879–93), v. 1–88.

MIRK, JOHN, *Instructions for Parish Priests*, ed. Gillis Kristensson (Lund, 1974).

Le Mort le roi Artu, ed. Jean Frappier, 3rd edn., TLF (Geneva, 1964).

Le Morte Arthur [Stanzaic], ed. P. F. Hissiger (The Hague, 1975).

Morte Arthure: A Critical Edition [Alliterative], ed. Mary Hamel (New York, 1984).

MORVAY, KARIN, *Die Albanuslegende: Deutsche Fassungen und ihre Beziehungen zur lateinischen Überlieferung* (Munich, 1977).

Mosaicarum et romanarum legum collatio, ed. and trans. M. Hyamson (London, 1913).

Nouveau recueil de contes, dits, fabliaux et autres pièces, ed. A. Jubinal, 2 vols. (Paris, 1839).

Novella della Figlia del Re di Dacia, ed. A. Wesselofsky (Pisa, 1866); repr. as 'La Favola della Fanciulla Perseguitata', in Veselovskij-Sade, *La Fanciulla Perseguitata*, ed. d'Arco Silvio Avalle (Milan, 1977), 35–101.

ORIGEN, *Contra Celsum*, trans. Henry Chadwick (Cambridge, 1953).

—— *Homilies on Genesis and Exodus*, trans. Ronald E. Heine, The Fathers of the Church, 71 (Washington, DC, 1982).

OROSIUS, *The Seven Books of History Against the Pagans*, trans. Roy J. Deferrari, The Fathers of the Church, 50 (Washington, DC, 1964).

Orson de Beauvais, ed. G. Paris, SATF (Paris, 1899).

ORTON, JOE, *What the Butler Saw* (London, 1969).

Ovide Moralisé, ed. C. de Boer, *Verhandelingen der Koninklijke Akademie van Wetenschapen te Amsterdam: Afdeeling Letterkunde*, 15, 21, 30, 36–7, 43 (Amsterdam, 1915–38).

Parise la Duchesse, Chanson de geste du XIIIe siècle, ed. May Plouzeau (= *Senefiance*, 17 and 18) (Aix-en-Provence, 1986).

Partonopeu de Blois, ed. J. Gildea, 2 vols. in 3 (Villanova, Pa., 1967–70).

Perlesvaus, ed. W. A. Nitze and T. A. Jenkins as *Le Haut Livre du Graal: Perlesvaus*, 2 vols. (Chicago, 1932–7).

PETER DAMIAN, *Die Briefe des Petrus Damiani*, ed. K. Reindel, 4 vols. (Munich, 1989).

PHILIPPE DE RÉMI. *See* Beaumanoir.

Philomena, ed. C. de Boer (Paris, 1909; repr. Geneva, 1974).

PIERRE DE SAINT-AUBERT, *Vita Sanctae Dympnae*, AASS Maii III (15 May), 477–97.

Die Pseudoklementinen, ed. B. Rehm and F. Paschke, vol. 1: *Homilien*, 2nd edn.; vol. 2: *Rekognitionen in Rufins Übersetzung*, Die griechischen christlichen Schriftsteller der ersten Jahrhunderte, 51 and 42 (Berlin, 1965–9).

La Queste del Saint Graal, ed. A. Pauphilet, CFMA (Paris, 1923).

RABANUS MAURUS, *Expositionum in Leviticum libri septem, PL* 108: 245–586.

*Rappresentazione di Santa Uliva, ed. Alessandro d'Ancona (Pisa, 1863); repr. in *Sacre Rappresentazioni dei Secoli XIV, XV e XVI*, ed. A. d'Ancona, 3 vols. (Florence, 1872), iii. 235–315; repr. in Veselovskij-Sade, *La Fanciulla*, 129–73.

—— ed. Luigi Banfi, in *Sacre Rappresentazioni del Quattrocento* (Turin, 1963), 739–845.

Recueil général et complet des fabliaux des XIIIe et XIVe siècles imprimés et inedités, ed. A. de Montaiglon and G. Reynaud, 6 vols. (Paris, 1872–90).

Registrum Hamonis Hethe, Diocensis Roffensis, ed. Charles Johnson, Kent Records 4, 2 vols. (Oxford, 1948).

Registrum Palatinum Dunelmense, The Register of Richard de Kellawe, Lord Palatine and Bishop of Durham, 1311–1316, ed. T. D. Hardy, Rolls Series, 4 vols. (London, 1873–8).

RÉGNIER-BOHLER, D., trans., *Le Cœur mangé: Récits érotiques et courtois* (Paris, 1979).

Richars li Biaus, ed. Anthony J. Holden, CFMA (Paris, 1983).

ROBERT OF FLAMBOROUGH, *Liber Poenitentialis*, ed. J. J. Firth, CSB (Toronto, 1971).

Le Roman du Comte d'Anjou. See Maillart, Jehan.

Le Roman de Lanvin, ed. L. Thorpe (Cambridge, 1960).

Le Roman de Renart, ed. M. Roques, CFMA, 6 vols. (Paris, 1955–69).

—— ed. and trans. J. Dufournet and A. Méline, 2 vols. (Paris, 1985).

Le Roman de Thèbes, ed. G. Raynaud de Lage, 2 vols., CFMA (Paris, 1966).

Le Roman de Tristan en prose, ed. R. L. Curtis, vol. i (Munich, 1963; repr. Cambridge, 1985).

Roncesvalles, poème épique provençal, ed. M. Roques in *Romania*, 58 (1932), 1–28 and 161–89.

ROY, É. (ed.), *Études sur le théâtre français du XIVe et du XVe siècle. La Comédie sans titre publiée pour la première fois d'après le manuscrit latin 8163 de la Bibliothèque nationale et les Miracles de Notre Dame par personnages* (Paris, 1902).

SADE, DONATIEN ALPHONSE FRANÇOIS, MARQUIS DE, *Justine, ou les malheurs de la vertu*, ed. M. Delon in *Œuvres*, 3 vols. (Paris, 1990–8), ii. 124–390.

—— *Justine*, trans Richard Seaver and Austryn Wainhouse in *Justine, Philosophy in the Bedroom, and Other Writings* (New York, 1965), 447–743.

The Saga of the Volsungs, ed. and trans. R. G. Finch (London, 1965).

The Sege of Thebes, ed. F. Brie in 'Zwei mittelenglische Prosaromane: *The Sege of Thebes* und *The Sege of Troy*', *Anglia*, 130 (1913), 40–52 and 269–85.

SERLO OF WILTON, *Summa de Penitentia*, ed. J. Goering, 'The *Summa de Penitentia* of Magister Serlo', *Mediaeval Studies*, 38 (1976), 1–53.

*SHAKESPEARE, WILLIAM, *Pericles*, ed. F. D. Hoeniger, Arden edition (London, 1963).

—— *Pericles*, ed. Philip Edwards, New Penguin Shakespeare (Harmondsworth, 1976).

SHELLEY, PERCY BYSSHE, *The Cenci*, ed. G. E. Woodberry (Boston, 1909).

—— *The Letters of Percy Bysshe Shelley*, ed. F. L. Jones, 2 vols. (Oxford, 1964).

Sir Degarre, ed. A. V. C. Schmidt and N. Jacobs in *Medieval English Romances*, 2 vols. (London, 1980), ii. 57–88.

*—— ed. G. Schleich, reproduced and corrected in N. Jacobs, *The Later Versions of Sir Degarre: A Study in Textual Degeneration*, Medium Aevum Monographs, NS 18 (Oxford, 1995), 12–37.

Sir Eglamour of Artois, ed. F. Richardson, EETS OS 256 (London, 1965).

SMART, ELIZABETH, *By Grand Central Station I Sat Down and Wept* (London, 1991).

STEWART, MARY, *The Wicked Day* (London, 1986).

STRAPAROLA, GIOVANNI FRANCESCO, *Le Piacevoli Notti*, ed. G. Rua (Rome, 1975).

Suite du Merlin, ed. G. Paris and J. Ulrich as *Merlin: Roman en prose du XIIIe siècle*, 2 vols., SATF (Paris, 1886).

THOMPSON, FRANCIS, *Poems*, ed. Wilfred Meynell (Oxford, 1937).

TIMONEDA, JUAN DE, *Patrañuelo*, ed. José Romera Castillo (Madrid, 1979).

Tristan de Nanteuil, ed. K. V. Sinclair (Assen, 1971).

Uliva. See *Rappresentazione di Santa Uliva*.

Vergogna. See *Leggenda di Vergogna*.

VESELOVSKIJ-SADE, *La Fanciulla Perseguitata*, ed. d'Arco Silvio Avalle (Milan, 1977).

La Vie du Pape Grégoire: 8 versions françaises médiévales de la légende du Bon Pécheur, ed. H. B. Sol (Amsterdam, 1977).

Vita Aegidii, AASS, Sept. I, 299–314.

The Vulgate Version of the Arthurian Romances, ed. H. O. Sommer, 8 vols. (Washington, DC, 1908–16; repr. 1983).

WACE, *Roman de Brut. A History of the British*, ed. and trans. Judith Weiss (Exeter, 1999).

WALKER, ALICE, *The Color Purple* (New York, 1982).

WAUQUELIN, JEAN, *La Belle Hélène de Constantinople*, trans. Marie-Claude de Crécy, in *Splendeurs de la cour de Bourgogne*, ed. Danielle Régnier-Bohler (Paris, 1995), 111–249.

WOLFRAM VON ESCHENBACH, *Parzival*, ed. Karl Lachmann, revised by Eberhard Nellmann, trans. Dieter Kuhn (Frankfurt, 1994).

—— *Parzival*, trans. A. T. Hatto (Harmondsworth, 1980).

Yde et Olive, ed. Max Schweigel in *Esclarmonde, Clarisse et Florent, Yde et Olive, Drei Fortsetzungen der chanson von Huon de Bordeaux, Ausgaben und Abhandlungen aus dem Gebiete der romanischen Philologie*, 83 (Marburg, 1889), 152–62.

Ysengrimus, ed. and trans. Jill Mann (Leiden, 1987).

Ystoria Regis Franchorum et Filie in qua Adulterium Comitere Voluit, ed. H. Suchier, in 'La Fille Sans Mains: II', *Romania*, 39 (1910), 61–76.

SECONDARY SOURCES

AARNE, A., *The Types of the Folktale*, trans. and enlarged Stith Thompson (Helsinki, 1961).

ADOLF, HELEN, 'The Concept of Original Sin as Reflected in Arthurian Romance', in M. Brahmer *et al.* (eds.), *Studies in Language and Literature in Honour of Margaret Schlauch* (Warsaw, 1966), 21–9.

ALEXANDER, FLORA, 'Late Medieval Scottish Attitudes to the Figure of King Arthur: A Reassessment', *Anglia*, 93 (1975), 17–34.

ALLEN, D. C., *Mysteriously Meant: The Rediscovery of Pagan Symbolism and Allegorical Interpretation in the Renaissance* (Baltimore, 1970).

APROBERTS, ROBERT, 'A Contribution to the Thirteenth Labour: Purging the *Troilus* of Incest', in J. Bakker *et al.* (eds.), *Essays on English and American Literature and a Sheaf of Poems Offered to David Wilkinson*, Costerus, NS 63 (Amsterdam, 1987), 11–25.

ARCHIBALD, ELIZABETH, 'The Flight from Incest: Two Late Classical Precursors of the Constance Theme', *Chaucer Review*, 20.4 (1985–6), 259–72.

—— 'Arthur and Mordred: Variations on an Incest Theme', in *Arthurian Literature*, 8 (1989), 1–27.

—— 'Incest in Medieval Literature and Society', *Forum for Modern Language Studies*, 25 (1989), 1–15.

—— 'Women and Romance', in Henk Aertsen and Alasdair MacDonald (eds.), *Companion to Middle English Romance* (Amsterdam, 1990), 153–69.

—— *Apollonius of Tyre. Medieval and Renaissance Themes and Variations, Including the Text of the* Historia Apollonii Regis Tyri *with an English Translation* (Cambridge, 1991).

—— 'Contextualizing Chaucer's Constance: Romance Modes and Family Values', in M. Teresa Tavormina and Robert F. Yeager (eds.), *The Endless Knot: Essays on Old and Middle English in Honor of Marie Borroff* (Cambridge, 1996), 161–75.

—— 'Gold in the Dungheap: Incest Stories and Family Values in the Middle Ages', *Journal of Family History*, 22 (1997), 133–49.

—— ' "The Price of Guilt": The Incest Theme in Thomas Hughes's *The Misfortunes of Arthur*', *Poetica*, 49 (Tokyo, 1998), 63–75.

—— 'The *Ide and Olive* Episode in Lord Berners's *Huon of Burdeux*', in Rosalind Field (ed.), *Tradition and Transformation in Medieval Romance* (Cambridge, 1999), 139–51.

—— '*Lai le Freine*: The Female Foundling and the Problem of Romance Genre', in Ad Putter and Jane Gilbert (eds.), *The Spirit of Medieval English Popular Romance*, (Harlow, 2000), 39–55.

—— 'Sex and Power in Thebes and Babylon: Oedipus and Semiramis in Classical and Medieval Texts', forthcoming in Gernot Wieland (ed.), *Classical Antiquity and the Middle Ages* (Kalamazoo, Mich.).

ARCHIBALD, ELIZABETH, 'Comedy and Tragedy in Arthurian Recognition Scenes', forthcoming.

—— ' "Worse then bogery": Incest Stories in Middle English Literature', forthcoming in *Arthurian Literature*.

ASTELL, ANN, *The Song of Songs in the Middle Ages* (Ithaca, 1990).

AXTON, RICHARD, 'Interpretations of Judas in Middle English Literature', in P. Boitani and A. Torti (eds.), *Religion in the Poetry and Drama of the Late Middle Ages in England* (Cambridge, 1990), 179–97.

BAASCH, KAREN, *Die Crescentialegende in der deutschen Dichtung des Mittelalters* (Stuttgart, 1968).

BALDWIN, JOHN, *Masters, Princes and Merchants: The Social Views of Peter the Chanter and his Circle*, 2 vols. (Princeton, 1970).

—— 'From the Ordeal to the Confession: In Search of Lay Religion in Early Thirteenth-Century France', in Biller and Minnis (eds.), *Handling Sin: Confession in the Middle Ages*, 191–209.

BARTLETT, ROBERT, *Gerald of Wales, 1146–1223* (Oxford, 1982).

BAUM. *See* Primary Sources.

BAUMGARTNER, E., *Le 'Tristan en Prose': Essai d'interpretation d'un roman médiéval* (Geneva, 1975).

BELL, ROBERT E., *The Dictionary of Classical Mythology: Symbols, Attributes, and Associations* (Oxford and Santa Barbara, 1982).

BELL, VICKI, *Interrogating Incest: Feminism, Foucault and the Law* (London and New York, 1993).

BENSON, C. DAVID, 'Incest and Moral Poetry in Gower's *Confessio Amantis*', *Chaucer Review*, 19 (1984), 100–9.

BERLIOZ, JACQUES, and POLO DE BEAULIEU, MARIE ANNE, *Les Exempla médiévaux* (Carcassonne, 1992).

BERNIER, HÉLÈNE, *La Fille aux mains coupées (conte-type 706)* (Quebec, 1971).

BILLER, PETER, and MINNIS, A. J. (eds.), *Handling Sin: Confession in the Middle Ages* (York, 1998).

BITEL, LISA, *Land of Women: Tales of Sex and Gender from Early Ireland* (Ithaca, 1996).

BLAESS, M., 'Arthur's Sisters', *Bulletin Bibliographique de la Société Internationale Arthurienne*, 8 (1956), 69–77.

BLOCH, R. HOWARD, 'Roland and Oedipus: A study of Paternity in *La Chanson de Roland*', in *French Review*, 46, special issue no. 5 (1973), 3–18.

—— *Etymologies and Genealogies: A Literary Anthropology of the French Middle Ages* (Chicago, 1983).

BLUMENFELD-KOSINSKI, RENATE, *Reading Myth: Classical Mythology and its Interpretation in Medieval French Literature* (Stanford, 1997).

BOEHRER, BRUCE T., *Monarchy and Incest in Renaissance England: Literature, Culture, Kinship, and Kingship* (Philadelphia, 1992).

BOGDANOW, FANNI, *The Romance of the Grail* (Manchester, 1966).

—— 'La Chute du royaume d'Arthur: Evolution d'un thème', *Romania*, 107 (1986), 504–19.

—— 'L'Amour illicite dans le *Roman du Graal* Post-Vulgate et la transformation du thème de la *Beste Glatissant*', in Buschinger and Spiewok (eds.), *Sexuelle Perversionen*, 17–28.

BOOSE, LYNDA E., 'The Father's House and the Daughter in It', in Lynda E. Boose and Betty S. Flowers (eds.), *Daughters and Fathers* (Baltimore, 1989), 19–74.

BORN, L. K., 'Ovid and Allegory', *Speculum*, 9 (1934), 362–79.

BOSSY, JOHN, 'Blood and Baptism: Kinship, Community and Christianity in Western Europe from the Fourteenth Century to the Seventeeth Century', in Derek Baker (ed.), *Sanctity and Secularity: The Church and the World* (Oxford, 1973), 129–43.

BOSWELL, JOHN, *The Kindness of Strangers: The Abandonment of Children in Western Europe from Late Antiquity to the Renaissance* (New York, 1988).

BOUCHÉ, THÉRÈSE, 'De "l'enfant trouvé" à "l'enfant prouvé": *Richars li Biau*, une mise en roman du mythe d'Œdipe', in *Les Relations de parenté dans le monde médiéval* (= *Senefiance*, 26) (1989), 145–59.

BOZÓKY, EDINA, 'La "Bête glatissant" et le Graal. Les Transformations d'un thème allégorique dans quelques romans arthuriens', *Revue de l'histoire des religions*, 86 (1974), 127–48.

BRASWELL, LAUREL, ' "Sir Isumbras" and the Legend of St. Eustace', *Medieval Studies*, 27 (1965), 128–51.

BREEZE, ANDREW, 'The Virgin Mary, Daughter of Her Son', *Études Celtiques*, 27 (1990), 267–83.

BREWER, D. S., *Symbolic Stories—Traditional Narratives of the Family Drama in English Literature* (Cambridge, 1980).

BREWSTER, PAUL G., *The Incest Theme in Folksong*, FF Communications, 212 (Helsinki, 1972), 1–35.

BROOKE, C., *The Medieval Idea of Marriage* (Oxford, 1989).

BROWN, PETER, *The Body and Society: Men, Women, and Sexual Renunciation in Early Christianity* (New York, 1988).

BRUCE, J. D., 'The Composition of the Old French *Lancelot*', *Romanic Review*, 9 (1918), 353–95.

—— 'Mordred's Incestuous Birth', in *Medieval Studies in Honor of Gertrude Schoepperle Loomis* (New York, 1927; repr. Geneva, 1974), 197–205.

BRUNDAGE, JAMES A., 'Carnal Delight: Canonistic Theories of Sexuality', in *Proceedings of the Fifth International Congress of Medieval Canon Law*, ed. Stephan Kuttner and Kenneth Pennington (Vatican City, 1980), 361–5; repr. in Brundage, *Sex, Law and Marriage in the Middle Ages* (Aldershot, 1993).

BRUNDAGE, JAMES A., *Law, Sex, and Christian Society in Medieval Europe* (Chicago, 1987).

BUELER, L., 'The Structural Uses of Incest in English Renaissance Drama', *Renaissance Drama*, NS 15 (1984), 115–45.

BULLÓN-FERNÁNDEZ, MARÍA, 'Confining the Daughter: Gower's "Tale of Canace and Machaire" and the Politics of the Body', in Allen J. Frantzen and David A. Robertson (eds.), *The Body in Medieval Art, History and Literature* (Chicago, 1995), 75–85; repr. with revisions as ch. 4 of Bullón-Fernández, *Fathers and Daughters in Gower's* Confessio Amantis (Cambridge, 2000), 130–72.

—— 'Engendering Authority: Father and Daughter, State and Church in Gower's "Tale of Constance" and Chaucer's "Man of Law's Tale"', in R. F. Yeager (ed.), *Re-Visioning Gower* (Asheville, NC, 1998), 129–46; repr. with revisions as ch. 2 of Bullón-Fernández, *Fathers and Daughters in Gower's* Confessio Amantis (Cambridge, 2000), 42–101.

BUSCHINGER, DANIELLE, and SPIEWOK, WOLFGANG (eds.), *Sexuelle Perversionen im Mittelalter/Les Perversions sexuelles dans le moyen âge* (Greifswald, 1994).

CARMICHAEL, CALUM M., *Law, Legend, and Incest in the Bible* (Ithaca, 1997).

CASTELLANI, MARIE-MADELEINE, 'L'Eau dans *La Manekine* de Philippe de Beaumanoir', in *L'Eau en moyen âge* (=*Senefiance*, 15) (1985), 79–90.

—— *Du conte populaire à l'exemplum: La Manekine de Philippe de Beaumanoir* (Lille, 1988).

CAVE, TERENCE, *Recognitions: A Study in Poetics* (Oxford, 1988).

CAZAURAN, NICOLE, 'La Trentième Nouvelle de l'*Heptaméron* ou la méditation d'un "exemple"', in *Mélanges de littérature du moyen âge au XXe siècle offerts à Mlle. Jeanne Lods*, 2 vols. (Paris, 1978), ii. 617–52.

CHADWICK, HENRY, 'Gregory the Great—the Mission to the Anglo-Saxons', in *Gregorio Magno e il suo tempo* (Rome, 1991), 199–212.

CHAMBERS, R. W., *Beowulf: An Introduction to the Study of the Poem with a Discussion of the Stories of Offa and Finn*, 2nd edn. (Cambridge, 1932).

CHRISTOPH, S., 'Guilt, Shame, Atonement, and Hartmann's *Gregorius*', *Euphorion*, 76 (1982), 207–21.

CINGANO, ETTORE, 'The Death of Oedipus in the Epic Tradition', *Phoenix*, 46.1 (1992), 1–11.

COLLOMP, DENIS, 'Le Parrainage: Une parenté spirituelle peu exploitée', in *Les Relations de parenté dans le monde médiéval* (= *Senefiance*, 26) (1989), 9–23.

CONSTANS, L., *La Légende d'Œdipe* (Paris, 1881).

COOPER, HELEN, 'Counter-Romance: Civil Strife and Father-Killing in the Prose Romances', in Helen Cooper and Sally Mapstone (eds.), *The Long Fifteenth Century: Essays for Douglas Gray* (Oxford, 1997), 141–62.

COPELAND, RITA, *Rhetoric, Hermeneutics, and Translation in the Middle Ages* (Cambridge, 1991).

COX, CHERYL ANNE, *Household Interests: Property, Marriage Strategies, and Family Dynamics in Ancient Athens* (Princeton, 1998).

COX, MARIAN ROALFE, *Cinderella: Three Hundred and Forty-Five Variants* (London, 1893).

CROUZEL, HENRI, ' "Pour former une seule chair": L'interprétation patristique de *Gn* 2,24, la "loi du mariage" ', in *Mélanges offerts à Jean Dauvillier* (Toulouse, 1979), 223–35.

DAUVILLIER, J., and CLERCQ, C. de, *Le Mariage en droit canonique oriental* (Paris, 1936).

DEANESLY, MARGARET, and GROSJEAN, PAUL, SJ, 'The Canterbury Editions of the Answers of Pope Gregory I to St. Augustine', *Journal of Ecclesiastical History*, 10 (1959), 1–49.

DEMATS, PAULE, *Fabula: Trois études de mythographie antique et médiévale* (Geneva, 1973).

Dictionnaire des antiquités grecques et romaines, 10 vols. in 5 (Paris, 1877–1919; repr. Graz, 1962–3).

Dictionnaire de théologie catholique, 15 vols. (Paris, 1899–1950).

DINSHAW, CAROLYN, 'The Law of Man and its "Abhomynacions" ', *Exemplaria*, 1.1 (1989), 117–48; repr. as ch. 3 of Dinshaw, *Chaucer's Sexual Poetics* (Madison, 1989), 88–112.

DONAVIN, GEORGIANA, *Incest Narratives and the Structure of Gower's Confessio Amantis* (Victoria, BC, 1993).

D'ONOFRIO, SALVATORE, 'La Parentela spirituale nel *Roman de Renart*', in Giovanni Ruffino (ed.), *Edizione e analisi linguistica dei testi letterari e documentari del medioevo: Paradigmi interpretativi della cultura medievale*, vol. vi of *Atti del XXI Congresso Internationale di Linguistica e Filologia Romanza* (Tübingen, 1998), 577–98.

DONOVAN, M. J., 'Middle English *Emaré* and the Cloth Worthily Wrought', in Larry D. Benson (ed.), *The Learned and the Lewed: Studies in Chaucer and Medieval Literature* (Cambridge, Mass., 1974), 373–42.

DORN, ERHARD, *Der Sündige Heilige in der Legende des Mittelalters* (Munich, 1967).

DOUGLAS, MARY, *Purity and Danger: An Analysis of the Concepts of Pollution and Taboo* (London, 1966; repr. 1984).

DUBY, Georges, *Medieval Marriage: Two Models from Twelfth-Century France*, trans. Elborg Forster (Baltimore, 1978).

—— *The Knight, The Priest and the Lady*, trans. B. Bray (London, 1984).

DUGGAN, CHARLES, 'Equity and Compassion in Papal Marriage Decretals to England', in W. van Hoecke and A. Welkenhuysen (eds.), *Love and Marriage in the Twelfth Century* (Leuven, 1981), 59–87.

DULAC, LILIANE, 'Un mythe didactique chez Christine de Pizan: Semiramis ou la veuve héroïque', in *Mélanges de philologie romane offerts à Charles Camproux*, 2 vols. (Montpellier, 1978), i. 315–43.

DUNDES, ALAN, ' "To Love My Father All": A Psychoanalytical Study of the Folktale Source of King Lear', in Alan Dundes (ed.), *Cinderella: A Folklore Casebook* (New York, 1982), 229–44.

EDMUNDS, LOWELL, 'Oedipus in the Middle Ages', *Antike und Abendland*, 22 (1976), 140–55.

—— and DUNDES, ALAN (eds.), *Oedipus: A Folklore Casebook* (New York, 1984).

ELLIS, DEBORAH S., '*The Color Purple* and the Patient Griselda', *College English*, 49 (1987), 188–201.

ELLIS, T. P., *Welsh Tribal Law in the Middle Ages*, 2 vols. (Oxford, 1926).

EMMERSON, RICHARD K., *Antichrist in the Middle Ages* (Seattle, 1981).

ESMEIN, A., *Le Mariage en droit canonique*, 2nd edn. revised by R. Genestal (Paris, 1929).

FABRIZIO, RICHARD, 'The Incest Theme', *Dictionary of Literary Themes and Motifs* (New York, 1988), 649–65.

FAUST, G., *Sir Degaré: A Study of the Texts and Narrative Structure* (Princeton, 1935).

FENSTER, THELMA, 'Joie mêlée de Tristouse: The Maiden with the Cut-off Hand in Epic Adaptation', *Neophilologus*, 65 (1981), 345–57.

—— 'Beaumanoir's *La Manekine*: Kin D(r)ead, Incest, Doubling, and Death', *American Imago*, 39 (1982), 41–58.

FIELD, P. J. C., 'Malory's Mordred and the *Morte Arthure*', in Jennifer Fellows *et al.* (eds.), *Romance Reading on the Book: Essays on Medieval Narrative presented to Maldwyn Mills* (Cardiff, 1996), 77–93; repr. (with revisions) in Field, *Malory: Texts and Contexts* (Cambridge, 1998), 89–102.

FLEURY, JEAN, *Recherches historiques sur les empêchements de parenté dans le mariage canonique* (Paris, 1933).

FLINKER, NOAM, 'Cinyras, Myrrha, and Adonis: Father–Daughter Incest from Ovid to Milton', *Milton Studies*, 14 (1980), 59–74.

FOEHR-JANSSENS, YASMINA, 'Quand la manchote se fait brodeuse', *Littérature*, 74 (1989), 63–75.

FOUCAULT, M., *History of Sexuality III: The Care of the Self*, trans. R. Hurley (Harmondsworth, 1990).

FRAPPIER, JEAN, *Étude sur* La Mort le roi Artu (Geneva, 1961).

FRIER, B. W., and BAGNALL, R. S., *The Demography of Roman Egypt* (Cambridge, 1999).

FRYE, NORTHROP, *The Secular Scripture: A Study of the Structure of Romance* (Cambridge, Mass., 1976).

FURTADO, ANTONIO L., 'The Questing Beast as Emblem of the Ruin of Logres in the *Post-Vulgate*', *Arthuriana*, 9.3 (1999), 27–48.

FUWA, YURI, 'Metaphors of Confusion: Incest and Illegitimacy in Thomas Hughes's *Misfortunes of Arthur*', *Poetica*, 49 (Tokyo, 1998), 77–95.

FYLER, JOHN, 'Domesticating the Exotic in the *Squire's Tale*', *English Literary History*, 55 (1988), 1–26.

GARDNER, JANE F., *Women in Roman Law and Society* (London, 1986).

GAUDEMET, JEAN, *Les Sources du droit canonique XIIIe-XXe siècles*, Repères canoniques, Sources occidentales (Paris, 1993).

GAUNT, SIMON, *Gender and Genre in Medieval French Literature* (Cambridge, 1995).

GILBERT, JANE, 'Unnatural Mothers and Monstrous Children in *The King of Tars* and *Sir Gowther*', in Jocelyn Wogan-Browne *et al.* (eds.), *Medieval Women: Texts and Contexts in Late Medieval Britain* (Turnhout, 2000), 329–44.

GOODALL, PETER, ' "Unkynde Abhomynacions" in Chaucer and Gower', *Parergon*, NS 5 (1987), 94–102.

GOODICH, MICHAEL, 'Sexuality, Family, and the Supernatural in the Fourteenth Century', *Journal of the History of Sexuality*, 4.4 (1994), 493–516.

GOODY, J., *The Development of the Family and Marriage in Europe* (Cambridge, 1983).

GRACIA, PALOMA, 'La Prehistoria del *Tristan en prose* y el incesto', *Romania*, 111 (1990), 385–98.

—— *Las Señales del destino heroico* (Madrid, 1991).

GRAVDAL, KATHRYN, 'Confessing Incests: Legal Erasures and Literary Celebrations in Medieval France', *Comparative Literature Studies*, 32.2 (1995), 280–95.

GRIMAL, PIERRE, *Dictionary of Classical Mythology*, trans. R. Maxwell-Hyslop (Oxford, 1986).

GRISWARD, JOËL, 'Un schème narratif du "Tristan en prose": le mythe d'Œdipe', in *Mélanges [. . .] Pierre Le Gentil* (Paris, 1973), 329–39.

GUERIN, M. VICTORIA, *The Fall of Kings and Princes: Structure and Destruction in Arthurian Tragedy* (Stanford, 1995).

GUERREAU-JALABERT, ANITA, 'Sur les structures de parenté dans l'Europe médiévale', *Annales ESC*, 36.6 (1981), 1028–49.

—— 'Inceste et sainteté: *La Vie de Saint Grégoire* en français', *Annales ESC*, 43.6 (1988), 1291–1319.

—— 'L'Arbre de Jessé et l'ordre chrétien de la parenté', in D. Iogna-Prat *et al.*, *Marie: La Culte de la vierge dans la société mediévale* (Paris, 1996), 137–70.

GULLETTE, MARGARET M., 'The Puzzling Case of the Deceased Wife's Sister: Nineteenth-Century England Deals with a Second-Chance Plot', *Representations*, 31 (1990), 142–66.

HAAS, LOUIS, 'Boccaccio, Baptismal Kinship, and Spiritual Incest', *Renaissance and Reformation*, 25 (1989), 343–56.

HÄGG, TOMAS, *The Novel in Antiquity* (Berkeley and Los Angeles, 1983).

HARES-STRYKER, CAROLYN, 'Adrift on the Seven Seas: The Medieval Topos of Exile at Sea', *Florilegium*, 12 (1993), 79–98.

HARRISON, A. R. W., *The Law of Athens* (Oxford, 1968).

HEINRICHS, KATHERINE, *The Myths of Love: Classical Lovers in Medieval Literature* (State Park, Pa., 1990).

HELMHOLZ, R.H, *Marriage Litigation in Medieval England* (Cambridge, 1974).

—— 'And were there Children's Rights in Early Modern England? The Canon Law and "Intra-Family violence" in England, 1400–1640', *International Journal of Children's Rights*, 1 (1993), 23–32.

—— 'The Bible in the Service of the Canon Law', *Chicago-Kent Law Review*, 70 (1995), 1557–81.

HÉRITIER, FRANÇOISE, *Les Deux Sœurs et leur mère: Anthropologie de l'inceste* (Paris, 1994).

HERLEM-PREY, Brigitte, 'Schuld oder Nichtschuld, das ist oft die Frage: Kritisches zur Diskussion der Schuld in Hartmanns "Gregorius" und in der "Vie du Pape Saint Grégoire"', *Germanisch-romanische Monatsschrift*, NS 39 (1989), 3–25.

HERLIHY, DAVID, 'Making Sense of Incest: Women and the Marriage Rules of the Early Middle Ages', in B. Bachrach and D. Nicholas (eds.), *Law, Custom and the Social Fabric in Medieval Europe: Essays in Honor of Bruce Lyon* (Kalamazoo, Mich., 1990), 1–16.

HERMAN, JUDITH, *Father–Daughter Incest* (Cambridge, Mass., and London, 1981).

HOFFNER, HARRY A., Jr., 'Incest, Sodomy and Bestiality in the Ancient Near East', *Alter Orient und Altes Testament*, 22 (1973), 81–90.

HOMAN, RICHARD L., 'Two *Exempla*: Analogues to the *Play of the Sacrament* and *Dux Moraud*', *Comparative Drama*, 18 (1984), 241–51.

HOPKINS, AMANDA, 'Veiling the Text: The True Role of the Cloth in *Emaré*', in Judith Weiss (ed.), *Medieval Insular Romance: Tradition and Innovation* (Cambridge, 2000), 71–82.

HOPKINS, KEITH, 'Brother–Sister Marriage in Roman Egypt', *Comparative Studies in Society and History*, 22 (1980), 303–55.

HORNSTEIN, L. H., 'Eustace-Constance-Florence-Griselda Legends', in *A Manual of the Writings in Middle English, 1000–1500*, ed. J. Burke Severs and Albert Hartung, vol. vii (New Haven, 1967), 120–32.

INGRAM, MARTIN, *Church Courts, Sex and Marriage in England, 1570–1640* (Cambridge, 1987).

JACOFF, RACHEL, 'Transgression and Transcendence: Figures of Female Desire in Dante's *Commedia*', *Romania*, 79 (1988), 129–42; repr. in Marina Brownlee, Kevin Brownlee, and Stephen G. Nichols (eds.), *The New Medievalism* (Baltimore and London, 1991), 183–200.

JOHNSON, ALLEN, and PRICE-WILLIAMS, DOUGLASS, *Oedipus Ubiquitous: The Family Complex in World Folk Literature* (Stanford, 1996).

JOHNSON, LESLEY, 'Return to Albion', *Arthurian Literature*, 13 (1995), 19–40.

JONG, MAYKE DE, 'To the Limits of Kinship: Anti-Incest Legislation in the Early Medieval West, 500–900', in J. Bremmer (ed.), *From Sappho to De Sade: Moments in the History of Sexuality* (London, 1989), 36–59.

JUST, ROGER, *Women in Athenian Law and Life* (London, 1989).

KARRAS, RUTH MAZO, 'Holy Harlots: Prostitute Saints in Medieval Legend', *Journal of the History of Sexuality*, 1.1 (1990), 3–32.

—— 'Gendered Sin: Misogyny in John of Bromyard's "Summa Predicantium"', *Traditio*, 47 (1992), 233–57.

KAY, SARAH, *The* Chansons de geste *in the Age of Romance: Political Fictions* (Oxford, 1995).

KELLY, H. A., 'Canonical Implications of Richard III's Plan to Marry his Niece', *Traditio*, 23 (1967), 269–311.

—— *Love and Marriage in the Age of Chaucer* (Ithaca, 1975).

—— *The Matrimonial Trials of Henry VIII* (Stanford, 1976).

—— 'Shades of Incest and Cuckoldry: Pandarus and John of Gaunt', *Studies in the Age of Chaucer*, 13 (1991), 121–40.

KERMODE, FRANK, *The Genesis of Secrecy* (London and Cambridge, Mass., 1979).

KING, K. C., 'The Mother's Guilt in Hartmann's *Gregorius*', in *Medieval German Studies presented to Frederick Norman* (London, 1965), 84–93.

KLAPISCH-ZUBER, CHRISTIANE, 'The Genesis of the Family Tree', *I Tatti Studies: Essays on the Renaissance*, 4 (1991), 105–29.

KLEIST, WOLFRAM, *Die erzählende französische Dit-Literaturen in 'quatrains alexandrins monorimes'* (Hamburg, 1973).

KOLVE, V. A., *Chaucer and the Imagery of Narrative: The First Five Canterbury Tales* (Stanford, 1984).

KRAPPE, A. H., 'Über die Sagen von der Geschwisterehe im Mittelalter', *Archiv für das Studium den neueren Sprache und Literatur*, 167 (1935), 161–76.

—— 'La Belle Hélène de Constantinople', *Romania*, 63 (1937), 324–53.

KRISTEVA, JULIA, 'Stabat Mater', trans. L. S. Roudiez, in *The Kristeva Reader*, ed. Toril Moi (Oxford, 1986), 160–86.

KULLMAN, Dorothea, *Verwandtschaft in epischer Dichtung: Untersuchungen zu den französischen* chansons de geste *und* Romanen *des 12. Jahrhunderts* (Tübingen, 1992).

—— 'Le Rôle de l'église dans les mariage épiques', in Philip E. Bennett, Anne Elizabeth Cobby, and Graham A. Runnals (eds.), *Charlemagne in the North* (London, 1993), 177–87.

LEACH, EDMUND, 'Genesis as Myth', in John Middleton (ed.), *Myth and Cosmos: Readings in Mythology and Symbolism* (Austin, 1967), 1–13.

LECLANCHE, JEAN-LUC, 'Biblis: Métamorphose médiévale d'un conte ovidien', in *Mélanges de langue et de littérature médiévales offerts à Alice Planche* (Nice, 1984), 287–97.

LEGROS, HUGUETTE, 'Parenté naturelle, alliance, parenté spirituelle: de l'inceste à la sainteté', in *Les Relations de parenté dans le monde médiéval* (= *Senefiance*, 26) (1989), 511–48.

LEHMANN, PAUL, 'Judas Iscariot in der lateinischen Legendenüberlieferung des Mittelalters', *Studi Medievali*, NS 2 (1929), 289–346.

LEJEUNE, RITA, 'Le Péché de Charlemagne et la *Chanson de Roland*', in *Studia Philologica: Homenaje ofrecido a Dámaso Alonso*, 3 vols. (Madrid, 1961), ii. 339–71.

LE ROY LADURIE, Emmanuel, *Montaillou*, trans. Barbara Bray (Harmondsworth, 1980).

LEVIN, EVE, *Sex and Society in the World of the Orthodox Slavs, 900–1700* (Ithaca, 1989).

LÉVI-STRAUSS, CLAUDE, *L'Homme nu* (Paris, 1971).

LOOMIS, R. S., *Celtic Myth and Arthurian Romance* (New York, 1927).

LÖSETH, E., *Le Roman en prose de Tristan: Analyse critique d'après les manuscrits de Paris* (Paris, 1890; repr. New York, 1970).

LYNCH, JOSEPH H., *Godparents and Kinship in Early Medieval Europe* (Princeton, 1986).

MCCABE, RICHARD, *Incest, Drama, and Nature's Law 1550–1700* (Cambridge, 1993).

MCLAUGHLIN, MEGAN, '"Abominable Mingling": Father–Daughter Incest and the Law', *Medieval Feminist Newsletter*, 24 (1997), 26–30.

MCLEOD, GLENDA, *Virtue and Venom: Catalogs of Women from Antiquity to the Renaissance* (Ann Arbor, 1991).

MANCINELLI, LAURA, 'Der guote sündaere: il problema della colpa nel *Gregorius* di Hartmann von Aue', *Romanobarbarica*, 10 (1988–9), 241–54.

MANDACH, ANDRÉ DE, 'L'Inceste et l'effondrement d'un monde: Tristan et Mordred', in Giovanna Angeli and Luciano Formisano (eds.), *L'Imaginaire courtois et son double* (Naples, 1991), 9–15.

MANSELLI, R., 'Vie familiale et éthique sexuelle dans les pénitentiels', in G. Duby and J. Le Goff (eds.), *Famille et parenté dans l'occident médiéval* (Rome, 1977), 363–78.

MARCHALONIS, SHIRLEY, 'Above Rubies: Popular Views of Medieval Women', *Journal of Popular Culture*, 14 (1980–1), 87–93.

MARTINET, SUZANNE, 'Le Péché de Charlemagne, Giselle, Roland et Ganelon', in D. Buschinger and A. Crepin (eds.), *Amour, mariage, et transgressions en moyen âge* (Göppingen, 1984), 9–16.

MAYER, ANTON, 'Mater et Filia: ein Versuch zur stilgeschichtlichen Entwicklung eines Gebetsausdrucks', *Jahrbuch für Liturgiewissenschaft*, 7 (1927), 60–82.

MEENS, ROB, 'The Frequency and Nature of Early Medieval Penance', in Biller and Minnis (eds.), *Handling Sin*, 35–61.

MÉLA, CHARLES, 'Œdipe, Judas, Osiris', in Giovanna Angeli and Luciano Formisano (eds.), *L'Imaginaire courtois et son double* (Naples, 1991), 17–37.

MELNIKAS, ANTHONY, *The Corpus of the Miniatures in the Manuscripts of the Decretum of Gratian*, 3 vols. (Rome, 1975).

MÉNARD, PHILIPPE, *Le Rire et le sourire dans le roman courtois en France au moyen âge* (Geneva, 1969).

MERTENS, V., *Gregorius Eremita* (Munich, 1978).

MESLIER, BERNARD, and MESLIER, MIREILLE, 'Le Thème de l'inceste dans la littérature française du moyen âge', unpub. thèse de troisième cycle (Tours, 1981).

MICHA, A., 'Deux sources de la *Mort Artu*: II, La Naissance incestueuse de Mordred', *Zeitschrift für romanische Philologie*, 66 (1950), 371–2.

—— 'La Femme injustement accusée dans les miracles de Notre-Dame par personnages', in *Mélanges d'histoire du théâtre au Moyen-Age et de la renaissance offerts à Gustave Cohen* (Paris, 1950), 85–92; repr. in Micha, *De la Chanson de geste au roman* (Geneva, 1976), 479–86.

MICHAUD-QUANTIN, P., *Sommes de casuistiques et manuels de confessions au moyen âge (XII–XVI siècles)* (Louvain, 1962).

MICKEL, EMMANUEL J., 'Tristan's Ancestry in the *Tristan en prose*', *Romania*, 109 (1988), 68–89.

MINNIS, A. J., *Medieval Theory of Authorship: Scholastic Literary Attitudes in the Later Middle Ages*, 2nd edn. (Philadelphia, 1988).

MITTERAUER, MICHAEL, 'Christianity and Endogamy', trans. Markus Cerman, *Continuity and Change*, 6.3 (1991), 295–333.

MÖLK, ULRICH, 'Zur Vorgeschichte der Gregoriuslegende: Vita und Kult des hl. Metro von Verona', in *Nachrichten der Akademie der Wissenschaften in Göttingen, I. Philologisch-historische Klasse* (1987), 5–54.

MORGAN, LESLIE Z., '*Berta ai piedi grandi*: Historical Figure and Literary Symbol', *Olifant*, 19.1–2 (1994–5), 37–56.

MORRIS, ROSEMARY, *The Character of King Arthur in Medieval Literature* (Cambridge, 1985).

—— 'Uther and Ygerne: A Study in Uncourtly Love', *Arthurian Literature*, 4 (1985), 70–92.

MUIR, LINETTE, 'The Questing Beast: Origin and Development', *Orpheus*, 4 (1957), 24–32.

MURRAY, JACQUELINE, 'Gendered Souls in Sexed Bodies: The Male Construction of Female Sexuality in Some Medieval Confessors', in Biller and Minnis (eds.), *Handling Sin*, 79–93.

NEWMAN, BARBARA, 'Intimate Pieties: Holy Trinity and Holy Family in the Late Middle Ages', *Religion and Literature*, 3.1 (1999), 77–101.

NOBEL, HILDEGARD, 'Schuld und Sühne in Hartmanns *Gregorius* und in der frühscholastischen Theologie', *Zeitschrift für deutsche Philologie*, 76 (1957), 42–79.

OHLY, FRIEDRICH, *The Damned and the Elect: Guilt in Western Culture*, trans. Linda Archibald (Cambridge, 1992).

OSBORN, MARIJANE, *Romancing the Goddess: Three Middle English Romances about Women* (Urbana and Chicago, 1998).

The Oxford Dictionary of Byzantium (Oxford, 1991).

PANOFSKY, E., 'Father Time', in *Studies in Iconology* (Oxford, 1939), 69–93.

PARKER, ROBERT, *Miasma: Pollution and Purification in Early Greek Religion* (Oxford, 1983; reissued 1996).

PAYEN, JEAN-CHARLES, *Le Motif du repentir dans la littérature française médiévale* (Geneva, 1967).

PAYER, PIERRE, *Sex and the Penitentials: The Development of a Sexual Code 550–1150* (Toronto, 1984).

PERRY, BEN EDWIN, *Secundus the Silent Philosopher* (Ithaca, 1964).

PHILIPPART, GUY, 'Le Récit miraculaire marial dans l'Occident médiéval', in D. Iogna-Prat et al. (eds.), *Marie: Le Culte de la Vierge dans la société médiévale* (Paris, 1996), 563–90.

PHILONENKO, MARC, 'Les Oxymores de Secundus', *Academie des Inscriptions et Belles Lettres*, comptes-rendus (1991), 373–8.

PINTO-MATHIEU, ELISABETH, 'Adultère et inceste dans *Tristan de Nanteuil*', in Buschinger and Spiewok (eds.), *Sexuelle Perversionen*, 169–81.

POIRION, DANIEL, 'Edyppus et l'enigme du roman médiéval', in *L'Enfant au moyen âge* (= *Senefiance*, 9) (1980), 285–97.

POMEROY, SARAH, *Families in Classical and Hellenistic Greece: Representations and Realities* (Oxford, 1997).

POTTER, M. A., *Sohrab and Rustum: The Epic Theme of a Combat between Father and Son* (London, 1902).

PRICE, S. R. F., 'The Future of Dreams: From Freud to Artemidorus', *Past and Present*, 113 (1986), 3–37.

PROPP, V., 'Oedipus in the Light of Folklore', trans. Polly Coote in Edmunds and Dundes (eds.), *Oedipus: A Folklore Casebook*, 76–121.

PUTTER, AD, 'The Narrative Logic of Emaré', in Ad Putter and Jane Gilbert (eds.), *The Spirit of Medieval English Popular Romance* (Harlow, 2000), 157–80.

QUILLIGAN, MAUREEN, *The Allegory of Female Authority: Christine de Pizan's Cité des Dames* (Ithaca, 1991).

RAMANUJAN, A. K., 'The Indian Oedipus', in Edmunds and Dundes (eds.), *Oedipus: A Folklore Casebook*, 234–61.

RAND, E. K., 'Medieval Lives of Judas Iscariot', in *Anniversary Papers by Pupils of G. L. Kittredge* (Boston, 1913), 305–16.

RANK, OTTO, *Das Inzest-Motif in Dichtung und Sage* (Leipzig and Vienna, 1912).

—— *The Myth of the Birth of the Hero: A Psychological Interpretation of Mythology*, trans. F. Robbins and S. E. Jelliffe (New York, 1957).

—— *The Incest Theme in Literature and Legend*, trans. Gregory C. Richter (Baltimore, 1992).

REDFORD, DONALD B., 'The Literary Motif of the Exposed Child', *Numen*, 14 (1967), 209–28.

RÉGNIER-BOHLER, DANIELLE, 'L'Inceste et les voies de la pénitence', in *Femmes—Mariages—Lignages: Mélanges offerts à Georges Duby* (Brussels, 1992), 289–303.

—— 'La Tragédie thébaine dans "La Mutacion de Fortune"', in Margarete Zimmermann and Dina De Rentis (eds.), *The City of Scholars: New Approaches to Christine de Pizan* (Berlin and New York, 1994), 127–47.

REIDER, NORMAN, 'Medieval Oedipal Legends about Judas', *Psychoanalytic Quarterly*, 29 (1960), 515–27.

REINHARD, J. R., 'Setting Adrift in Medieval Law and Literature', *PMLA* 56 (1941), 33–68.

RICHLIN, AMY, *The Garden of Priapus: Sexuality and Aggression in Roman Humor*, rev. edn. (Oxford, 1992).

RICKERT, EDITH, 'The Old English Offa Saga', *Modern Philology*, 2 (1904–5), 321–76.

ROBSON, MARGARET, 'Cloaking Desire: Re-reading *Emaré*', in Jennifer Fellows *et al.* (eds.), *Romance Reading on the Book: Essays on Medieval Narrative Presented to Maldwyn Mills* (Cardiff, 1996), 64–76.

ROCHER, DANIEL, 'Das Motiv der "felix culpa" und des betrogenen Teufels in der "Vie du pape Grégoire" und in Hartmanns "Gregorius"', *Germanisch-romanische Monatsschrift*, NS 38 (1988), 57–66.

RONCAGLIA, AURELIO, 'Roland e il peccato di Carlomagno', in *Symposium in honorem prof. M. de Riquer* (Barcelona, 1984), 315–47.

ROOTH, A. B., *The Cinderella Cycle* (Lund, 1951; repr. New York, 1980).

ROUBAUD, JACQUES, 'Généalogie morale des rois-pêcheurs', *Change*, 16 (1973), 228–47.

ROUSSEL, CLAUDE, 'Chanson de geste et roman: remarques sur deux adaptations littéraires du conte de "La fille aux mains coupées"', in *Essor et fortune de la chanson de geste dans l'Europe et l'Orient Latin. Actes du IXe Congrès International de la Société Rencesvals* (Modena, 1984), 565–82.

—— 'Aspects du père incestueux dans la littérature médiévale', in D. Buschinger and A. Crepin (eds.), *Amour, mariage et transgressions au moyen âge* (Göppingen, 1984), 47–62.

—— *Conter de geste au XIVe siècle: Inspiration folklorique et écriture épique dans* La Belle Hélène de Constantinople (Geneva, 1998).

ROUSSELLE, ALINE, *Porneia: On Desire and the Body in Antiquity*, trans. Felicia Pheasant (Oxford, 1988).

RUBIN, GAYLE, 'The Traffic in Women: Notes on the Political Economy of Sex', in Rayna R. Reiter (ed.), *Toward an Anthropology of Women* (New York, 1975), 157–210.

RUDHARDT, JEAN, 'De l'inceste dans la mythologie grecque', *Revue française de psychoanalyse*, 46 (1982), 731–63.

RUH, K., *Höfische Epik des deutschen Mittelalters*, 2nd edn. (Berlin, 1977).

SAMUEL, IRENE, 'Semiramis in the Middle Ages', *Medievalia et Humanistica*, 2 (1944), 32–44.

SAVAGE, ANNE, 'Clothing Paternal Incest in *The Clerk's Tale, Emaré* and the *Life of St Dympna*', in Jocelyn Wogan-Browne *et al.* (eds.), *Medieval Women: Texts and Contexts in Late Medieval Britain* (Turnhout, 2000), 345–61.

SCALA, ELIZABETH, 'Canacee and the Chaucer Canon: Incest and Other Unnarratables', *Chaucer Review*, 30.1 (1995), 15–39.

SCANLON, LARRY, 'The Riddle of Incest: John Gower and the Problem of Medieval Sexuality', in R. F. Yeager (ed.), *Re-Visioning Gower* (Ashville, NC, 1998), 93–127.

SCHLAUCH, MARGARET, *Chaucer's Constance and Accused Queens* (New York, 1927; repr. 1973).

SCHNEIDEGGER, JEAN R., 'Pères et filles dans *Apollonius de Tyre*', in *Les Relations de parenté dans le monde médiéval* (= *Senefiance*, 26) (1989), 259–71.

SCHROEDER, HORST, *Der Topos der Nine Worthies in Literatur und bildender Kunst* (Göttingen, 1971).

SEZNEC, JEAN, *The Survival of the Pagan Gods: The Mythological Tradition and Its Place in Renaissance Humanism*, trans. Barbara F. Sessions (New York, 1953).

SHAPIRO, SHANTI, 'Self-Mutilation and Self-Blame in Incest Victims', *American Journal of Psychotherapy*, 41.1 (1987), 46–54.

SHAW, BRENT, 'Explaining Incest: Brother–Sister Marriage in Graeco-Roman Egypt', *Man*, NS 27 (1992), 267–99.

—— and SALLER, RICHARD, 'Close-Kin Marriage in Roman Society', *Man*, NS 19 (1984), 432–44.

SHAW, JUDITH, 'The Role of the Shared Bed in John Gower's *Tales of Incest*', *English Language Notes*, 26 (1989), 4–7.

SHEEHAN, MICHAEL M., 'The Formation and Stability of Marriage in Fourteenth-Century England: Evidence of an Ely Register', *Medieval Studies*, 33 (1971), 228–63.

SHEEHY, MICHAEL, *When the Normans Came to Ireland* (Cork and Dublin, 1975).

SHELL, MARC, 'The Want of Incest in the Human Family, Or, Kin and Kind in Christian Thought', *Journal of the American Academy of Religion*, 52 (1994), 625–50.

SHEPHERD, M., *Tradition and Recreation in Thirteenth-Century Romance: 'La Manekine' and 'Jehan and Blonde' by Philippe de Rémi* (Amsterdam, 1990).

SIMPSON, JAMES, 'Violence, Narrative and Proper Name: *Sir Degaré*, "The Tale of Sir Gareth of Orkney", and the Anglo-Norman *Folie Tristan d'Oxford*', in Ad Putter and Jane Gilbert (eds.), *The Spirit of Medieval English Popular Romance* (Harlow, 2000), 122–41.

SMITH, CHARLES E., *Papal Enforcement of Some Medieval Marriage Laws* (Port Washington, NY, and London, 1940; repr. 1972).

SPEARING, A. C., 'Canace and Machaire', *Medievalia*, 16 (1993), 211–21.

SUARD, FRANÇOIS, 'Chanson de geste et roman devant le materiau folklorique: le conte de la *Fille aux mains coupées* dans la *Belle Hélène de Constantinople*, *Lion de Bourges*, et *La Manekine*', in E. Ruhe and R. Behrens (eds.), *Mittelalterbilder aus neuer Perspektive* (Munich, 1985), 364–79.

TAUBENSCHLAG, RAPHAEL, *The Law of Greco-Roman Egypt in the Light of the Papyri 332BC–640AD*, 2nd edn. (Warsaw, 1955).

TAYLOR, ARCHER, 'Riddles dealing with Family Relationships', *Journal of American Folklore*, 51 (1938), 25–37.

THOMPSON, RAYMOND H., 'Gawain against Arthur: The Impact of a Mythological Pattern upon Arthurian Tradition in Accounts of the Birth of Gawain', *Folklore*, 85 (1974), 113–21.

TOBIN, FRANK J., 'Fallen Man and Hartmann's *Gregorius*', *Germanic Review*, 50 (1970), 85–98.

TRAXLER, JEANINE P., 'Observations on the Importance of the Prehistory in the *Tristan en prose*', *Romania*, 108.4 (1987), 539–48.

TREGGIARI, SUSAN, *Roman Marriage* (Oxford, 1991).

TRENKNER, SOPHIE, *The Greek Novella in the Classical Period* (Cambridge, 1958).

TUBACH, F., *Index Exemplorum: A Handbook of Medieval Religious Tales*, FF Communications, 204 (Helsinki, 1969).

VAUGHAN, R., *Matthew Paris* (Cambridge, 1979).

VERDUCCI, FLORENCE, *Ovid's Toyshop of the Heart* (Princeton, 1985).

VERNANT, J.-P. , 'Le Tyran boiteux: d'Œdipe à Périandre', in J.-P. Vernant and P. Vidal-Naquet, *Mythe et tragédie en grèce ancienne II* (Paris, 1986), 45–77.

VERNIER, BERNARD, 'Théorie de l'inceste et construction d'objet: Françoise Héritier, la Grèce antique et les Hittites', *Annales ESC*, 51.1 (1996), 173–200.

VESELOVSKIJ [WESSELOFSKY]-SADE, *La Fanciulla Perseguitata*, ed. d'Arco Silvio Avalle (Milan, 1977).

VISSER-VAN TERWISGA, MARIJKE DER, 'Œdipe, victime du destin, homme perverti ou préfiguration divin?' in Buschinger and Spiewok (eds.), *Sexuelle Perversionen*, 57–69.

VITZ, EVELYN BIRGE, *Medieval Narrative and Modern Narratology: Subjects and Objects of Desire* (New York, 1989).

WALLENSKÖLD, A., *Le Conte de la femme chaste convoitée par son beau-frère* (Helsinki, 1907).

WARNER, MARINA, *Alone of All Her Sex: The Myth and Cult of the Virgin Mary* (London, 1976).

—— *From the Beast to the Blonde: On Fairytales and their Tellers* (London, 1994).

WATSON, ALAN, *Society and Legal Change* (Edinburgh, 1977).

WATT, DIANE, 'Behaving like a Man? Incest, Lesbian Desire, and Gender Play in *Yde et Olive* and its Adaptations', *Comparative Literature*, 50.4 (1998), 265–85.

WELSH, ANDREW, 'Doubling and Incest in the *Mabinogi*', *Speculum*, 65 (1990), 344–62.

WETHERBEE, WINTHROP, 'Constance and the World in Chaucer and Gower', in *John Gower: Recent Readings*, ed. R. F. Yeager (Kalamazoo, Mich., 1989), 65–93.

WOLFRAM, SYBIL, *In-Laws and Outlaws* (London, 1987).

WOOLF, ROSEMARY, *The English Religious Lyric in the Middle Ages* (Oxford, 1968).

ZIPES, JACK, *Fairy Tales and the Art of Subversion* (London, 1983).

ZISKIND, JONATHAN R., 'Legal Rules on Incest in the Ancient Near East', *Revue internationale des droits de l'antiquité*, 3rd ser. 35 (1988), 79–109.

Index

This index contains the authors and (where appropriate) the titles of all primary texts cited in this book, as well as references to topics and themes. Modern scholars are included only when discussed or quoted in the text, or cited on points of importance in the footnotes. All secondary sources are included in the bibliography.

Fenster, Thelma 156, 170, 176 n. 65
Field, P. J. C. 208 n. 44, 213 n. 59
filicide 56–8, 89–91, 133, 187, 214–15,
    218
    see also infanticide; parricide
La Fille du Comte de Pontieu 176
Fingal Rónáin 221
Flight from Incestuous Father motif XIII,
    62, 68, 135, 146–83, 235, 245–56
    see also father-daughter incest
Flinker, Noam 239 n. 23
Foehr-Janssens, Yasmina 156 n.
folklore 62, 147, 172, 185 n. 84, 193, 229
    see also ballads
Ford, John:
    'Tis Pity She's a Whore 144, 189, 192,
        195, 236–7
foundlings 82, 105, 112, 129, 166, 187,
    189, 196, 235
    see also exposure
Frisch, Max:
    Homo Faber 185 n. 84
Frappier, Jean 217
Froissart:
    Meliador 196
Frye, Northrop 105 n.
Fulgentius:
    On the Thebaid 77 n. 39
    Mythologies 87

Gaius:
    Institutes 14, 15
Galahad 197, 198–9, 210, 213 n. 59
Ganelon 202 n. 26, 215, 219
Gardner, Jane F. 14 n. 23
Garin le Loherain 224–5
Gaunt, Simon 116, 117
Gautier de Coincy 222
Gawain 195, 203, 208, 218, 240
Generides 221
Geoffrey of Monmouth 132, 144 n. 82,
    203 & n. 30, 209 n. 48, 210, 214,
    218, 223
Gerald of Wales 51
Germanic lawcodes, *see* barbarians
Germanus, St 186 n., 202
Gesta Romanorum 209
    Albanus 125
    Apollonius 99–100
    Crescentia 222
    Gregorius 124–5
    incestuous mother 135–7
    incestuous siblings 194

see also allegorical interpretations of
    incest stories
giants 144 n. 82, 187
Gilles, St 169 n. 45, 200–2, 216, 225
Giraldus Cambrensis, *see* Gerald of
    Wales
Gobi, Jean:
    Scala coeli 149–50, 175 n. 62, 176, 222,
        247
godparents and godchildren:
    in lawcodes 16, 30–2, 37–9, 47, 48–9
    in literature 226–8
    see also spiritual incest and kinship
Goodich, Michael 49
Goody, J. 49
Gottfried von Strassburg:
    Tristan 79
Gower, John:
    Confessio Amantis 25, 100–1, 243–4;
        Apollonius 93–101, 185–7, 190,
        243–4; Canace 80–85; Constance
        175 n. 64, 177 n. 67; Philomena 90
    Mirour de l'Omme 39, 239 n. 23
Gracia, Paloma 197
Grail Quest 117, 197, 198, 210, 213 n. 59
grandparent-grandchild incest:
    in lawcodes 9–10, 14
    in medieval literature 225
Des Granz Geanz 144 n. 82
    see also giants
Gratian 25, 31 n. 83, 35–7, 38 n. 99,
    40
Gregorius legend:
    in Arnold of Lübeck 115
    compared with other incest stories
        106, 121–2, 123, 127–9, 132–4, 137,
        139, 140–1, 144, 145, 148, 152 n.,
        157, 165, 168 n., 169, 184, 194–5,
        200, 208–9, 210, 213, 216, 218, 230,
        233–4, 238
    in *Gesta Romanorum* 124–5
    in Hartmann von Aue 111–19, 124,
        126 n. 50, 133, 154, 194, 233
    in Old French version 111, 116, 118,
        126 n. 50
    in Timoneda 131–2
Grimm's Tales:
    'The Girl Without Hands' 169 n. 44
Griselda 161, 182
Guerin, M. Victoria 203 n. 30, 209 n. 48,
    210, 217
Guerreau-Jalabert, Anita 31 n. 81, 41 n.
    106, 116

Lightning Source UK Ltd.
Milton Keynes UK
UKHW041352270819
348511UK00004B/2/P